ELFQUEST:
THE GRAND
QUEST
VOLUME FOUR

ELFQUEST CREATED BY
**WENDY &
RICHARD PINI**

ELFQUEST:
**THE GRAND
QUEST**
VOLUME FOUR

WRITTEN BY
WENDY & RICHARD PINI

ART AND LETTERING BY
WENDY PINI

ELFQUEST: THE GRAND QUEST VOLUME FOUR
Published by DC Comics. Cover, timeline, character
bios and compilation copyright © 2004 Warp
Graphics, Inc. All Rights Reserved.

Originally published in single magazine form in
ELFQUEST 11-15. Copyright © 1981, 1982 Warp
Graphics, Inc. All Rights Reserved. All characters,
their distinctive likenesses and related elements
featured in this publication are trademarks of
Warp Graphics, Inc. The stories, characters and
incidents featured in this publication are
entirely fictional. DC Comics does not read
or accept unsolicited submissions of ideas,
stories or artwork.

DC Comics, 1700 Broadway, New York, NY 10019
A Warner Bros. Entertainment Company
Printed in Canada. First Printing.
ISBN: 1-4012-0141-5

Cover illustration by Wendy Pini
Publication design by John J. Hill

The ElfQuest Saga is an ever-unfolding story spanning countless millennia that follows the adventures of humans, trolls and various elfin tribes. Some of the events that occur prior to the time of this volume are outlined below using the very first published ElfQuest story as a benchmark.

OUR STORY BEGINS HERE...

7 YEARS LATER

Recognition has given Cutter and Leetah twin children, Ember and Suntop, and the two tribes at last live in peace. The arrival of nomadic humans, though, alerts the elves to the continuing threat. Cutter and Skywise, seeking strength in numbers, set out to find other elfin tribes. Their journey leads them through the mysterious Forbidden Grove where they encounter fairylike Petalwing, one of the Preservers.

Cutter and Skywise are reunited with Leetah, the cubs and the Wolfriders. Together, they enter the fabled Blue Mountain where they meet bizarre, winged Tyldak and the beautiful, enigmatic Winnowill.

2,000 - 3000 YEARS BEFORE

Goodtree, eighth chief of the Wolfriders, founds a new Holt deep in the woods and creates the Father Tree where the Wolfriders can all live. Her son, *Mantricker,* is the first in several generations to have to deal with nomadic humans again.

Mantricker's son, *Bearclaw,* discovers Greymung's trolls who live in the caverns and tunnels beneath the Holt. Bearclaw becomes the Wolfriders' tenth chief.

In the distant Forbidden Grove near Blue Mountain, *Petalwing* and the preservers tirelessly protect their mysterious wrapstuff bundles.

Among the Wolfriders, *Treestump, Clearbrook, Moonshade, Strongbow, One-Eye, Redlance, Pike, Rainsong* and *Woodlock* are born.

4,000 YEARS BEFORE

Freefoot leads the Wolfriders during a prosperous time. Game is plentiful, and life is easy.

Freefoot's son, Oakroot, subsequently becomes chief and later takes the name *Tanner.*

9,000 YEARS BEFORE

Wolfrider chief Timmorn feels the conflict between his elf and wolf sides, and leaves the tribe to find his own destiny. *Rahnee the She-Wolf* takes over as leader, followed by her son *Prey-Pacer.*

10,000 YEARS BEFORE

Over time, the early High Ones become too many for their faraway planet to support. *Timmain's* group discovers the World of Two Moons, but as the crystalline ship approaches, the trolls revolt. The High Ones lose control and crash-land far in the new world's past. Ape-like primitive humans greet them with brutality, and the elfin High Ones scatter into the surrounding forest.

In order to survive, Timmain magically takes on a wolf's form and hunts for the other elves. In time, the High Ones adapt, making a spartan life for themselves. *Timmorn,* first chief of the Wolfriders, is born to Timmain and a true wolf.

10,000 YEARS BEFORE

0

1,000

2,000

3,000

4,000

5,000

6,000

7,000

8,000

9,000

10,000

0	
475	
600	
1,000	

FIRE & FLIGHT

The peace is an illusion, and humans burn the Wolfriders from their forest home. Cutter and his band are driven into a vast desert where, at the end of their strength, they discover a second tribe of elves, the Sun Folk. Cutter recognizes the Sun Folks' healer Leetah, and the two groups unite in an uneasy alliance.

6 YEARS BEFORE

The feud between elves and humans ends – seemingly – with the death of Bearclaw. Cutter takes the chief's lock and assumes leadership of the tribe.

| 2,000 | |

25 YEARS BEFORE

Joyleaf gives birth to a son, *Cutter*, who forms a fast friendship with Skywise. The two become brothers "in all but blood."

| 3,000 | |

475 YEARS BEFORE

Bearclaw begins a long feud with a tribe of humans who have claimed the land near the Wolfriders' Holt. Though both sides suffer over the years, neither can prevail, and neither will give in.

| 4,000 | |

7,000 YEARS BEFORE

Swift-Spear, fourth chief, goes to war for the first time against the humans of a nearby village. The humans are forced to leave, and he earns the name *Two-Spear*.

Two-Spear has strange dreams of the humans returning and believes the elves are no longer safe. He becomes obsessed by the dreams and tries repeatedly to convince the Wolfriders they must wipe out the human threat for all time. When his sister Huntress Skyfire challenges his chieftainship, the tribe splits. Two-Spear leaves with his followers, and Skyfire becomes chief of the remaining tribe.

| 5,000 | |

600 YEARS BEFORE

In an oasis called the Sun Village deep in the desert to the south of the Holt, *Rayek* is born to villagers Jarrah and Ingen. *Leetah* is born to Suntoucher and Toorah twelve years later.

| 6,000 | |
| 7,000 | |

10,000 - 8,000 YEARS BEFORE

In a long diaspora, descendants of the High Ones wander the world. *Savah* and her family settle the Sun Village in the desert at Sorrow's End. Lord Voll and the Gliders move into Blue Mountain and shut themselves away from the world.

Guttlekraw becomes king of the trolls, who have fled to the cold north.

Ekuar and two rock-shaper companions discover the abandoned palace-ship of the High Ones but are enslaved by Guttlekraw. Glaciers force the trolls to move south, tunneling under the future Holt of the Wolfriders.

Greymung rebels against Guttlekraw. Guttlekraw and his cohorts return north, and the three rock-shaper elves escape in the melee.

Winnowill leaves Blue Mountain, finds the troll, seduces him and gives birth to *Two-Edge*. She later kills the troll.

8,000	
9,000	
10,000	

The ElfQuest saga spans thousands of years and to date has introduced readers to hundreds of characters. At the time of the stories in this volume, these are the major characters you will meet and get to know.

THE ELVES

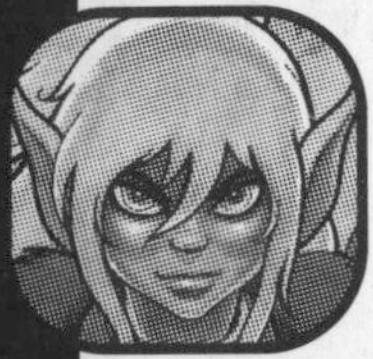

CUTTER

While his name denotes his skill with a sword, Cutter is not a cold and merciless death-dealer. Strong in his beliefs, he will nevertheless bend even the most fundamental of them if the well-being of his tribe is at stake. Skywise believes that what sets Cutter apart from all past Wolfrider chieftains is his imagination and ability to not only accept change, but take advantage of it.

LEETAH

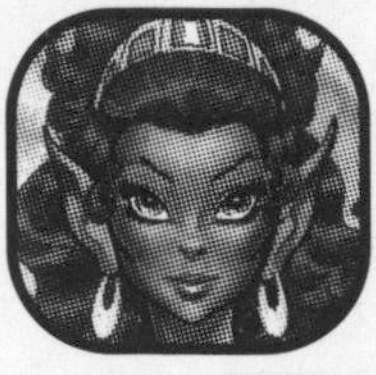

Her name means "healing light" and – as the Sun Folks' healer – she is the village's most precious resource. For over 600 years she has lived a sheltered life, surrounded by love and admiration, knowing little of the world beyond her desert oasis. Though delicate-seeming, beneath her beauty lies a wellspring of strength that has yet to be tested.

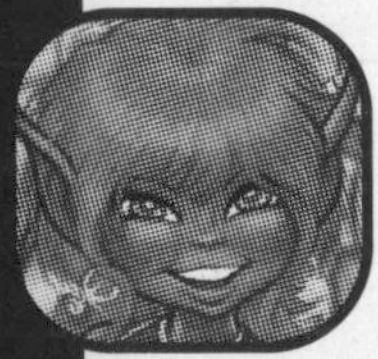

EMBER

Named for her fire-red hair, Ember is destined to be the next chief of the Wolfriders. As such, she constantly watches and learns from her father's actions; she also learns gentler skills from Leetah. As Cutter was a unique blend of his own parents' qualities, so too is Ember. She shares a close bond with her twin brother Suntop, giving her strength.

SUNTOP

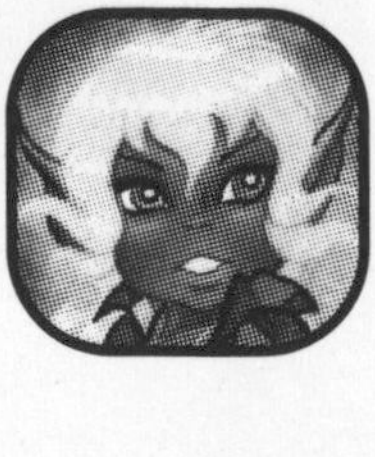

Suntop is the gentler, enigmatic son of Cutter and Leetah. Although a true Wolfrider, Suntop was born in the Sun Village and considers it home. Content that Ember will become chief of the Wolfriders, he says of himself, "I'll be what I'll be." Suntop has powerful mental abilities; his "magic feeling," as he calls it, alerts him when magic is being used by other elves.

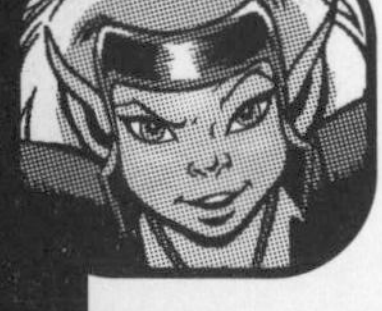

SKYWISE

Orphaned at birth, Skywise is the resident stargazer of the Wolfriders, and only his interest in elf maidens rivals his passion for understanding the mysteries of the universe. Skywise is Cutter's counselor, confidant, and closest friend. While he is capable of deep seriousness, nothing can diminish Skywise's jovial and rakish manner.

TREESTUMP

Seemingly gruff and no-nonsense, Treestump also has a vulnerable side, especially when it comes to protecting the well-being of his tribemates. More than a thousand years of living with "the Way" has given Treestump a wellspring of wisdom, allowing him to find calm even in the face of great danger. He is something of a father figure to the entire tribe.

STRONGBOW

Strongbow is the reserved, silent master archer of the Wolfriders. Ever the devil's advocate, he is often proved right but finds no value in saying "I told you so." Strongbow is extremely serious, rarely smiles, and prefers sending to audible speech. He is completely devoted to his lifemate, Moonshade, and intensely proud of their son Dart, who has remained in the Sun Village to train its people in the art of combat.

NIGHTFALL

Nightfall is the beautiful counterpoint to her lifemate, Redlance, and one of the most skilled hunters in the tribe. She is cool and calculated, neither vengeful nor violent unless absolutely necessary. The relationship between Nightfall and Redlance is very much one of yin and yang. Nightfall grew up with Cutter and is strongly loyal to the young chief.

REDLANCE

Redlance is the sweet-natured plantshaper of the Wolfriders. Indeed, he will only use his talents defensively to protect the tribe. Redlance is too much a pacifist at heart to do willful harm, and this gentleness makes him a natural to care for the cubs of the tribe. Redlance is a master of the soft counsel, gently prodding other, more headstrong elves in the right direction.

MOONSHADE

Moonshade is the Wolfriders' tanner. Though the process can be lengthy and tedious, she enjoys the quiet hours spent bringing the beauty out of a supple hide. Moonshade, like her lifemate Strongbow, is very much a traditionalist, strong-minded and with unshakable beliefs. Completely devoted to her mate, Moonshade will defend him even when she knows he's wrong.

SCOUTER

Scouter has the sharpest eyes of all the Wolfriders. He is steadfast, loyal, and often overprotective. He is also extremely intolerant of anyone, tribemates included, whom he perceives as putting his loved ones in jeopardy. Dewshine and Scouter have been lovemates for most of their lives, yet are not Recognized.

ONE-EYE

Woodhue gained his new sobriquet after his right eye was put out by humans. Needless to say, this seeded a lifelong hatred and distrust of the "five-fingers." Although he still considers Cutter a cub, One-Eye never questions Cutter's judgments; Cutter is chief and that is that. One-Eye is fierce in battle, especially when his cub, Scouter, or his lifemate, Clearbrook, is endangered.

PIKE

Pike is the Wolfriders' resident storyteller, taking his name from his preferred weapon. The most ordinary and happy-go-lucky of the Wolfriders, Pike has no grand ideals or desires for quests – he is a follower and rarely questions his chief's orders. Fully immersed in "the now of wolf thought," he clings through thick and thin to his two greatest loves: dreamberries and taking the easy path.

SAVAH

By far the eldest elf known to either the Wolfriders or Sun Folk, Savah – the "Mother of Memory" for the village – is a child of the original High Ones who first came to the World of Two Moons. Infinitely wise and compassionate, she is the keeper of both history and ritual for the desert elves, yet all her years have not dimmed the twinkle of humor in her eyes.

OTHERS

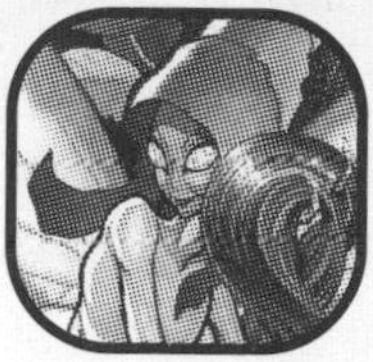

PETALWING

Petalwing is a Preserver – a carefree, fairylike creature that arrived on the World of Two Moons with the original High Ones. Petalwing lives under the grand illusion that "highthings" (elves) cannot live without it, and must be watched over and protected. Petalwing is the closest thing that the Preservers have to a leader. Cutter considers Petalwing to be a major annoyance; the sprite is unperturbed by this.

LORD VOLL

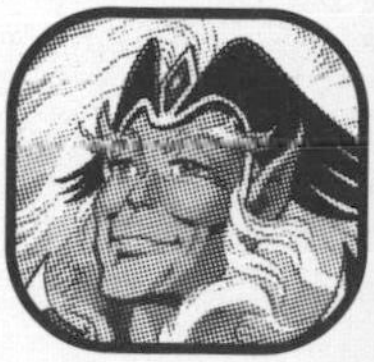

Lord Voll is a firstborn of the High Ones and the leader of the Glider elves who live within Blue Mountain. By the time the Wolfriders arrived, Voll had suffered the effects of centuries of apathy and has an air of melancholy about him. Though he still sees himself as lord, Winnowill effectively rules in his name.

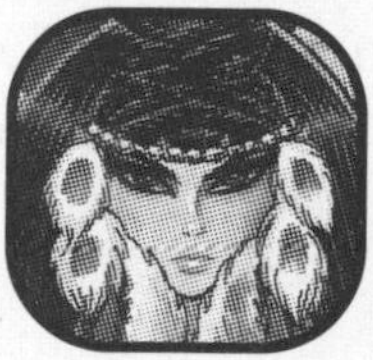

WINNOWILL

Beautiful, seductive, manipulative, enigmatic, black-hearted... Winnowill is all this, but she was not always thus. Countless centuries of boredom and uselessness have caused her healing powers to fester and turn in on themselves, taking her down into a subtle madness. Her only known child is the half elf/half troll Two-Edge, and she is not above lying, abduction, or even murder in order to achieve her ends.

TYLDAK

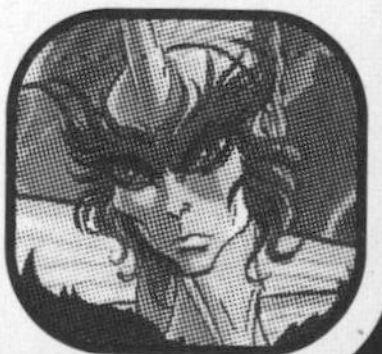

Tyldak is a Glider elf who wished desperately to fly, rather than merely glide or levitate as the rest of his folk do. He begged Winnowill to use her flesh-shaping powers to give him true wings that he might ride on air currents and soar with the birds.

IN THE PREVIOUS VOLUME

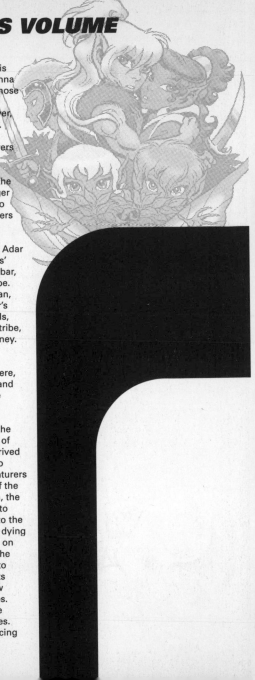

Cutter, feverish from an animal bite, finds his
way to the camp of two exiled humans, Nonna
and Adar. Nonna helps heal the elf chief, whose
eyes are opened for the first time to human
kindness. Suspicious of the humans, however,
Skywise is slow to accept their selfless acts.

In the Sun Village, Savah has used her powers
to help guide Cutter, but her spirit form has
traveled too far and now her physical body
seems paralyzed. Suntop links minds with the
Mother of Memory and discovers that danger
awaits his father. Leetah decides it is time to
find her lifemate and his friend; the Wolfriders
choose to go with her and offer protection.

Cutter and Skywise accompany Nonna and Adar
back to their homeland and use the humans'
superstitions of spirits to force the chief, Olbar,
to accept Nonna and Adar back into the tribe.
The power-hungry shamaness, Bone Woman,
attempts to save face, scheming with Olbar's
brother to kill the elves. But the scheme fails,
the two exiles are welcomed back into the tribe,
and Cutter and Skywise continue their journey.

The Wolfriders trace Cutter's path, the trail
leading them into the Forbidden Grove. There,
several members of the tribe are attacked and
taken away by giant hawks. Leetah and the
two children escape to an uncertain fate.

Sometime later, Cutter and Skywise enter the
Forbidden Grove and encounter Petalwing of
the Preservers, a race that like the elves arrived
on the world of Two Moons ages past. Also
within the Forbidden Grove, the two adventurers
find Leetah, the twins, and the remnants of the
Wolfriders. With the sprite as a companion, the
united elves arrive at Blue Mountain, only to
discover that their friends serve as slaves to the
Gliders, a new group of elves, ancient and dying
out. Lord Voll, leader of the Gliders, egged on
by the icy, beautiful Winnowill, considers the
Wolfriders expendable, as life has ceased to
have meaning for him. Cutter then presents
Ember and Suntop to Lord Voll who is now
convinced that new life is possible for elves.
Cutter shares his dream of reuniting all the
elfin tribes, all the children of the High Ones.
Winnowill stuns the Wolfriders by announcing
that the Gliders are the High Ones.

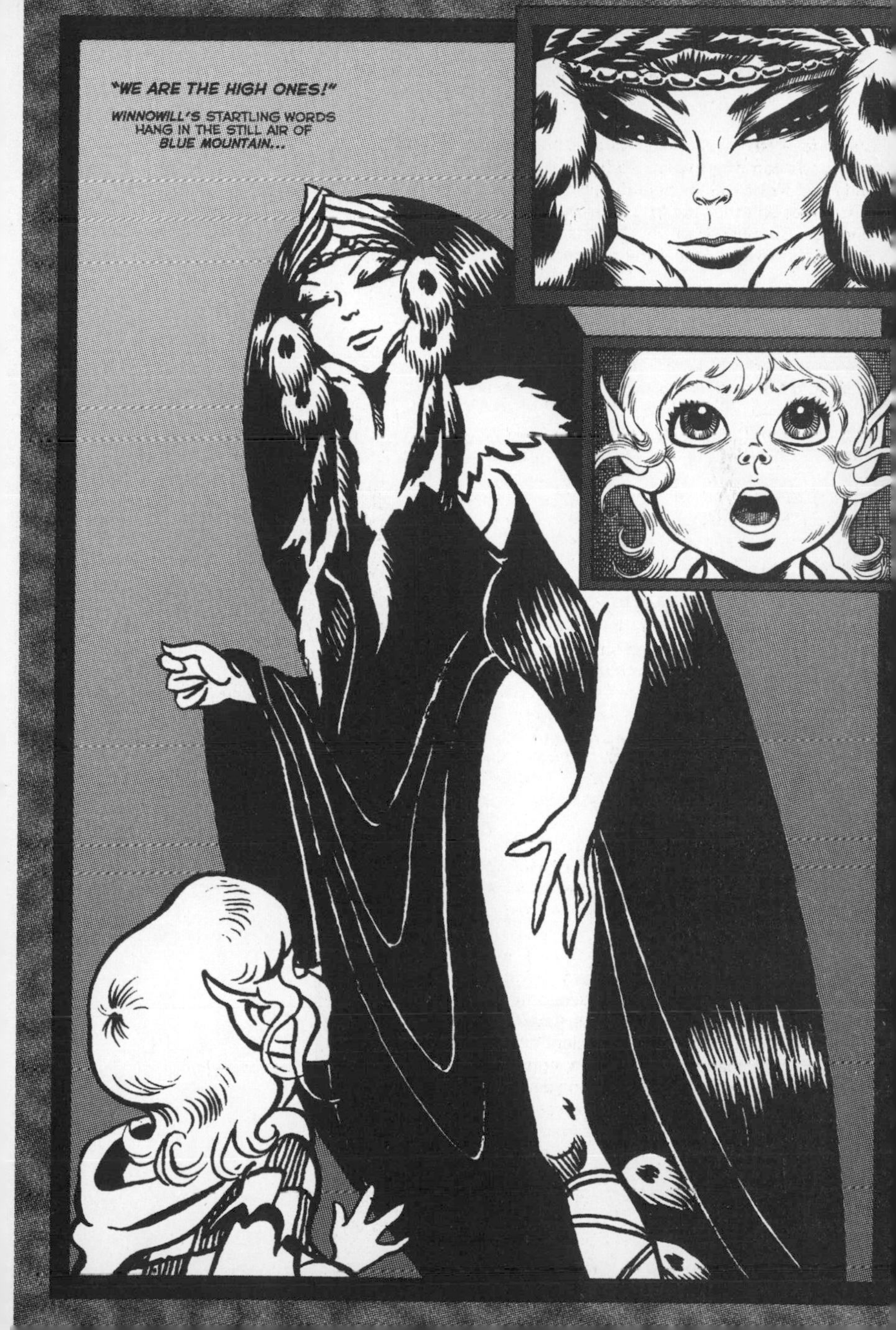
"WE ARE THE HIGH ONES!"
WINNOWILL'S STARTLING WORDS HANG IN THE STILL AIR OF BLUE MOUNTAIN...

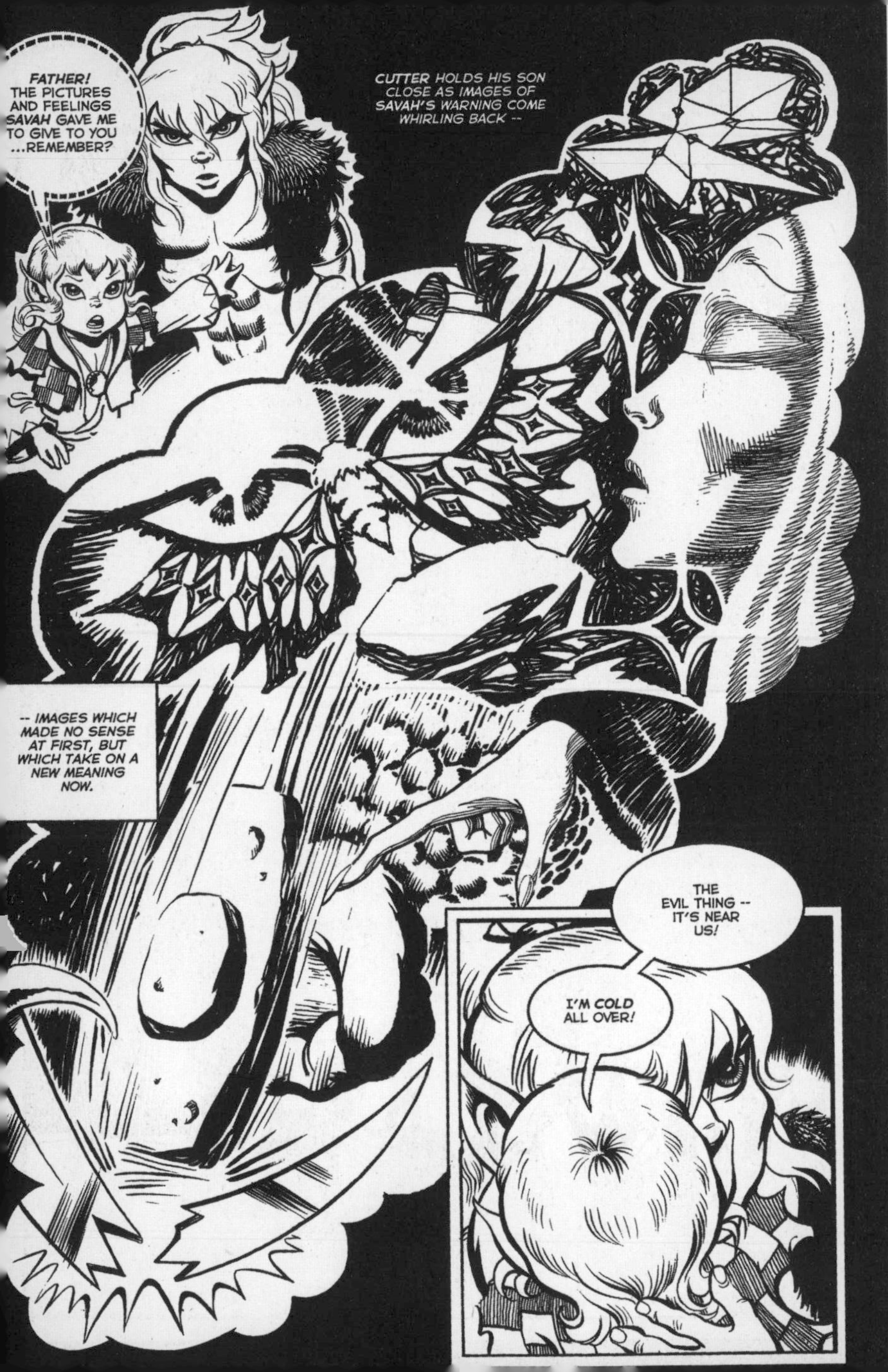
FATHER! THE PICTURES AND FEELINGS SAVAH GAVE ME TO GIVE TO YOU ...REMEMBER?
CUTTER HOLDS HIS SON CLOSE AS IMAGES OF SAVAH'S WARNING COME WHIRLING BACK --
-- IMAGES WHICH MADE NO SENSE AT FIRST, BUT WHICH TAKE ON A NEW MEANING NOW.
THE EVIL THING -- IT'S NEAR US!
I'M COLD ALL OVER!

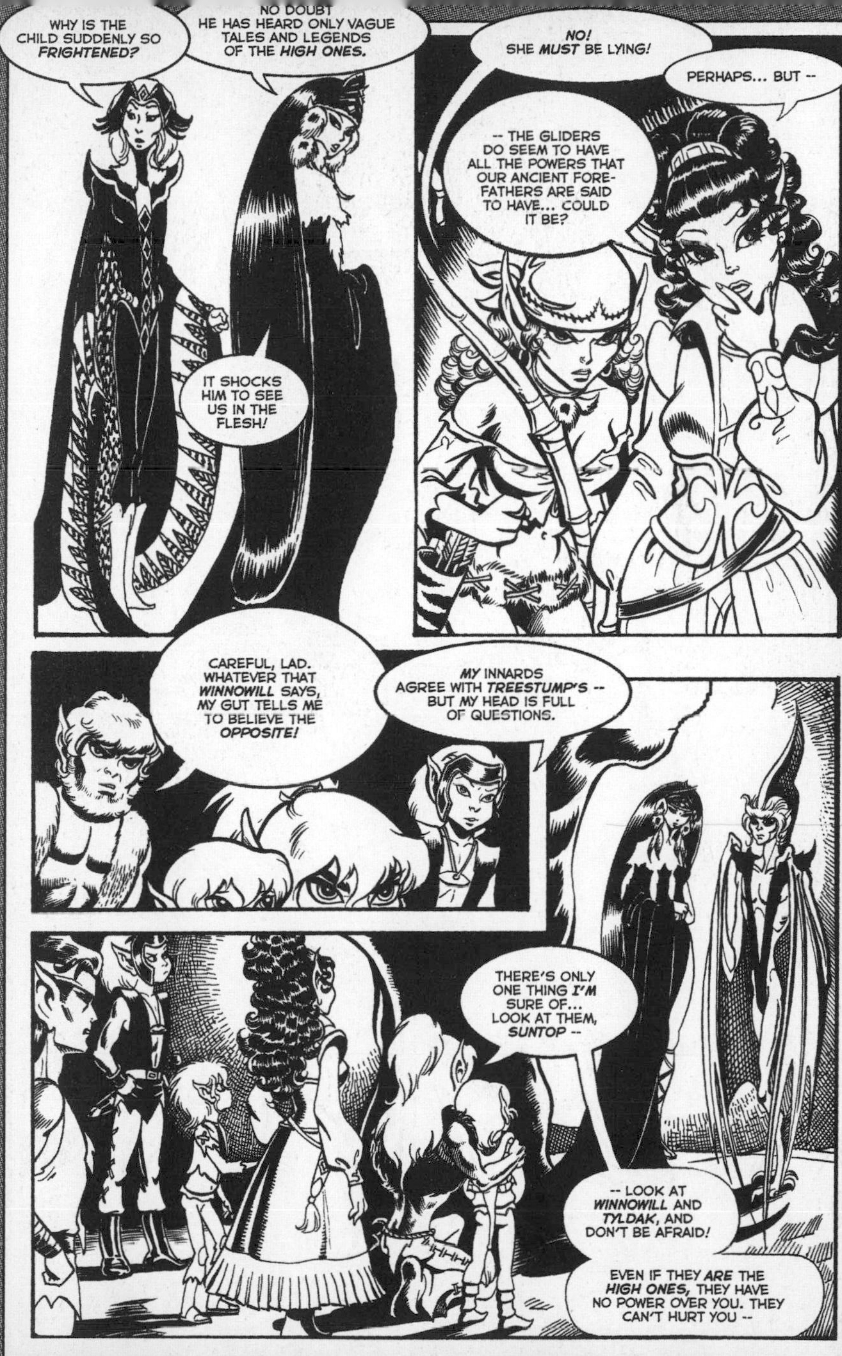
WHY IS THE CHILD SUDDENLY SO *FRIGHTENED?*
NO DOUBT HE HAS HEARD ONLY VAGUE TALES AND LEGENDS OF THE *HIGH ONES.*
IT SHOCKS HIM TO SEE US IN THE FLESH!
NO! SHE *MUST* BE LYING!
PERHAPS... BUT --
-- THE GLIDERS DO SEEM TO HAVE ALL THE POWERS THAT OUR ANCIENT FORE-FATHERS ARE SAID TO HAVE... COULD IT BE?
CAREFUL, LAD. WHATEVER THAT *WINNOWILL* SAYS, MY GUT TELLS ME TO BELIEVE THE *OPPOSITE!*
MY INNARDS AGREE WITH *TREESTUMP'S* -- BUT MY HEAD IS FULL OF QUESTIONS.
THERE'S ONLY ONE THING *I'M* SURE OF... LOOK AT THEM, *SUNTOP* --
-- LOOK AT *WINNOWILL* AND *TYLDAK*, AND DON'T BE AFRAID!
EVEN IF THEY *ARE* THE *HIGH ONES*, THEY HAVE NO POWER OVER YOU. THEY CAN'T HURT YOU --

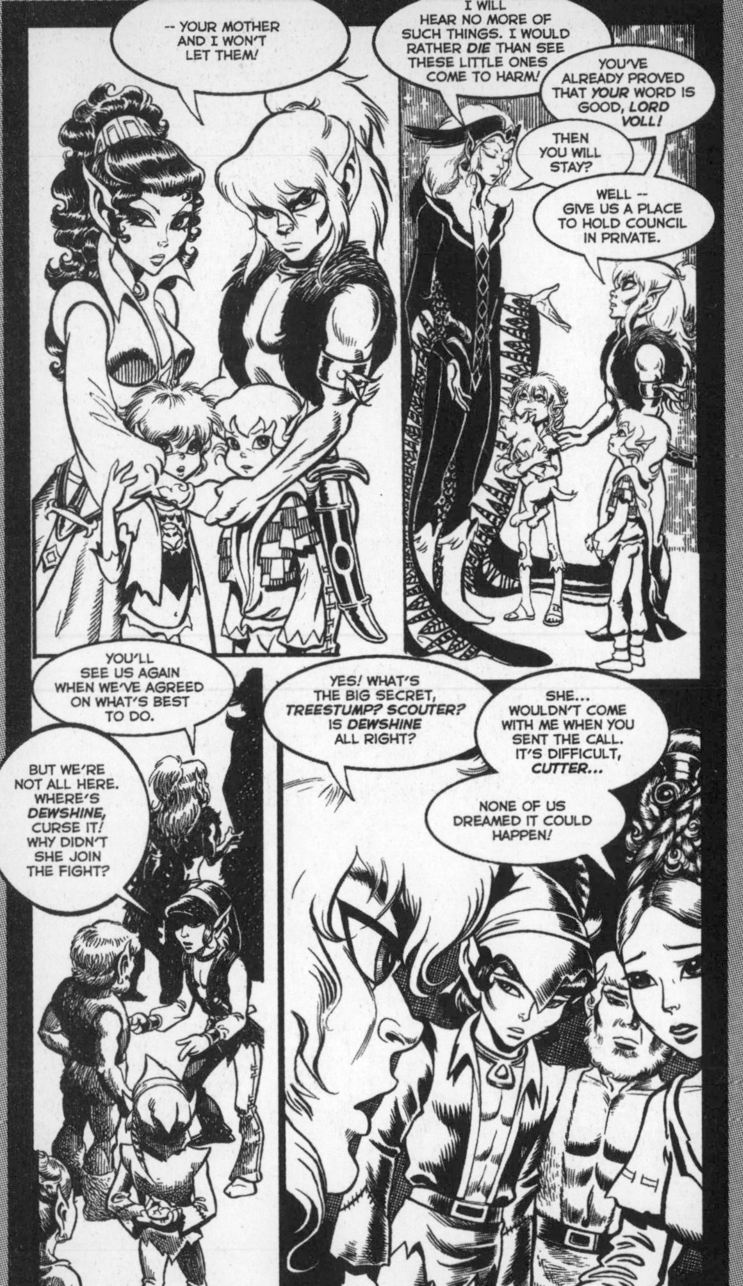
-- YOUR MOTHER AND I WON'T LET THEM!
I WILL HEAR NO MORE OF SUCH THINGS. I WOULD RATHER *DIE* THAN SEE THESE LITTLE ONES COME TO HARM!
YOU'VE ALREADY PROVED THAT *YOUR* WORD IS GOOD, ***LORD VOLL!***
THEN YOU WILL STAY?
WELL -- GIVE US A PLACE TO HOLD COUNCIL IN PRIVATE.
YOU'LL SEE US AGAIN WHEN WE'VE AGREED ON WHAT'S BEST TO DO.
BUT WE'RE NOT ALL HERE. WHERE'S ***DEWSHINE,*** CURSE IT! WHY DIDN'T SHE JOIN THE FIGHT?
YES! WHAT'S THE BIG SECRET, ***TREESTUMP? SCOUTER?*** IS ***DEWSHINE*** ALL RIGHT?
SHE... WOULDN'T COME WITH ME WHEN YOU SENT THE CALL. IT'S DIFFICULT, ***CUTTER...***
NONE OF US DREAMED IT COULD HAPPEN!

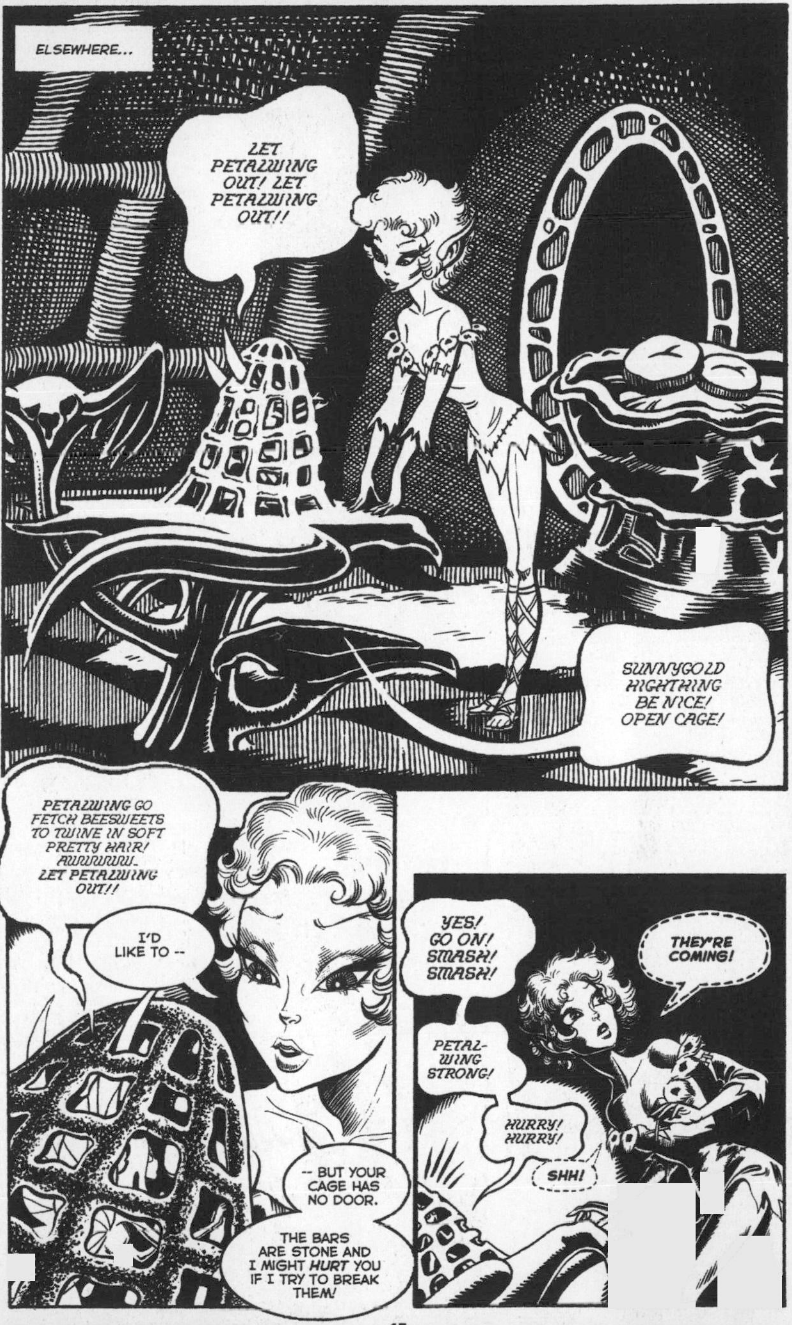
ELSEWHERE...
LET PETALWING OUT! LET PETALWING OUT!!
SUNNYGOLD HIGHTHING BE NICE! OPEN CAGE!
PETALWING GO FETCH BEESWEETS TO TWINE IN SOFT PRETTY HAIR! AWWWWWW... LET PETALWING OUT!!
I'D LIKE TO --
-- BUT YOUR CAGE HAS NO DOOR.
THE BARS ARE STONE AND I MIGHT HURT YOU IF I TRY TO BREAK THEM!
YES! GO ON! SMASH! SMASH!
PETAL-WING STRONG!
HURRY! HURRY!
SHH!
THEY'RE COMING!

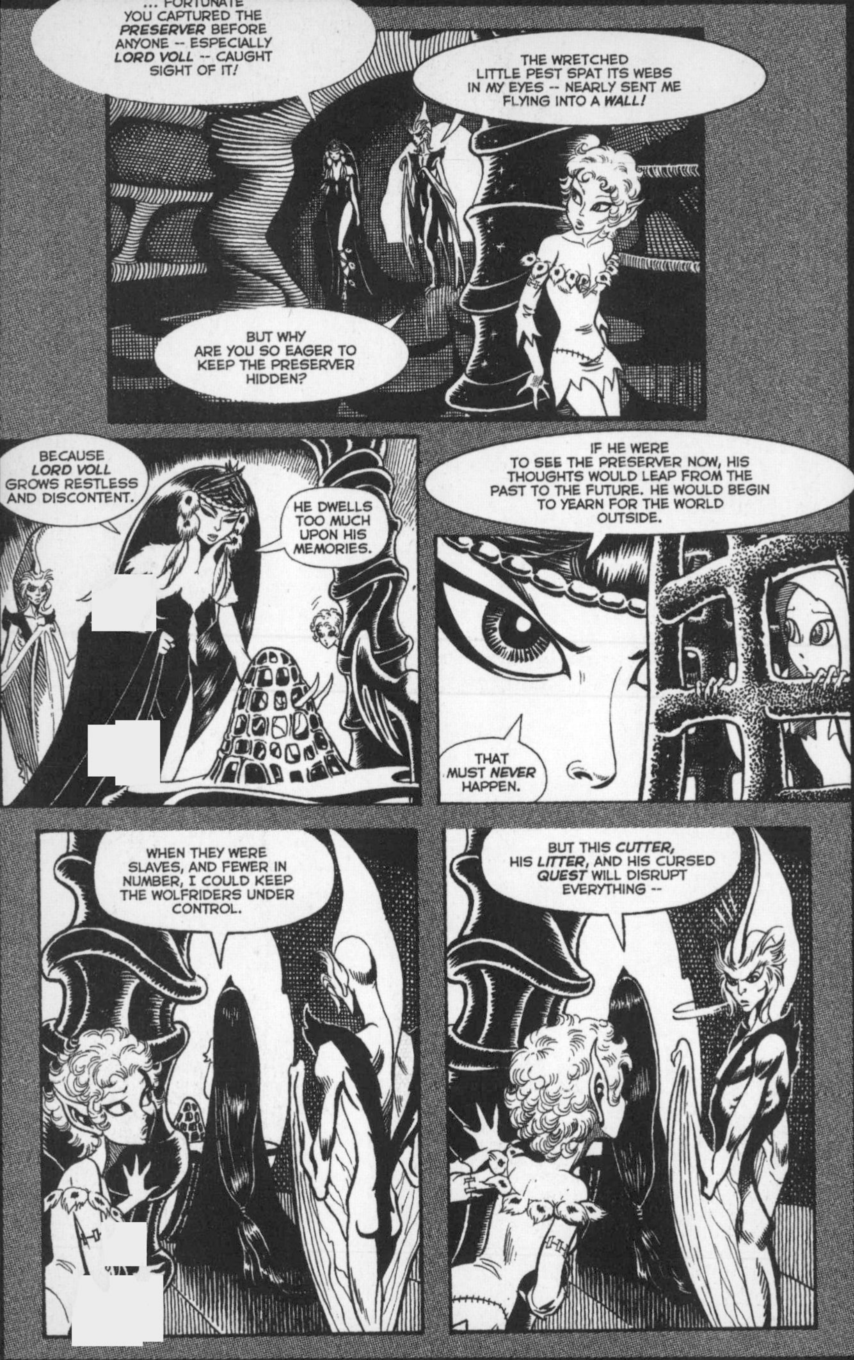
... FORTUNATE YOU CAPTURED THE PRESERVER BEFORE ANYONE -- ESPECIALLY LORD VOLL -- CAUGHT SIGHT OF IT!
THE WRETCHED LITTLE PEST SPAT ITS WEBS IN MY EYES -- NEARLY SENT ME FLYING INTO A WALL!
BUT WHY ARE YOU SO EAGER TO KEEP THE PRESERVER HIDDEN?
BECAUSE LORD VOLL GROWS RESTLESS AND DISCONTENT.
HE DWELLS TOO MUCH UPON HIS MEMORIES.
IF HE WERE TO SEE THE PRESERVER NOW, HIS THOUGHTS WOULD LEAP FROM THE PAST TO THE FUTURE. HE WOULD BEGIN TO YEARN FOR THE WORLD OUTSIDE.
THAT MUST NEVER HAPPEN.
WHEN THEY WERE SLAVES, AND FEWER IN NUMBER, I COULD KEEP THE WOLFRIDERS UNDER CONTROL.
BUT THIS CUTTER, HIS LITTER, AND HIS CURSED QUEST WILL DISRUPT EVERYTHING --

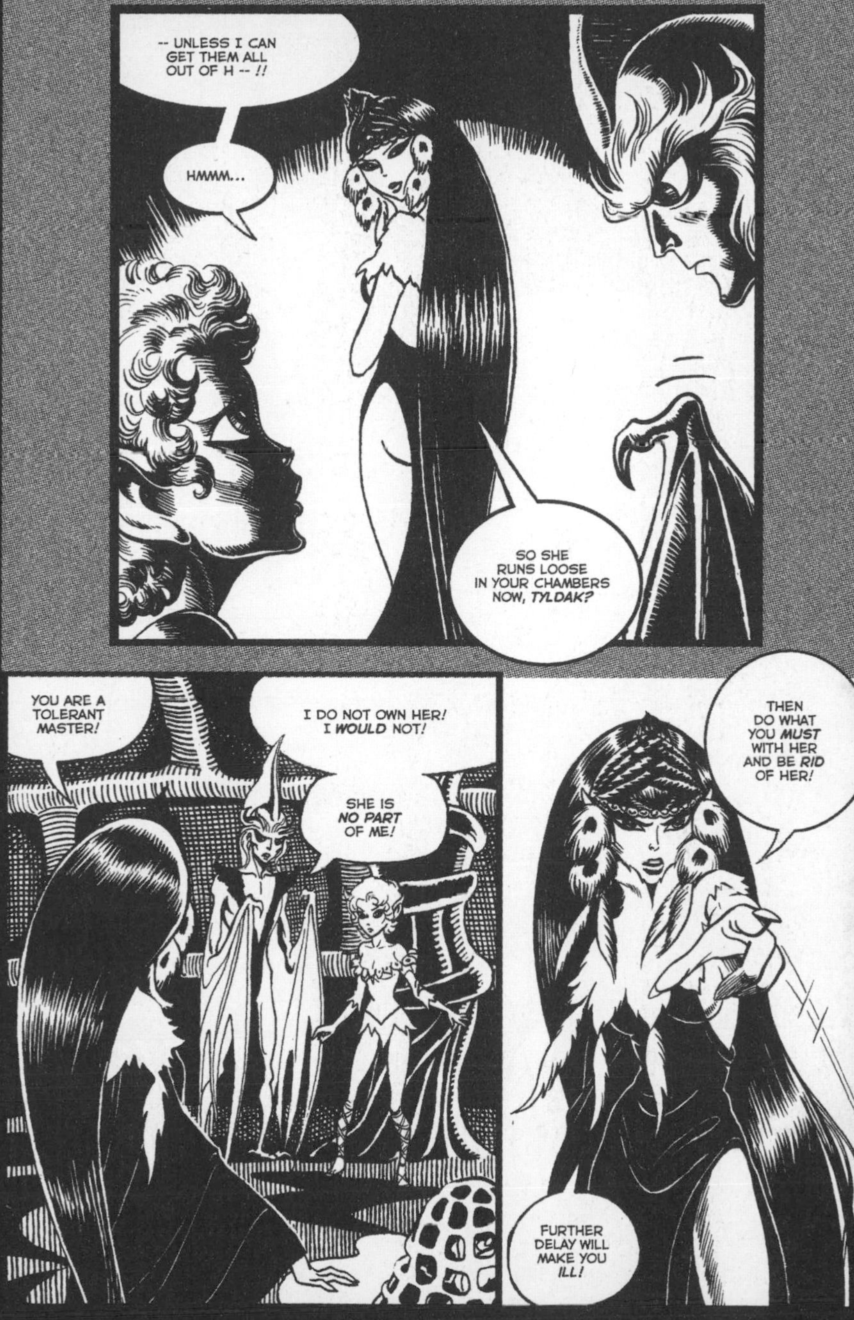
-- UNLESS I CAN GET THEM ALL OUT OF H -- !!
HMMM...
SO SHE RUNS LOOSE IN YOUR CHAMBERS NOW, TYLDAK?
YOU ARE A TOLERANT MASTER!
I DO NOT OWN HER! I WOULD NOT!
SHE IS NO PART OF ME!
THEN DO WHAT YOU MUST WITH HER AND BE RID OF HER!
FURTHER DELAY WILL MAKE YOU ILL!

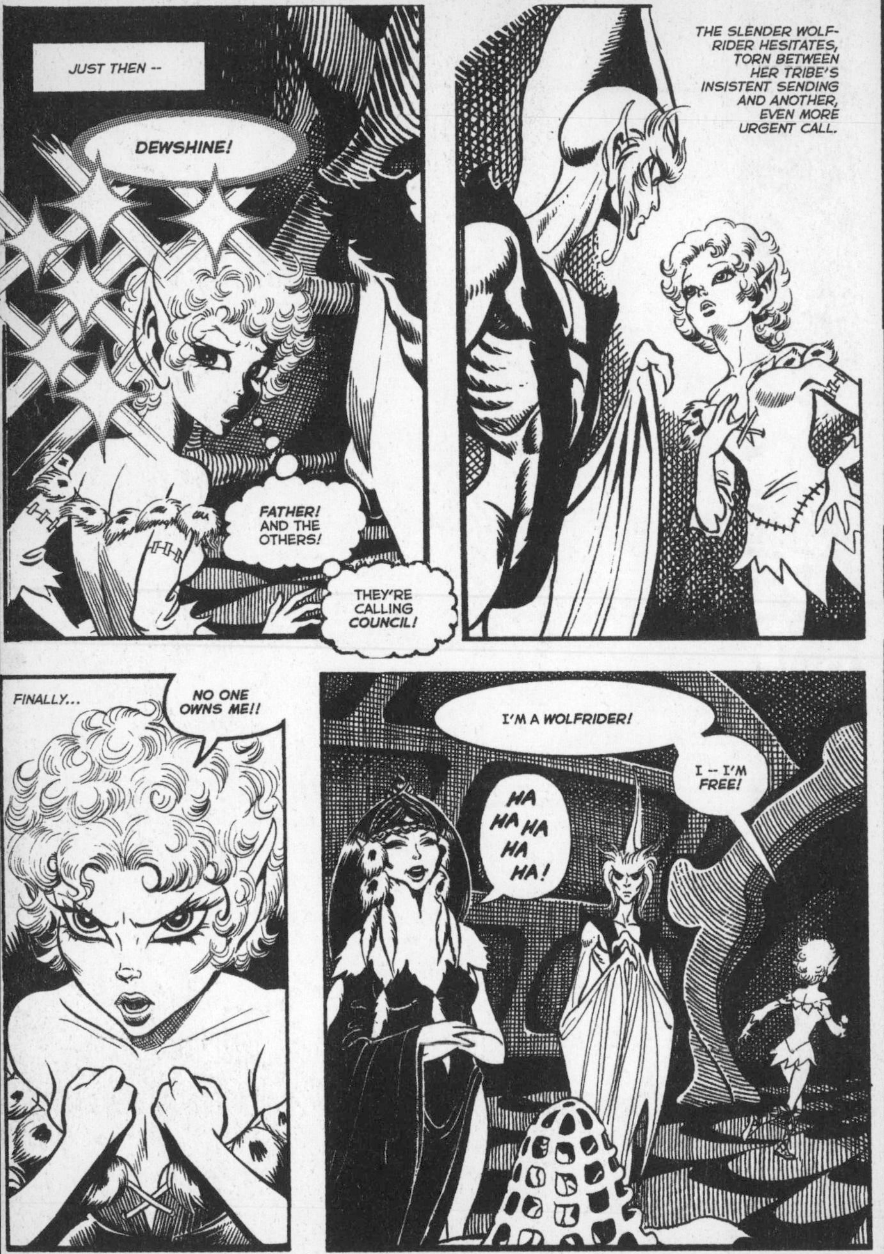
JUST THEN --
DEWSHINE!
FATHER! AND THE OTHERS!
THEY'RE CALLING COUNCIL!
THE SLENDER WOLF-RIDER HESITATES, TORN BETWEEN HER TRIBE'S INSISTENT SENDING AND ANOTHER, EVEN MORE URGENT CALL.
FINALLY...
NO ONE OWNS ME!!
I'M A WOLFRIDER!
I -- I'M FREE!
HA HA HA HA HA!

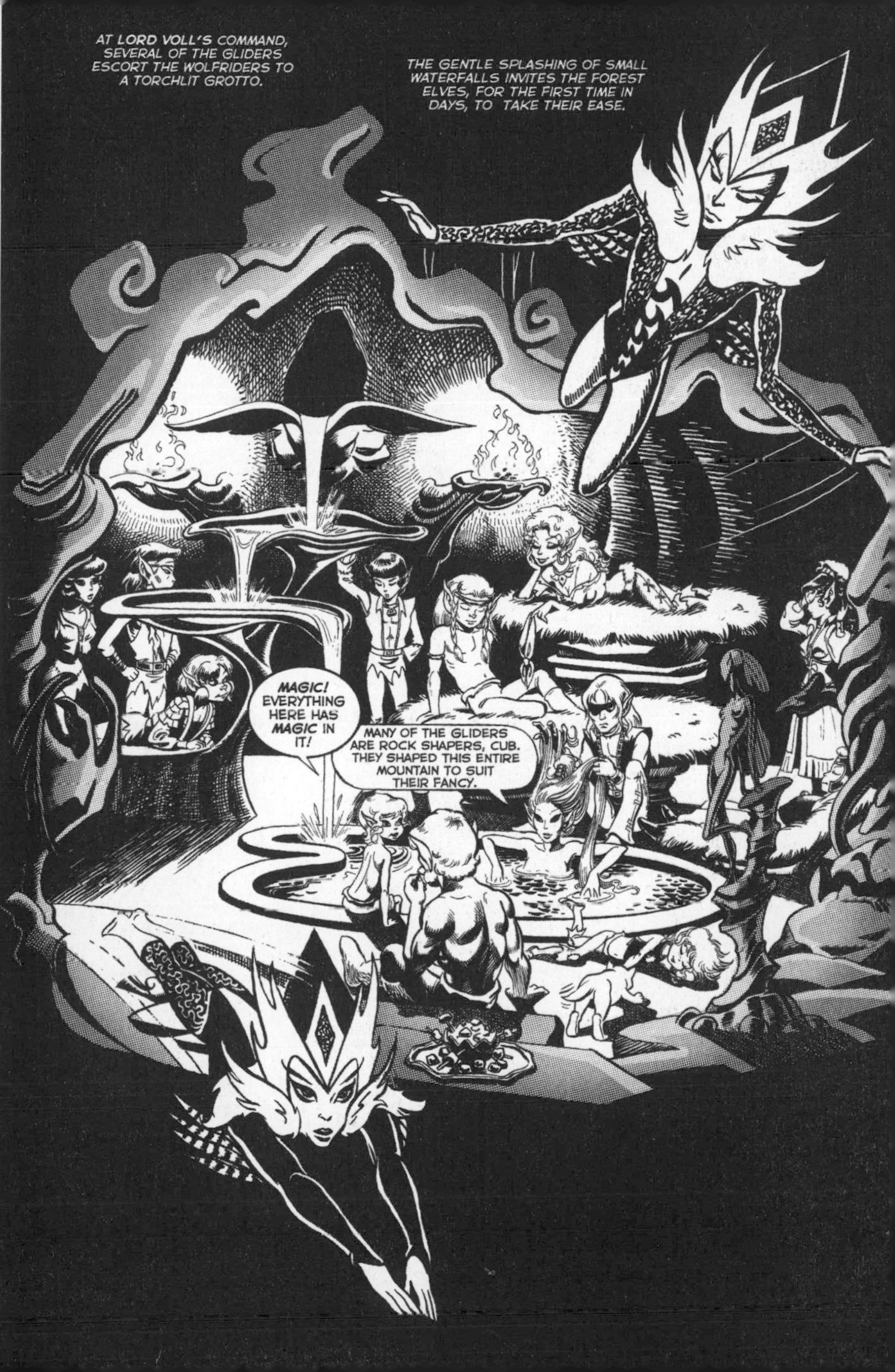
AT LORD VOLL'S COMMAND, SEVERAL OF THE GLIDERS ESCORT THE WOLFRIDERS TO A TORCHLIT GROTTO.
THE GENTLE SPLASHING OF SMALL WATERFALLS INVITES THE FOREST ELVES, FOR THE FIRST TIME IN DAYS, TO TAKE THEIR EASE.
MAGIC! EVERYTHING HERE HAS MAGIC IN IT!
MANY OF THE GLIDERS ARE ROCK SHAPERS, CUB. THEY SHAPED THIS ENTIRE MOUNTAIN TO SUIT THEIR FANCY.

GRUMBLE THEY CAN'T LEAVE WELL ENOUGH ALONE!

GIVE ME A TREE TO SHAPE ANY DAY -- ROCKS DON'T *BREATHE!*

FATHER...?

TREESTUMP'S EYES LIGHT UP AS HIS DAUGHTER SHYLY COMES TO HIM.

PRETTY CUB, I MISSED YOU! WE ALL DID! WHY...?

PLEASE, FATHER...

JUST LET ME SIT QUIETLY WITH YOU.

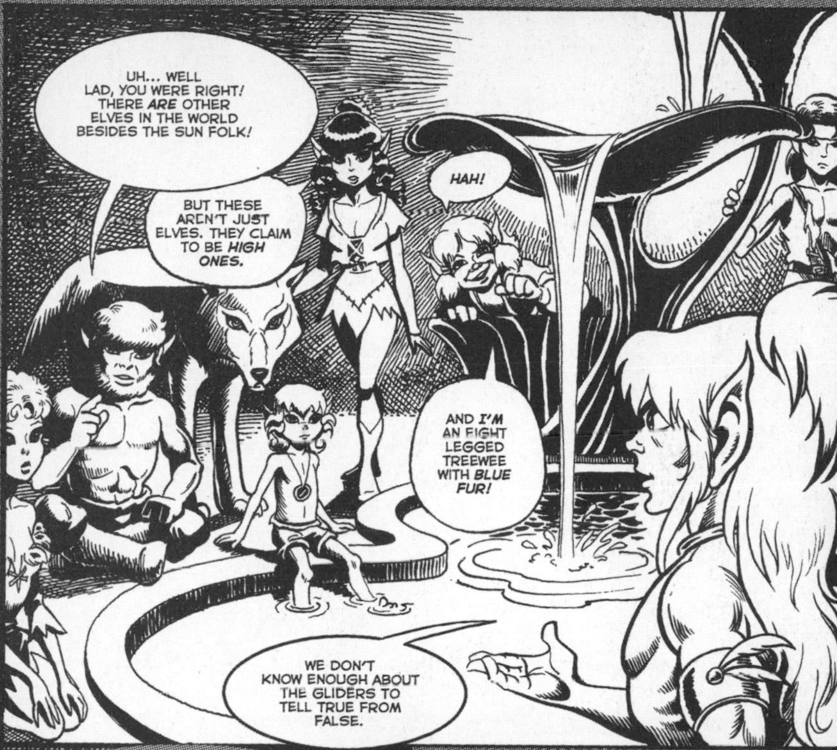
UH... WELL LAD, YOU WERE RIGHT! THERE ARE OTHER ELVES IN THE WORLD BESIDES THE SUN FOLK!
BUT THESE AREN'T JUST ELVES. THEY CLAIM TO BE HIGH ONES.
HAH!
AND I'M AN EIGHT LEGGED TREEWEE WITH BLUE FUR!
WE DON'T KNOW ENOUGH ABOUT THE GLIDERS TO TELL TRUE FROM FALSE.

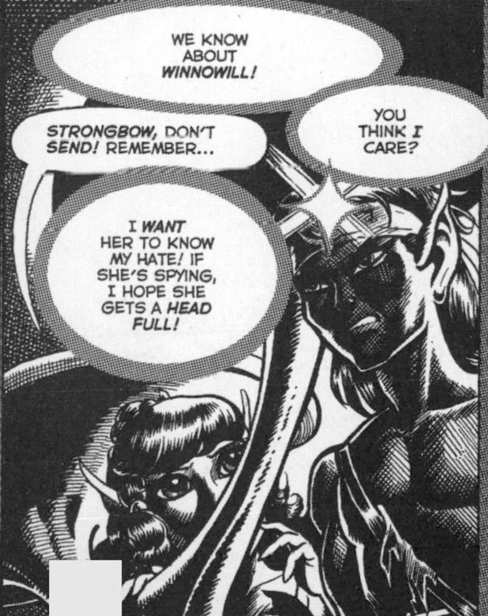
WE KNOW ABOUT WINNOWILL!
STRONGBOW, DON'T SEND! REMEMBER...
YOU THINK I CARE?
I WANT HER TO KNOW MY HATE! IF SHE'S SPYING, I HOPE SHE GETS A HEAD FULL!

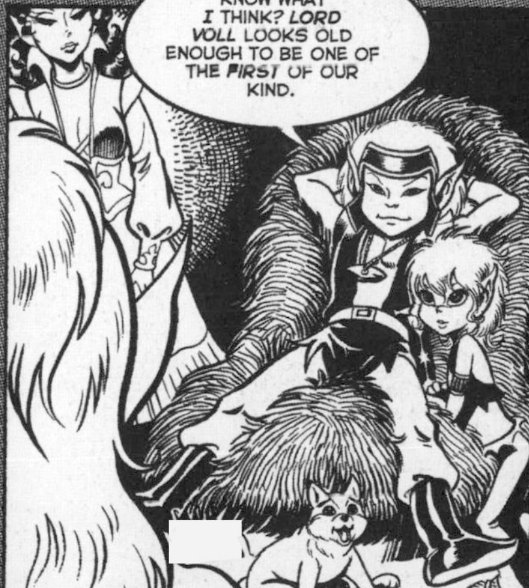
KNOW WHAT I THINK? LORD VOLL LOOKS OLD ENOUGH TO BE ONE OF THE FIRST OF OUR KIND.

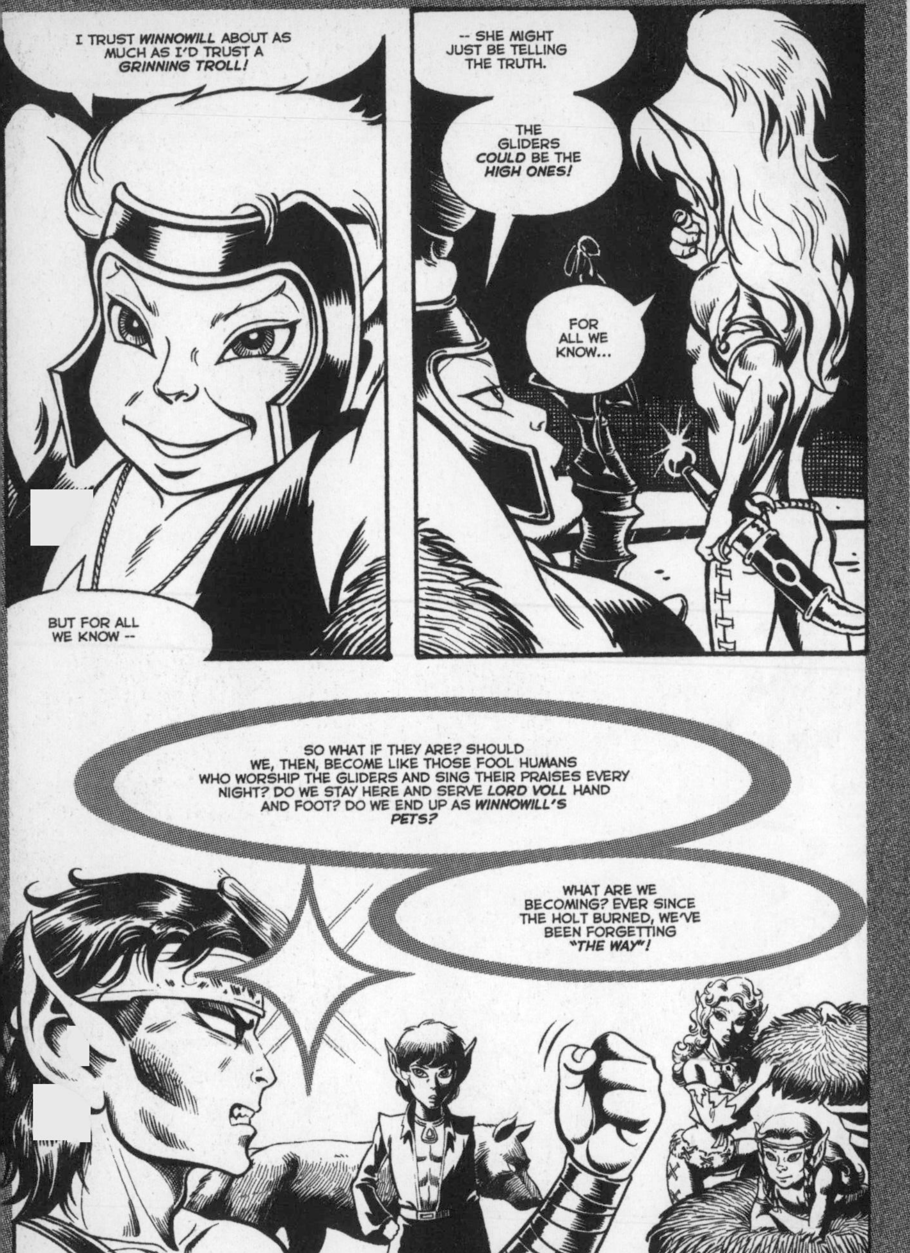

I TRUST WINNOWILL ABOUT AS MUCH AS I'D TRUST A GRINNING TROLL!
BUT FOR ALL WE KNOW --
-- SHE MIGHT JUST BE TELLING THE TRUTH.
THE GLIDERS COULD BE THE HIGH ONES!
FOR ALL WE KNOW...
SO WHAT IF THEY ARE? SHOULD WE, THEN, BECOME LIKE THOSE FOOL HUMANS WHO WORSHIP THE GLIDERS AND SING THEIR PRAISES EVERY NIGHT? DO WE STAY HERE AND SERVE LORD VOLL HAND AND FOOT? DO WE END UP AS WINNOWILL'S PETS?
WHAT ARE WE BECOMING? EVER SINCE THE HOLT BURNED, WE'VE BEEN FORGETTING "THE WAY"!

BUT REMEMBER HOW IT WAS *BEFORE* THE FIRE, WHEN THE HOLT WAS GREEN --
-- WHEN WE KNEW WHO WE WERE!
REMEMBER THE HUNTS AND HOWLS --
-- THE TASTE OF FRESH BLOOD SHARED WITH OUR FOREST BROTHERS!
REMEMBER HOW SELDOM WE WORRIED ABOUT TOMORROW.
WE LIVED LIKE *WOLVES!*
WE KNEW OUR TERRITORY AND WE DEFENDED IT!

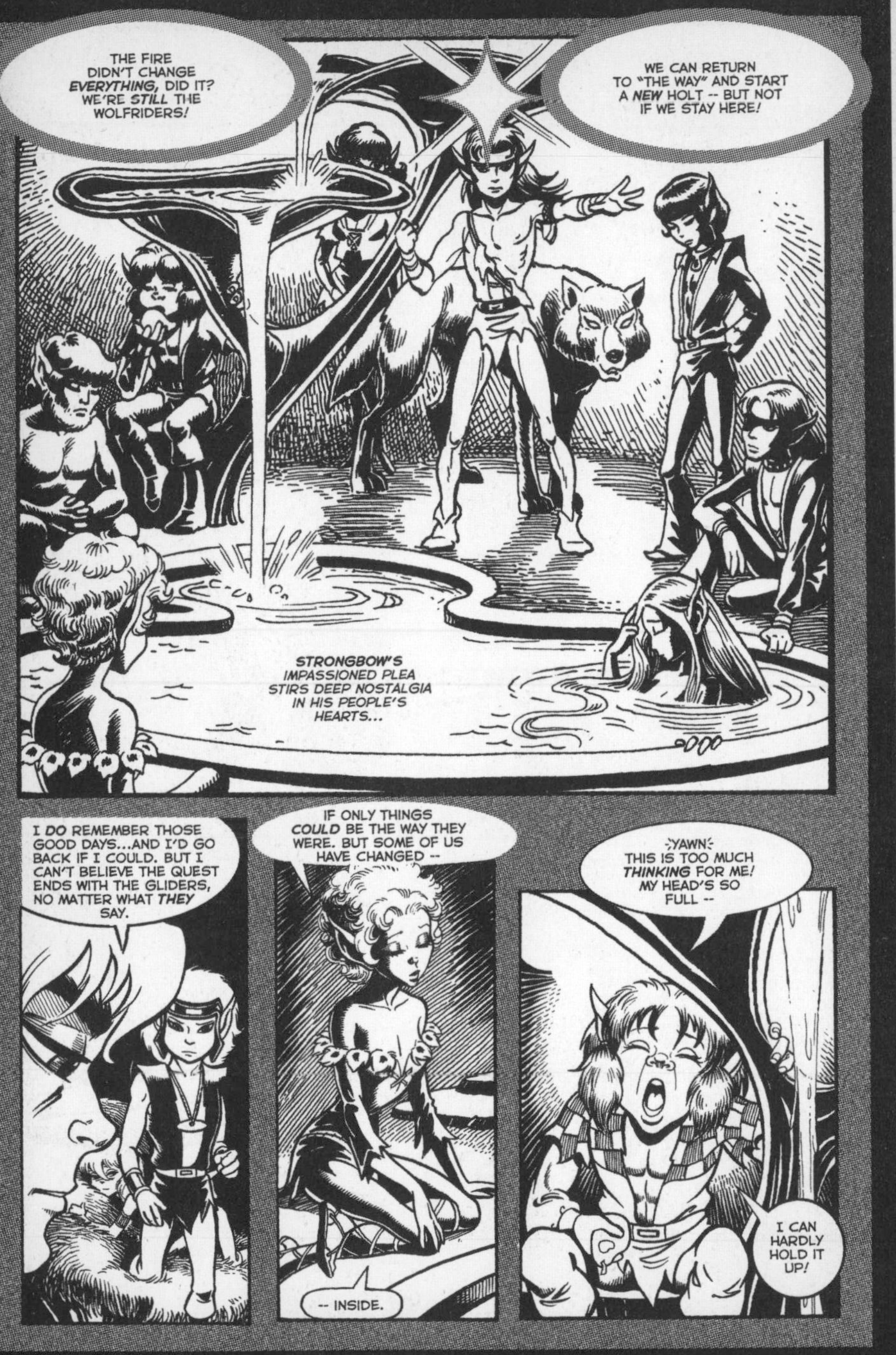

THE FIRE DIDN'T CHANGE *EVERYTHING*, DID IT? WE'RE *STILL* THE WOLFRIDERS!
WE CAN RETURN TO "THE WAY" AND START A *NEW* HOLT -- BUT NOT IF WE STAY HERE!
STRONGBOW'S IMPASSIONED PLEA STIRS DEEP NOSTALGIA IN HIS PEOPLE'S HEARTS...
I *DO* REMEMBER THOSE GOOD DAYS...AND I'D GO BACK IF I COULD. BUT I CAN'T BELIEVE THE QUEST ENDS WITH THE GLIDERS, NO MATTER WHAT *THEY* SAY.
IF ONLY THINGS *COULD* BE THE WAY THEY WERE. BUT SOME OF US HAVE CHANGED --
-- INSIDE.
YAWN
THIS IS TOO MUCH *THINKING* FOR ME! MY HEAD'S SO FULL --
I CAN HARDLY HOLD IT UP!

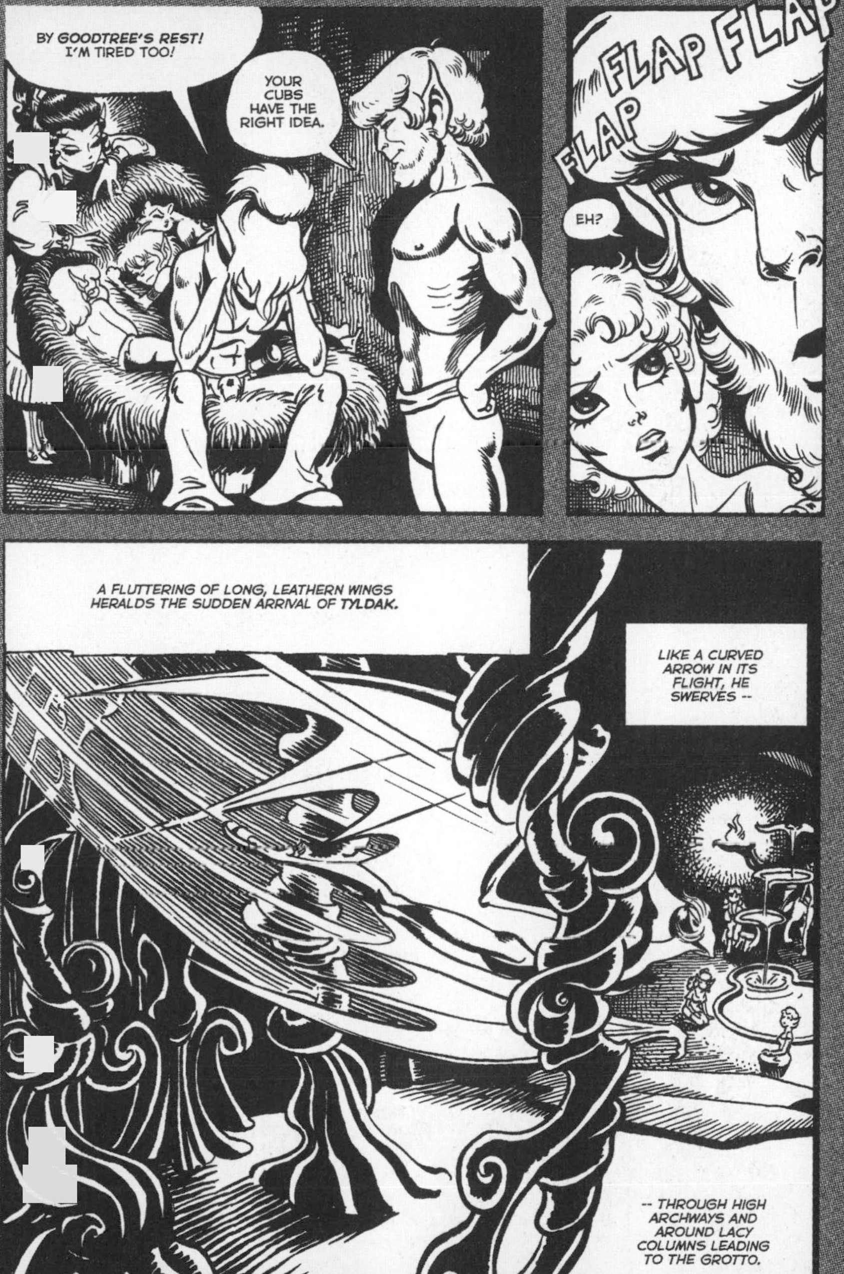
BY GOODTREE'S REST! I'M TIRED TOO!
YOUR CUBS HAVE THE RIGHT IDEA.
FLAP FLAP FLAP FLAP
EH?
A FLUTTERING OF LONG, LEATHERN WINGS HERALDS THE SUDDEN ARRIVAL OF TYLDAK.
LIKE A CURVED ARROW IN ITS FLIGHT, HE SWERVES --
-- THROUGH HIGH ARCHWAYS AND AROUND LACY COLUMNS LEADING TO THE GROTTO.

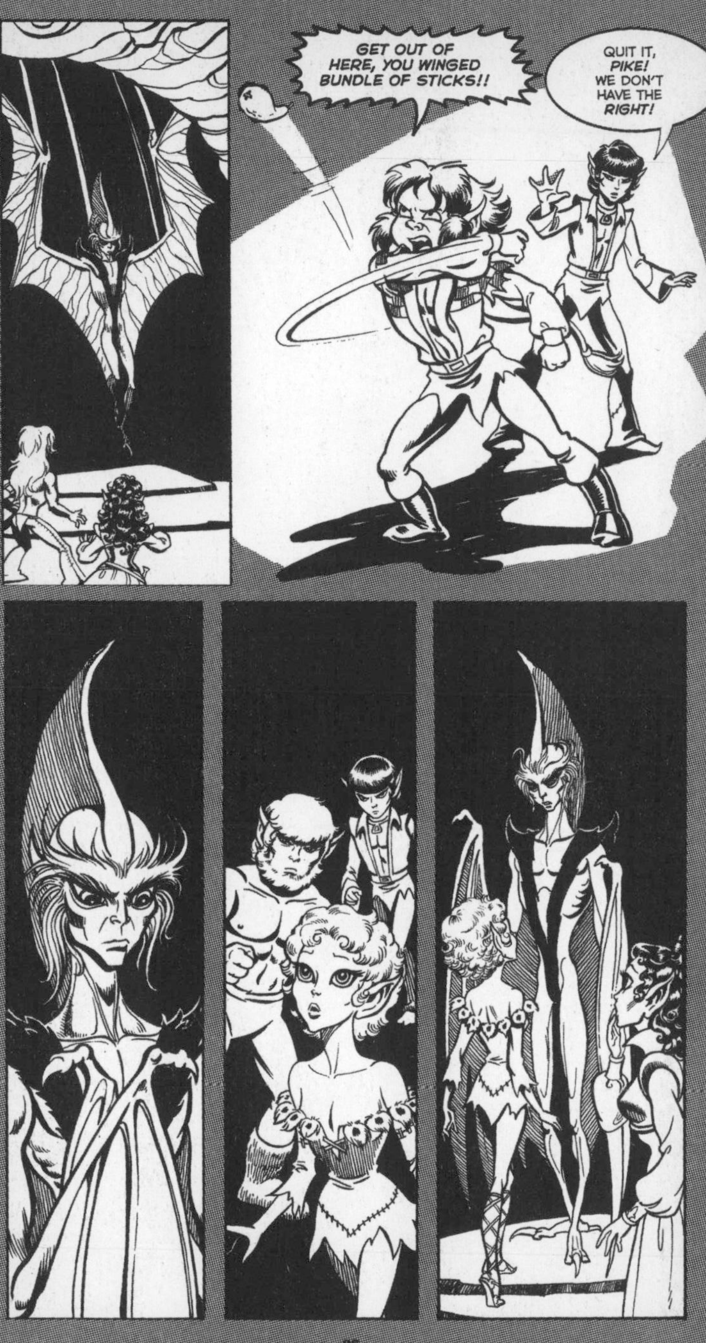
GET OUT OF HERE, YOU WINGED BUNDLE OF STICKS!!
QUIT IT, PIKE! WE DON'T HAVE THE RIGHT!

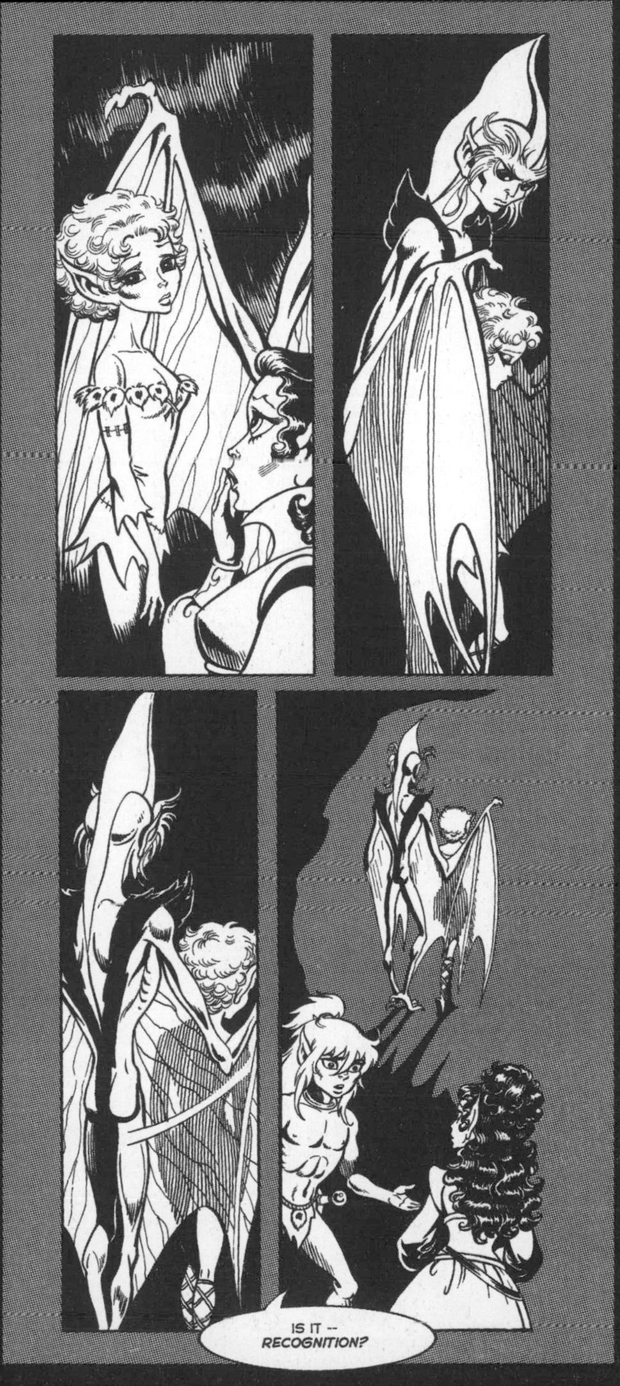
IS IT --
RECOGNITION?

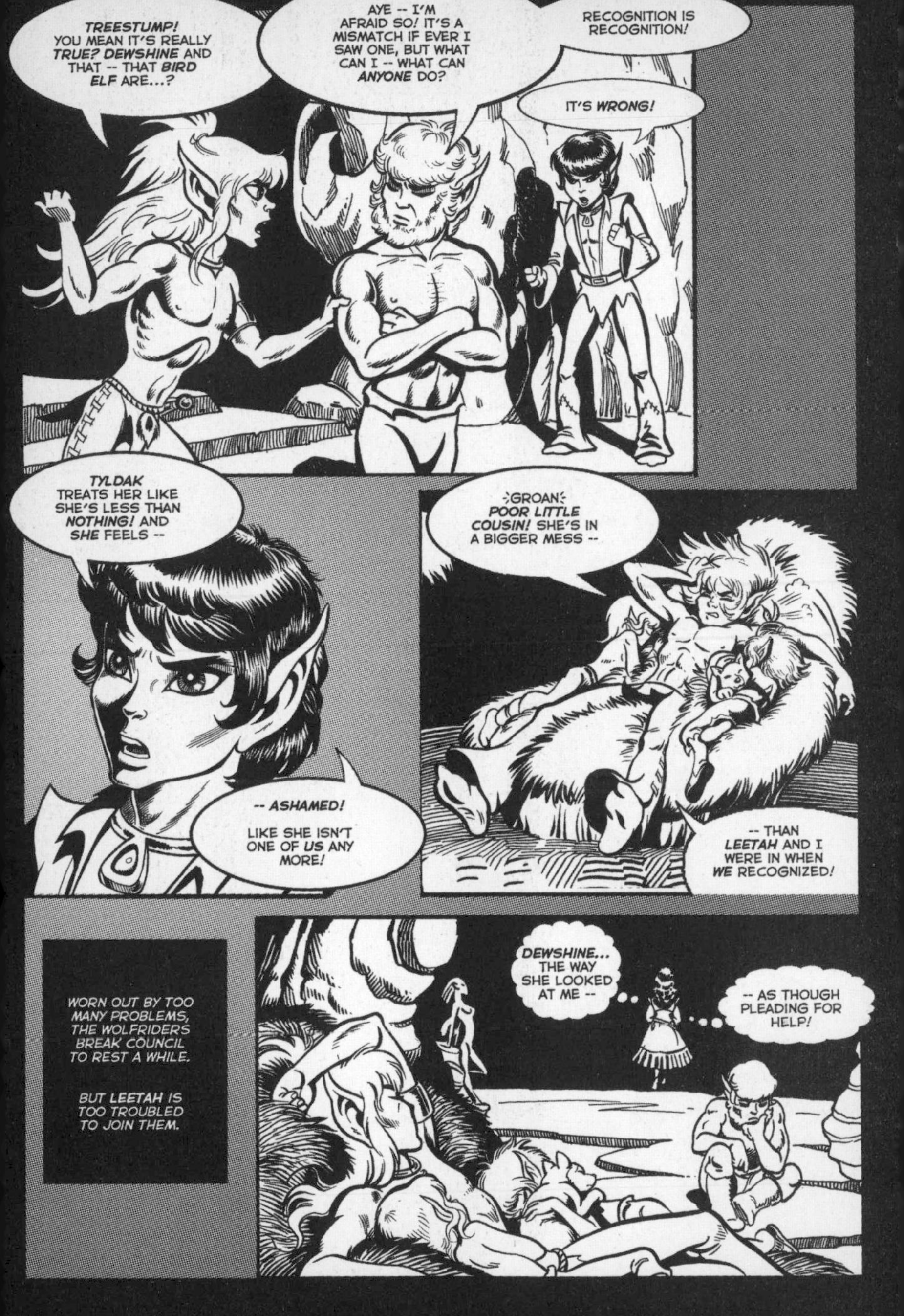
TREESTUMP! YOU MEAN IT'S REALLY TRUE? DEWSHINE AND THAT -- THAT BIRD ELF ARE...?
AYE -- I'M AFRAID SO! IT'S A MISMATCH IF EVER I SAW ONE, BUT WHAT CAN I -- WHAT CAN ANYONE DO?
RECOGNITION IS RECOGNITION!
IT'S WRONG!
TYLDAK TREATS HER LIKE SHE'S LESS THAN NOTHING! AND SHE FEELS --
-- ASHAMED!
LIKE SHE ISN'T ONE OF US ANY MORE!
GROAN POOR LITTLE COUSIN! SHE'S IN A BIGGER MESS --
-- THAN LEETAH AND I WERE IN WHEN WE RECOGNIZED!
WORN OUT BY TOO MANY PROBLEMS, THE WOLFRIDERS BREAK COUNCIL TO REST A WHILE.
BUT LEETAH IS TOO TROUBLED TO JOIN THEM.
DEWSHINE... THE WAY SHE LOOKED AT ME --
-- AS THOUGH PLEADING FOR HELP!

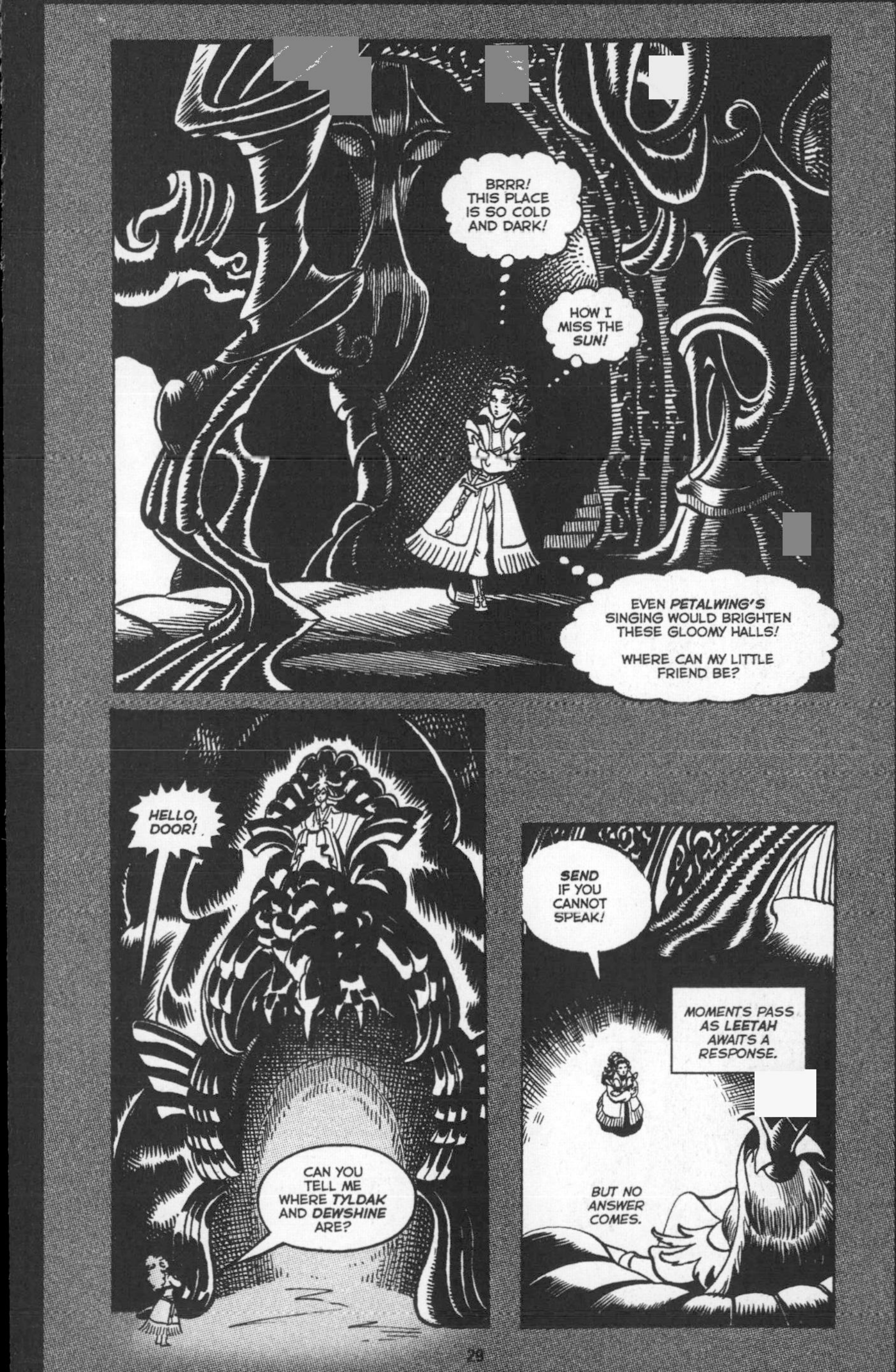
BRRR! THIS PLACE IS SO COLD AND DARK!
HOW I MISS THE SUN!
EVEN PETALWING'S SINGING WOULD BRIGHTEN THESE GLOOMY HALLS!
WHERE CAN MY LITTLE FRIEND BE?
HELLO, DOOR!
CAN YOU TELL ME WHERE TYLDAK AND DEWSHINE ARE?
SEND IF YOU CANNOT SPEAK!
MOMENTS PASS AS LEETAH AWAITS A RESPONSE.
BUT NO ANSWER COMES.

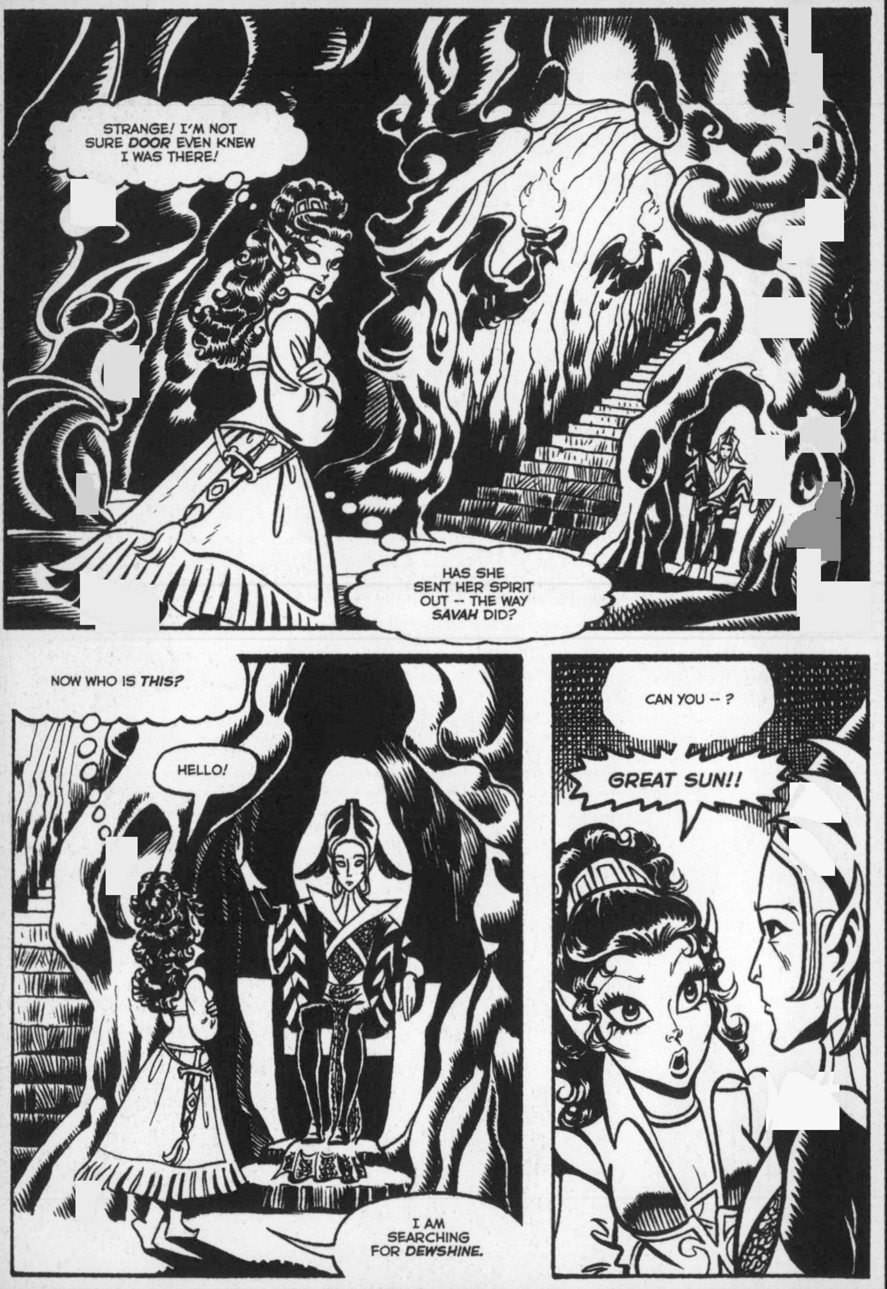

STRANGE! I'M NOT SURE DOOR EVEN KNEW I WAS THERE!
HAS SHE SENT HER SPIRIT OUT -- THE WAY SAVAH DID?
NOW WHO IS THIS?
HELLO!
I AM SEARCHING FOR DEWSHINE.
CAN YOU -- ?
GREAT SUN!!

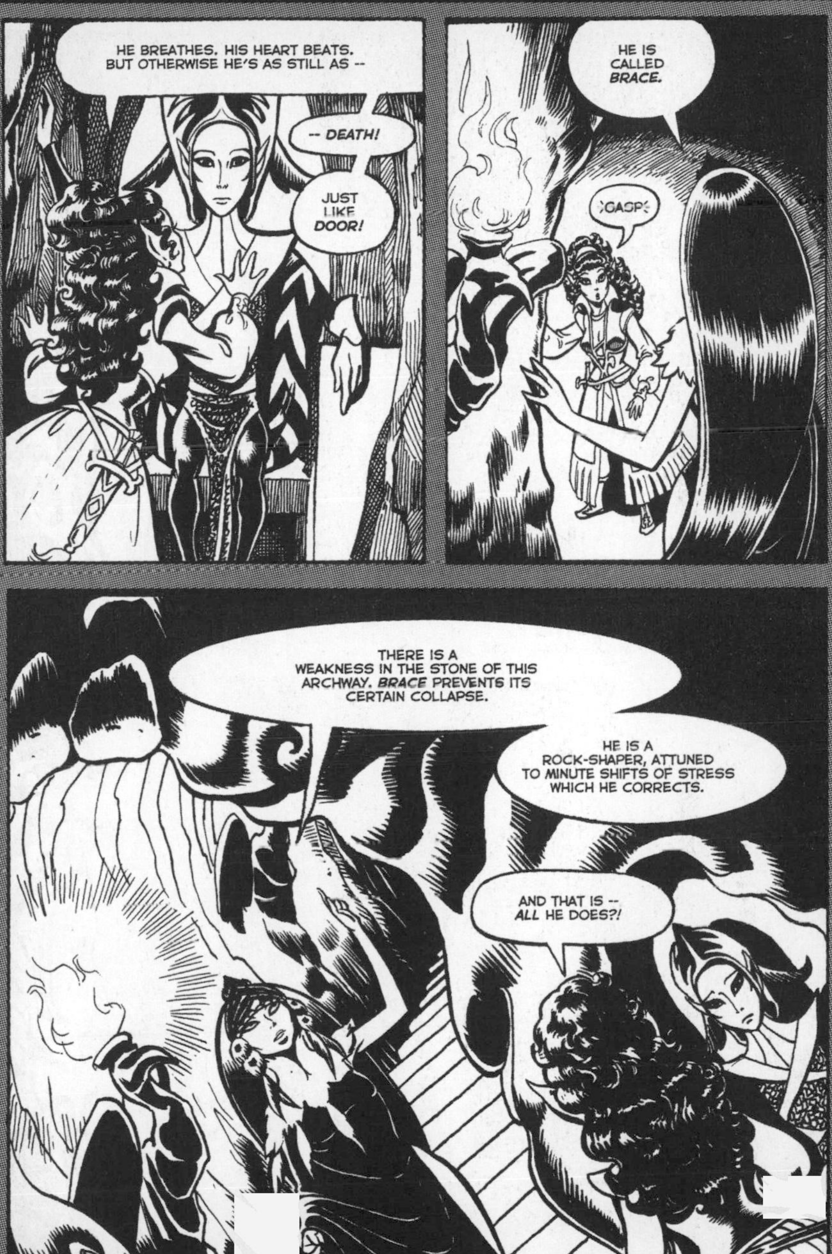
HE BREATHES. HIS HEART BEATS. BUT OTHERWISE HE'S AS STILL AS --
-- DEATH!
JUST LIKE DOOR!
HE IS CALLED BRACE.
GASP
THERE IS A WEAKNESS IN THE STONE OF THIS ARCHWAY. BRACE PREVENTS ITS CERTAIN COLLAPSE.
HE IS A ROCK-SHAPER, ATTUNED TO MINUTE SHIFTS OF STRESS WHICH HE CORRECTS.
AND THAT IS -- ALL HE DOES?!

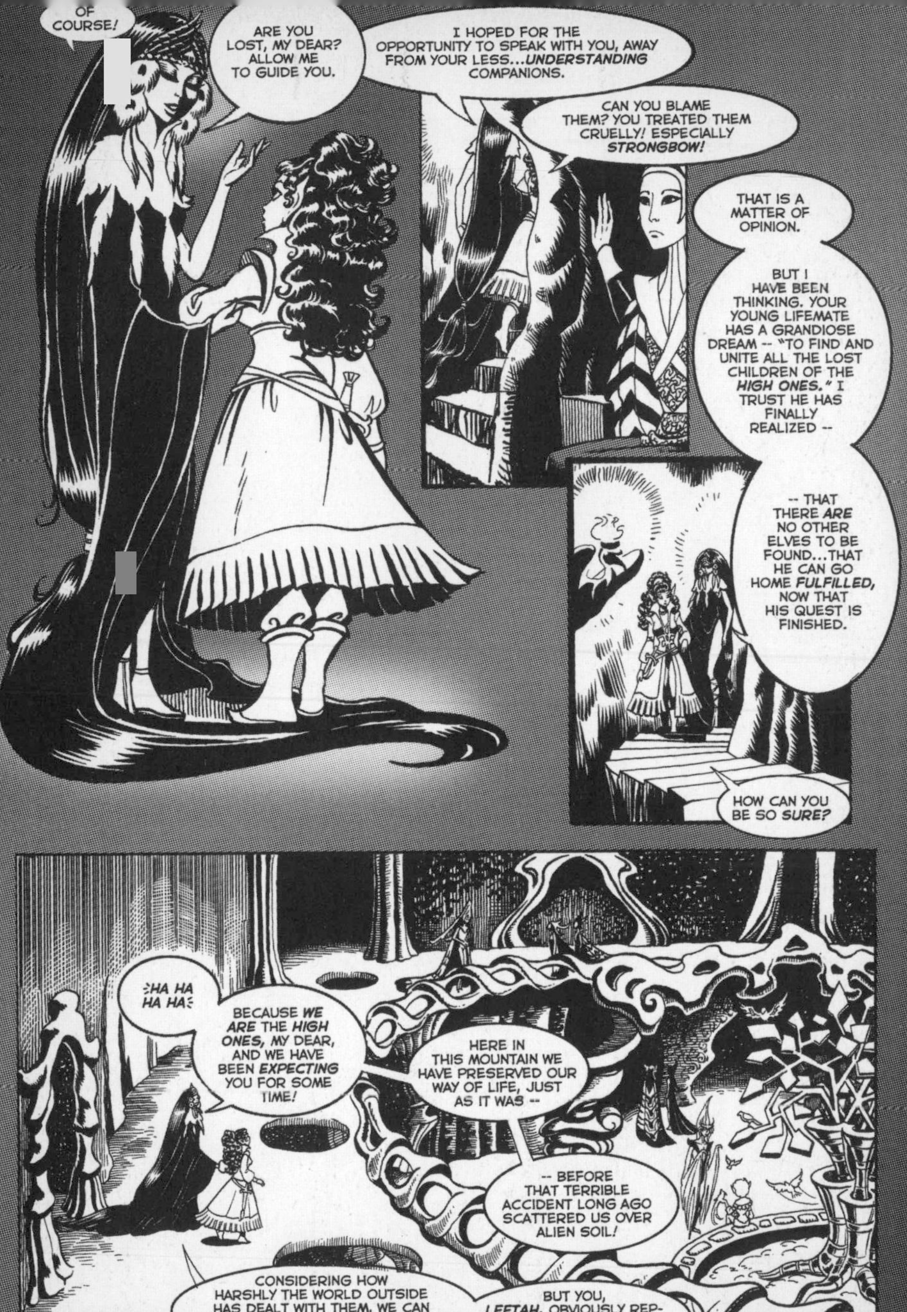

OF COURSE!
ARE YOU LOST, MY DEAR? ALLOW ME TO GUIDE YOU.
I HOPED FOR THE OPPORTUNITY TO SPEAK WITH YOU, AWAY FROM YOUR LESS...UNDERSTANDING COMPANIONS.
CAN YOU BLAME THEM? YOU TREATED THEM CRUELLY! ESPECIALLY STRONGBOW!
THAT IS A MATTER OF OPINION.
BUT I HAVE BEEN THINKING. YOUR YOUNG LIFEMATE HAS A GRANDIOSE DREAM -- "TO FIND AND UNITE ALL THE LOST CHILDREN OF THE HIGH ONES." I TRUST HE HAS FINALLY REALIZED --
-- THAT THERE ARE NO OTHER ELVES TO BE FOUND...THAT HE CAN GO HOME FULFILLED, NOW THAT HIS QUEST IS FINISHED.
HOW CAN YOU BE SO SURE?
HA HA HA HA
BECAUSE WE ARE THE HIGH ONES, MY DEAR, AND WE HAVE BEEN EXPECTING YOU FOR SOME TIME!
HERE IN THIS MOUNTAIN WE HAVE PRESERVED OUR WAY OF LIFE, JUST AS IT WAS --
-- BEFORE THAT TERRIBLE ACCIDENT LONG AGO SCATTERED US OVER ALIEN SOIL!
CONSIDERING HOW HARSHLY THE WORLD OUTSIDE HAS DEALT WITH THEM, WE CAN FORGIVE THE WOLFRIDERS FOR THEIR MURDEROUS SAVAGERY.
BUT YOU, LEETAH, OBVIOUSLY REPRESENT THE FAR LESS "DAMAGED" GROUP.

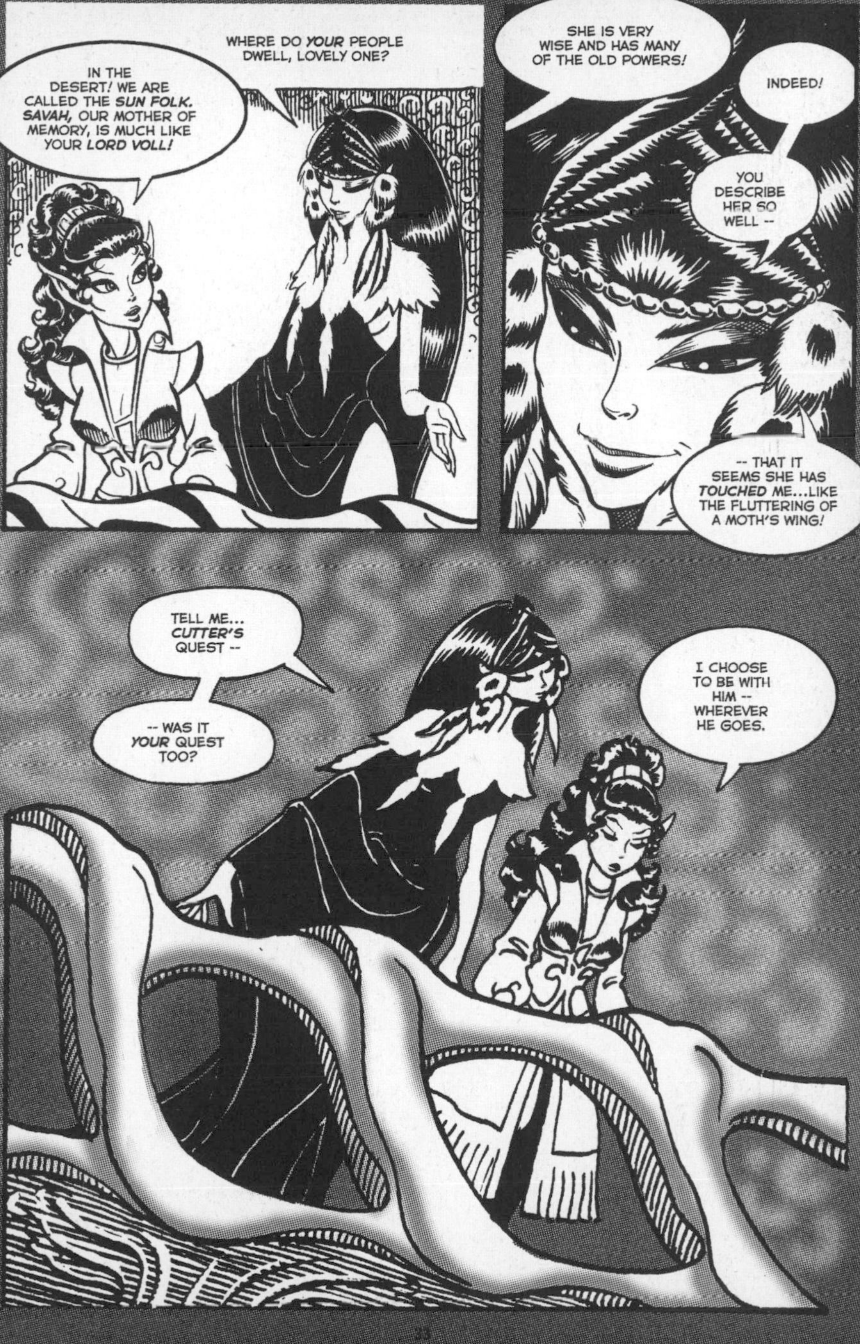

IN THE DESERT! WE ARE CALLED THE SUN FOLK. SAVAH, OUR MOTHER OF MEMORY, IS MUCH LIKE YOUR LORD VOLL!
WHERE DO YOUR PEOPLE DWELL, LOVELY ONE?
SHE IS VERY WISE AND HAS MANY OF THE OLD POWERS!
INDEED!
YOU DESCRIBE HER SO WELL --
-- THAT IT SEEMS SHE HAS TOUCHED ME...LIKE THE FLUTTERING OF A MOTH'S WING!
TELL ME... CUTTER'S QUEST --
-- WAS IT YOUR QUEST TOO?
I CHOOSE TO BE WITH HIM -- WHEREVER HE GOES.

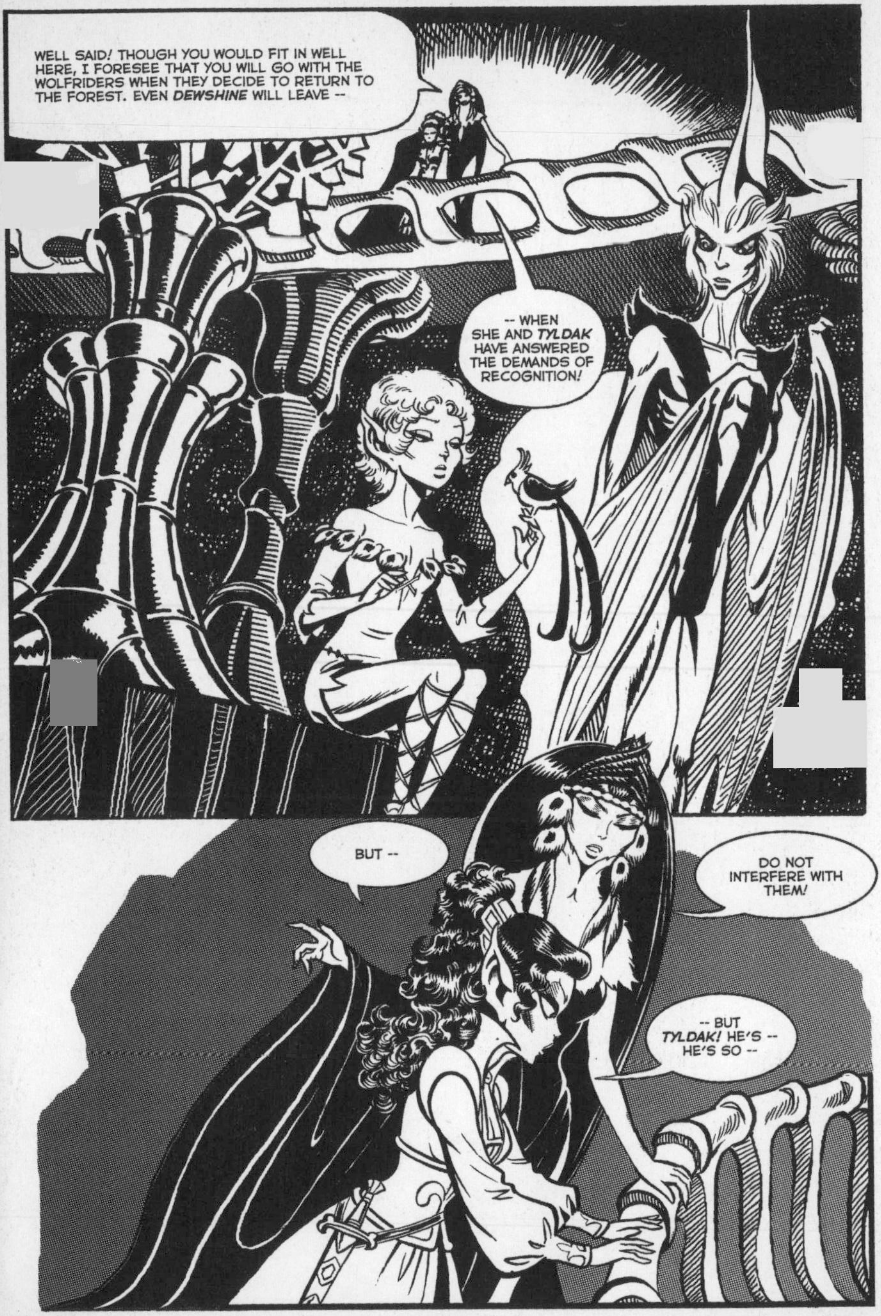

WELL SAID! THOUGH YOU WOULD FIT IN WELL HERE, I FORESEE THAT YOU WILL GO WITH THE WOLFRIDERS WHEN THEY DECIDE TO RETURN TO THE FOREST. EVEN *DEWSHINE* WILL LEAVE --
-- WHEN SHE AND *TYLDAK* HAVE ANSWERED THE DEMANDS OF RECOGNITION!
BUT --
DO NOT INTERFERE WITH THEM!
-- BUT *TYLDAK!* HE'S -- HE'S SO --

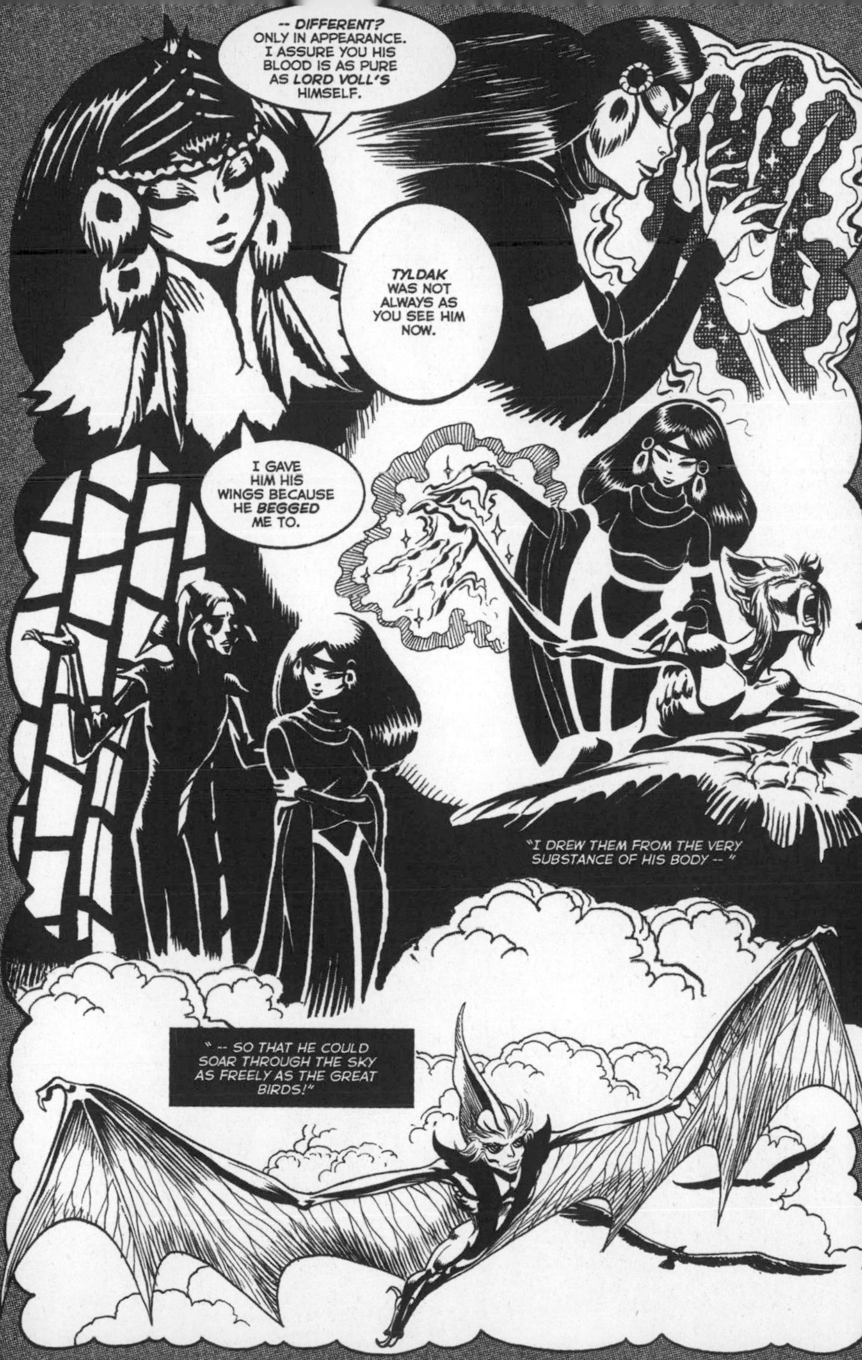
-- DIFFERENT? ONLY IN APPEARANCE. I ASSURE YOU HIS BLOOD IS AS PURE AS LORD VOLL'S HIMSELF.
TYLDAK WAS NOT ALWAYS AS YOU SEE HIM NOW.
I GAVE HIM HIS WINGS BECAUSE HE BEGGED ME TO.
"I DREW THEM FROM THE VERY SUBSTANCE OF HIS BODY -- "
" -- SO THAT HE COULD SOAR THROUGH THE SKY AS FREELY AS THE GREAT BIRDS!"

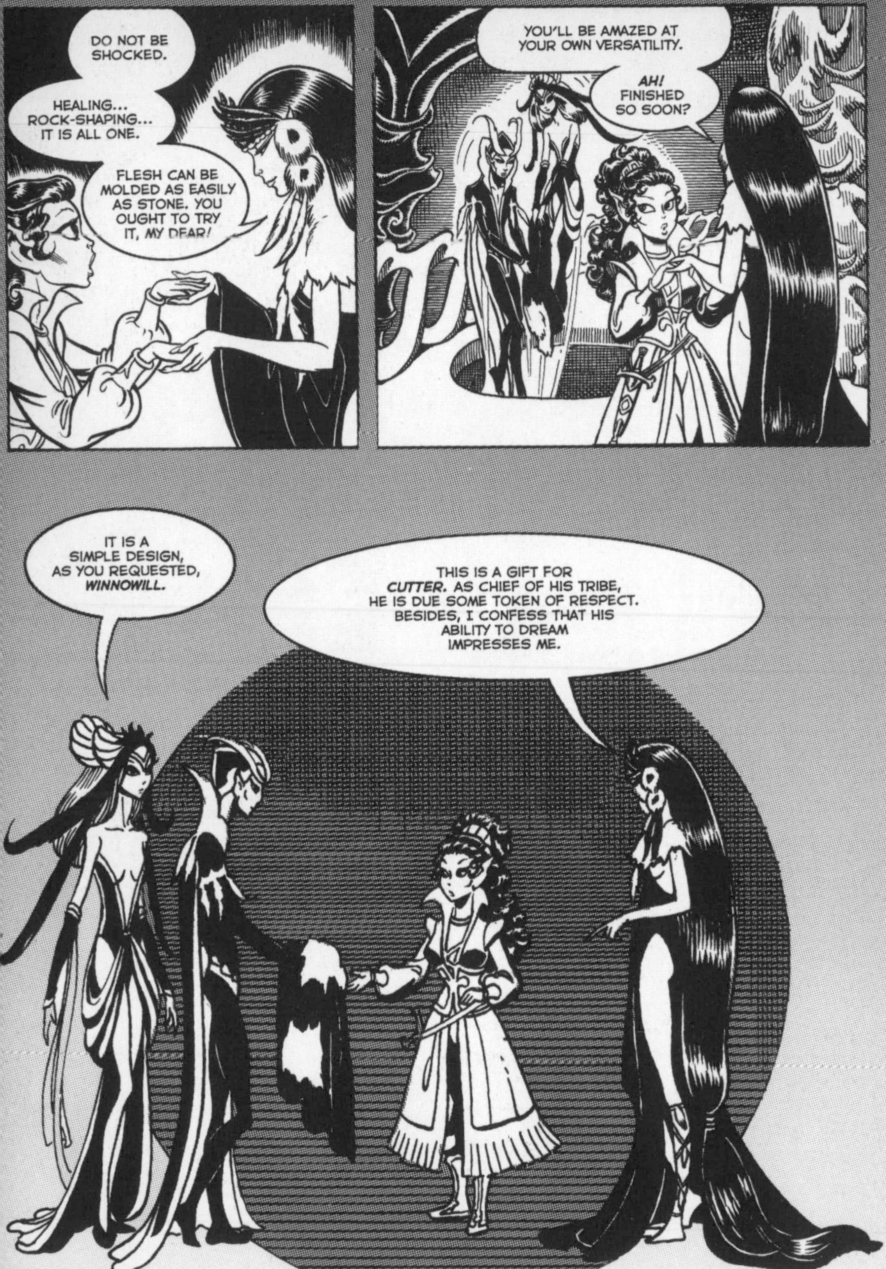
DO NOT BE SHOCKED.
HEALING... ROCK-SHAPING... IT IS ALL ONE.
FLESH CAN BE MOLDED AS EASILY AS STONE. YOU OUGHT TO TRY IT, MY DEAR!
YOU'LL BE AMAZED AT YOUR OWN VERSATILITY.
AH! FINISHED SO SOON?
IT IS A SIMPLE DESIGN, AS YOU REQUESTED, WINNOWILL.
THIS IS A GIFT FOR CUTTER. AS CHIEF OF HIS TRIBE, HE IS DUE SOME TOKEN OF RESPECT. BESIDES, I CONFESS THAT HIS ABILITY TO DREAM IMPRESSES ME.

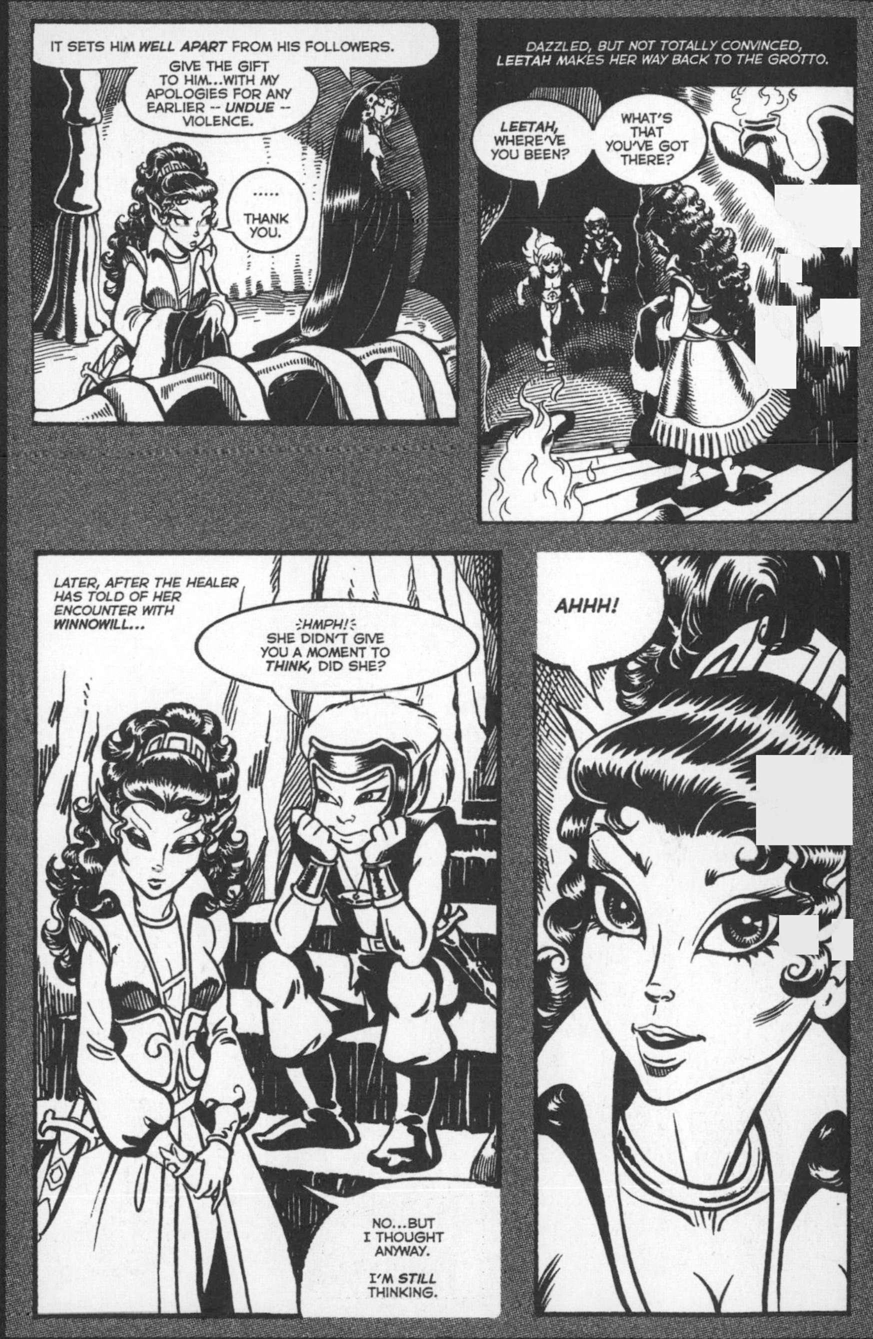
IT SETS HIM WELL APART FROM HIS FOLLOWERS.
GIVE THE GIFT TO HIM...WITH MY APOLOGIES FOR ANY EARLIER -- UNDUE -- VIOLENCE.
..... THANK YOU.
DAZZLED, BUT NOT TOTALLY CONVINCED, LEETAH MAKES HER WAY BACK TO THE GROTTO.
LEETAH, WHERE'VE YOU BEEN?
WHAT'S THAT YOU'VE GOT THERE?
LATER, AFTER THE HEALER HAS TOLD OF HER ENCOUNTER WITH WINNOWILL...
HMPH! SHE DIDN'T GIVE YOU A MOMENT TO THINK, DID SHE?
NO...BUT I THOUGHT ANYWAY.
I'M STILL THINKING.
AHHH!

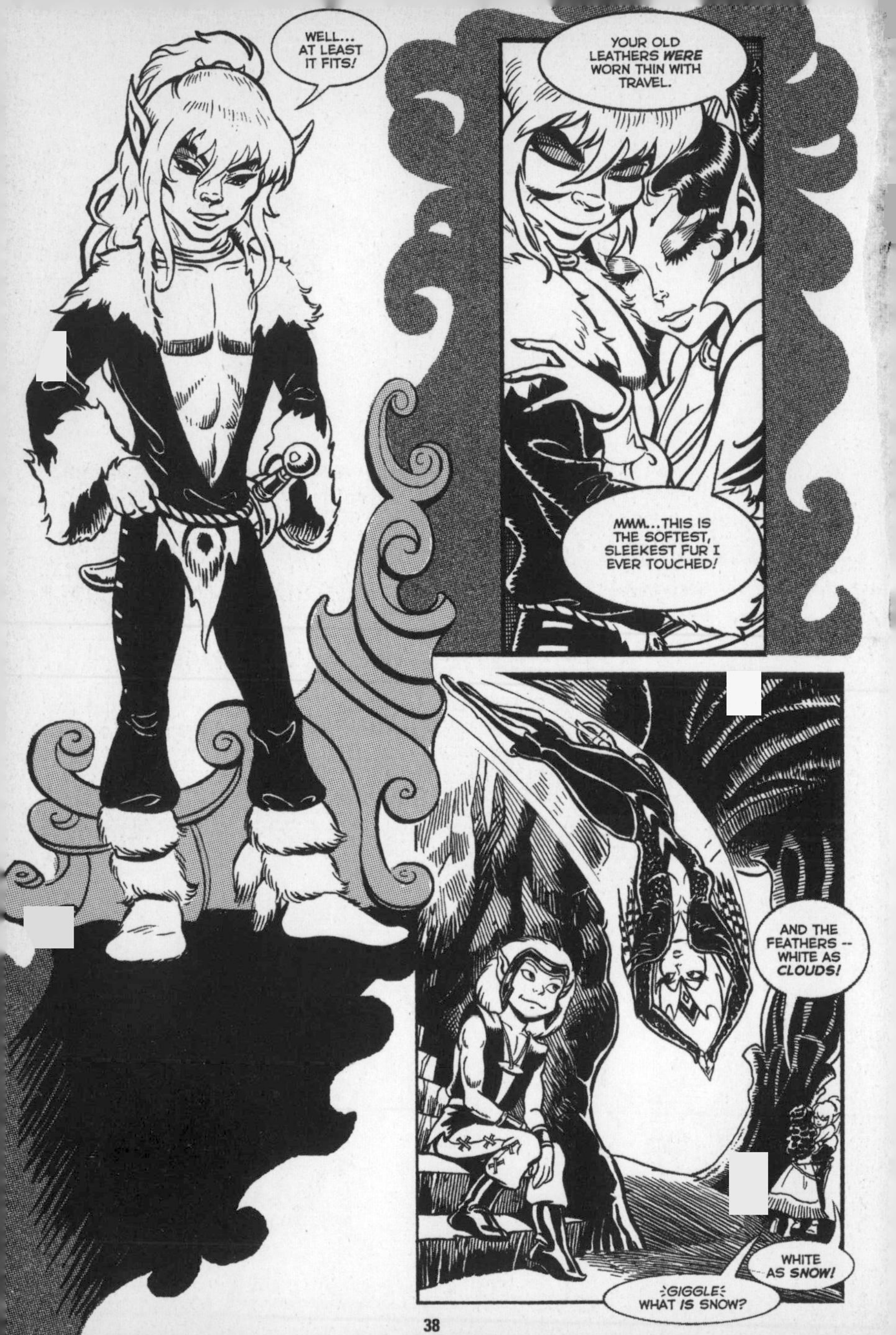
WELL... AT LEAST IT FITS!
YOUR OLD LEATHERS WERE WORN THIN WITH TRAVEL.
MMM...THIS IS THE SOFTEST, SLEEKEST FUR I EVER TOUCHED!
AND THE FEATHERS -- WHITE AS CLOUDS!
WHITE AS SNOW!
GIGGLE WHAT IS SNOW?

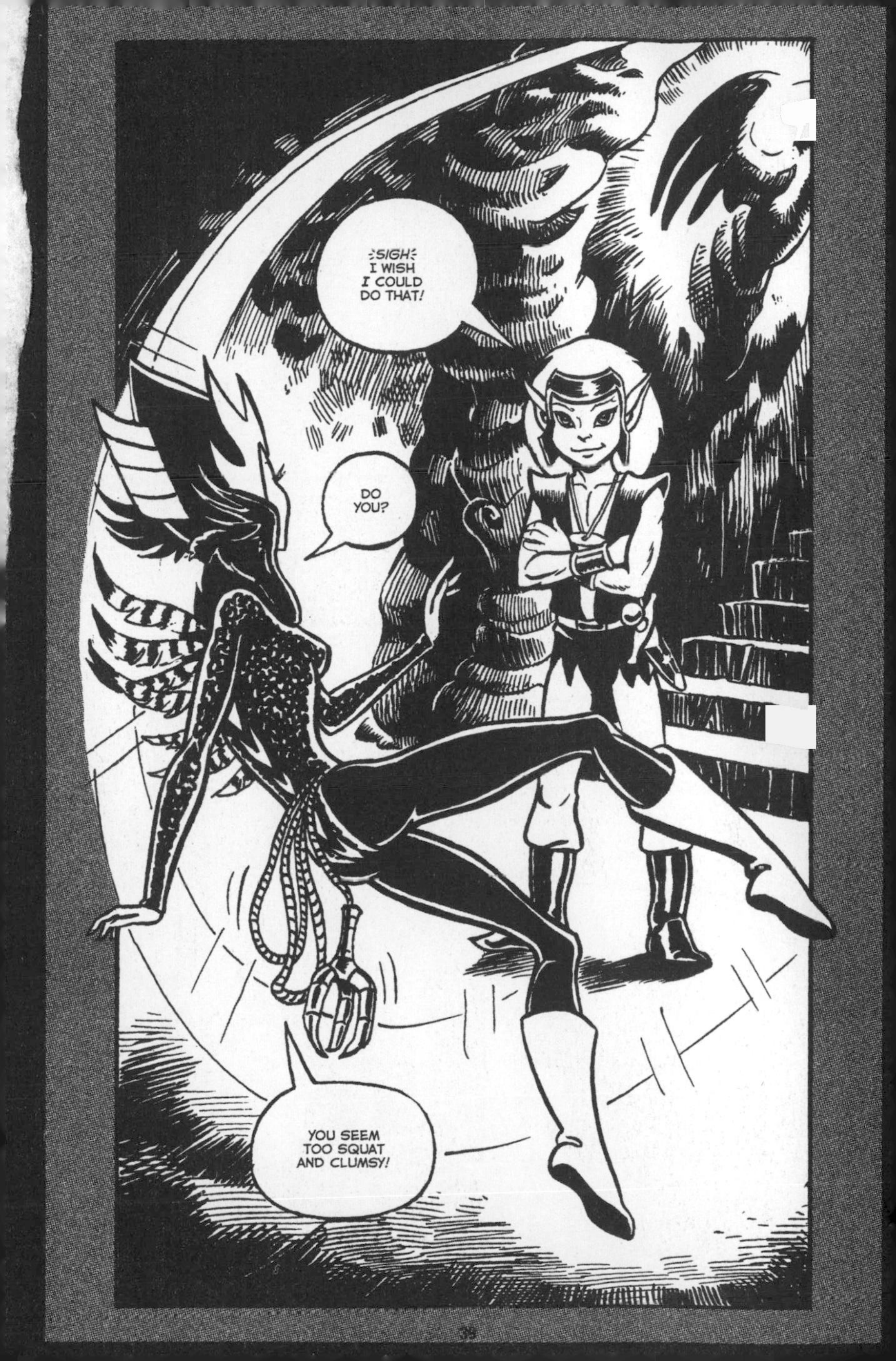

SIGH I WISH I COULD DO THAT!
DO YOU?
YOU SEEM TOO SQUAT AND CLUMSY!

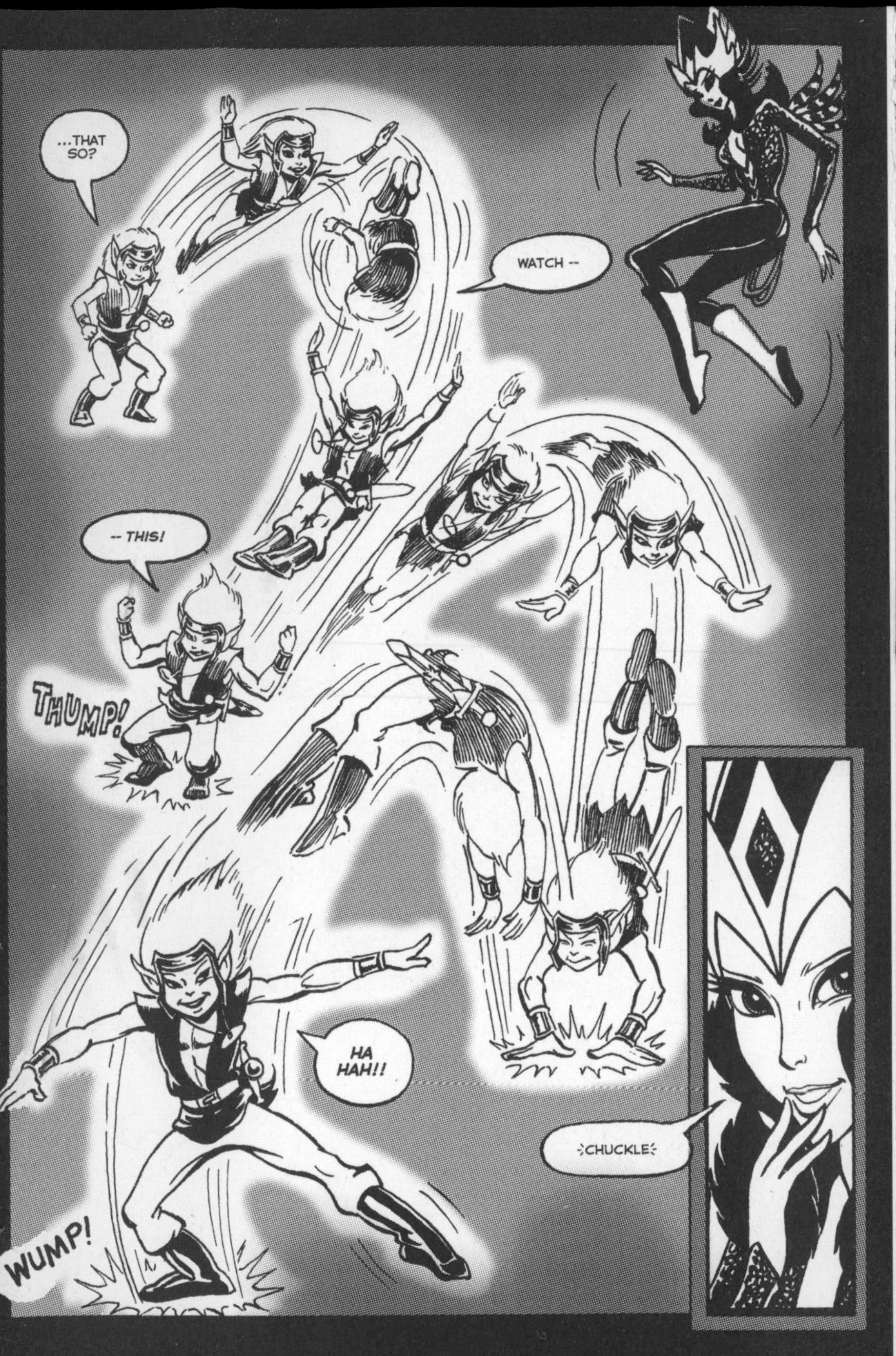

...THAT SO?
WATCH --
-- THIS!
THUMP!
HA HAH!!
WUMP!
CHUCKLE

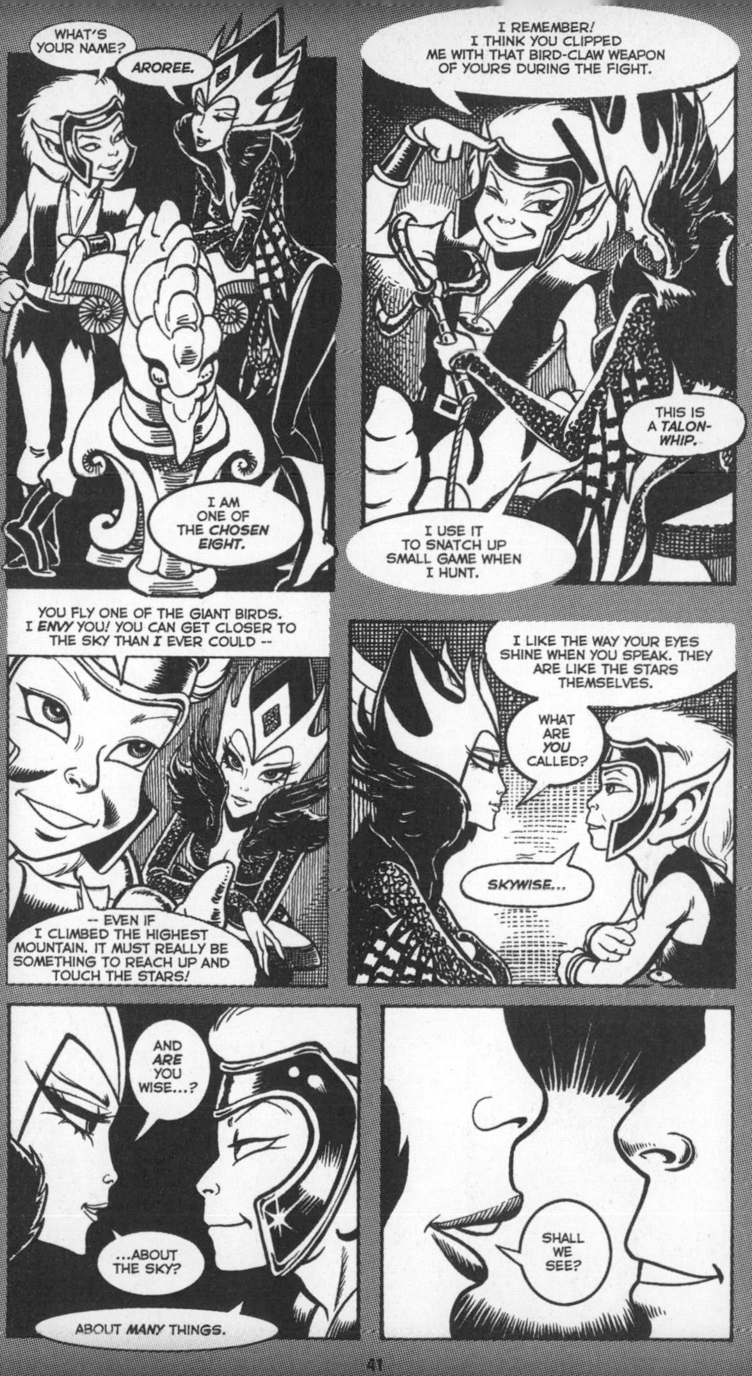
WHAT'S YOUR NAME?
AROREE.
I AM ONE OF THE CHOSEN EIGHT.
I REMEMBER! I THINK YOU CLIPPED ME WITH THAT BIRD-CLAW WEAPON OF YOURS DURING THE FIGHT.
THIS IS A TALON-WHIP.
I USE IT TO SNATCH UP SMALL GAME WHEN I HUNT.
YOU FLY ONE OF THE GIANT BIRDS. I ENVY YOU! YOU CAN GET CLOSER TO THE SKY THAN I EVER COULD --
-- EVEN IF I CLIMBED THE HIGHEST MOUNTAIN. IT MUST REALLY BE SOMETHING TO REACH UP AND TOUCH THE STARS!
I LIKE THE WAY YOUR EYES SHINE WHEN YOU SPEAK. THEY ARE LIKE THE STARS THEMSELVES.
WHAT ARE YOU CALLED?
SKYWISE...
AND ARE YOU WISE...?
...ABOUT THE SKY?
ABOUT MANY THINGS.
SHALL WE SEE?

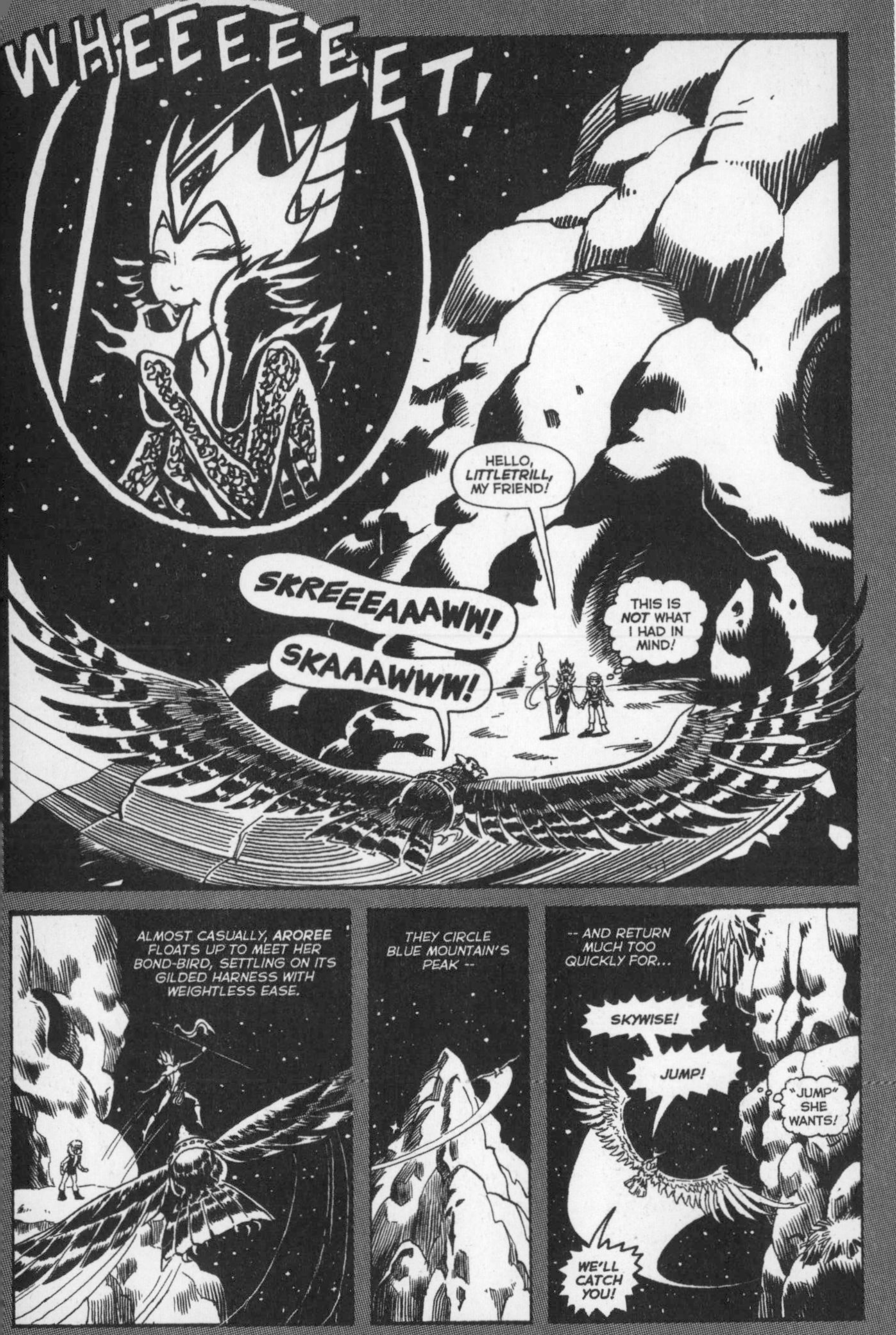
WHEEEEEEET!
HELLO, LITTLETRILL, MY FRIEND!
SKREEEAAAWW!
SKAAAWWW!
THIS IS NOT WHAT I HAD IN MIND!
ALMOST CASUALLY, AROREE FLOATS UP TO MEET HER BOND-BIRD, SETTLING ON ITS GILDED HARNESS WITH WEIGHTLESS EASE.
THEY CIRCLE BLUE MOUNTAIN'S PEAK --
-- AND RETURN MUCH TOO QUICKLY FOR...
SKYWISE!
JUMP!
"JUMP" SHE WANTS!
WE'LL CATCH YOU!

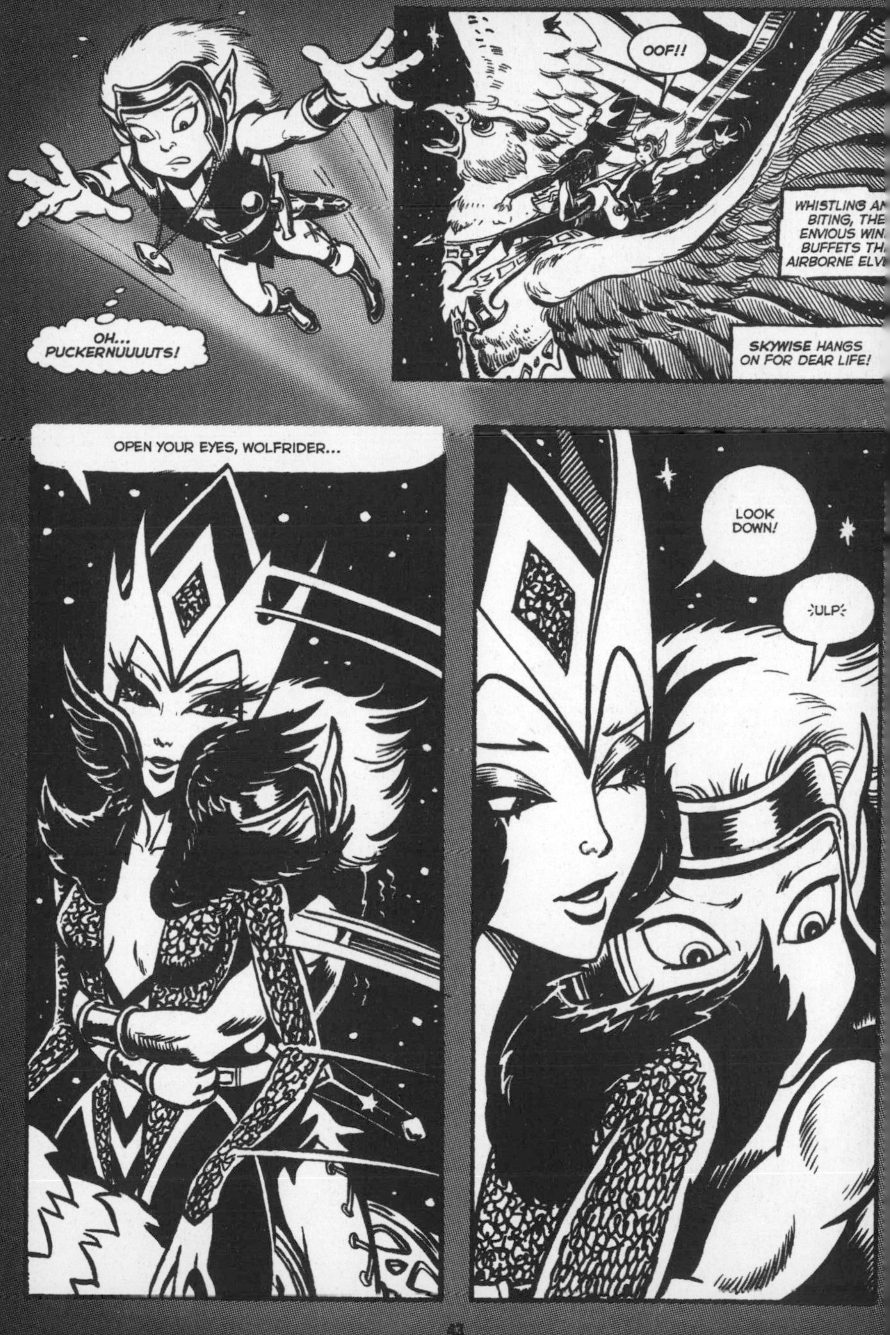

OH... PUCKERNUUUUTS!
OOF!!
WHISTLING AN BITING, THE ENVIOUS WIN BUFFETS TH AIRBORNE ELV
SKYWISE HANGS ON FOR DEAR LIFE!
OPEN YOUR EYES, WOLFRIDER...
LOOK DOWN!
ULP

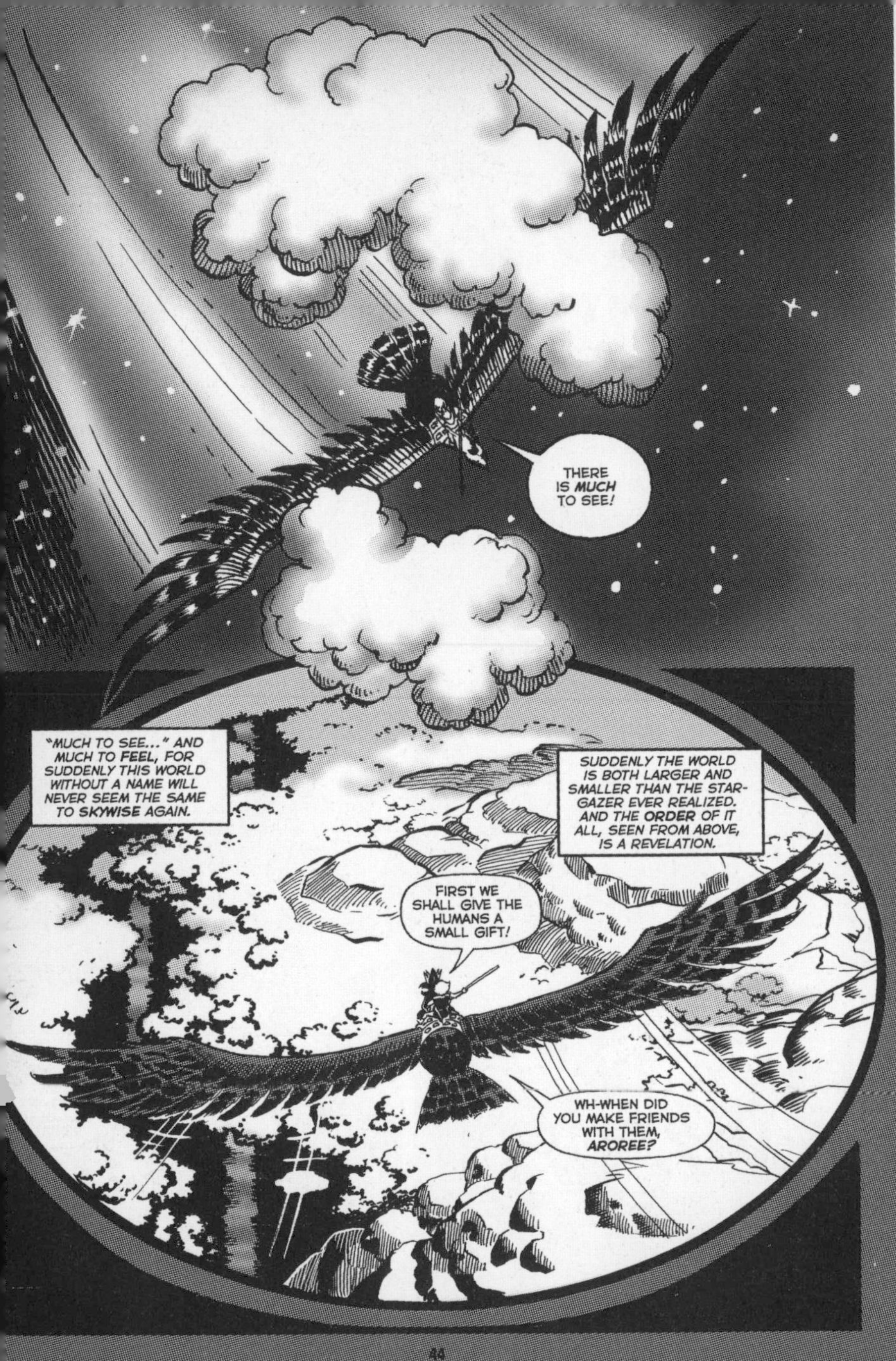
THERE IS MUCH TO SEE!
"MUCH TO SEE..." AND MUCH TO FEEL, FOR SUDDENLY THIS WORLD WITHOUT A NAME WILL NEVER SEEM THE SAME TO SKYWISE AGAIN.
SUDDENLY THE WORLD IS BOTH LARGER AND SMALLER THAN THE STAR-GAZER EVER REALIZED. AND THE ORDER OF IT ALL, SEEN FROM ABOVE, IS A REVELATION.
FIRST WE SHALL GIVE THE HUMANS A SMALL GIFT!
WH-WHEN DID YOU MAKE FRIENDS WITH THEM, AROREE?

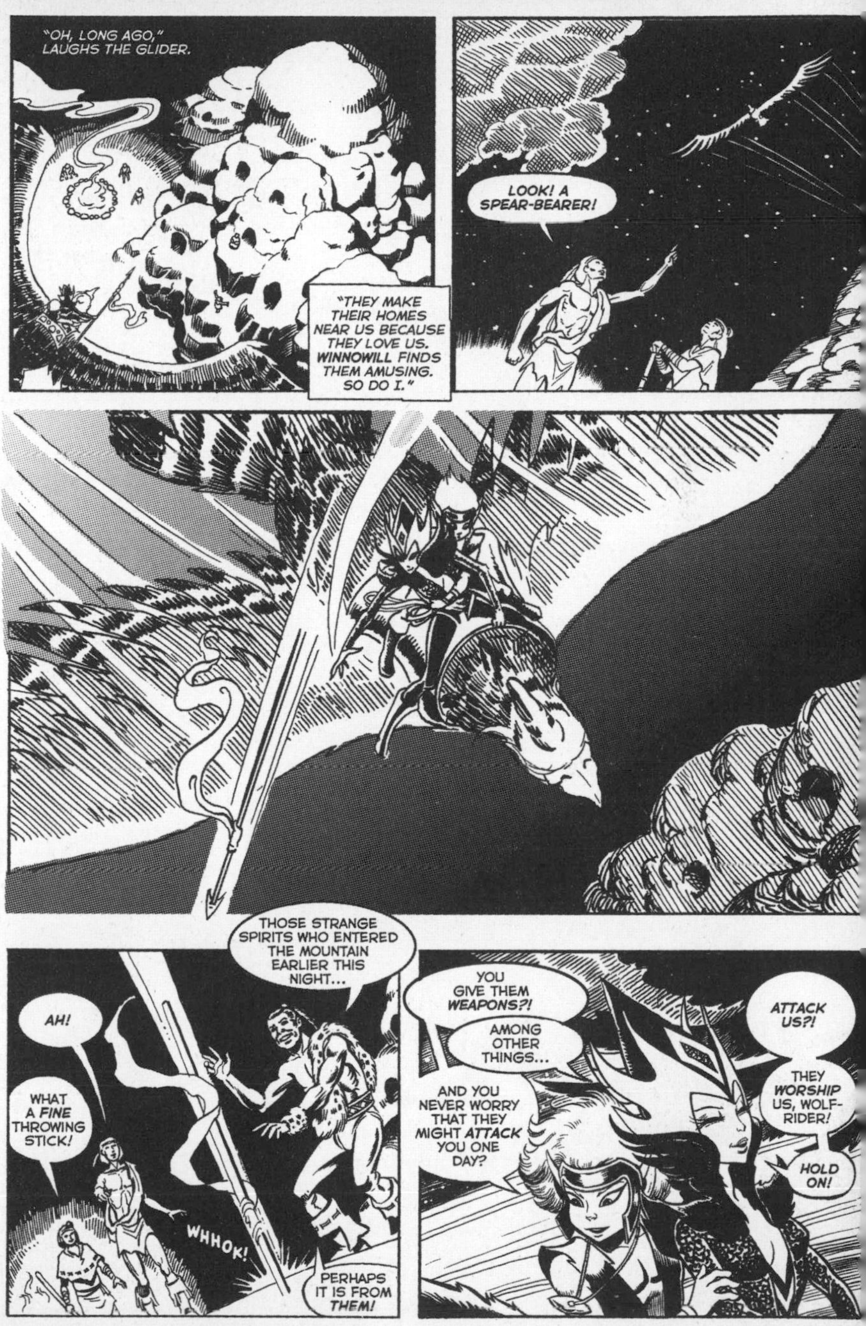
"OH, LONG AGO," LAUGHS THE GLIDER.
"THEY MAKE THEIR HOMES NEAR US BECAUSE THEY LOVE US. WINNOWILL FINDS THEM AMUSING. SO DO I."
LOOK! A SPEAR-BEARER!
THOSE STRANGE SPIRITS WHO ENTERED THE MOUNTAIN EARLIER THIS NIGHT...
AH!
WHAT A FINE THROWING STICK!
WHHOK!
PERHAPS IT IS FROM THEM!
YOU GIVE THEM WEAPONS?!
AMONG OTHER THINGS...
AND YOU NEVER WORRY THAT THEY MIGHT ATTACK YOU ONE DAY?
ATTACK US?!
THEY WORSHIP US, WOLF-RIDER!
HOLD ON!

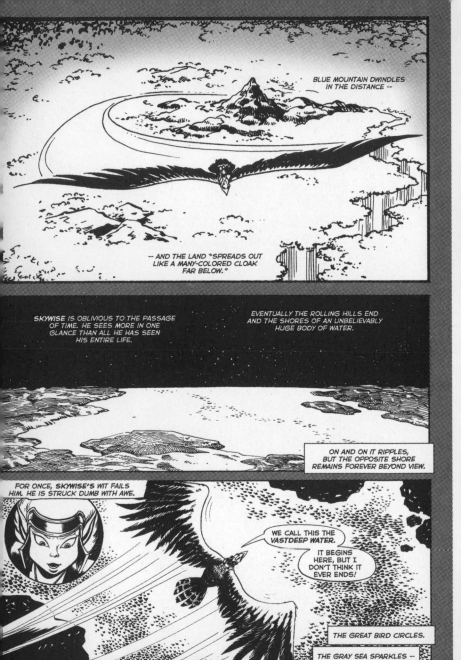

BLUE MOUNTAIN DWINDLES IN THE DISTANCE --

-- AND THE LAND "SPREADS OUT LIKE A MANY-COLORED CLOAK FAR BELOW."

SKYWISE IS OBLIVIOUS TO THE PASSAGE OF TIME. HE SEES MORE IN ONE GLANCE THAN ALL HE HAS SEEN HIS ENTIRE LIFE.

EVENTUALLY THE ROLLING HILLS END AND THE SHORES OF AN UNBELIEVABLY HUGE BODY OF WATER.

ON AND ON IT RIPPLES, BUT THE OPPOSITE SHORE REMAINS FOREVER BEYOND VIEW.

FOR ONCE, SKYWISE'S WIT FAILS HIM. HE IS STRUCK DUMB WITH AWE.

WE CALL THIS THE VASTDEEP WATER.

IT BEGINS HERE, BUT I DON'T THINK IT EVER ENDS!

THE GREAT BIRD CIRCLES.

THE GRAY SEA SPARKLES --

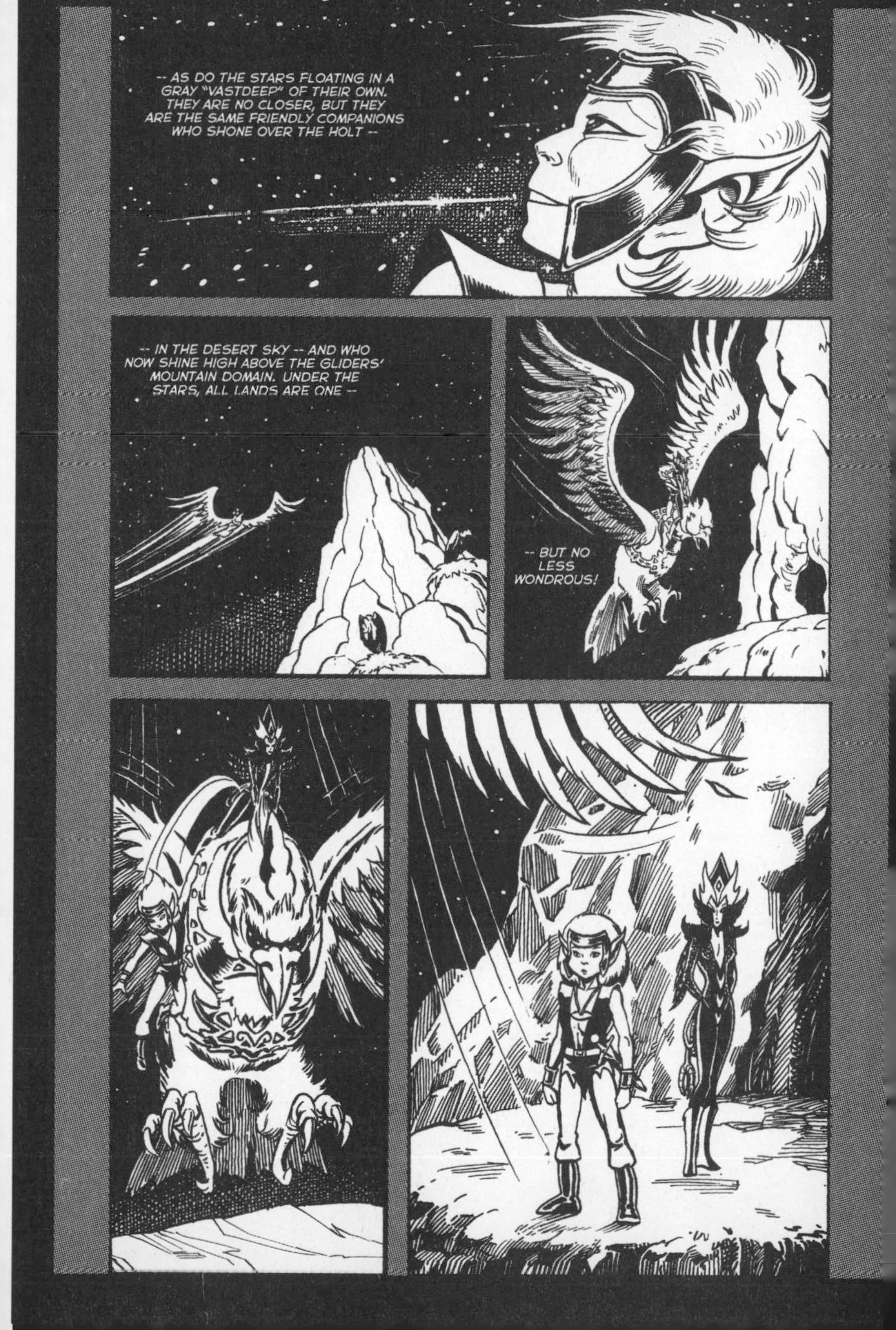
-- AS DO THE STARS FLOATING IN A GRAY "VASTDEEP" OF THEIR OWN. THEY ARE NO CLOSER, BUT THEY ARE THE SAME FRIENDLY COMPANIONS WHO SHONE OVER THE HOLT --
-- IN THE DESERT SKY -- AND WHO NOW SHINE HIGH ABOVE THE GLIDERS' MOUNTAIN DOMAIN. UNDER THE STARS, ALL LANDS ARE ONE --
-- BUT NO LESS WONDROUS!

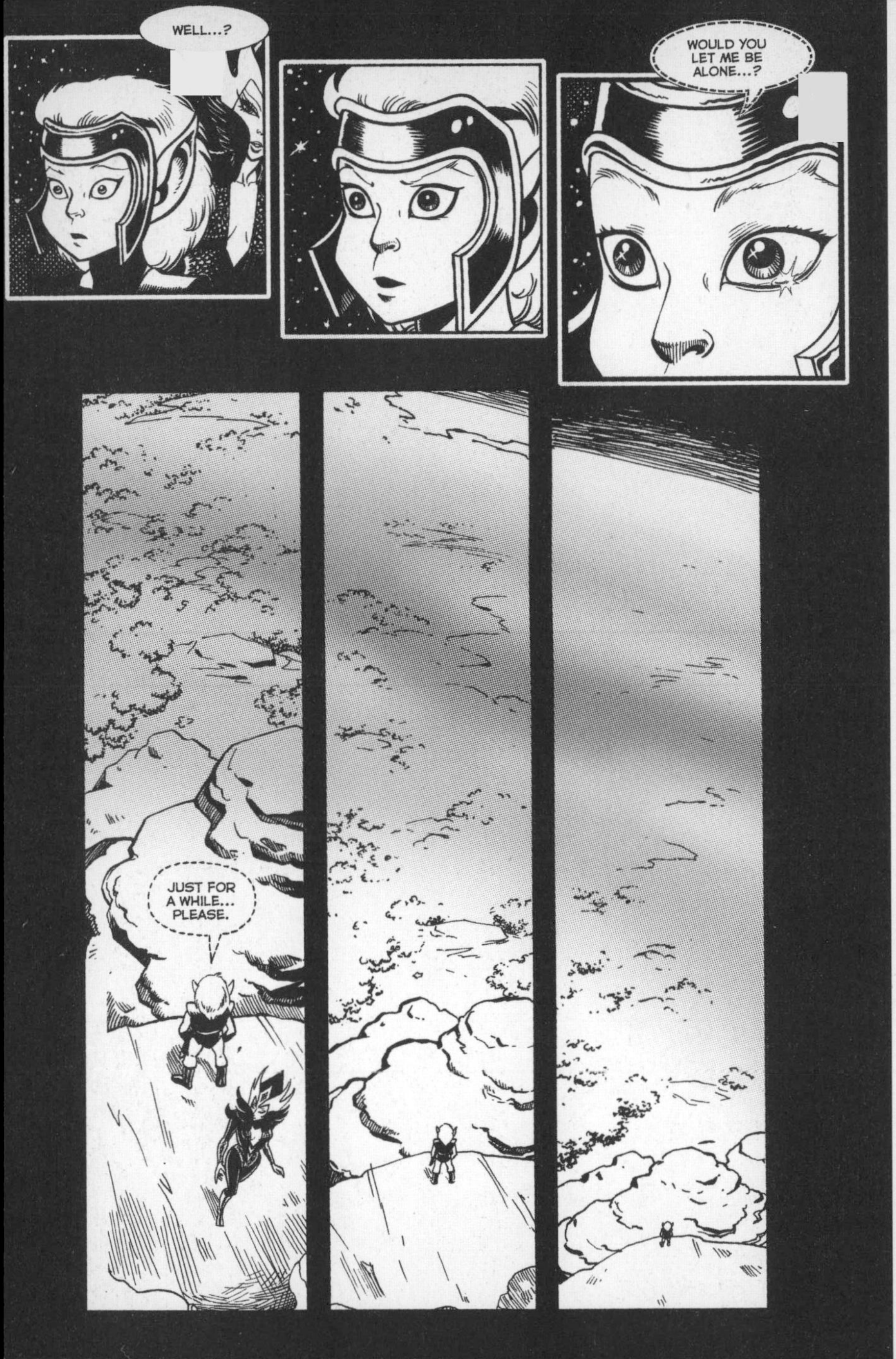
WELL...?
WOULD YOU LET ME BE ALONE...?
JUST FOR A WHILE... PLEASE.

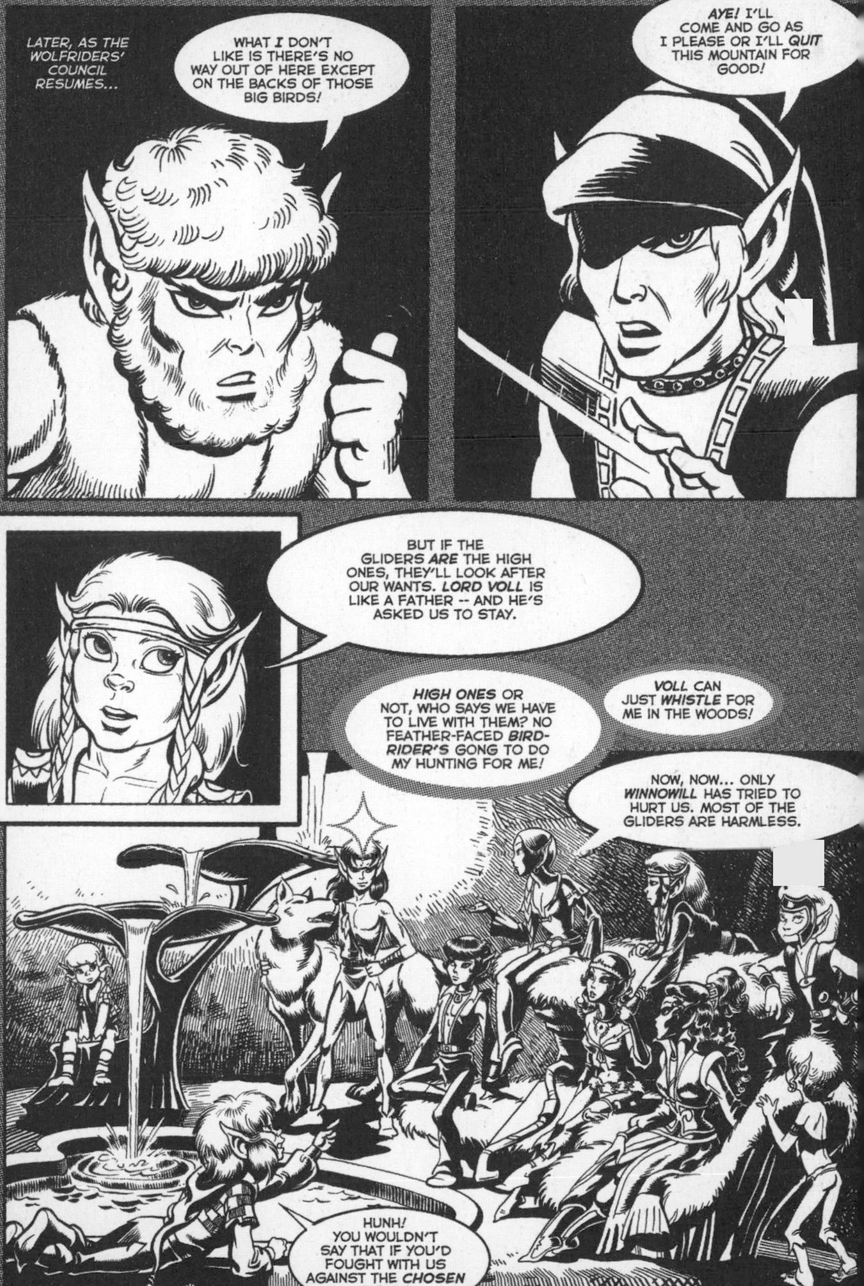
LATER, AS THE WOLFRIDERS' COUNCIL RESUMES...
WHAT *I* DON'T LIKE IS THERE'S NO WAY OUT OF HERE EXCEPT ON THE BACKS OF THOSE BIG BIRDS!
AYE! I'LL COME AND GO AS I PLEASE OR I'LL *QUIT* THIS MOUNTAIN FOR GOOD!
BUT IF THE GLIDERS *ARE* THE HIGH ONES, THEY'LL LOOK AFTER OUR WANTS. *LORD VOLL* IS LIKE A FATHER -- AND HE'S ASKED US TO STAY.
HIGH ONES OR NOT, WHO SAYS WE HAVE TO LIVE WITH THEM? NO FEATHER-FACED *BIRD-RIDER'S* GONG TO DO *MY* HUNTING FOR ME!
VOLL CAN JUST *WHISTLE* FOR ME IN THE WOODS!
NOW, NOW... ONLY *WINNOWILL* HAS TRIED TO HURT US. MOST OF THE GLIDERS ARE HARMLESS.
HUNH! YOU WOULDN'T SAY THAT IF YOU'D FOUGHT WITH US AGAINST THE *CHOSEN EIGHT!*

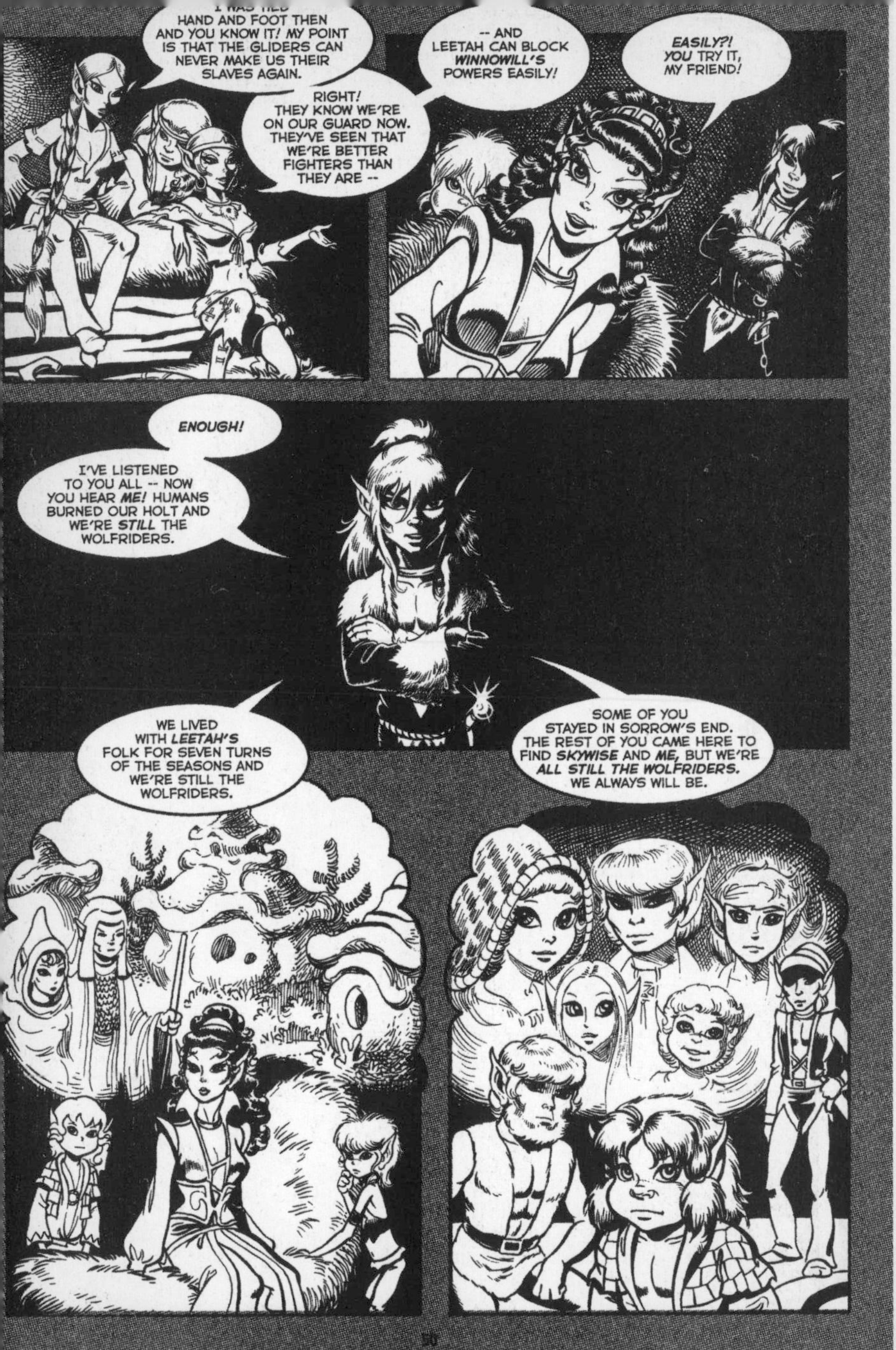
HAND AND FOOT THEN AND YOU KNOW IT! MY POINT IS THAT THE GLIDERS CAN NEVER MAKE US THEIR SLAVES AGAIN.
RIGHT! THEY KNOW WE'RE ON OUR GUARD NOW. THEY'VE SEEN THAT WE'RE BETTER FIGHTERS THAN THEY ARE --
-- AND LEETAH CAN BLOCK WINNOWILL'S POWERS EASILY!
EASILY?! YOU TRY IT, MY FRIEND!
ENOUGH!
I'VE LISTENED TO YOU ALL -- NOW YOU HEAR ME! HUMANS BURNED OUR HOLT AND WE'RE STILL THE WOLFRIDERS.
WE LIVED WITH LEETAH'S FOLK FOR SEVEN TURNS OF THE SEASONS AND WE'RE STILL THE WOLFRIDERS.
SOME OF YOU STAYED IN SORROW'S END. THE REST OF YOU CAME HERE TO FIND SKYWISE AND ME, BUT WE'RE ALL STILL THE WOLFRIDERS. WE ALWAYS WILL BE.

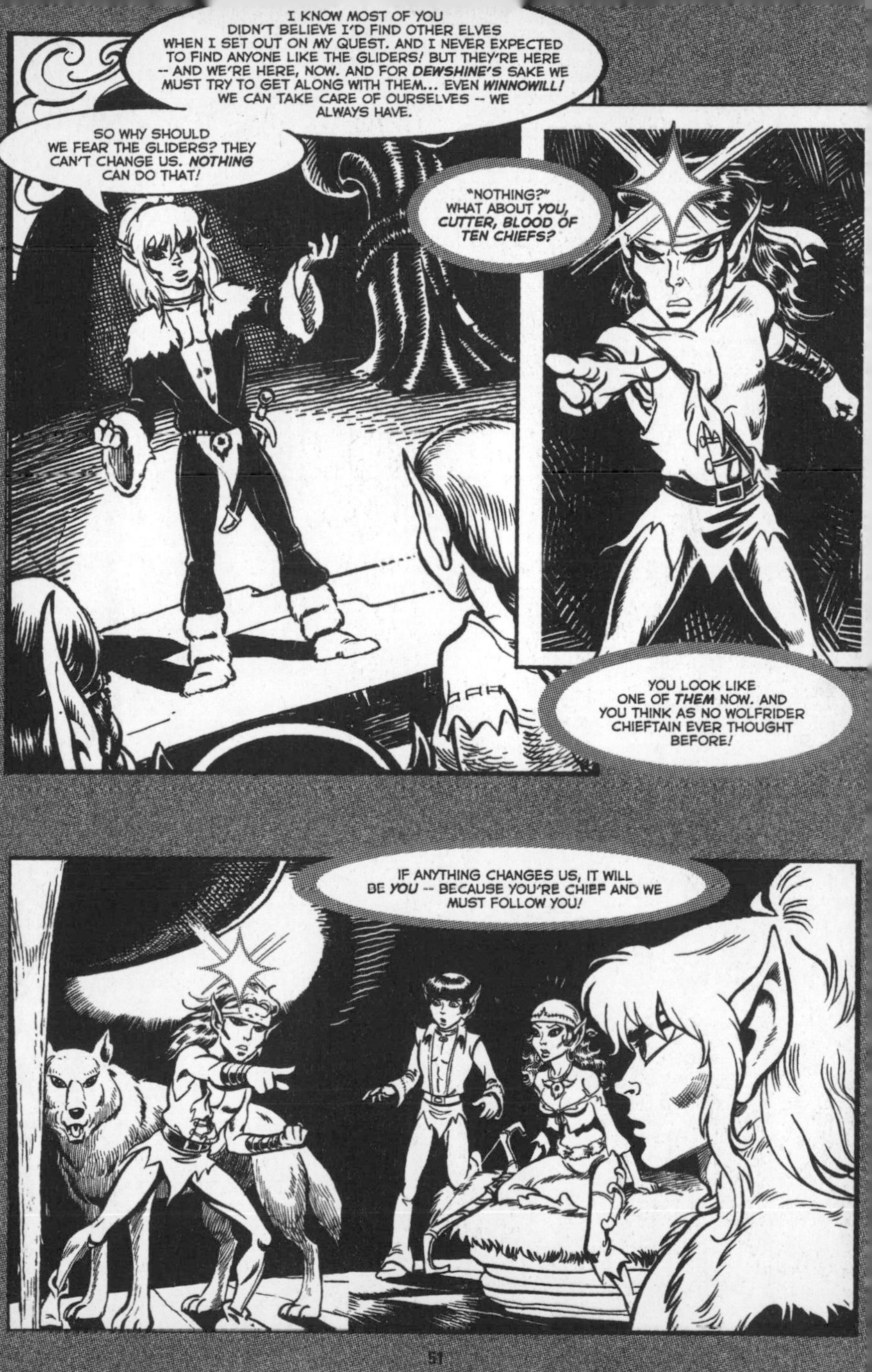
I KNOW MOST OF YOU DIDN'T BELIEVE I'D FIND OTHER ELVES WHEN I SET OUT ON MY QUEST. AND I NEVER EXPECTED TO FIND ANYONE LIKE THE GLIDERS! BUT THEY'RE HERE -- AND WE'RE HERE, NOW. AND FOR DEWSHINE'S SAKE WE MUST TRY TO GET ALONG WITH THEM... EVEN WINNOWILL! WE CAN TAKE CARE OF OURSELVES -- WE ALWAYS HAVE.
SO WHY SHOULD WE FEAR THE GLIDERS? THEY CAN'T CHANGE US. NOTHING CAN DO THAT!
"NOTHING?" WHAT ABOUT YOU, CUTTER, BLOOD OF TEN CHIEFS?
YOU LOOK LIKE ONE OF THEM NOW. AND YOU THINK AS NO WOLFRIDER CHIEFTAIN EVER THOUGHT BEFORE!
IF ANYTHING CHANGES US, IT WILL BE YOU -- BECAUSE YOU'RE CHIEF AND WE MUST FOLLOW YOU!

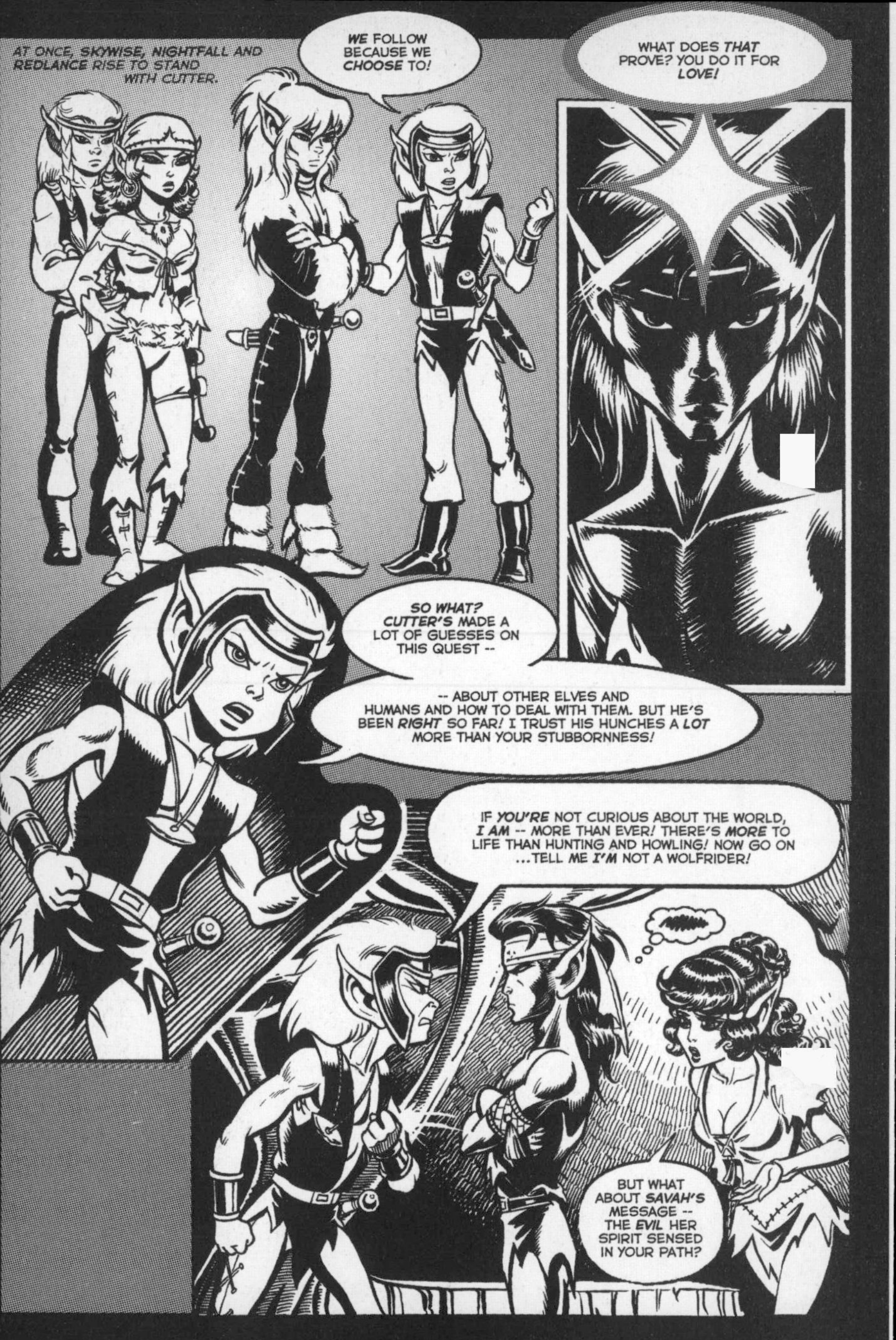
AT ONCE, SKYWISE, NIGHTFALL AND REDLANCE RISE TO STAND WITH CUTTER.
WE FOLLOW BECAUSE WE CHOOSE TO!
WHAT DOES THAT PROVE? YOU DO IT FOR LOVE!
SO WHAT? CUTTER'S MADE A LOT OF GUESSES ON THIS QUEST --
-- ABOUT OTHER ELVES AND HUMANS AND HOW TO DEAL WITH THEM. BUT HE'S BEEN RIGHT SO FAR! I TRUST HIS HUNCHES A LOT MORE THAN YOUR STUBBORNNESS!
IF YOU'RE NOT CURIOUS ABOUT THE WORLD, I AM -- MORE THAN EVER! THERE'S MORE TO LIFE THAN HUNTING AND HOWLING! NOW GO ON ...TELL ME I'M NOT A WOLFRIDER!
BUT WHAT ABOUT SAVAH'S MESSAGE -- THE EVIL HER SPIRIT SENSED IN YOUR PATH?

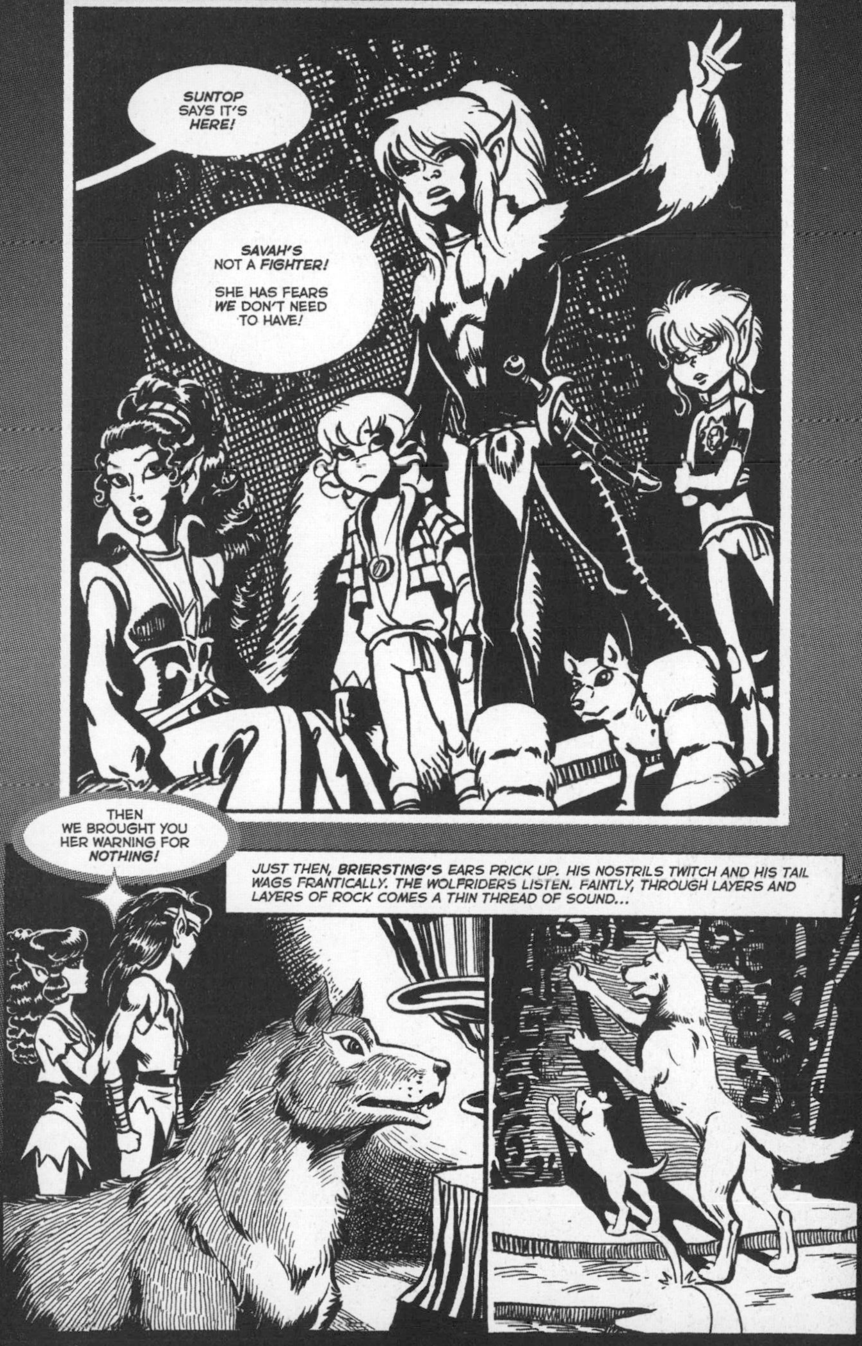
SUNTOP SAYS IT'S HERE!
SAVAH'S NOT A FIGHTER!
SHE HAS FEARS WE DON'T NEED TO HAVE!
THEN WE BROUGHT YOU HER WARNING FOR NOTHING!
JUST THEN, BRIERSTING'S EARS PRICK UP. HIS NOSTRILS TWITCH AND HIS TAIL WAGS FRANTICALLY. THE WOLFRIDERS LISTEN. FAINTLY, THROUGH LAYERS AND LAYERS OF ROCK COMES A THIN THREAD OF SOUND...

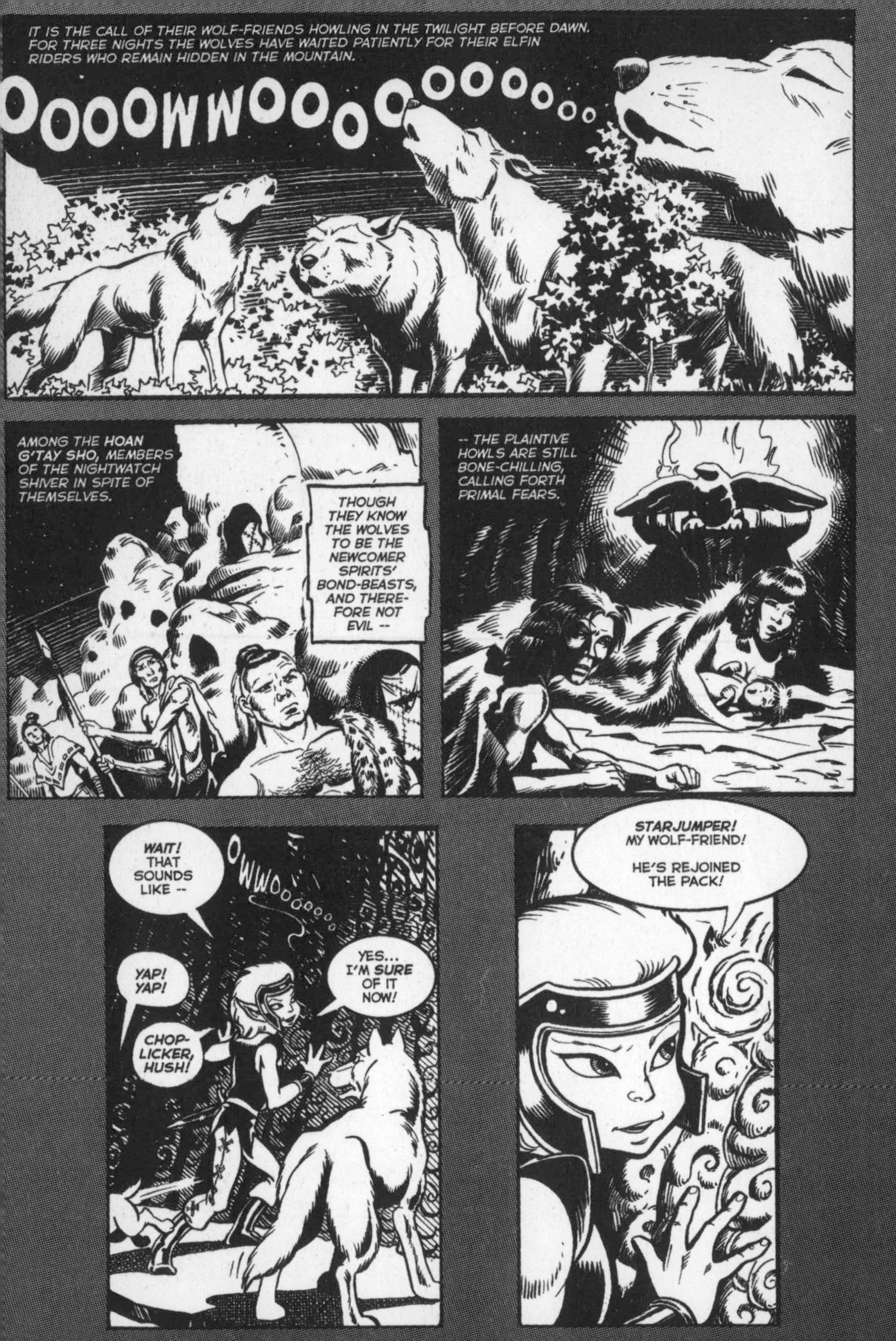
IT IS THE CALL OF THEIR WOLF-FRIENDS HOWLING IN THE TWILIGHT BEFORE DAWN. FOR THREE NIGHTS THE WOLVES HAVE WAITED PATIENTLY FOR THEIR ELFIN RIDERS WHO REMAIN HIDDEN IN THE MOUNTAIN.
OOOOWWOOOOOOOOOOO...
AMONG THE HOAN G'TAY SHO, MEMBERS OF THE NIGHTWATCH SHIVER IN SPITE OF THEMSELVES.
THOUGH THEY KNOW THE WOLVES TO BE THE NEWCOMER SPIRITS' BOND-BEASTS, AND THEREFORE NOT EVIL --
-- THE PLAINTIVE HOWLS ARE STILL BONE-CHILLING, CALLING FORTH PRIMAL FEARS.
WAIT! THAT SOUNDS LIKE --
OWWOOoooooo
YAP! YAP!
YES... I'M SURE OF IT NOW!
CHOP-LICKER, HUSH!
STARJUMPER! MY WOLF-FRIEND!
HE'S REJOINED THE PACK!

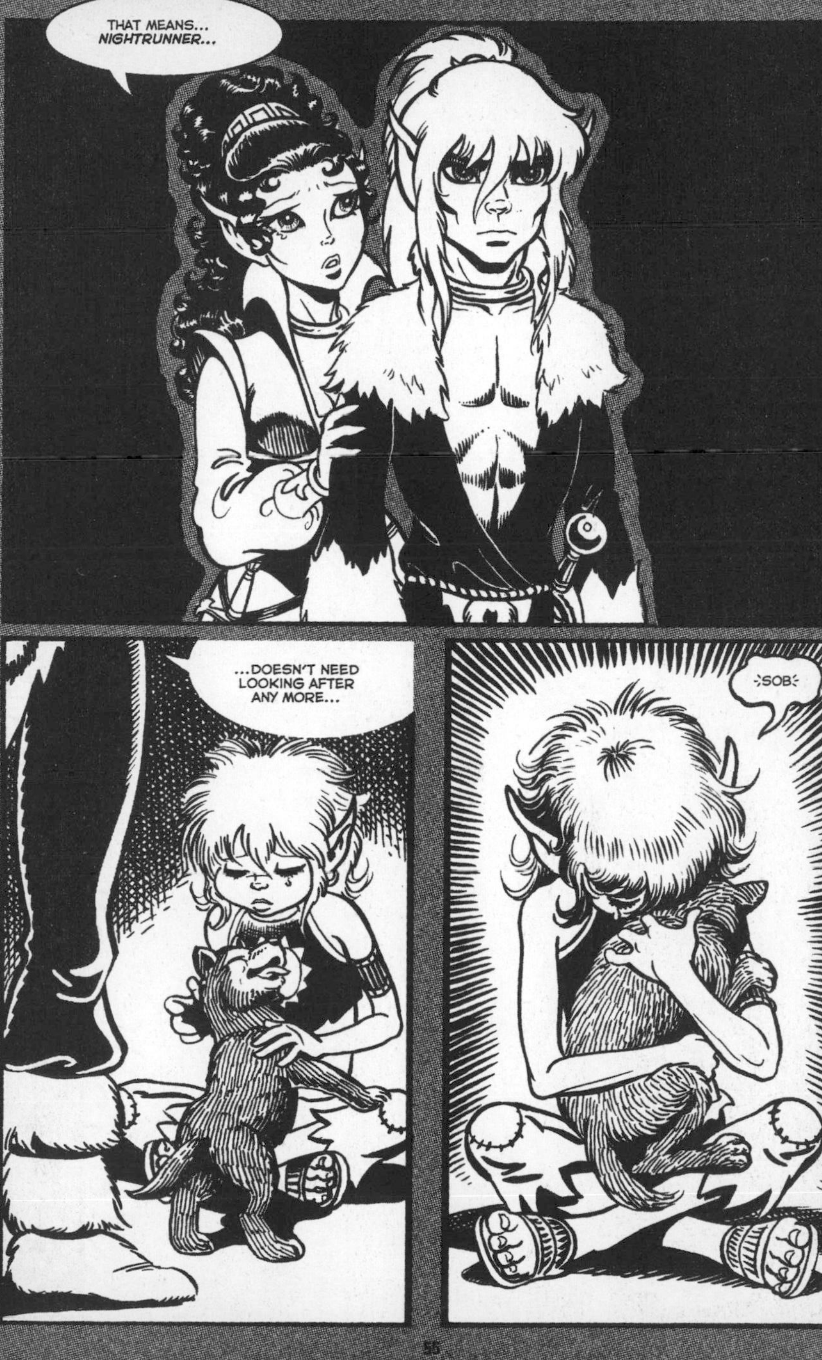
THAT MEANS... NIGHTRUNNER...
...DOESN'T NEED LOOKING AFTER ANY MORE...
SOB

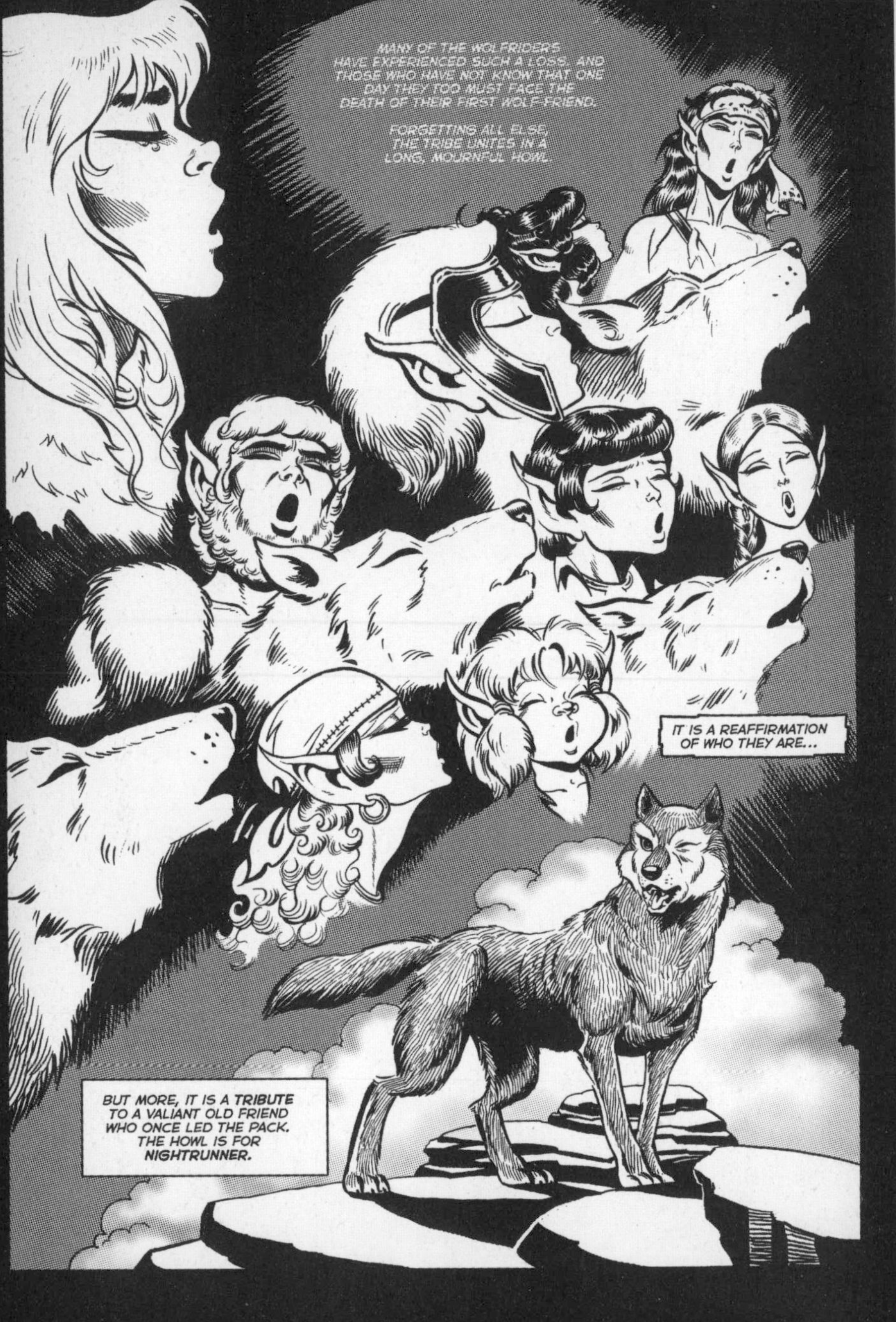
MANY OF THE WOLFRIDERS HAVE EXPERIENCED SUCH A LOSS, AND THOSE WHO HAVE NOT KNOW THAT ONE DAY THEY TOO MUST FACE THE DEATH OF THEIR FIRST WOLF-FRIEND.
FORGETTING ALL ELSE, THE TRIBE UNITES IN A LONG, MOURNFUL HOWL.
IT IS A REAFFIRMATION OF WHO THEY ARE...
BUT MORE, IT IS A TRIBUTE TO A VALIANT OLD FRIEND WHO ONCE LED THE PACK. THE HOWL IS FOR NIGHTRUNNER.

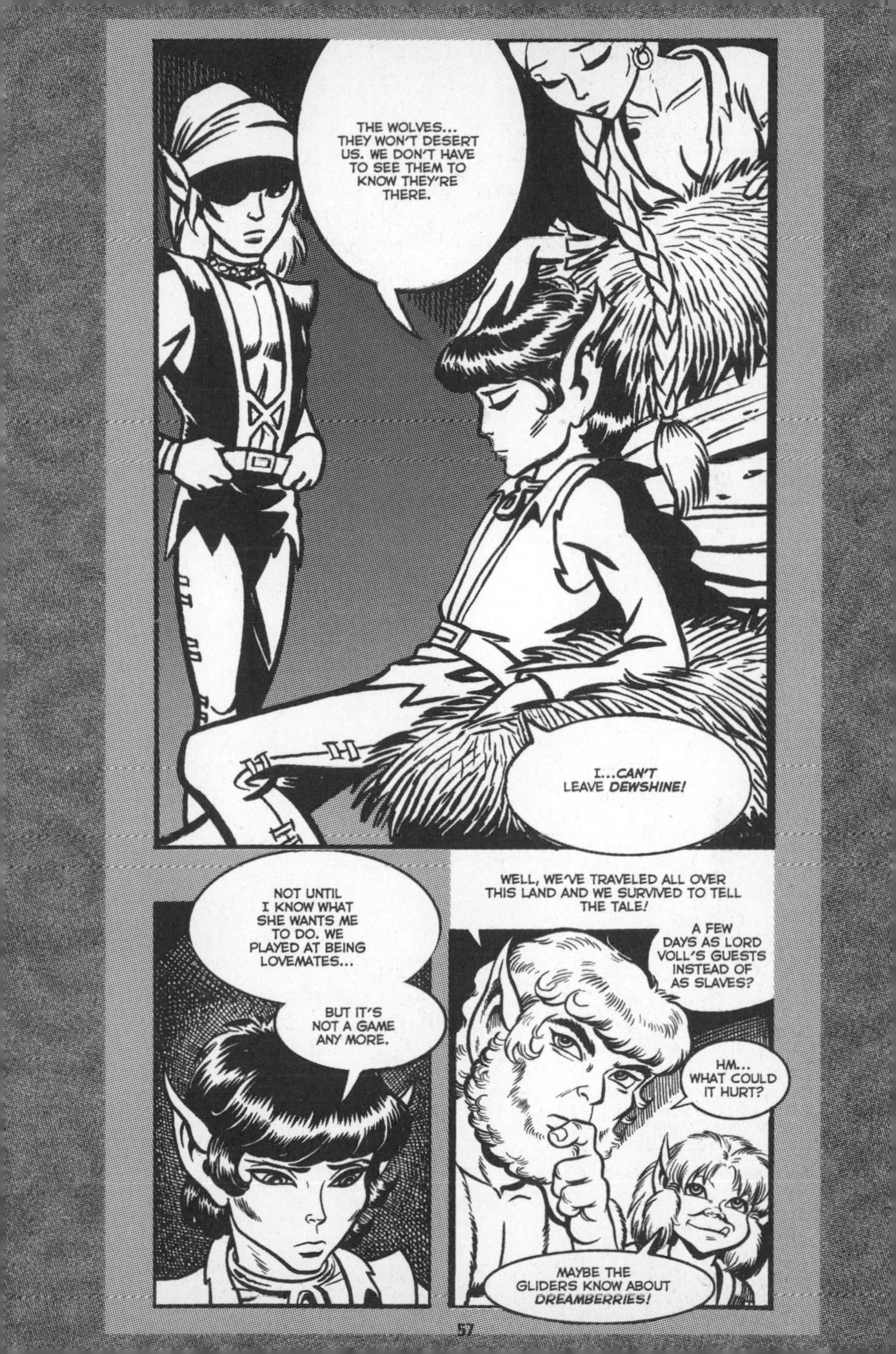

THE WOLVES... THEY WON'T DESERT US. WE DON'T HAVE TO SEE THEM TO KNOW THEY'RE THERE.
I...*CAN'T* LEAVE *DEWSHINE!*
NOT UNTIL I KNOW WHAT SHE WANTS ME TO DO. WE PLAYED AT BEING LOVEMATES...
BUT IT'S NOT A GAME ANY MORE.
WELL, WE'VE TRAVELED ALL OVER THIS LAND AND WE SURVIVED TO TELL THE TALE!
A FEW DAYS AS LORD VOLL'S GUESTS INSTEAD OF AS SLAVES?
HM... WHAT COULD IT HURT?
MAYBE THE GLIDERS KNOW ABOUT *DREAMBERRIES!*

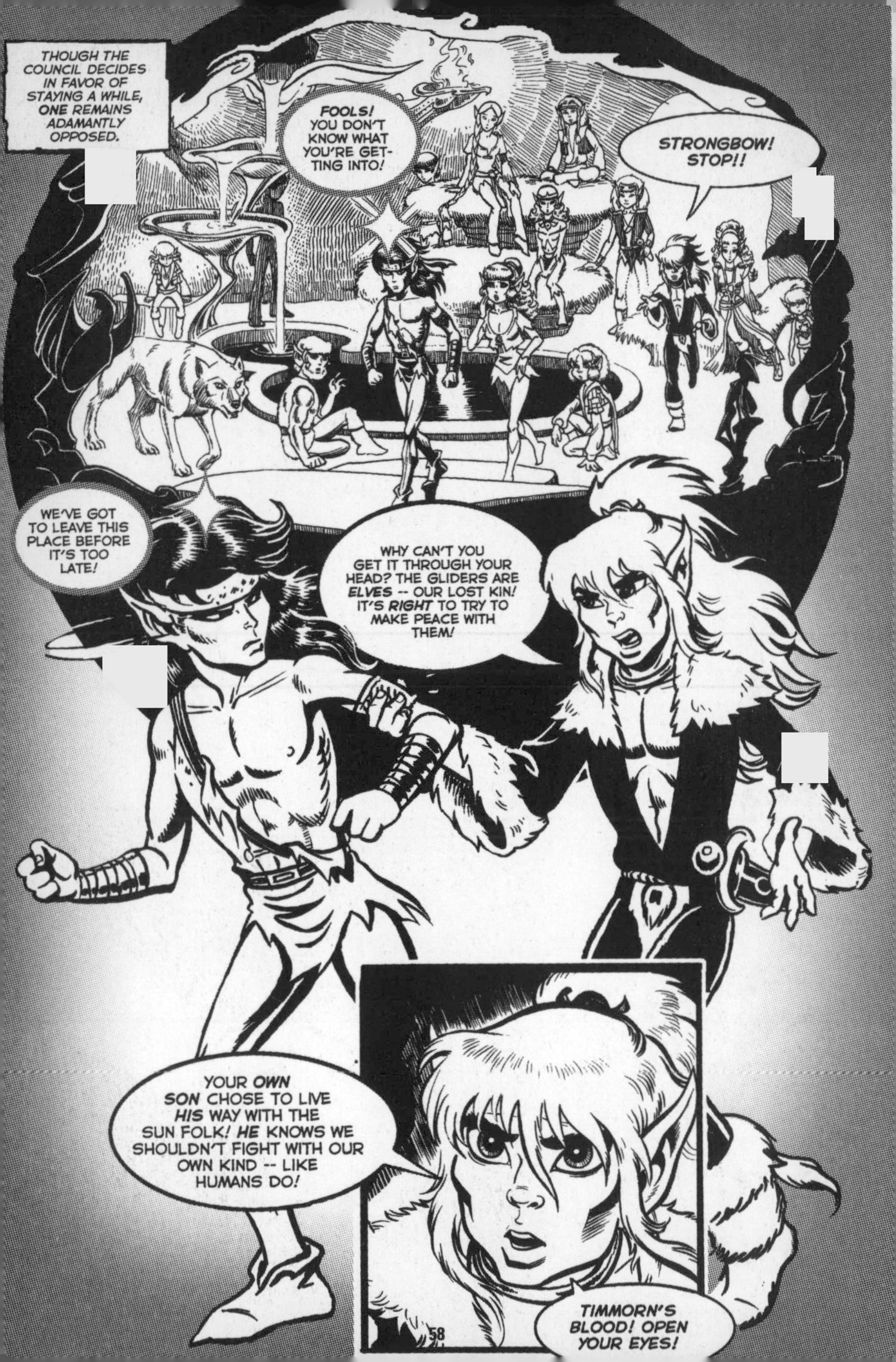
THOUGH THE COUNCIL DECIDES IN FAVOR OF STAYING A WHILE, ONE REMAINS ADAMANTLY OPPOSED.
FOOLS! YOU DON'T KNOW WHAT YOU'RE GETTING INTO!
STRONGBOW! STOP!!
WE'VE GOT TO LEAVE THIS PLACE BEFORE IT'S TOO LATE!
WHY CAN'T YOU GET IT THROUGH YOUR HEAD? THE GLIDERS ARE ELVES -- OUR LOST KIN! IT'S RIGHT TO TRY TO MAKE PEACE WITH THEM!
YOUR OWN SON CHOSE TO LIVE HIS WAY WITH THE SUN FOLK! HE KNOWS WE SHOULDN'T FIGHT WITH OUR OWN KIND -- LIKE HUMANS DO!
TIMMORN'S BLOOD! OPEN YOUR EYES!

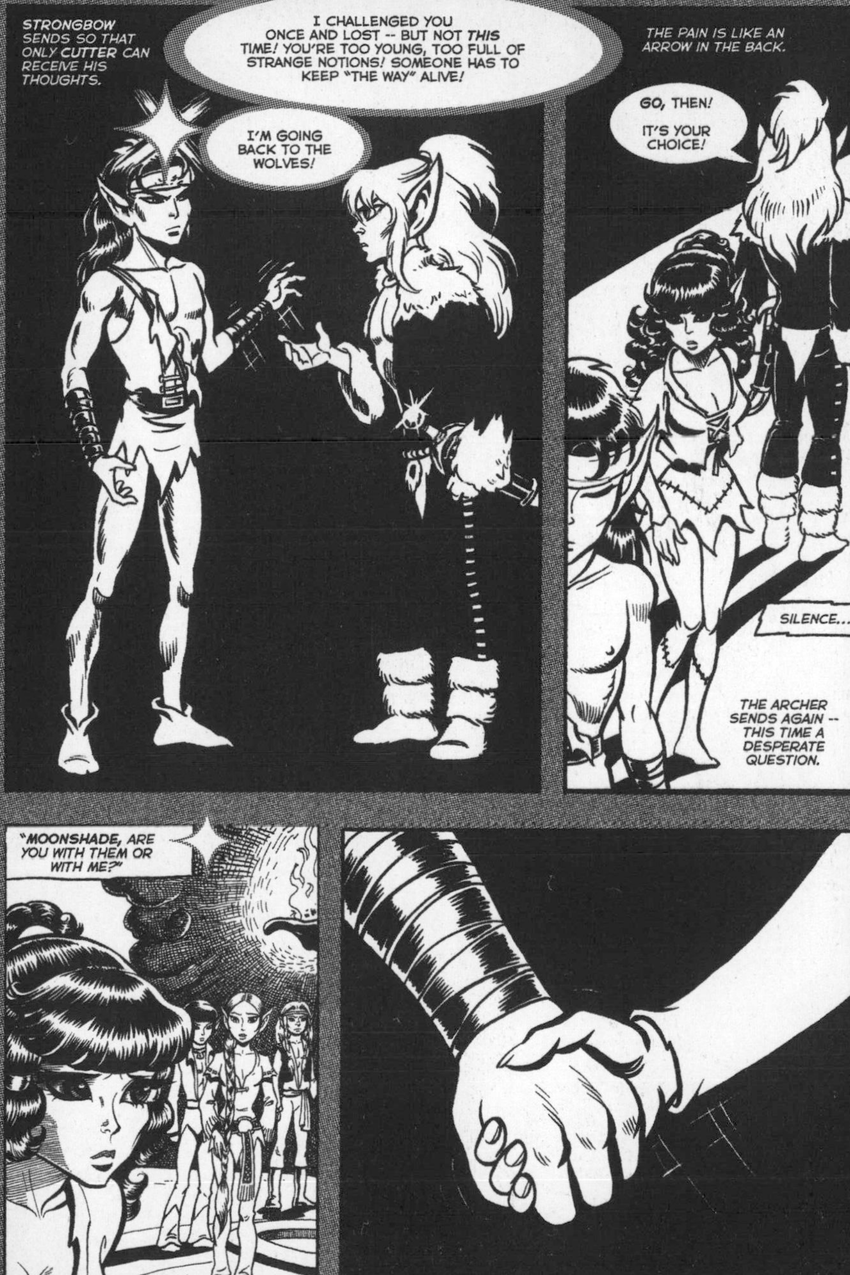
STRONGBOW SENDS SO THAT ONLY CUTTER CAN RECEIVE HIS THOUGHTS.
I CHALLENGED YOU ONCE AND LOST -- BUT NOT THIS TIME! YOU'RE TOO YOUNG, TOO FULL OF STRANGE NOTIONS! SOMEONE HAS TO KEEP "THE WAY" ALIVE!
I'M GOING BACK TO THE WOLVES!
THE PAIN IS LIKE AN ARROW IN THE BACK.
GO, THEN!
IT'S YOUR CHOICE!
SILENCE...
THE ARCHER SENDS AGAIN -- THIS TIME A DESPERATE QUESTION.
"MOONSHADE, ARE YOU WITH THEM OR WITH ME?"

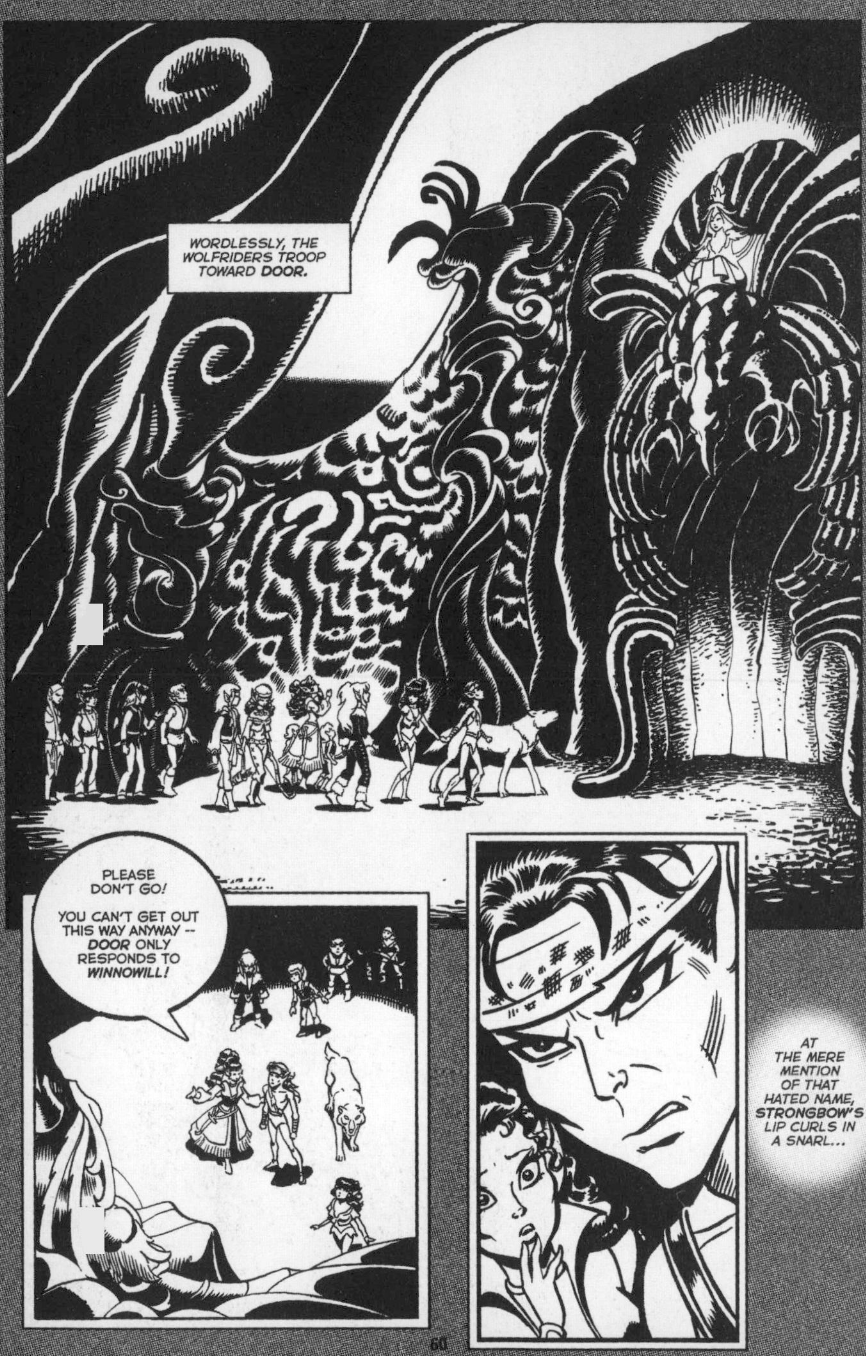
WORDLESSLY, THE WOLFRIDERS TROOP TOWARD DOOR.
PLEASE DON'T GO!
YOU CAN'T GET OUT THIS WAY ANYWAY -- DOOR ONLY RESPONDS TO WINNOWILL!
AT THE MERE MENTION OF THAT HATED NAME, STRONGBOW'S LIP CURLS IN A SNARL...

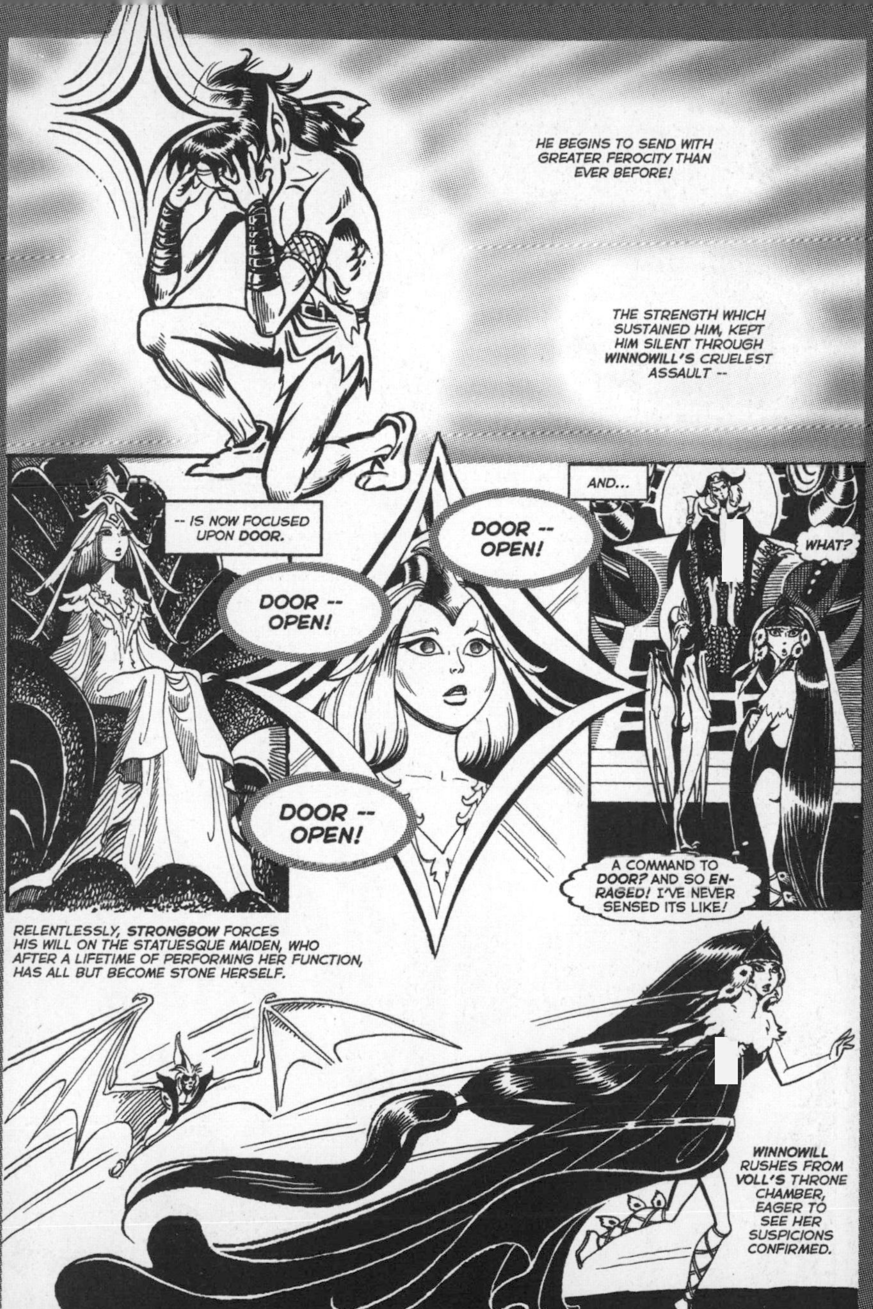
HE BEGINS TO SEND WITH GREATER FEROCITY THAN EVER BEFORE!
THE STRENGTH WHICH SUSTAINED HIM, KEPT HIM SILENT THROUGH WINNOWILL'S CRUELEST ASSAULT --
-- IS NOW FOCUSED UPON DOOR.
DOOR -- OPEN!
DOOR -- OPEN!
DOOR -- OPEN!
AND...
WHAT?
A COMMAND TO DOOR? AND SO EN-RAGED! I'VE NEVER SENSED ITS LIKE!
RELENTLESSLY, STRONGBOW FORCES HIS WILL ON THE STATUESQUE MAIDEN, WHO AFTER A LIFETIME OF PERFORMING HER FUNCTION, HAS ALL BUT BECOME STONE HERSELF.
WINNOWILL RUSHES FROM VOLL'S THRONE CHAMBER, EAGER TO SEE HER SUSPICIONS CONFIRMED.

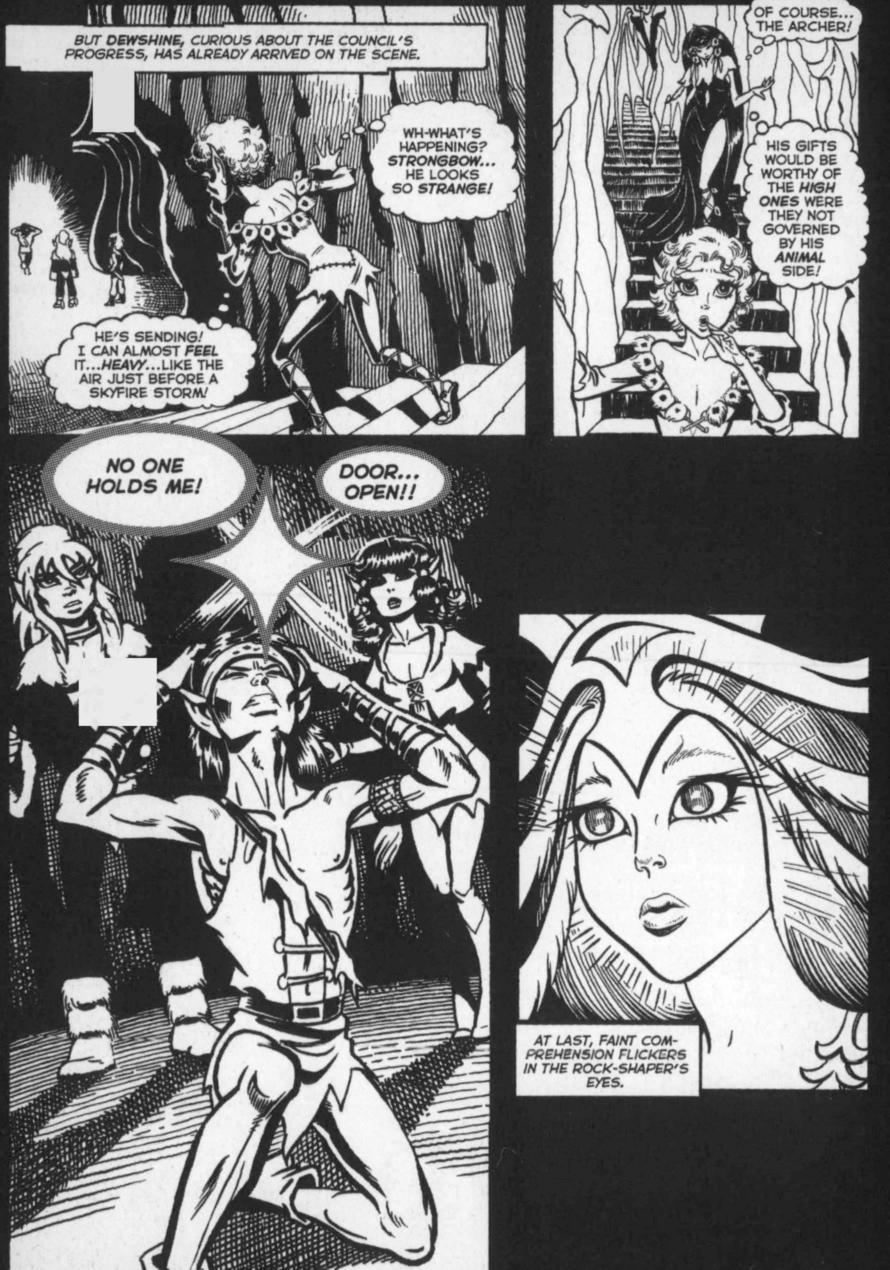

BUT DEWSHINE, CURIOUS ABOUT THE COUNCIL'S PROGRESS, HAS ALREADY ARRIVED ON THE SCENE.
WH-WHAT'S HAPPENING? STRONGBOW... HE LOOKS SO STRANGE!
HE'S SENDING! I CAN ALMOST FEEL IT...HEAVY...LIKE THE AIR JUST BEFORE A SKYFIRE STORM!
OF COURSE... THE ARCHER!
HIS GIFTS WOULD BE WORTHY OF THE HIGH ONES WERE THEY NOT GOVERNED BY HIS ANIMAL SIDE!
NO ONE HOLDS ME!
DOOR... OPEN!!
AT LAST, FAINT COMPREHENSION FLICKERS IN THE ROCK-SHAPER'S EYES.

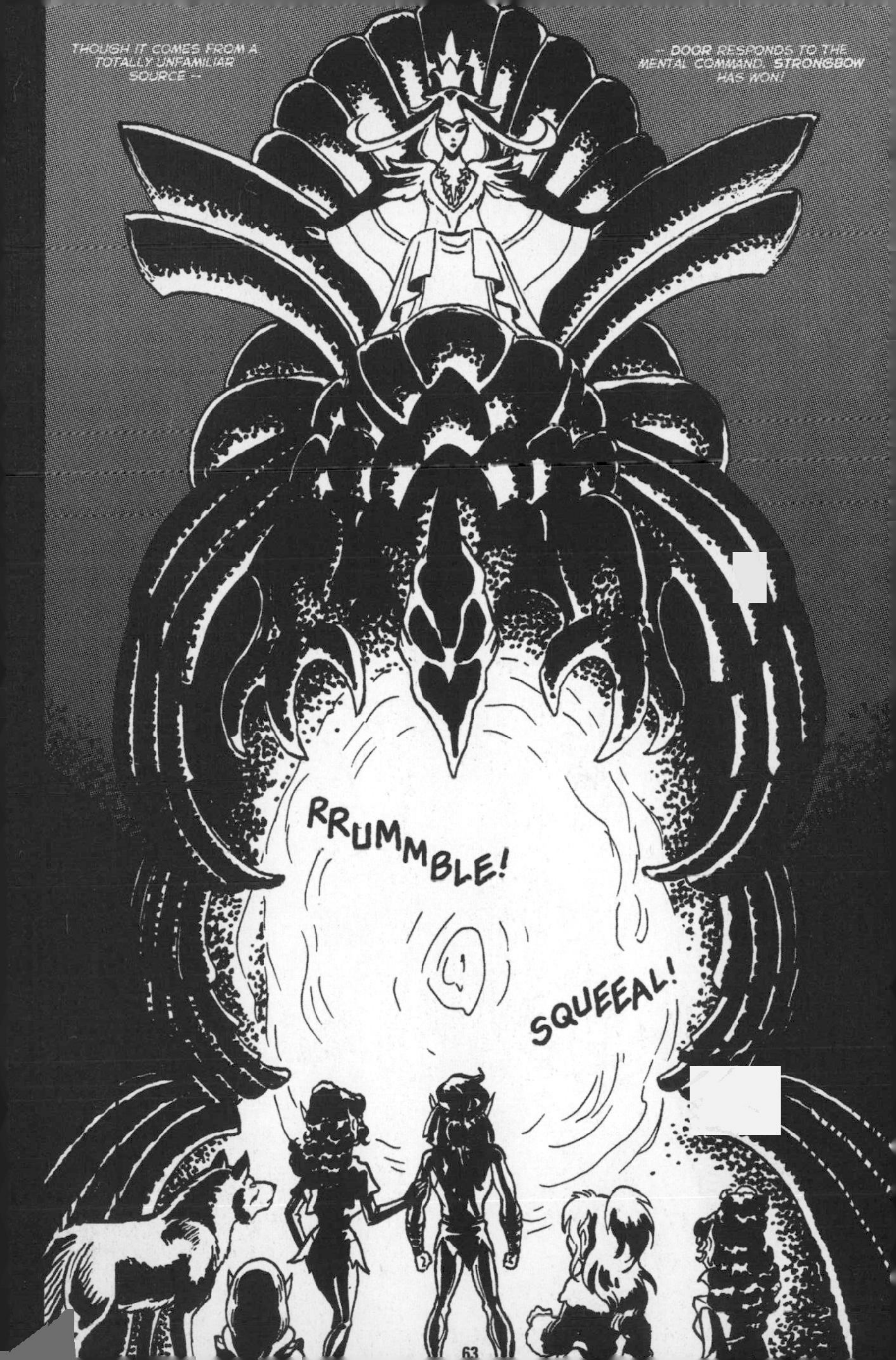
THOUGH IT COMES FROM A TOTALLY UNFAMILIAR SOURCE --
-- DOOR RESPONDS TO THE MENTAL COMMAND. STRONGBOW HAS WON!
RRUMMBLE!
SQUEEAL!

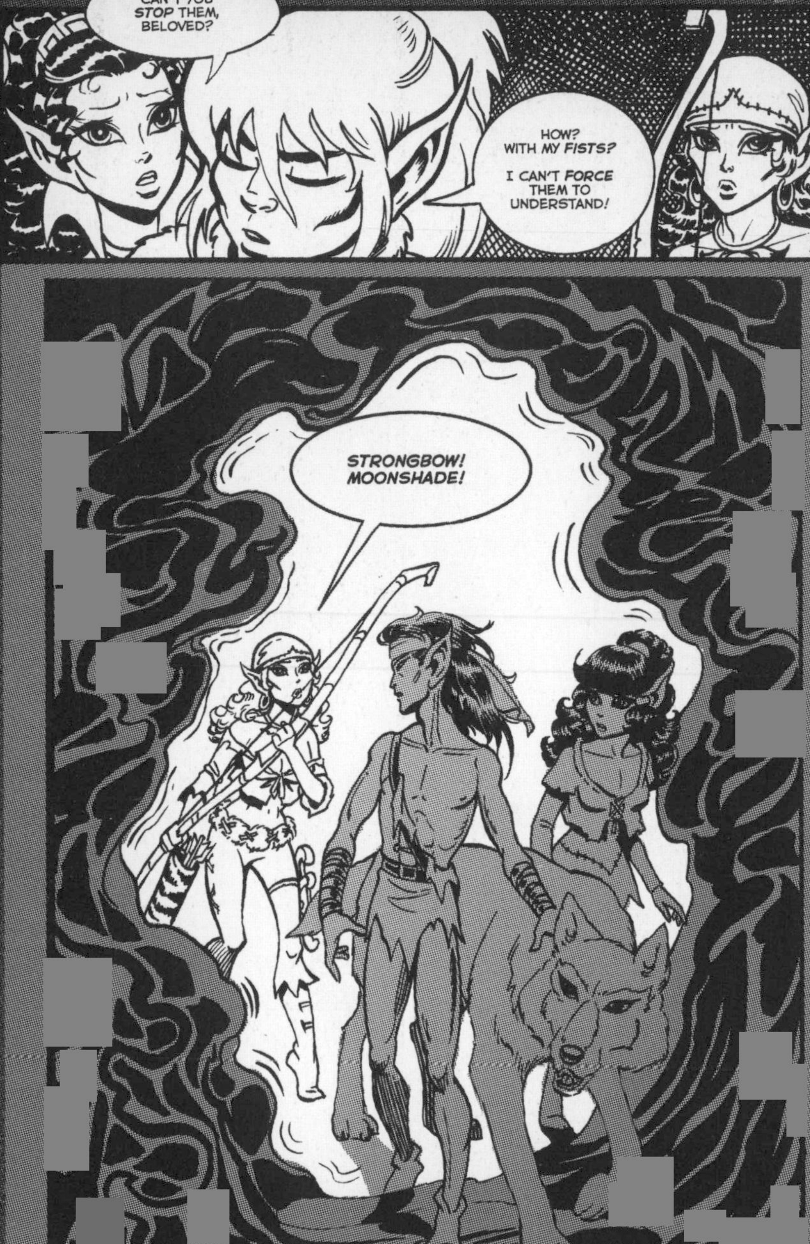
CAN'T YOU STOP THEM, BELOVED?
HOW? WITH MY FISTS?
I CAN'T FORCE THEM TO UNDERSTAND!
STRONGBOW! MOONSHADE!

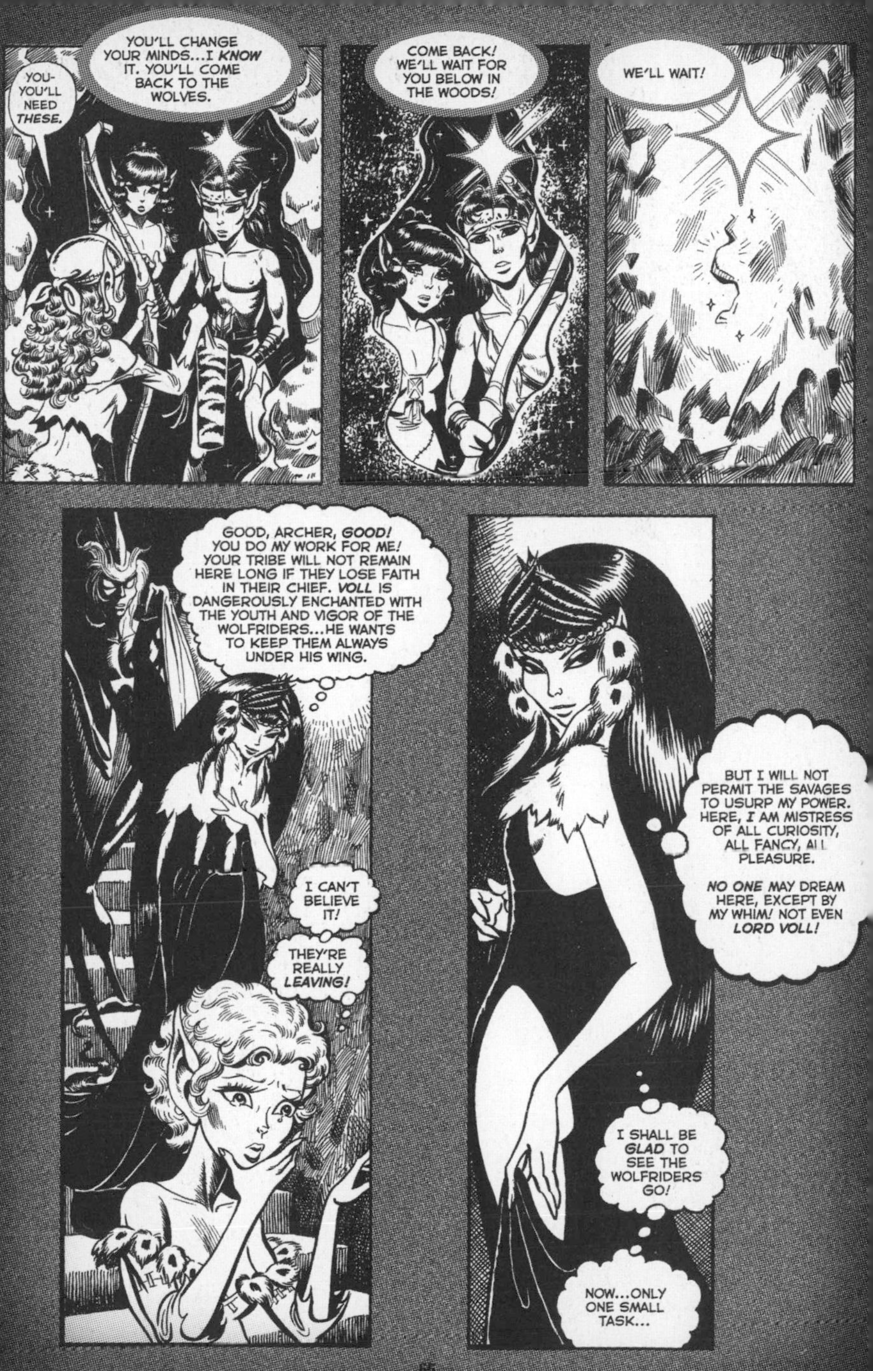
YOU- YOU'LL NEED *THESE.*
YOU'LL CHANGE YOUR MINDS...I *KNOW* IT. YOU'LL COME BACK TO THE WOLVES.
COME BACK! WE'LL WAIT FOR YOU BELOW IN THE WOODS!
WE'LL WAIT!
GOOD, ARCHER, *GOOD!* YOU DO MY WORK FOR ME! YOUR TRIBE WILL NOT REMAIN HERE LONG IF THEY LOSE FAITH IN THEIR CHIEF. *VOLL* IS DANGEROUSLY ENCHANTED WITH THE YOUTH AND VIGOR OF THE WOLFRIDERS...HE WANTS TO KEEP THEM ALWAYS UNDER HIS WING.
I CAN'T BELIEVE IT!
THEY'RE REALLY *LEAVING!*
BUT I WILL NOT PERMIT THE SAVAGES TO USURP MY POWER. HERE, *I* AM MISTRESS OF ALL CURIOSITY, ALL FANCY, ALL PLEASURE.
NO ONE MAY DREAM HERE, EXCEPT BY MY WHIM! NOT EVEN *LORD VOLL!*
I SHALL BE *GLAD* TO SEE THE WOLFRIDERS GO!
NOW...ONLY ONE SMALL TASK...

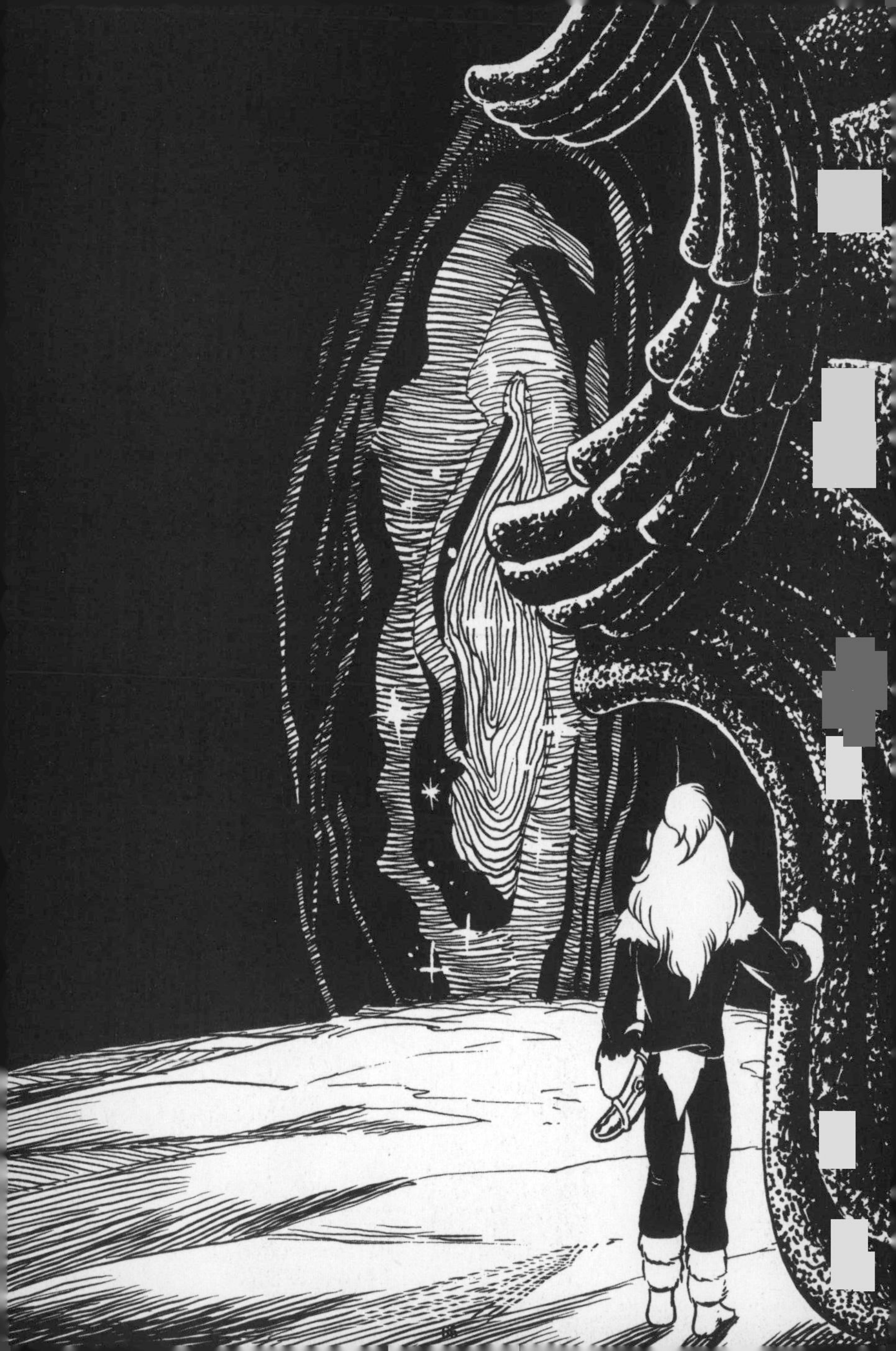

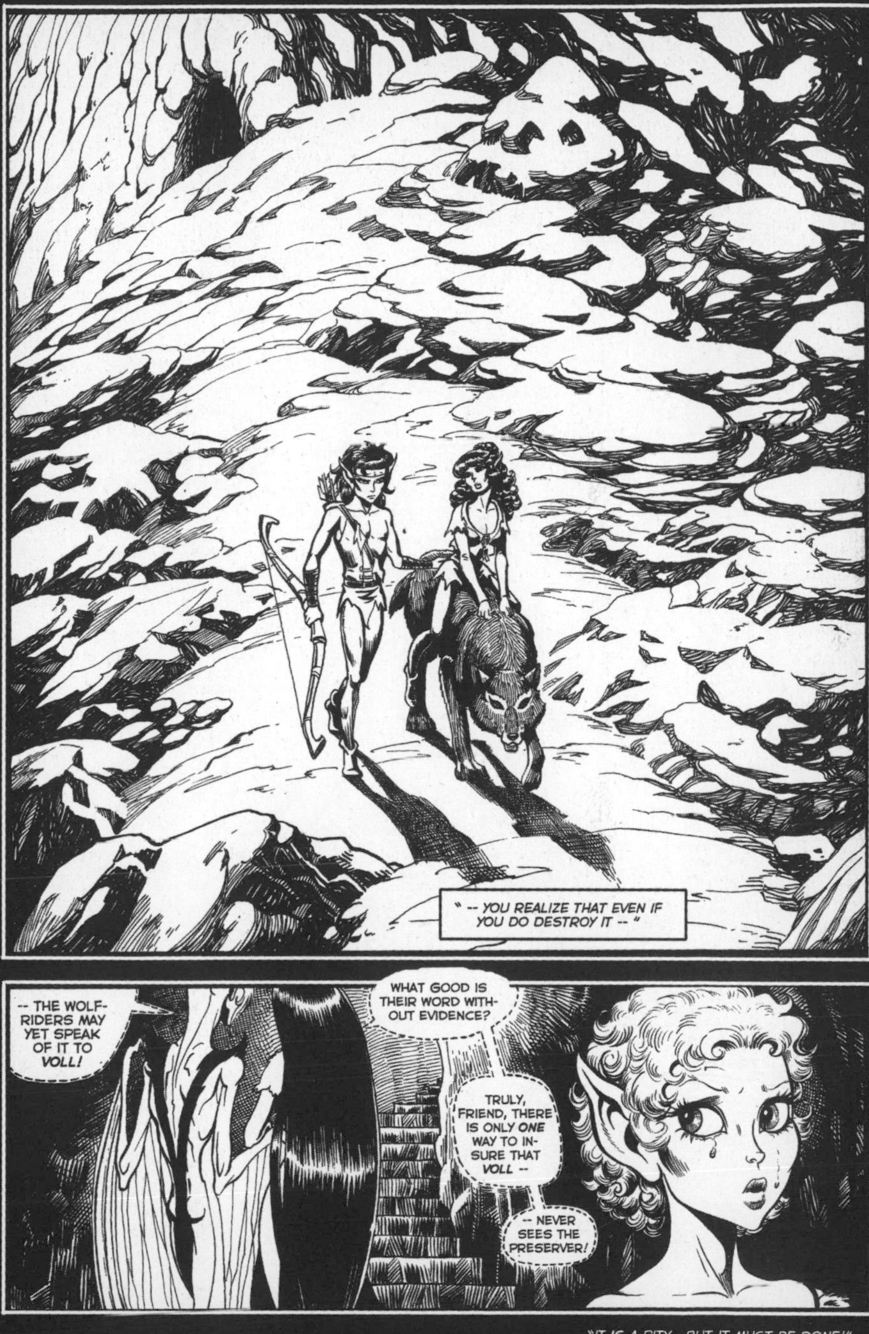
" -- *YOU REALIZE THAT EVEN IF YOU DO DESTROY IT* -- "
-- THE WOLF-RIDERS MAY YET SPEAK OF IT TO *VOLL!*
WHAT GOOD IS THEIR WORD WITH-OUT EVIDENCE?
TRULY, FRIEND, THERE IS ONLY *ONE* WAY TO IN-SURE THAT *VOLL* --
-- NEVER SEES THE PRESERVER!

"IT IS A PITY...BUT IT MUST BE DONE!"

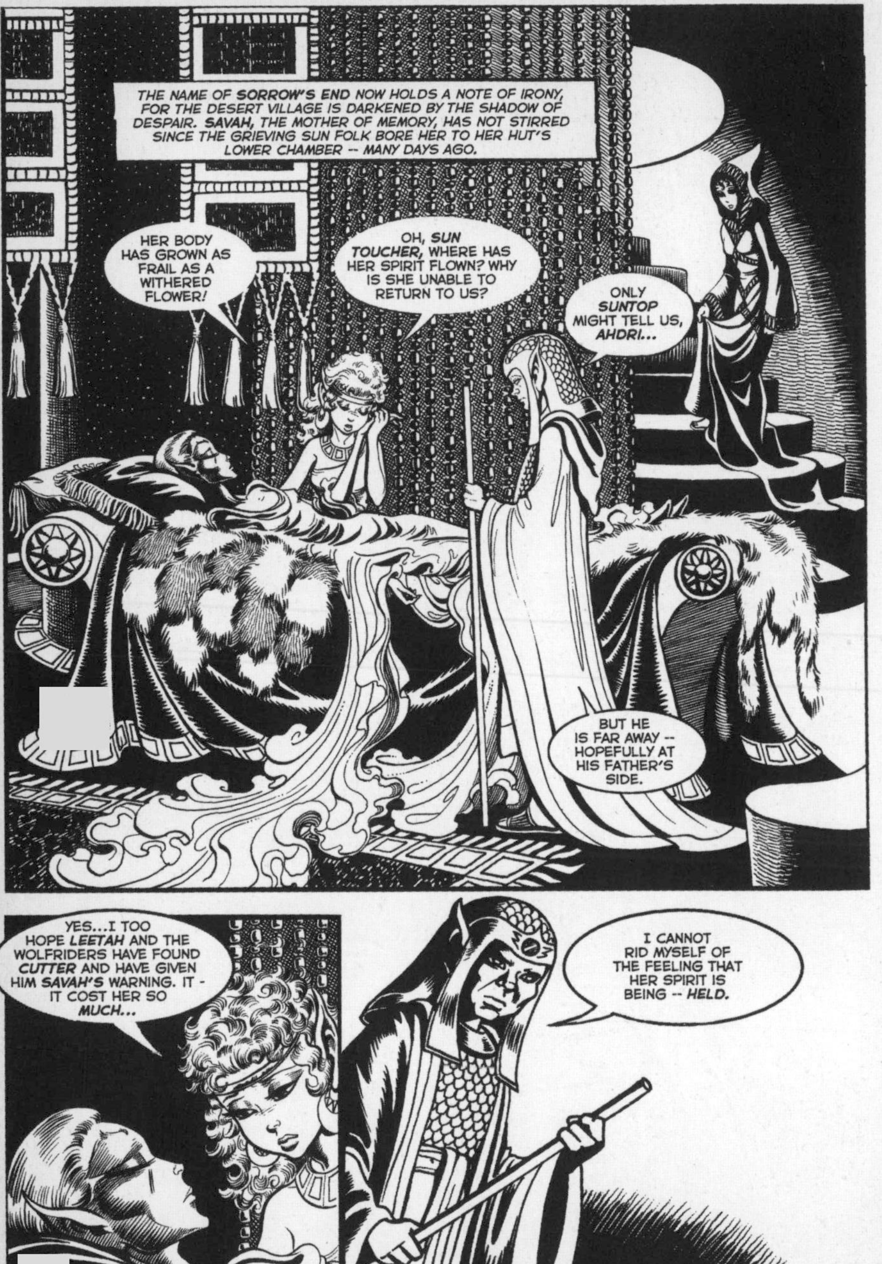
THE NAME OF SORROW'S END NOW HOLDS A NOTE OF IRONY, FOR THE DESERT VILLAGE IS DARKENED BY THE SHADOW OF DESPAIR. SAVAH, THE MOTHER OF MEMORY, HAS NOT STIRRED SINCE THE GRIEVING SUN FOLK BORE HER TO HER HUT'S LOWER CHAMBER -- MANY DAYS AGO.
HER BODY HAS GROWN AS FRAIL AS A WITHERED FLOWER!
OH, SUN TOUCHER, WHERE HAS HER SPIRIT FLOWN? WHY IS SHE UNABLE TO RETURN TO US?
ONLY SUNTOP MIGHT TELL US, AHDRI...
BUT HE IS FAR AWAY -- HOPEFULLY AT HIS FATHER'S SIDE.
YES...I TOO HOPE LEETAH AND THE WOLFRIDERS HAVE FOUND CUTTER AND HAVE GIVEN HIM SAVAH'S WARNING. IT - IT COST HER SO MUCH...
I CANNOT RID MYSELF OF THE FEELING THAT HER SPIRIT IS BEING -- HELD.

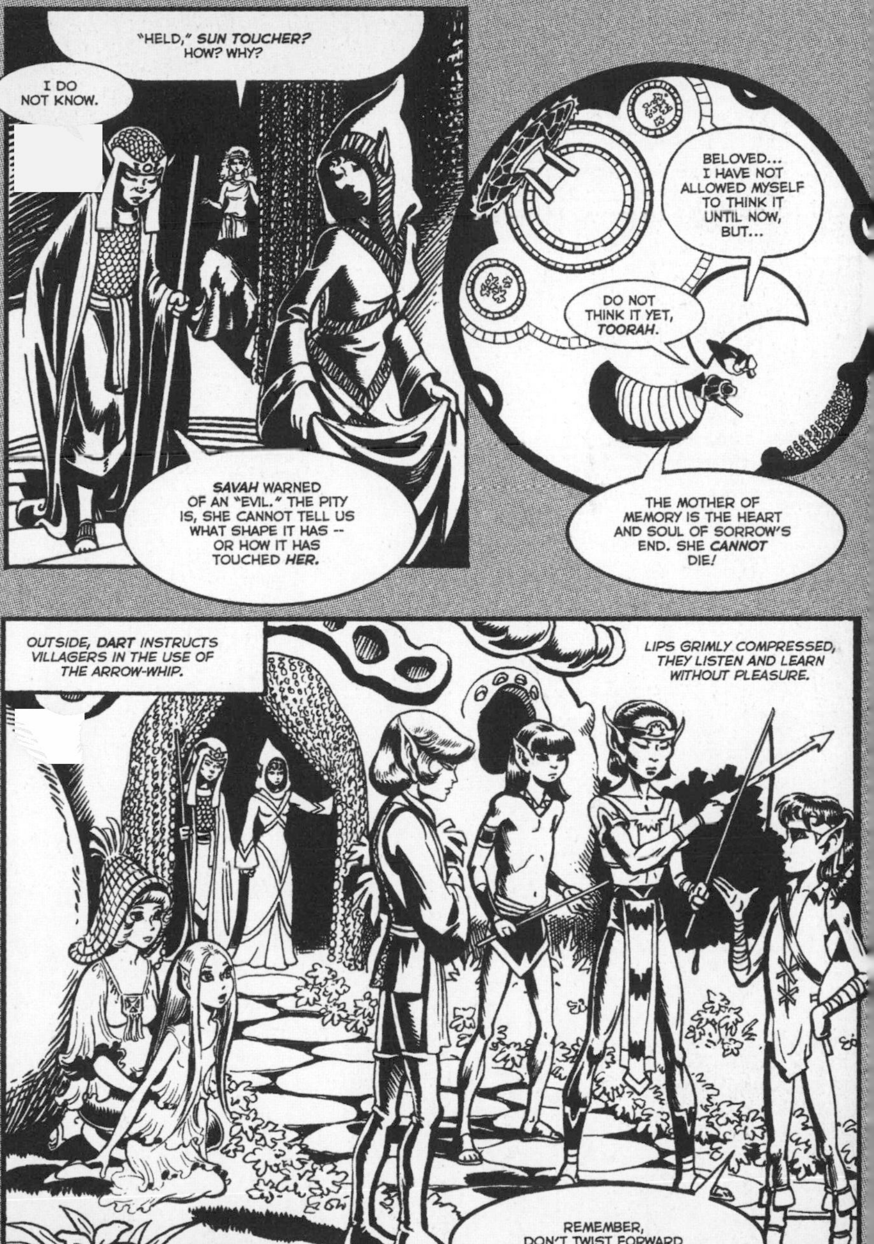
"HELD," SUN TOUCHER? HOW? WHY?
I DO NOT KNOW.
SAVAH WARNED OF AN "EVIL." THE PITY IS, SHE CANNOT TELL US WHAT SHAPE IT HAS -- OR HOW IT HAS TOUCHED HER.
BELOVED... I HAVE NOT ALLOWED MYSELF TO THINK IT UNTIL NOW, BUT...
DO NOT THINK IT YET, TOORAH.
THE MOTHER OF MEMORY IS THE HEART AND SOUL OF SORROW'S END. SHE CANNOT DIE!
OUTSIDE, DART INSTRUCTS VILLAGERS IN THE USE OF THE ARROW-WHIP.
LIPS GRIMLY COMPRESSED, THEY LISTEN AND LEARN WITHOUT PLEASURE.
REMEMBER, DON'T TWIST FORWARD WHEN YOU SHOOT.

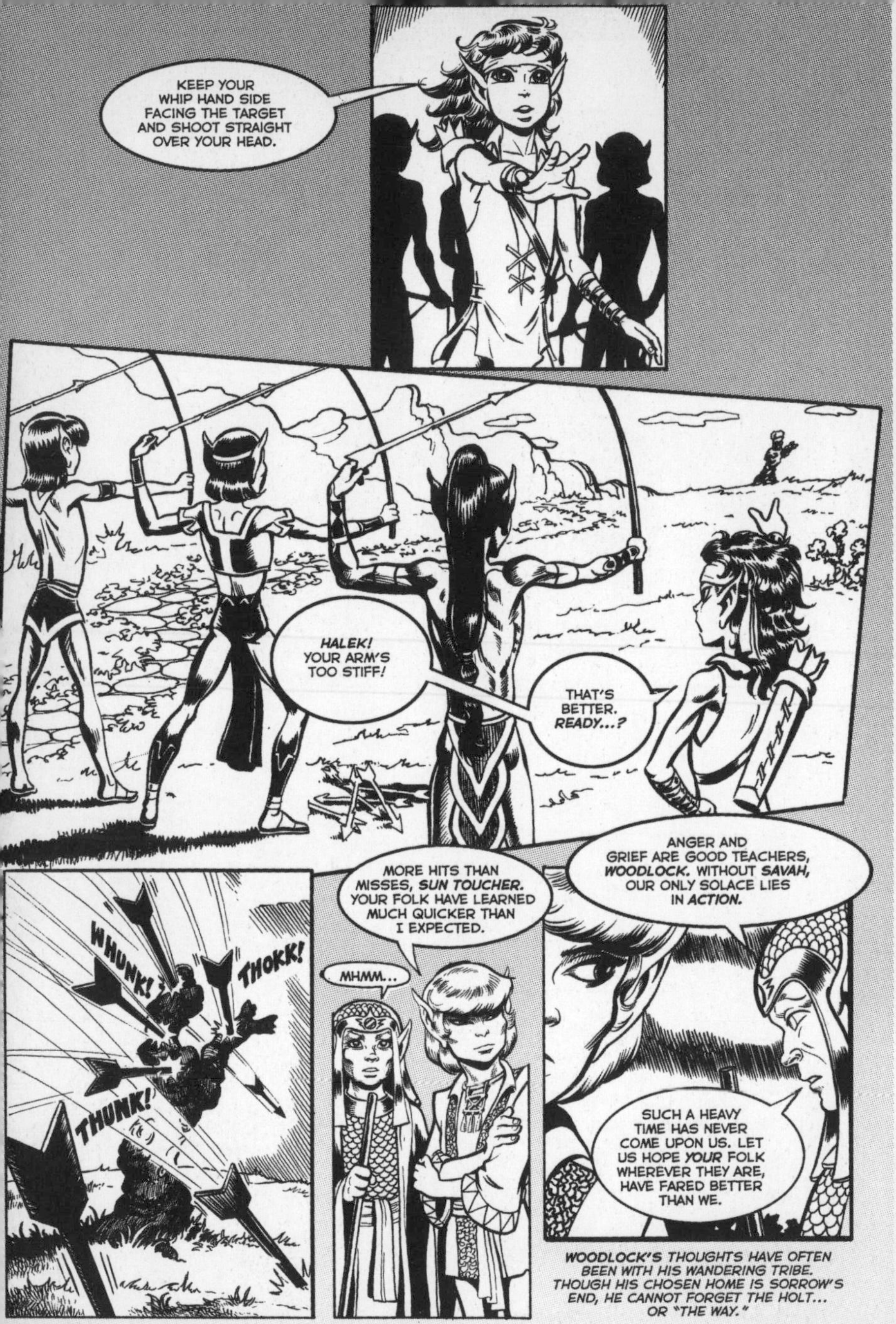

KEEP YOUR WHIP HAND SIDE FACING THE TARGET AND SHOOT STRAIGHT OVER YOUR HEAD.
HALEK! YOUR ARM'S TOO STIFF!
THAT'S BETTER. READY...?
WHUNK!
THOKK!
THUNK!
MORE HITS THAN MISSES, SUN TOUCHER. YOUR FOLK HAVE LEARNED MUCH QUICKER THAN I EXPECTED.
MHMM...
ANGER AND GRIEF ARE GOOD TEACHERS, WOODLOCK. WITHOUT SAVAH, OUR ONLY SOLACE LIES IN ACTION.
SUCH A HEAVY TIME HAS NEVER COME UPON US. LET US HOPE YOUR FOLK WHEREVER THEY ARE, HAVE FARED BETTER THAN WE.
WOODLOCK'S THOUGHTS HAVE OFTEN BEEN WITH HIS WANDERING TRIBE. THOUGH HIS CHOSEN HOME IS SORROW'S END, HE CANNOT FORGET THE HOLT... OR "THE WAY."

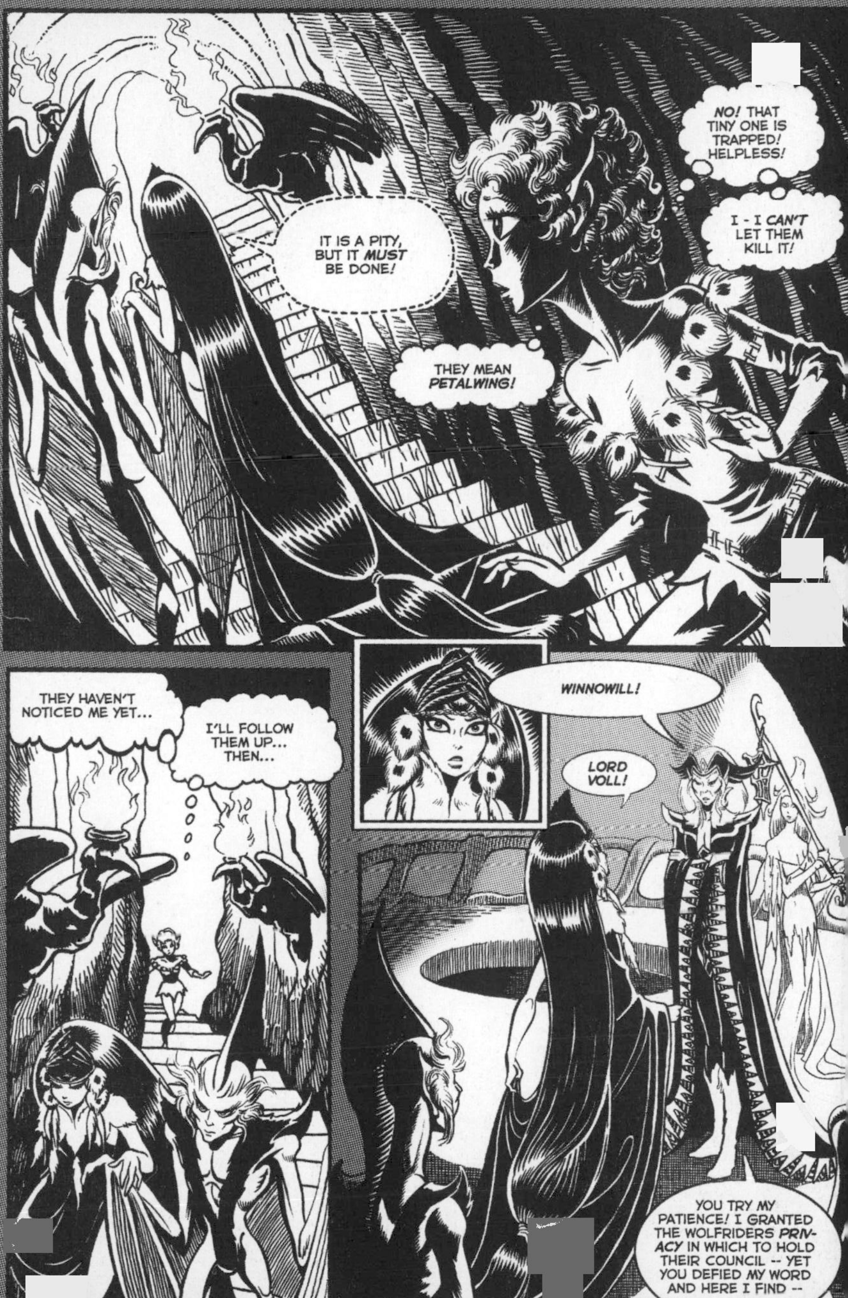
IT IS A PITY, BUT IT *MUST* BE DONE!
THEY MEAN *PETALWING!*
NO! THAT TINY ONE IS TRAPPED! HELPLESS!
I - I *CAN'T* LET THEM KILL IT!
THEY HAVEN'T NOTICED ME YET...
I'LL FOLLOW THEM UP... THEN...
WINNOWILL!
LORD VOLL!
YOU TRY MY PATIENCE! I GRANTED THE WOLFRIDERS *PRIVACY* IN WHICH TO HOLD THEIR COUNCIL -- YET YOU DEFIED *MY* WORD AND HERE I FIND --

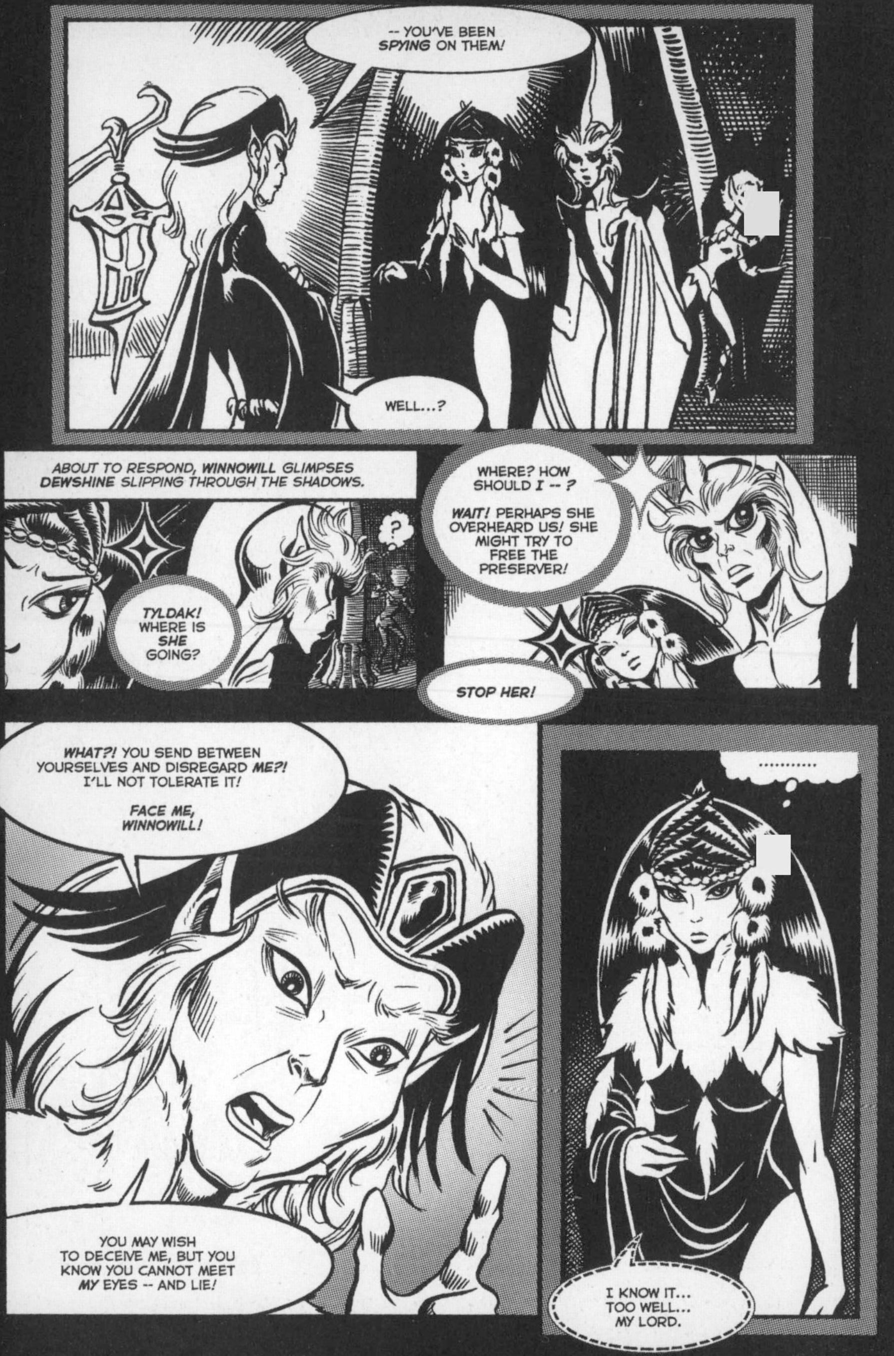
-- YOU'VE BEEN SPYING ON THEM!
WELL...?
ABOUT TO RESPOND, WINNOWILL GLIMPSES DEWSHINE SLIPPING THROUGH THE SHADOWS.
TYLDAK! WHERE IS SHE GOING?
?
WHERE? HOW SHOULD I -- ?
WAIT! PERHAPS SHE OVERHEARD US! SHE MIGHT TRY TO FREE THE PRESERVER!
STOP HER!
WHAT?! YOU SEND BETWEEN YOURSELVES AND DISREGARD ME?! I'LL NOT TOLERATE IT!
FACE ME, WINNOWILL!
YOU MAY WISH TO DECEIVE ME, BUT YOU KNOW YOU CANNOT MEET MY EYES -- AND LIE!
....
I KNOW IT... TOO WELL... MY LORD.

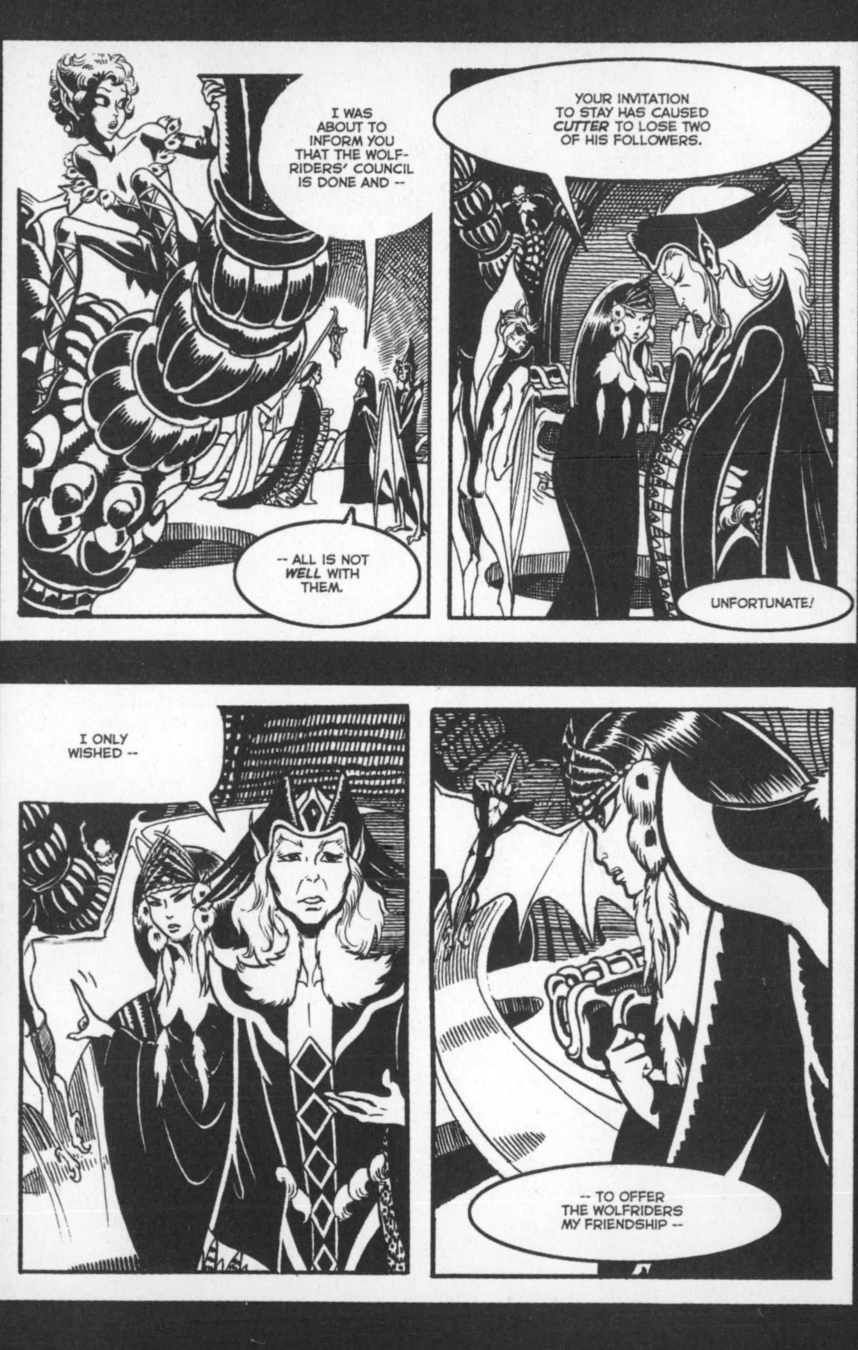
I WAS ABOUT TO INFORM YOU THAT THE WOLF-RIDERS' COUNCIL IS DONE AND --
-- ALL IS NOT *WELL* WITH THEM.
YOUR INVITATION TO STAY HAS CAUSED *CUTTER* TO LOSE TWO OF HIS FOLLOWERS.
UNFORTUNATE!
I ONLY WISHED --
-- TO OFFER THE WOLFRIDERS MY FRIENDSHIP --

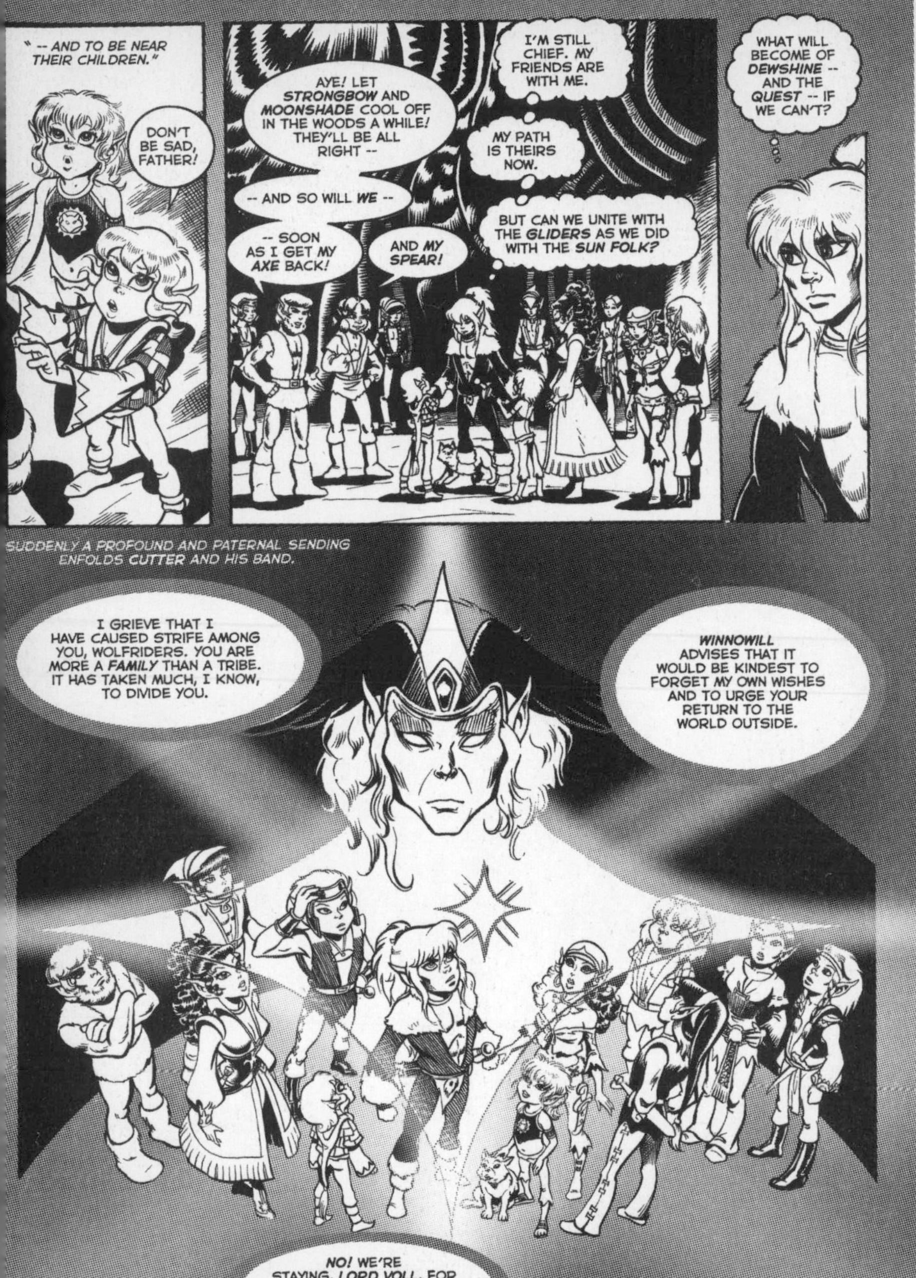
"-- AND TO BE NEAR THEIR CHILDREN."
DON'T BE SAD, FATHER!
AYE! LET STRONGBOW AND MOONSHADE COOL OFF IN THE WOODS A WHILE! THEY'LL BE ALL RIGHT --
-- AND SO WILL WE --
-- SOON AS I GET MY AXE BACK!
AND MY SPEAR!
I'M STILL CHIEF. MY FRIENDS ARE WITH ME.
MY PATH IS THEIRS NOW.
BUT CAN WE UNITE WITH THE GLIDERS AS WE DID WITH THE SUN FOLK?
WHAT WILL BECOME OF DEWSHINE -- AND THE QUEST -- IF WE CAN'T?
SUDDENLY A PROFOUND AND PATERNAL SENDING ENFOLDS CUTTER AND HIS BAND.
I GRIEVE THAT I HAVE CAUSED STRIFE AMONG YOU, WOLFRIDERS. YOU ARE MORE A FAMILY THAN A TRIBE. IT HAS TAKEN MUCH, I KNOW, TO DIVIDE YOU.
WINNOWILL ADVISES THAT IT WOULD BE KINDEST TO FORGET MY OWN WISHES AND TO URGE YOUR RETURN TO THE WORLD OUTSIDE.
NO! WE'RE STAYING, LORD VOLL, FOR MORE ANSWERS -- AND FOR THE SAKE OF ONE OF OUR OWN --

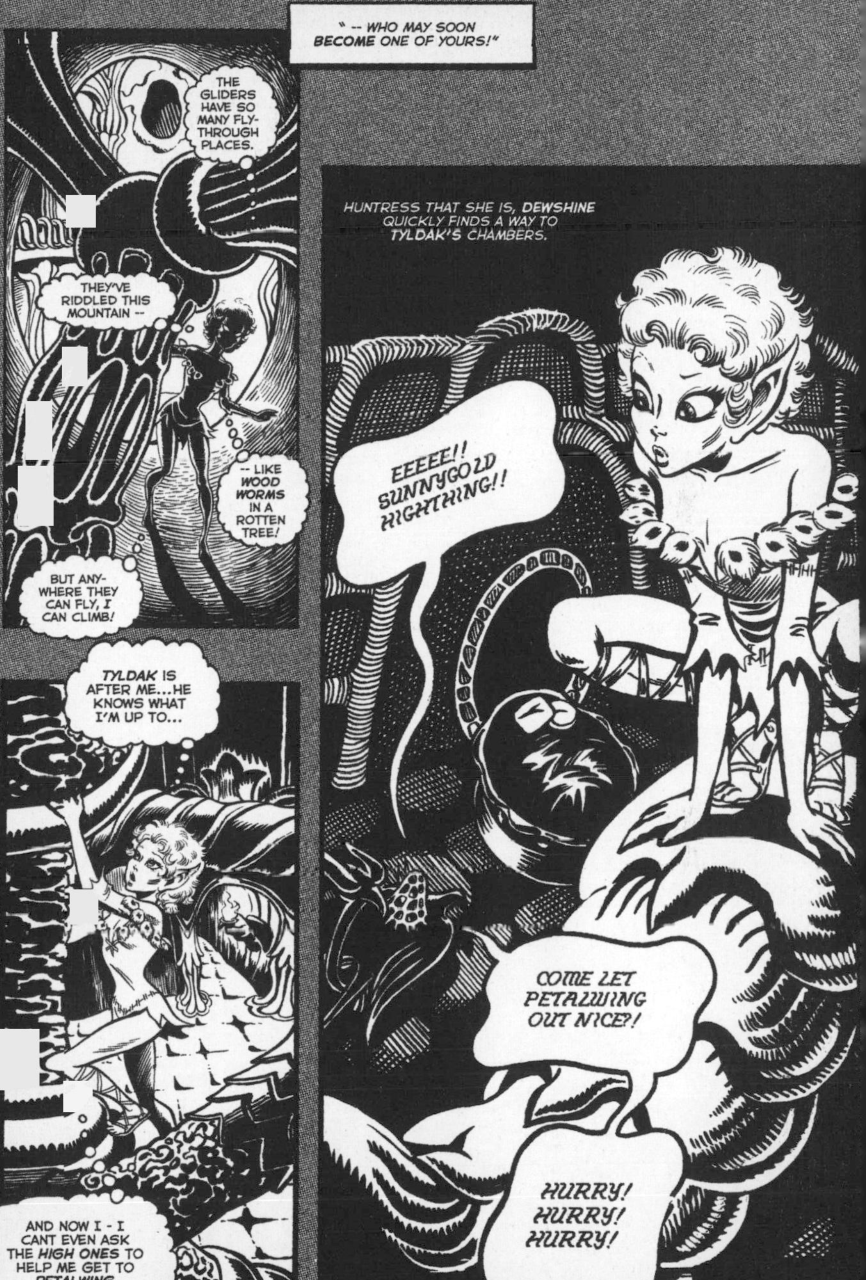
" -- WHO MAY SOON BECOME ONE OF YOURS!"
THE GLIDERS HAVE SO MANY FLY-THROUGH PLACES.
THEY'VE RIDDLED THIS MOUNTAIN --
-- LIKE WOOD WORMS IN A ROTTEN TREE!
BUT ANYWHERE THEY CAN FLY, I CAN CLIMB!
TYLDAK IS AFTER ME...HE KNOWS WHAT I'M UP TO...
AND NOW I - I CANT EVEN ASK THE HIGH ONES TO HELP ME GET TO PETALWING FIRST!
HUNTRESS THAT SHE IS, DEWSHINE QUICKLY FINDS A WAY TO TYLDAK'S CHAMBERS.
EEEEE!! SUNNYGOLD HIGHTHING!!
COME LET PETALWING OUT NICE?!
HURRY! HURRY! HURRY!

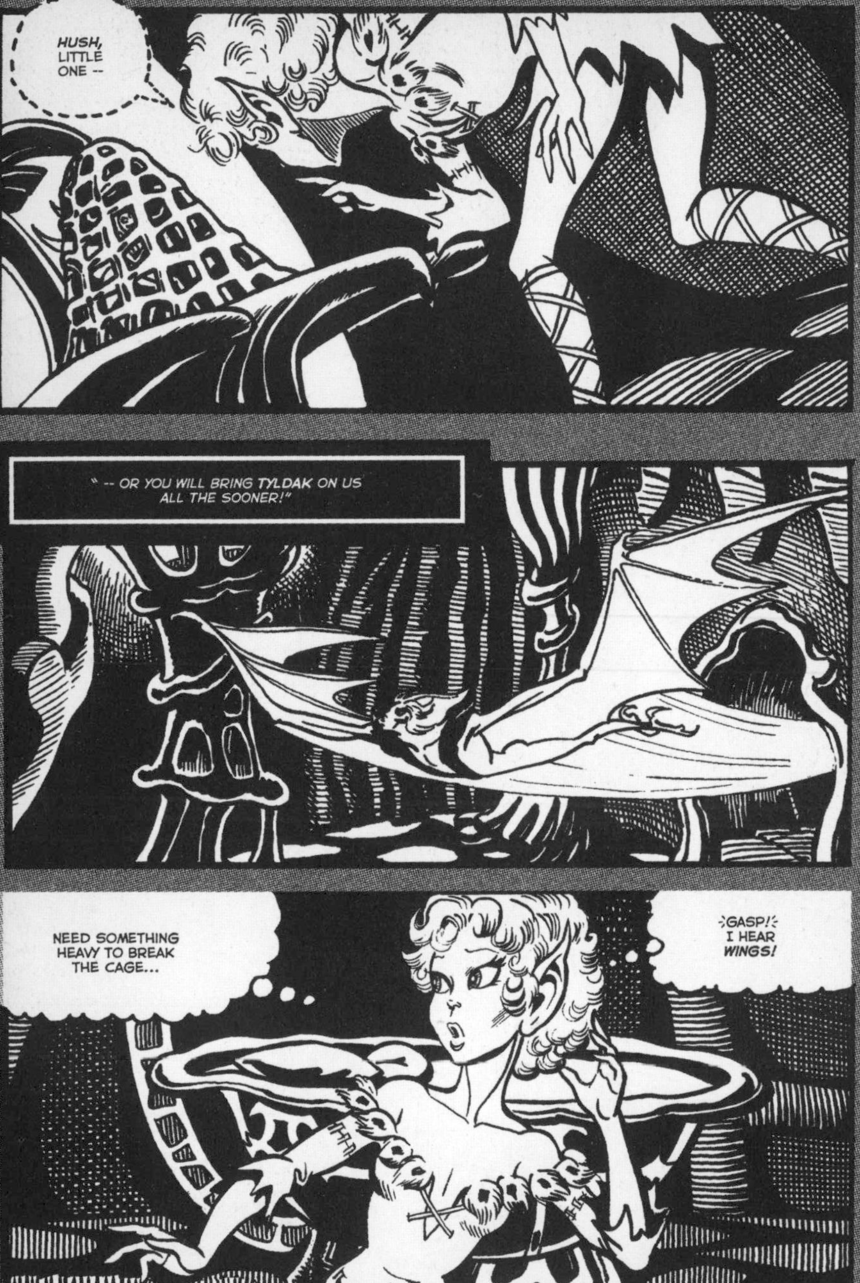

HUSH, LITTLE ONE --
" -- OR YOU WILL BRING TYLDAK ON US ALL THE SOONER!"
NEED SOMETHING HEAVY TO BREAK THE CAGE...
GASP! I HEAR WINGS!

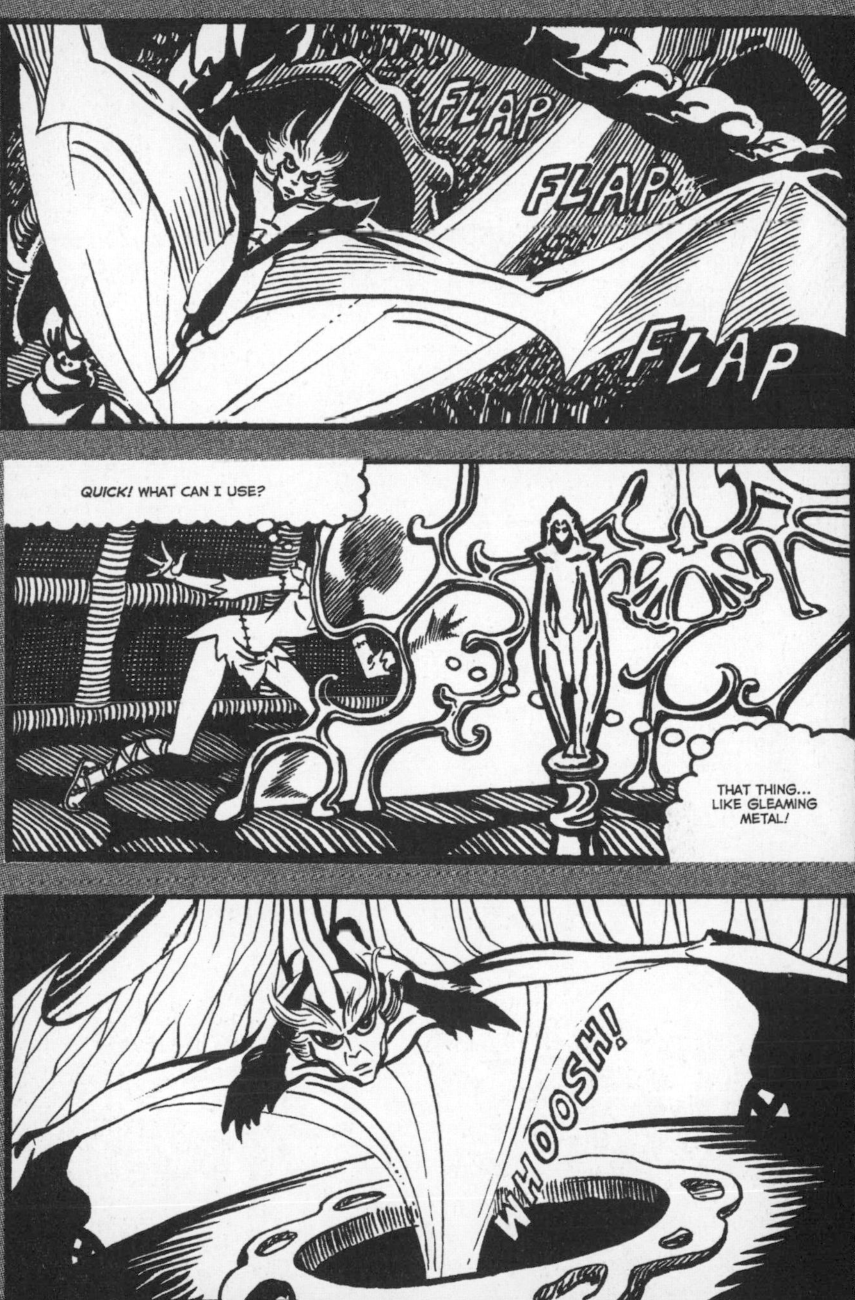
FLAP
FLAP
FLAP
QUICK! WHAT CAN I USE?
THAT THING... LIKE GLEAMING METAL!
WHOOSH!

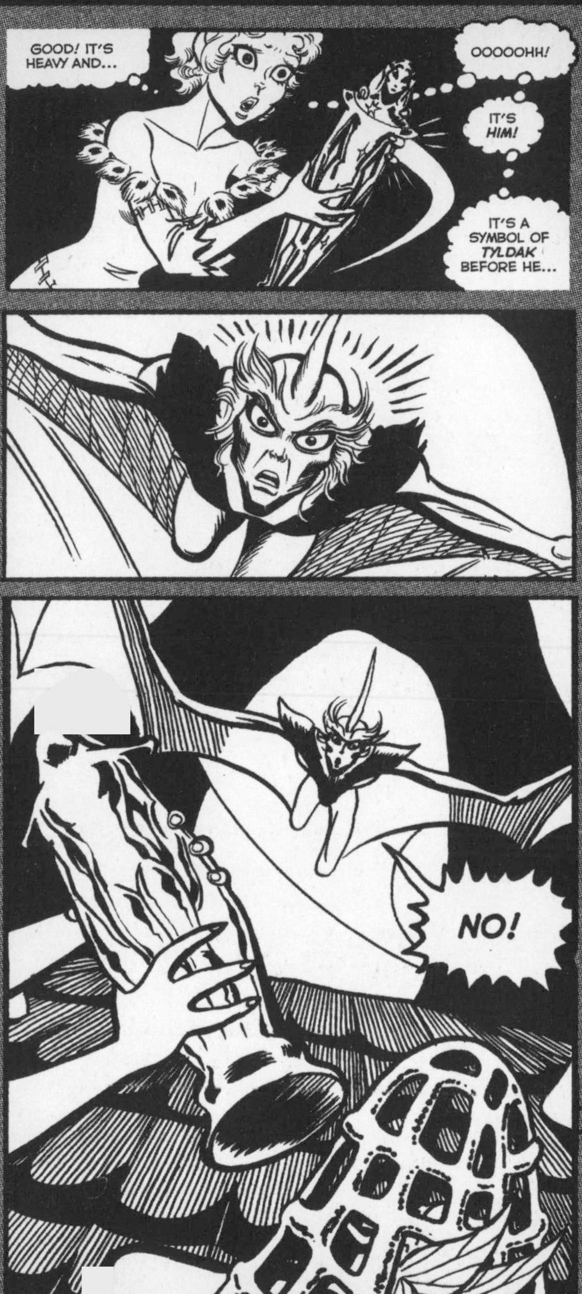
GOOD! IT'S HEAVY AND...
OOOOOHH!
IT'S HIM!
IT'S A SYMBOL OF TYLDAK BEFORE HE...
NO!

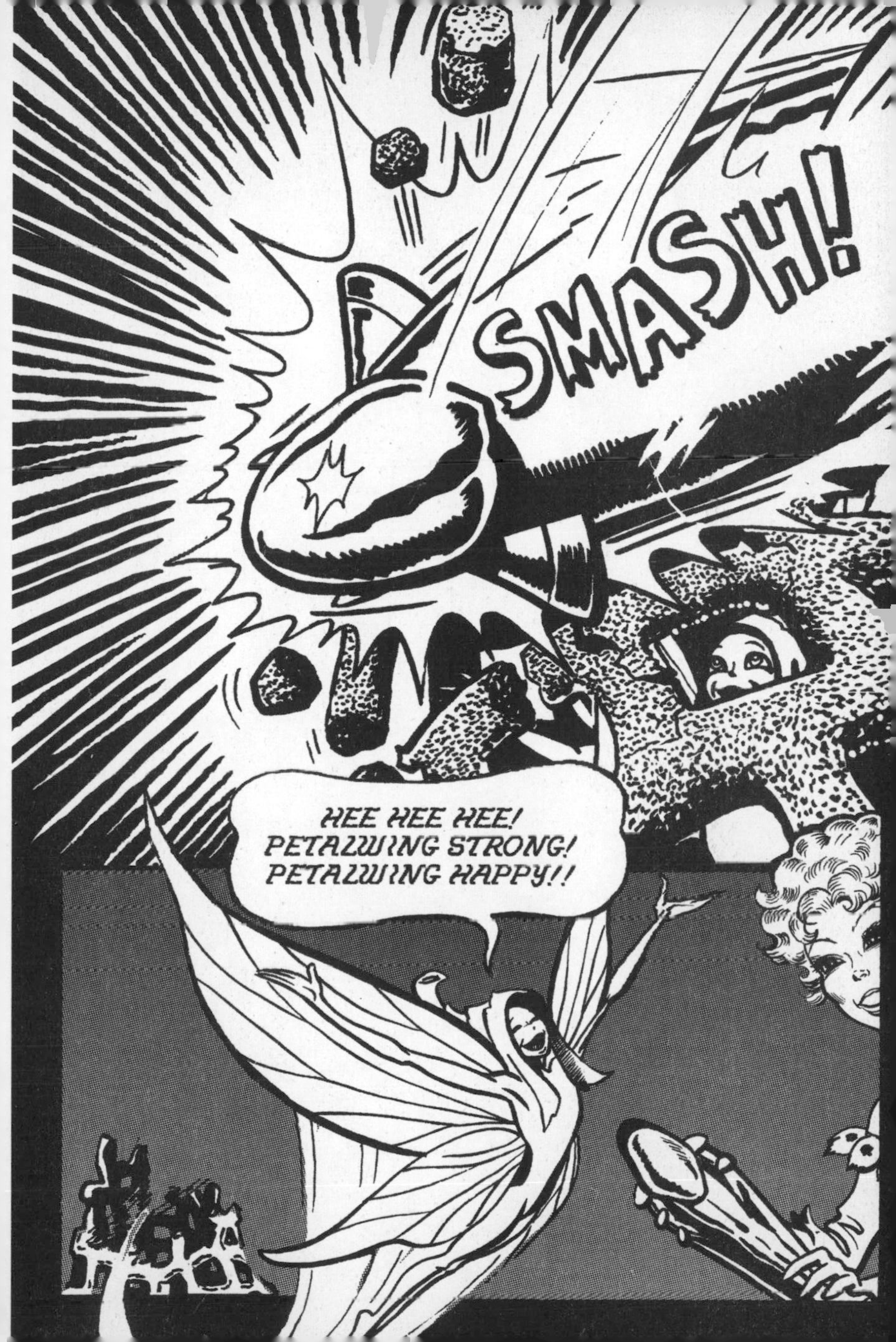
SMASH!
HEE HEE HEE! PETALWING STRONG! PETALWING HAPPY!!

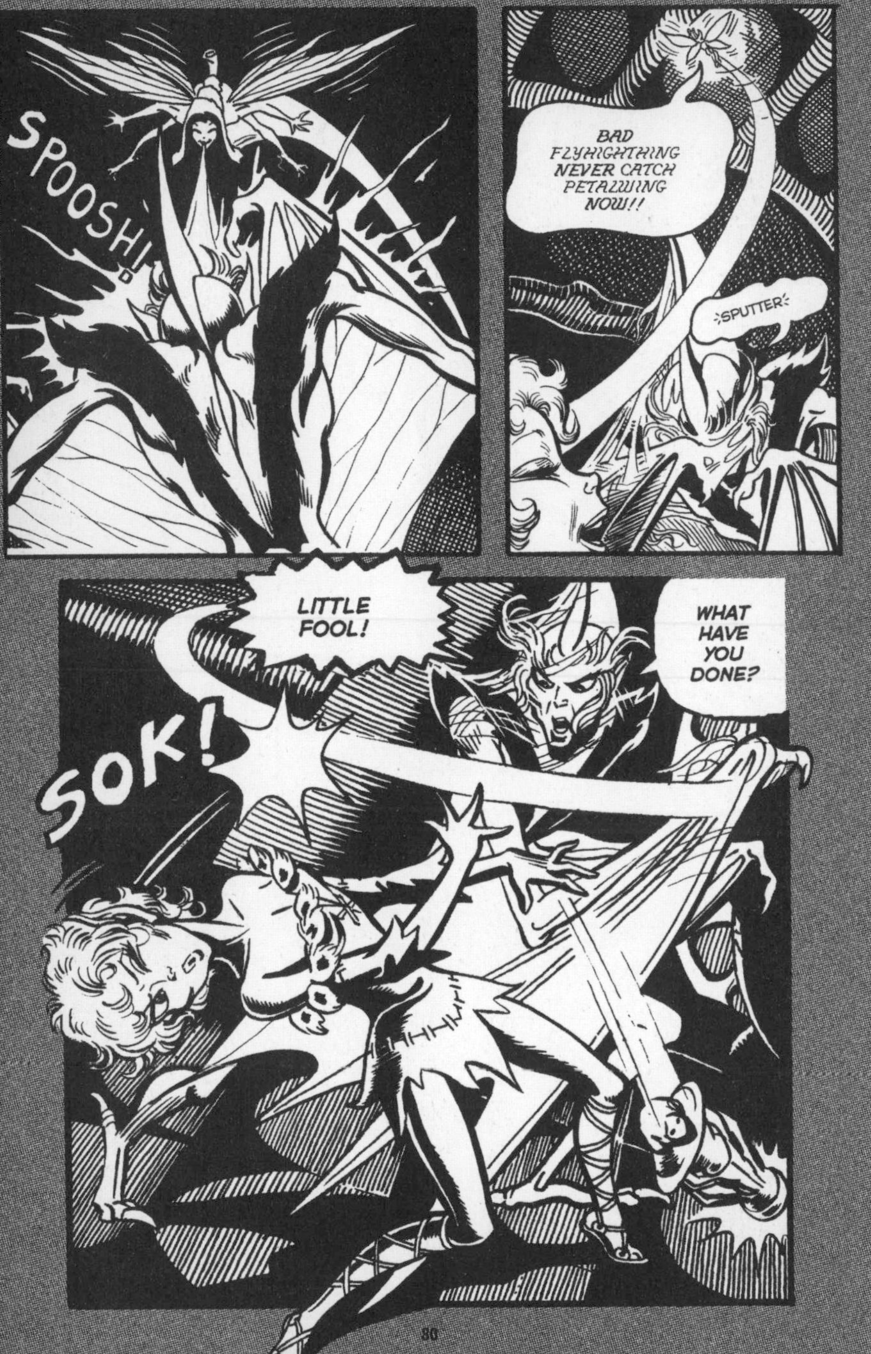
SPOOSH!
BAD FLYHIGHTHING NEVER CATCH PETALWING NOW!!
SPUTTER
LITTLE FOOL!
WHAT HAVE YOU DONE?
SOK!

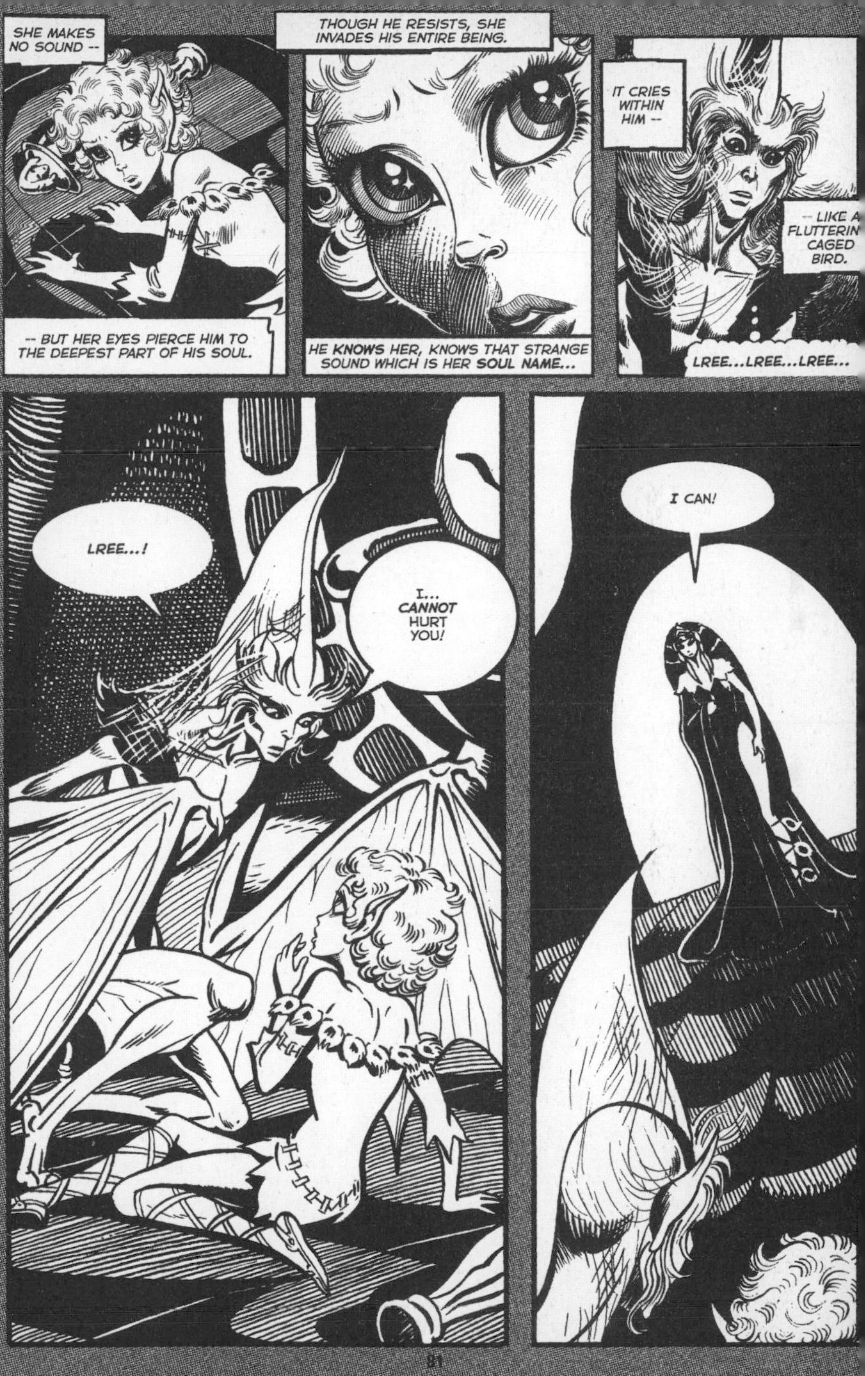
SHE MAKES NO SOUND --
-- BUT HER EYES PIERCE HIM TO THE DEEPEST PART OF HIS SOUL.
THOUGH HE RESISTS, SHE INVADES HIS ENTIRE BEING.
HE KNOWS HER, KNOWS THAT STRANGE SOUND WHICH IS HER SOUL NAME...
IT CRIES WITHIN HIM --
-- LIKE A FLUTTERIN CAGED BIRD.
LREE...LREE...LREE...
LREE...!
I... CANNOT HURT YOU!
I CAN!

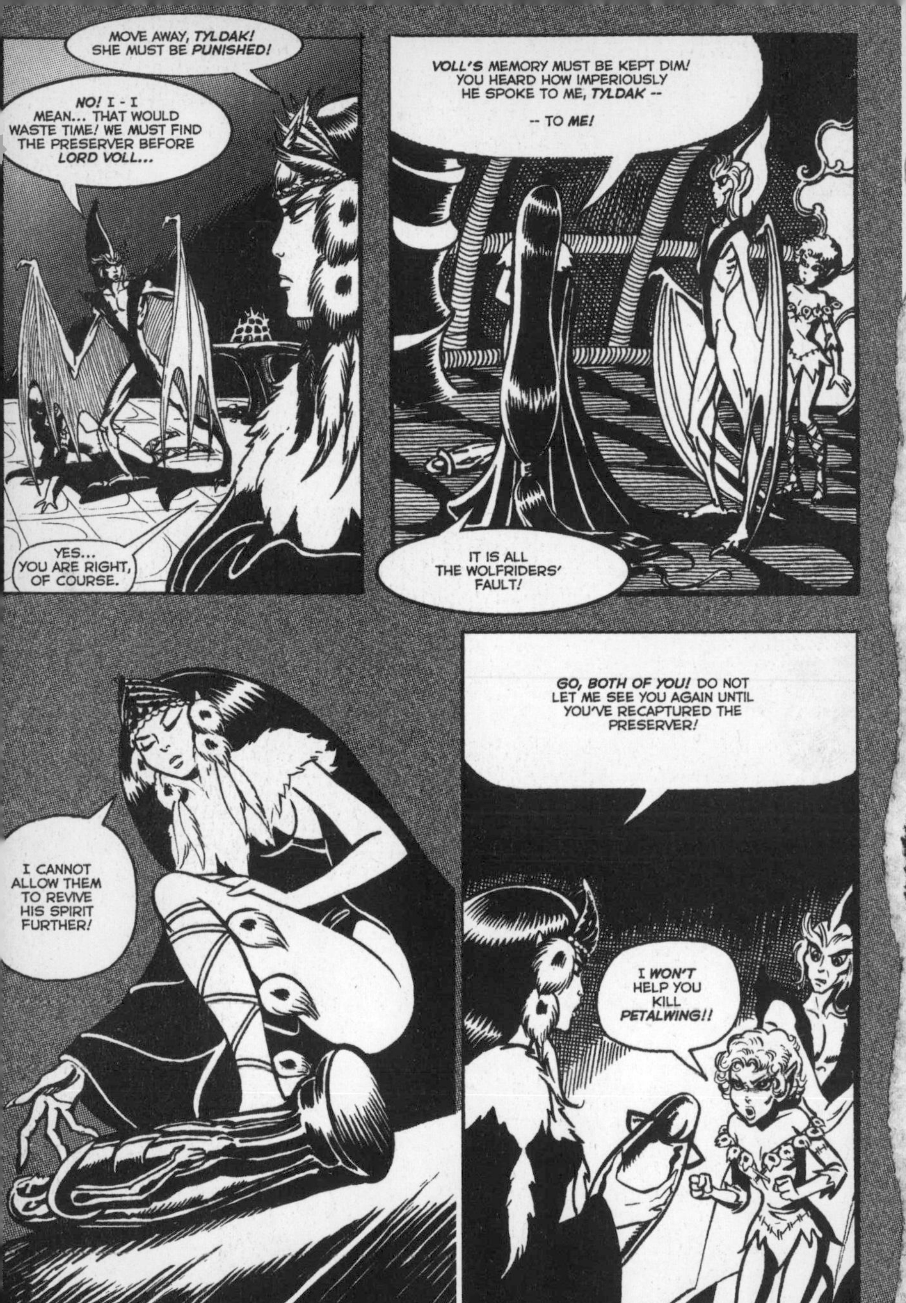
MOVE AWAY, TYLDAK! SHE MUST BE PUNISHED!
NO! I - I MEAN... THAT WOULD WASTE TIME! WE MUST FIND THE PRESERVER BEFORE LORD VOLL...
YES... YOU ARE RIGHT, OF COURSE.
VOLL'S MEMORY MUST BE KEPT DIM! YOU HEARD HOW IMPERIOUSLY HE SPOKE TO ME, TYLDAK --
-- TO ME!
IT IS ALL THE WOLFRIDERS' FAULT!
I CANNOT ALLOW THEM TO REVIVE HIS SPIRIT FURTHER!
GO, BOTH OF YOU! DO NOT LET ME SEE YOU AGAIN UNTIL YOU'VE RECAPTURED THE PRESERVER!
I WON'T HELP YOU KILL PETALWING!!

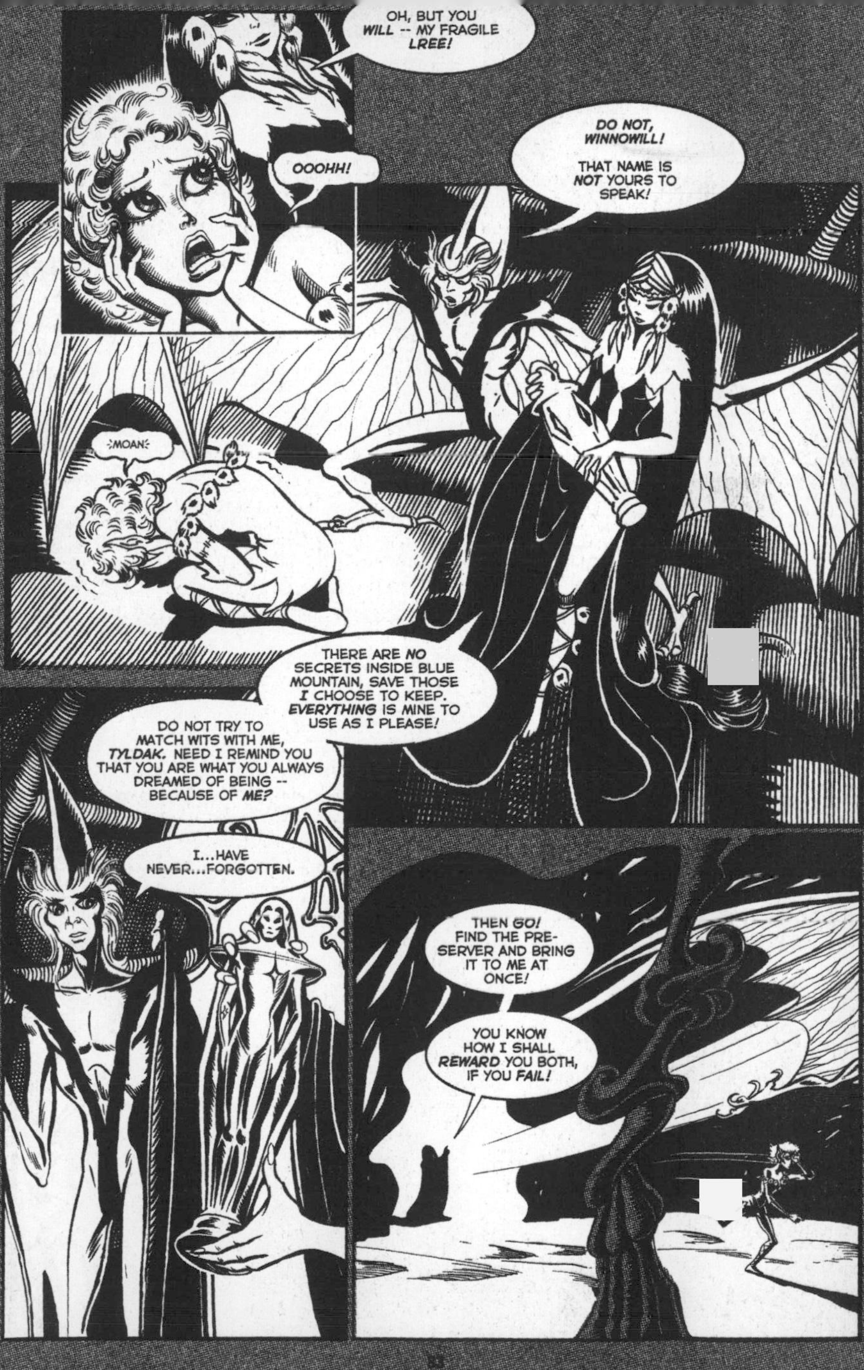

OH, BUT YOU WILL -- MY FRAGILE LREE!
OOOHH!
DO NOT, WINNOWILL!
THAT NAME IS NOT YOURS TO SPEAK!
MOAN
THERE ARE NO SECRETS INSIDE BLUE MOUNTAIN, SAVE THOSE I CHOOSE TO KEEP. EVERYTHING IS MINE TO USE AS I PLEASE!
DO NOT TRY TO MATCH WITS WITH ME, TYLDAK. NEED I REMIND YOU THAT YOU ARE WHAT YOU ALWAYS DREAMED OF BEING -- BECAUSE OF ME?
I...HAVE NEVER...FORGOTTEN.
THEN GO! FIND THE PRE-SERVER AND BRING IT TO ME AT ONCE!
YOU KNOW HOW I SHALL REWARD YOU BOTH, IF YOU FAIL!

MEANWHILE...

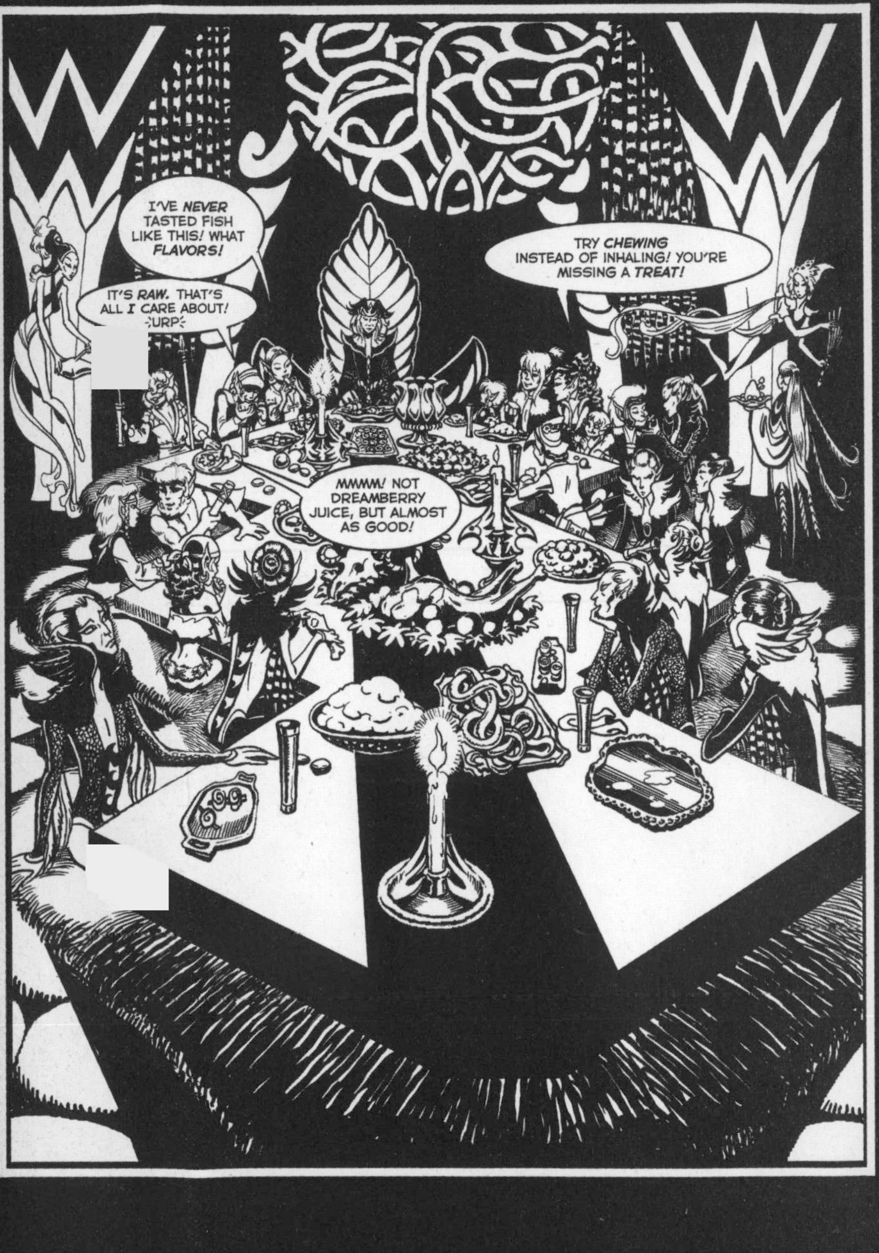

I'VE NEVER TASTED FISH LIKE THIS! WHAT FLAVORS!
IT'S RAW. THAT'S ALL I CARE ABOUT! URP
TRY CHEWING INSTEAD OF INHALING! YOU'RE MISSING A TREAT!
MMMM! NOT DREAMBERRY JUICE, BUT ALMOST AS GOOD!

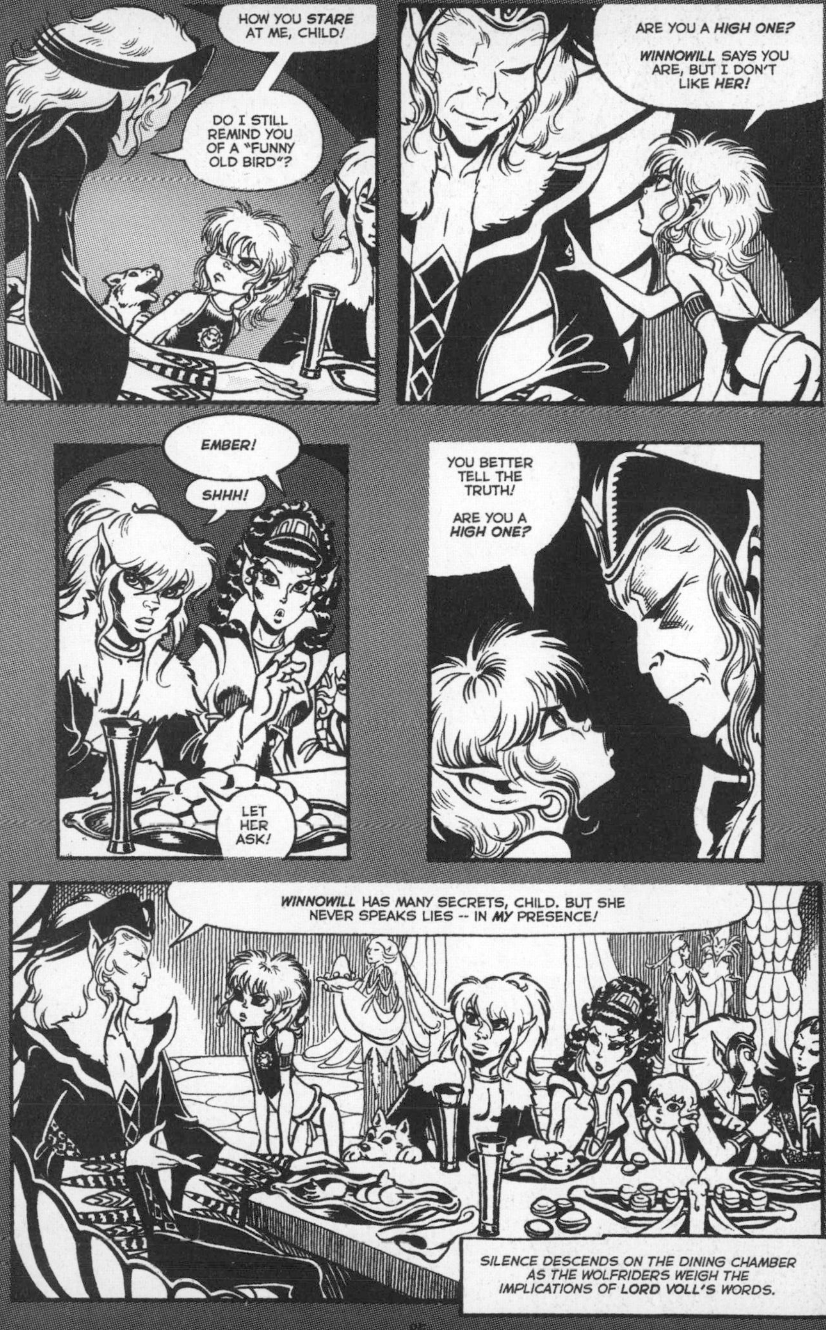

HOW YOU STARE AT ME, CHILD!
DO I STILL REMIND YOU OF A "FUNNY OLD BIRD"?
ARE YOU A HIGH ONE?
WINNOWILL SAYS YOU ARE, BUT I DON'T LIKE HER!
EMBER!
SHHH!
LET HER ASK!
YOU BETTER TELL THE TRUTH!
ARE YOU A HIGH ONE?
WINNOWILL HAS MANY SECRETS, CHILD. BUT SHE NEVER SPEAKS LIES -- IN MY PRESENCE!
SILENCE DESCENDS ON THE DINING CHAMBER AS THE WOLFRIDERS WEIGH THE IMPLICATIONS OF LORD VOLL'S WORDS.

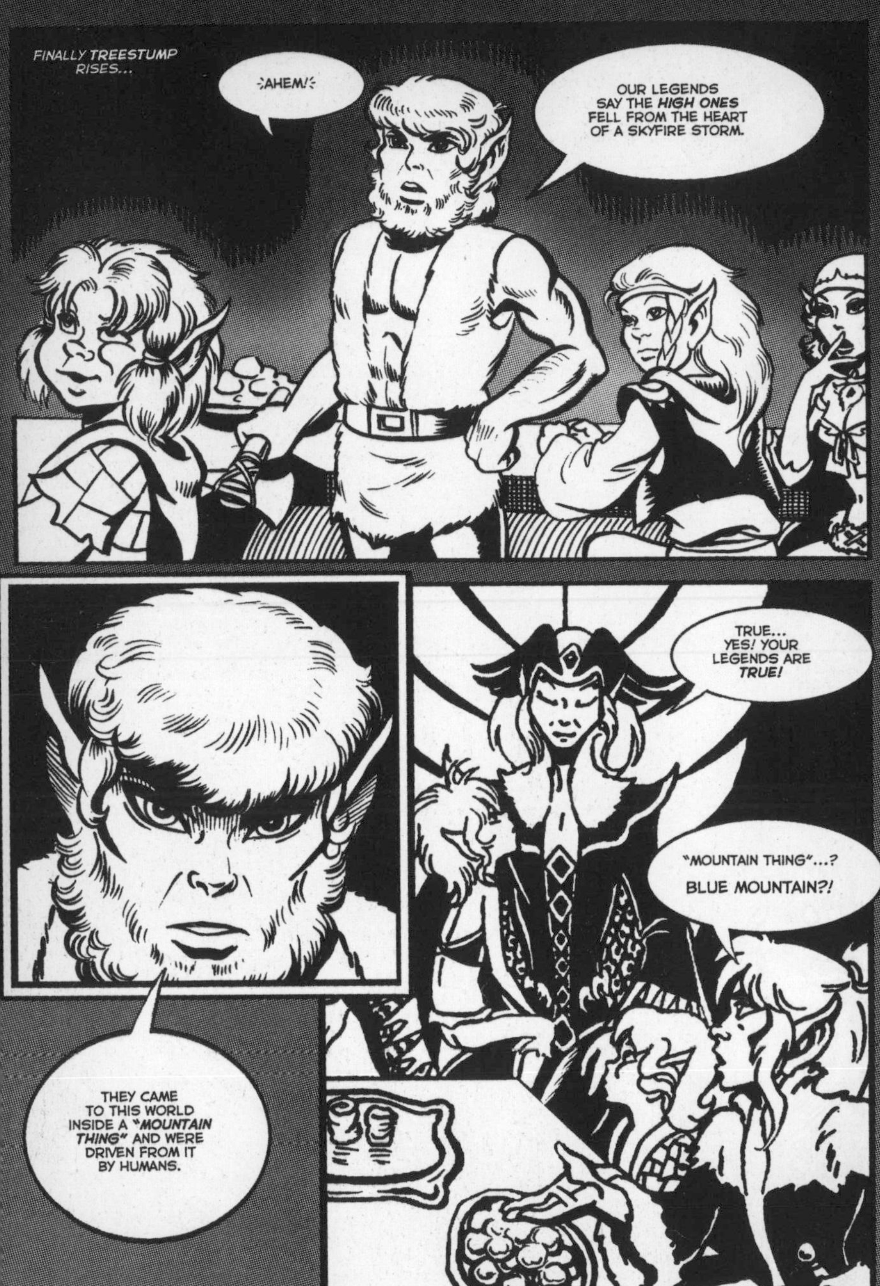
FINALLY TREESTUMP RISES...
AHEM!
OUR LEGENDS SAY THE HIGH ONES FELL FROM THE HEART OF A SKYFIRE STORM.
THEY CAME TO THIS WORLD INSIDE A "MOUNTAIN THING" AND WERE DRIVEN FROM IT BY HUMANS.
TRUE... YES! YOUR LEGENDS ARE TRUE!
"MOUNTAIN THING"...?
BLUE MOUNTAIN?!

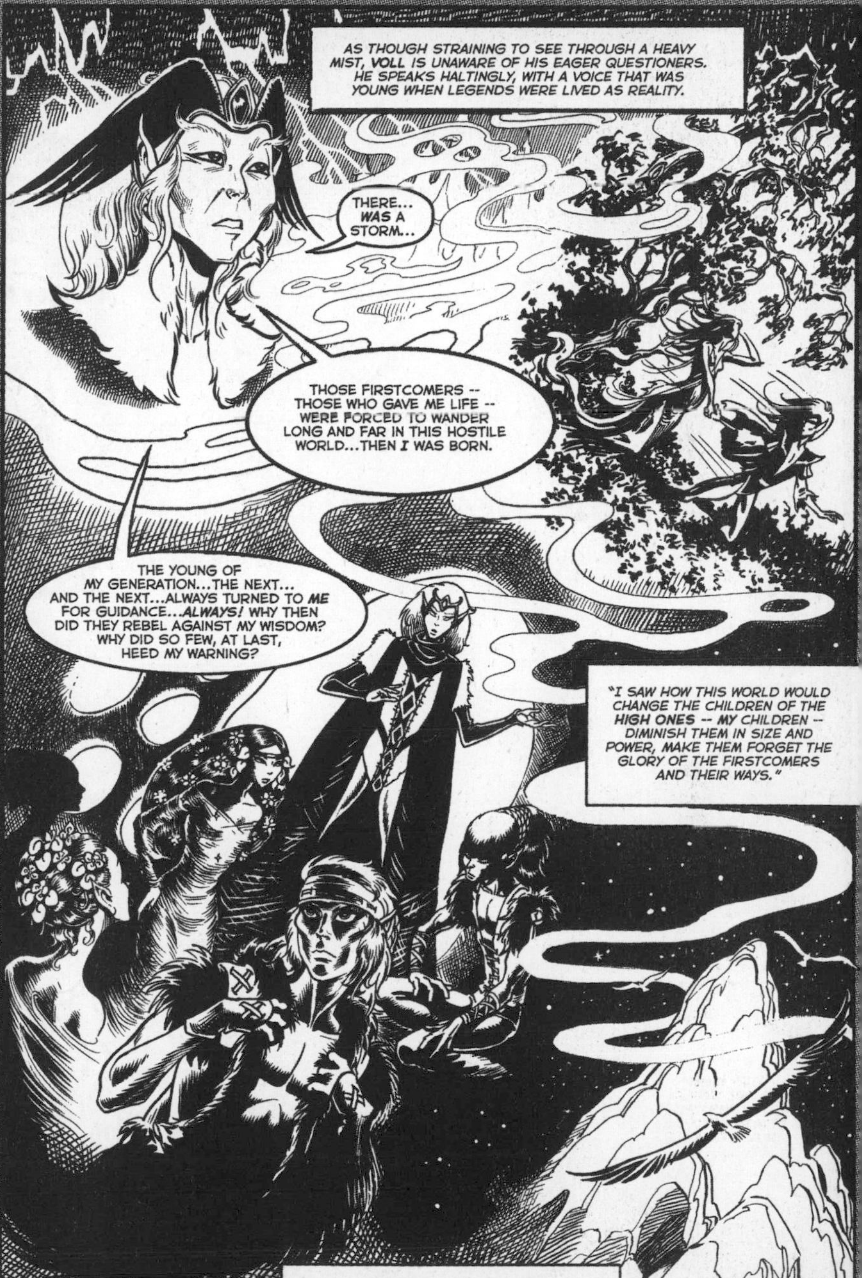
AS THOUGH STRAINING TO SEE THROUGH A HEAVY MIST, VOLL IS UNAWARE OF HIS EAGER QUESTIONERS. HE SPEAKS HALTINGLY, WITH A VOICE THAT WAS YOUNG WHEN LEGENDS WERE LIVED AS REALITY.
THERE... WAS A STORM...
THOSE FIRSTCOMERS -- THOSE WHO GAVE ME LIFE -- WERE FORCED TO WANDER LONG AND FAR IN THIS HOSTILE WORLD...THEN I WAS BORN.
THE YOUNG OF MY GENERATION...THE NEXT... AND THE NEXT...ALWAYS TURNED TO ME FOR GUIDANCE...ALWAYS! WHY THEN DID THEY REBEL AGAINST MY WISDOM? WHY DID SO FEW, AT LAST, HEED MY WARNING?
"I SAW HOW THIS WORLD WOULD CHANGE THE CHILDREN OF THE HIGH ONES -- MY CHILDREN -- DIMINISH THEM IN SIZE AND POWER, MAKE THEM FORGET THE GLORY OF THE FIRSTCOMERS AND THEIR WAYS."
"BLUE MOUNTAIN IS A HAVEN FOR THOSE WHO REFUSED TO BE CHANGED."

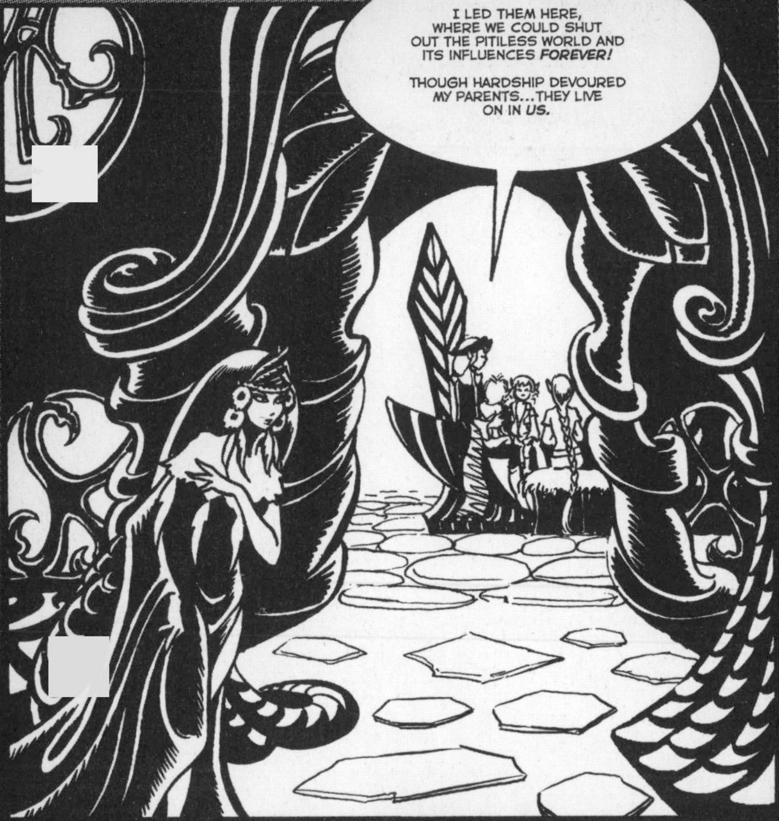
I LED THEM HERE, WHERE WE COULD SHUT OUT THE PITILESS WORLD AND ITS INFLUENCES *FOREVER!*
THOUGH HARDSHIP DEVOURED MY PARENTS...THEY LIVE ON IN *US.*

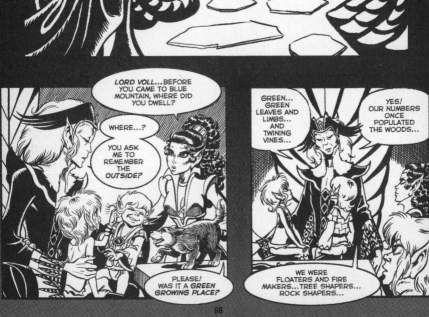

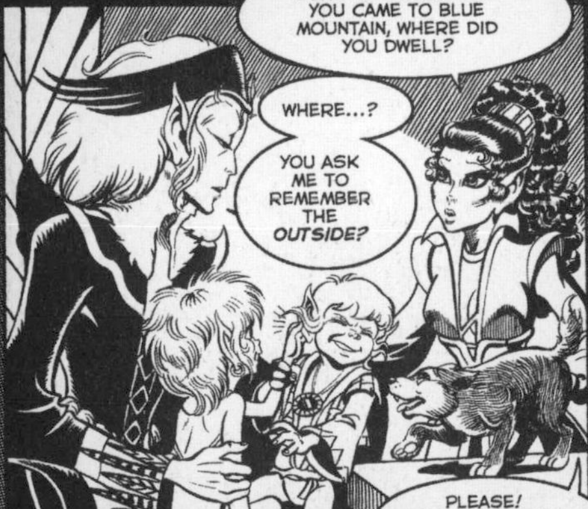
*LORD VOLL...*BEFORE YOU CAME TO BLUE MOUNTAIN, WHERE DID YOU DWELL?
WHERE...?
YOU ASK ME TO REMEMBER THE *OUTSIDE?*
PLEASE! WAS IT A *GREEN GROWING PLACE?*

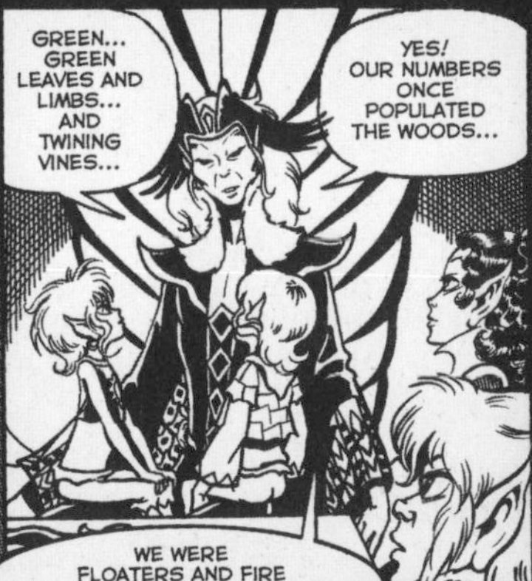
GREEN... GREEN LEAVES AND LIMBS... AND TWINING VINES...
YES! OUR NUMBERS ONCE POPULATED THE WOODS...
WE WERE FLOATERS AND FIRE MAKERS...TREE SHAPERS... ROCK SHAPERS...

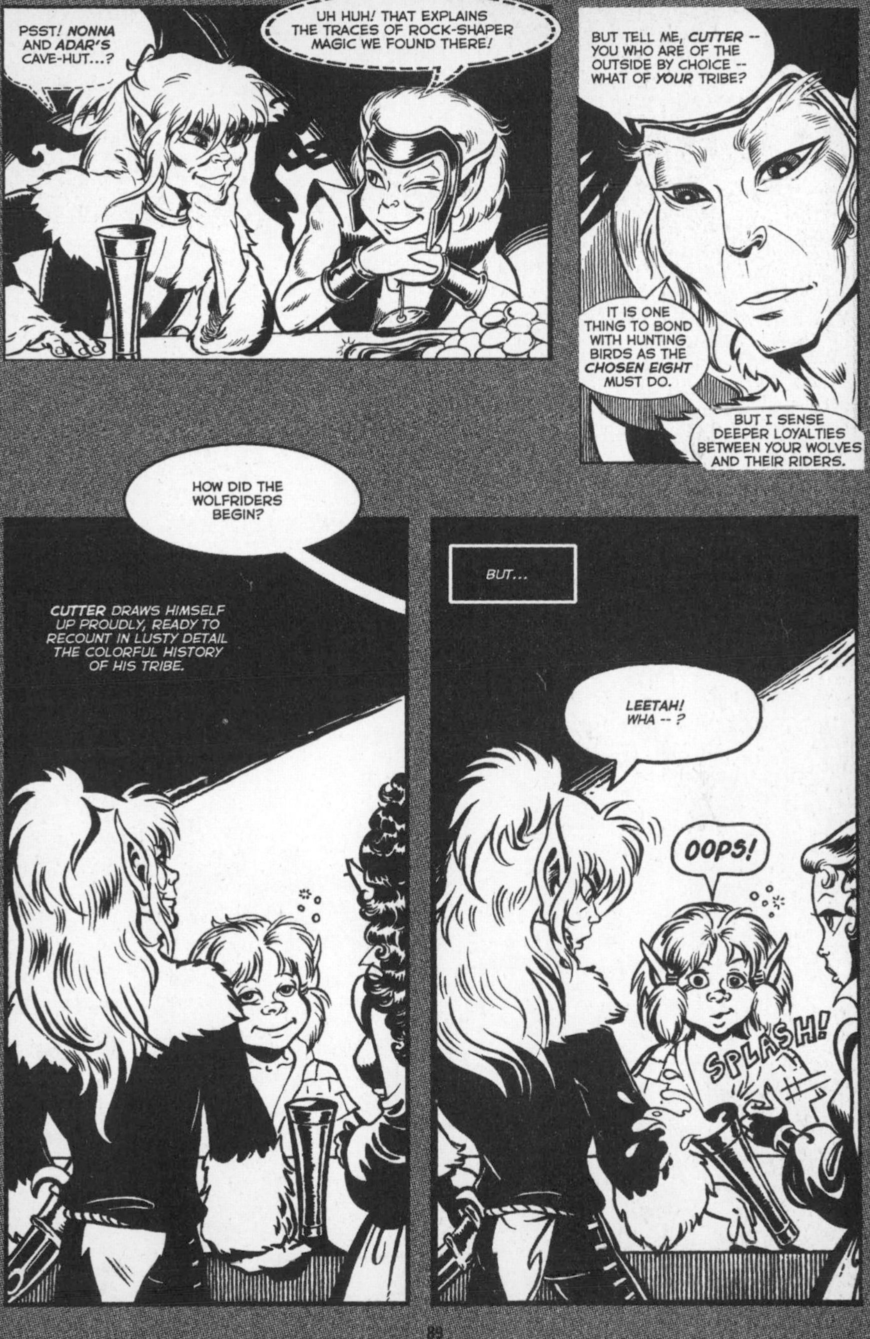
PSST! NONNA AND ADAR'S CAVE-HUT...?
UH HUH! THAT EXPLAINS THE TRACES OF ROCK-SHAPER MAGIC WE FOUND THERE!
BUT TELL ME, CUTTER -- YOU WHO ARE OF THE OUTSIDE BY CHOICE -- WHAT OF YOUR TRIBE?
IT IS ONE THING TO BOND WITH HUNTING BIRDS AS THE CHOSEN EIGHT MUST DO.
BUT I SENSE DEEPER LOYALTIES BETWEEN YOUR WOLVES AND THEIR RIDERS.
HOW DID THE WOLFRIDERS BEGIN?
CUTTER DRAWS HIMSELF UP PROUDLY, READY TO RECOUNT IN LUSTY DETAIL THE COLORFUL HISTORY OF HIS TRIBE.
BUT...
LEETAH! WHA -- ?
OOPS!
SPLASH!

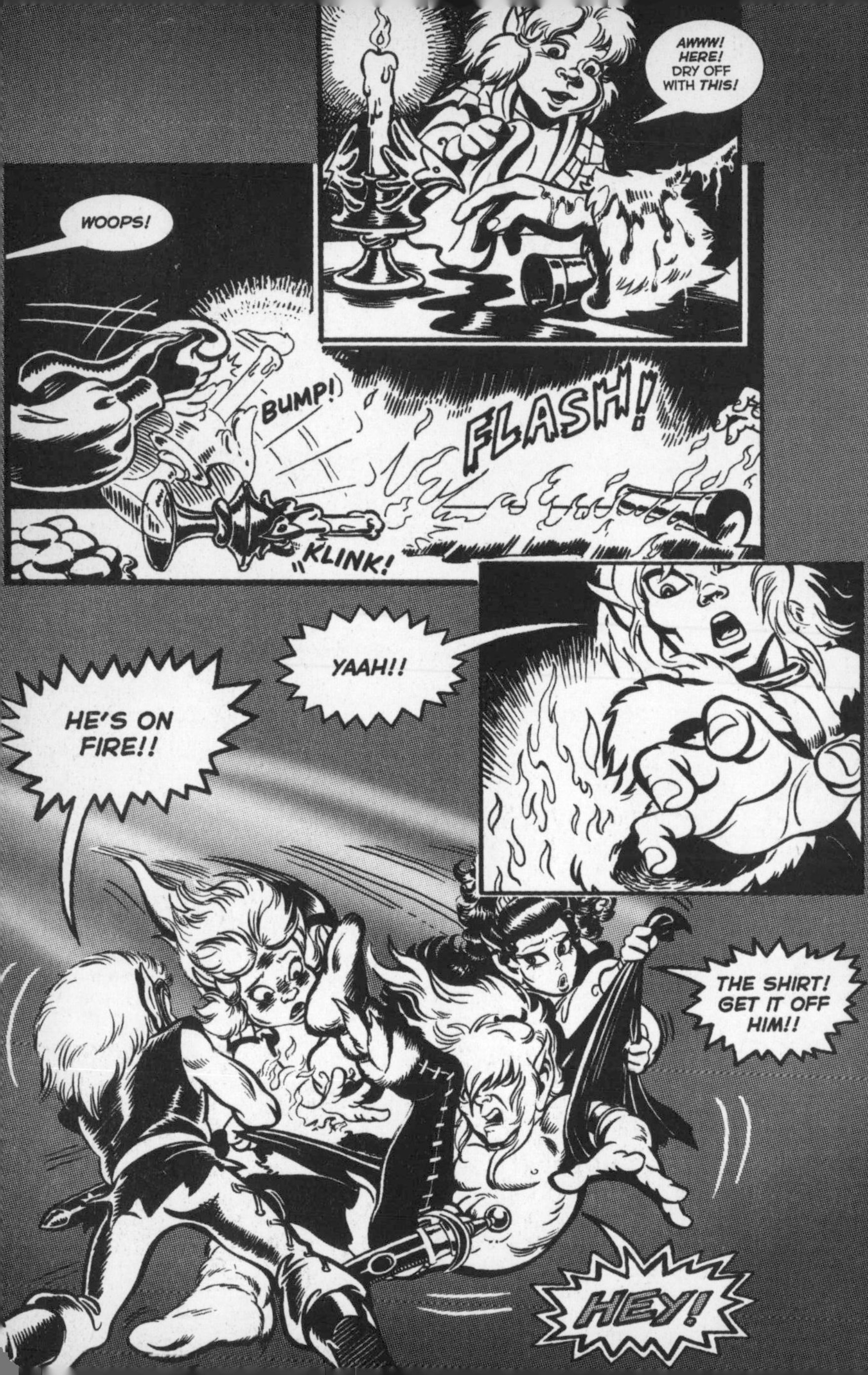
AWWW! HERE! DRY OFF WITH THIS!
WOOPS!
BUMP!
FLASH!
KLINK!
YAAH!!
HE'S ON FIRE!!
THE SHIRT! GET IT OFF HIM!!
HEY!

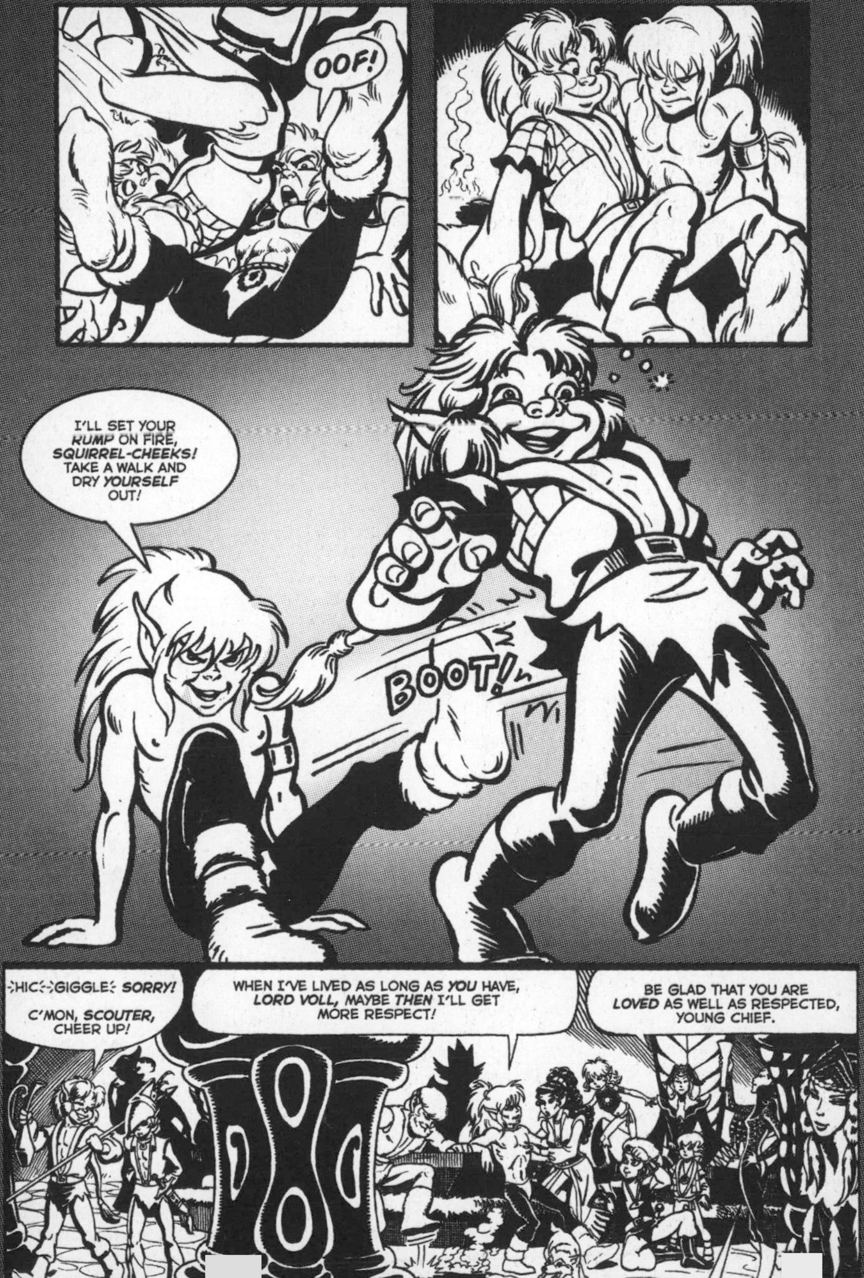
OOF!
I'LL SET YOUR *RUMP* ON FIRE, *SQUIRREL-CHEEKS!* TAKE A WALK AND DRY *YOURSELF* OUT!
BOOT!
HIC GIGGLE *SORRY!*
C'MON, *SCOUTER*, CHEER UP!
WHEN I'VE LIVED AS LONG AS *YOU* HAVE, *LORD VOLL*, MAYBE *THEN* I'LL GET MORE RESPECT!
BE GLAD THAT YOU ARE *LOVED* AS WELL AS RESPECTED, YOUNG CHIEF.
AS ARE *YOU, VOLL, LORD OF THE GLIDERS!*

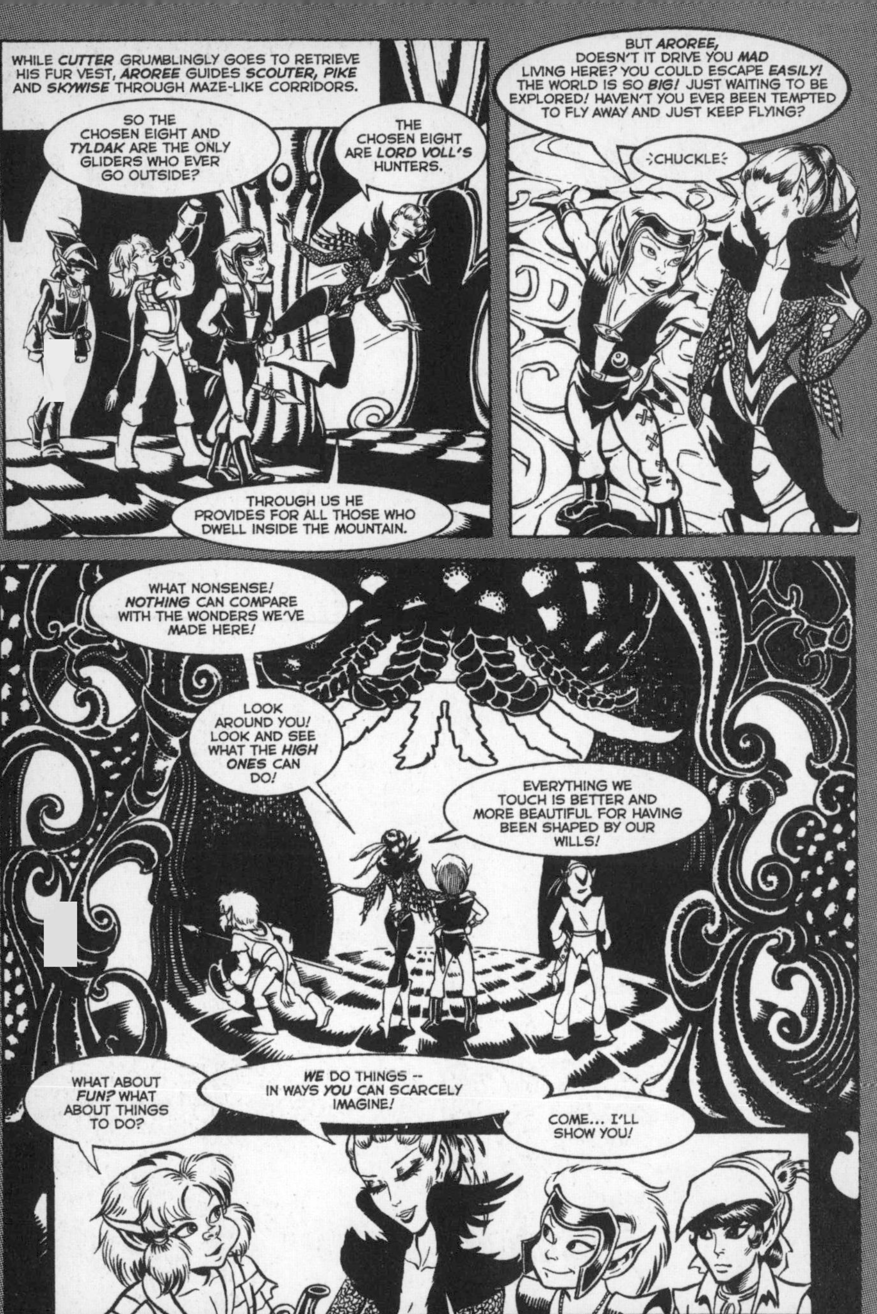

WHILE CUTTER GRUMBLINGLY GOES TO RETRIEVE HIS FUR VEST, AROREE GUIDES SCOUTER, PIKE AND SKYWISE THROUGH MAZE-LIKE CORRIDORS.
SO THE CHOSEN EIGHT AND TYLDAK ARE THE ONLY GLIDERS WHO EVER GO OUTSIDE?
THE CHOSEN EIGHT ARE LORD VOLL'S HUNTERS.
THROUGH US HE PROVIDES FOR ALL THOSE WHO DWELL INSIDE THE MOUNTAIN.
BUT AROREE, DOESN'T IT DRIVE YOU MAD LIVING HERE? YOU COULD ESCAPE EASILY! THE WORLD IS SO BIG! JUST WAITING TO BE EXPLORED! HAVEN'T YOU EVER BEEN TEMPTED TO FLY AWAY AND JUST KEEP FLYING?
CHUCKLE
WHAT NONSENSE! NOTHING CAN COMPARE WITH THE WONDERS WE'VE MADE HERE!
LOOK AROUND YOU! LOOK AND SEE WHAT THE HIGH ONES CAN DO!
EVERYTHING WE TOUCH IS BETTER AND MORE BEAUTIFUL FOR HAVING BEEN SHAPED BY OUR WILLS!
WHAT ABOUT FUN? WHAT ABOUT THINGS TO DO?
WE DO THINGS -- IN WAYS YOU CAN SCARCELY IMAGINE!
COME... I'LL SHOW YOU!

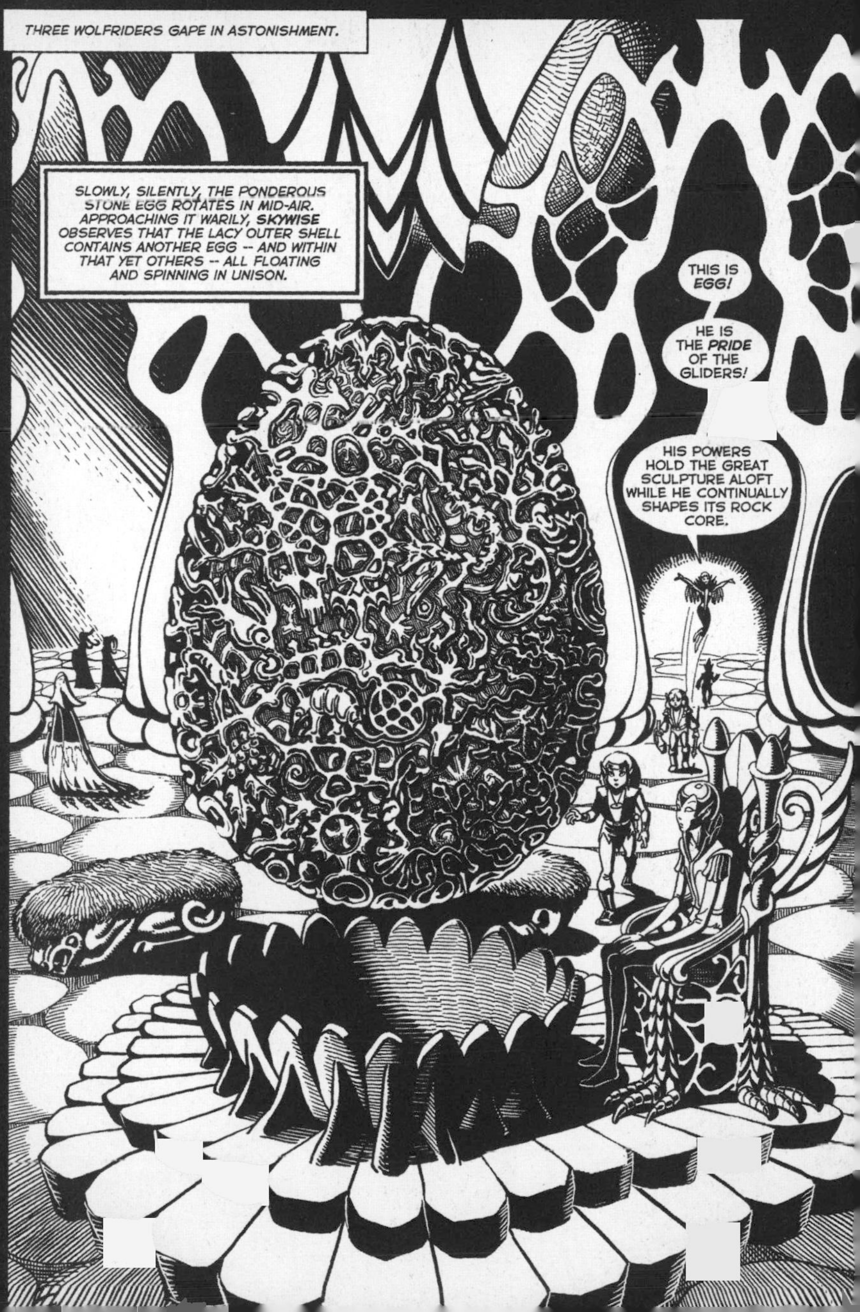
THREE WOLFRIDERS GAPE IN ASTONISHMENT.
SLOWLY, SILENTLY, THE PONDEROUS STONE EGG ROTATES IN MID-AIR. APPROACHING IT WARILY, SKYWISE OBSERVES THAT THE LACY OUTER SHELL CONTAINS ANOTHER EGG -- AND WITHIN THAT YET OTHERS -- ALL FLOATING AND SPINNING IN UNISON.
THIS IS EGG!
HE IS THE PRIDE OF THE GLIDERS!
HIS POWERS HOLD THE GREAT SCULPTURE ALOFT WHILE HE CONTINUALLY SHAPES ITS ROCK CORE.

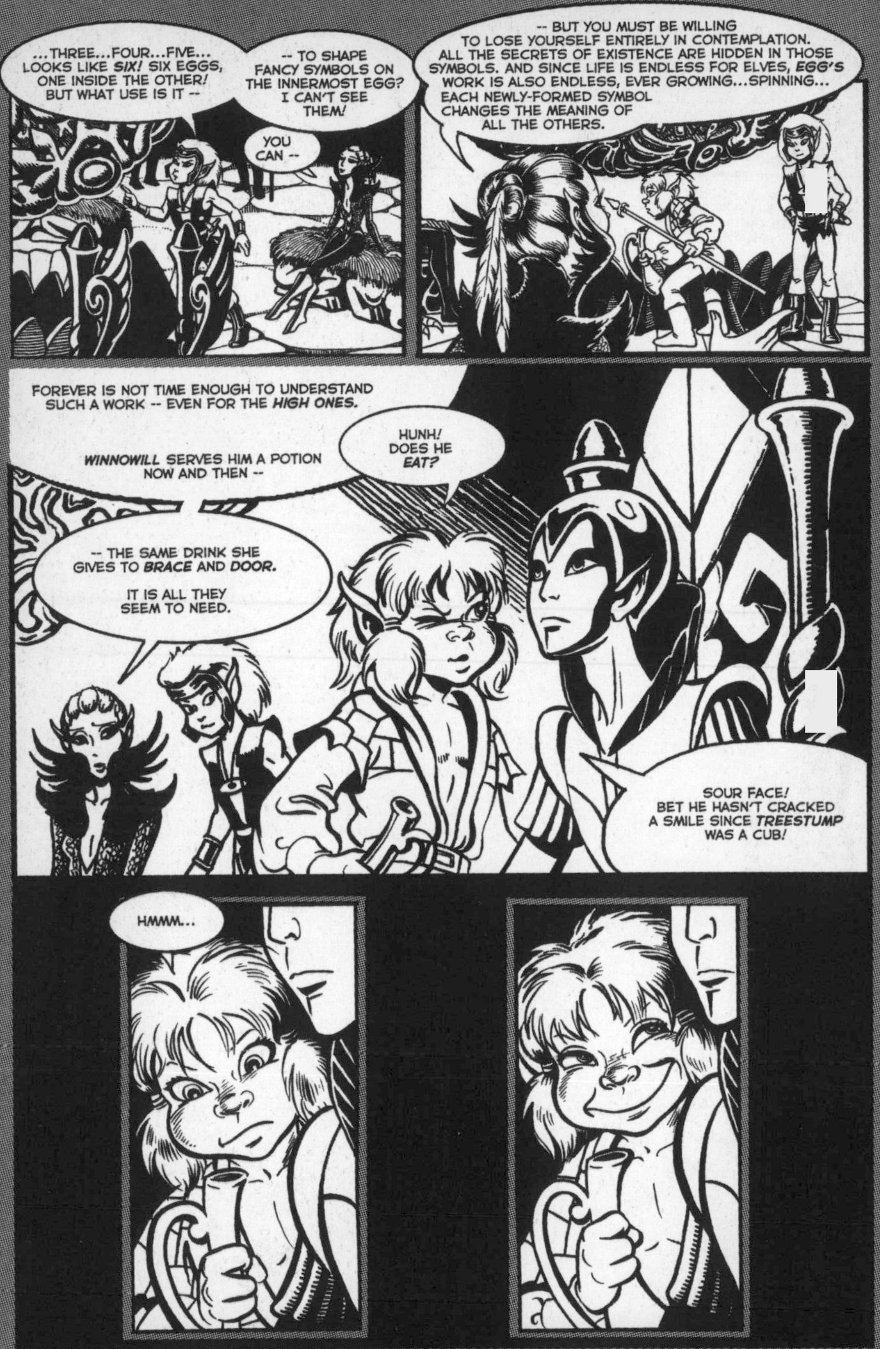
...THREE...FOUR...FIVE... LOOKS LIKE SIX! SIX EGGS, ONE INSIDE THE OTHER! BUT WHAT USE IS IT --
-- TO SHAPE FANCY SYMBOLS ON THE INNERMOST EGG? I CAN'T SEE THEM!
YOU CAN --
-- BUT YOU MUST BE WILLING TO LOSE YOURSELF ENTIRELY IN CONTEMPLATION. ALL THE SECRETS OF EXISTENCE ARE HIDDEN IN THOSE SYMBOLS. AND SINCE LIFE IS ENDLESS FOR ELVES, EGG'S WORK IS ALSO ENDLESS, EVER GROWING...SPINNING... EACH NEWLY-FORMED SYMBOL CHANGES THE MEANING OF ALL THE OTHERS.
FOREVER IS NOT TIME ENOUGH TO UNDERSTAND SUCH A WORK -- EVEN FOR THE HIGH ONES.
WINNOWILL SERVES HIM A POTION NOW AND THEN --
HUNH! DOES HE EAT?
-- THE SAME DRINK SHE GIVES TO BRACE AND DOOR.
IT IS ALL THEY SEEM TO NEED.
SOUR FACE! BET HE HASN'T CRACKED A SMILE SINCE TREESTUMP WAS A CUB!
HMMM...

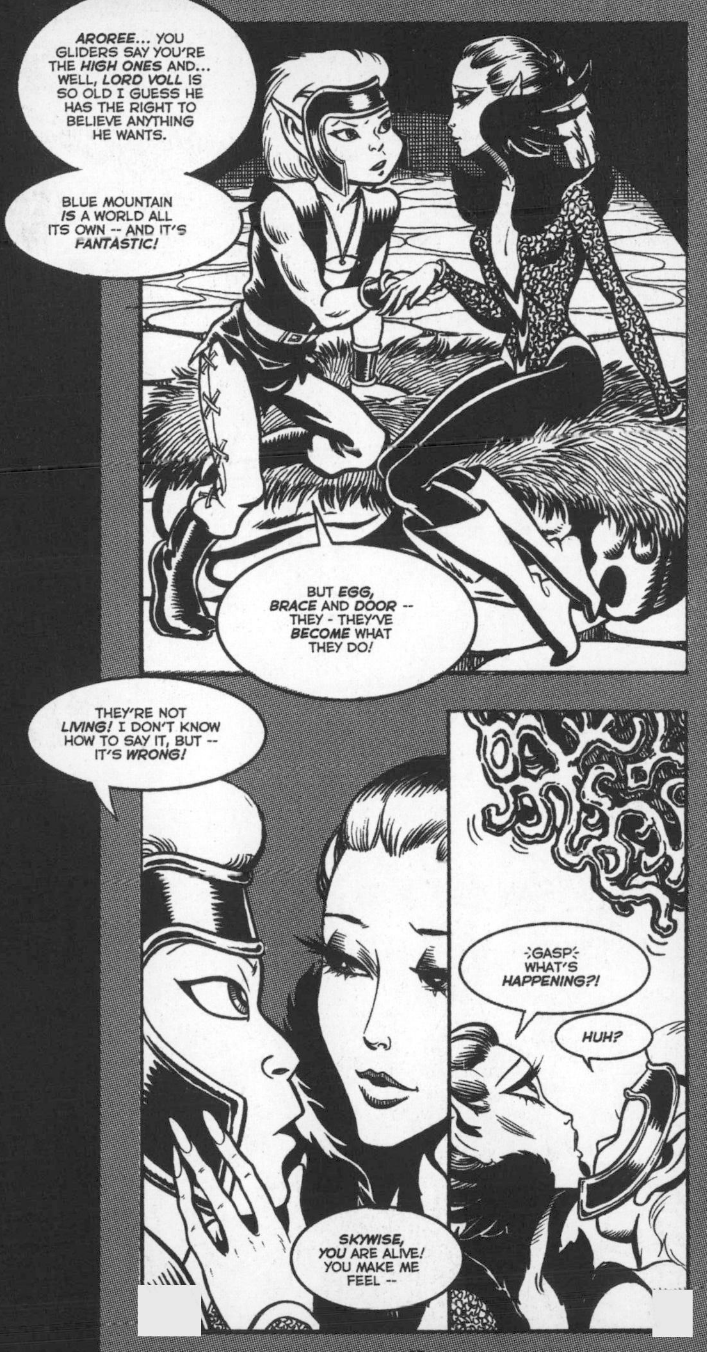
AROREE... YOU GLIDERS SAY YOU'RE THE HIGH ONES AND... WELL, LORD VOLL IS SO OLD I GUESS HE HAS THE RIGHT TO BELIEVE ANYTHING HE WANTS.
BLUE MOUNTAIN IS A WORLD ALL ITS OWN -- AND IT'S FANTASTIC!
BUT EGG, BRACE AND DOOR -- THEY - THEY'VE BECOME WHAT THEY DO!
THEY'RE NOT LIVING! I DON'T KNOW HOW TO SAY IT, BUT -- IT'S WRONG!
SKYWISE, YOU ARE ALIVE! YOU MAKE ME FEEL --
GASP WHAT'S HAPPENING?!
HUH?

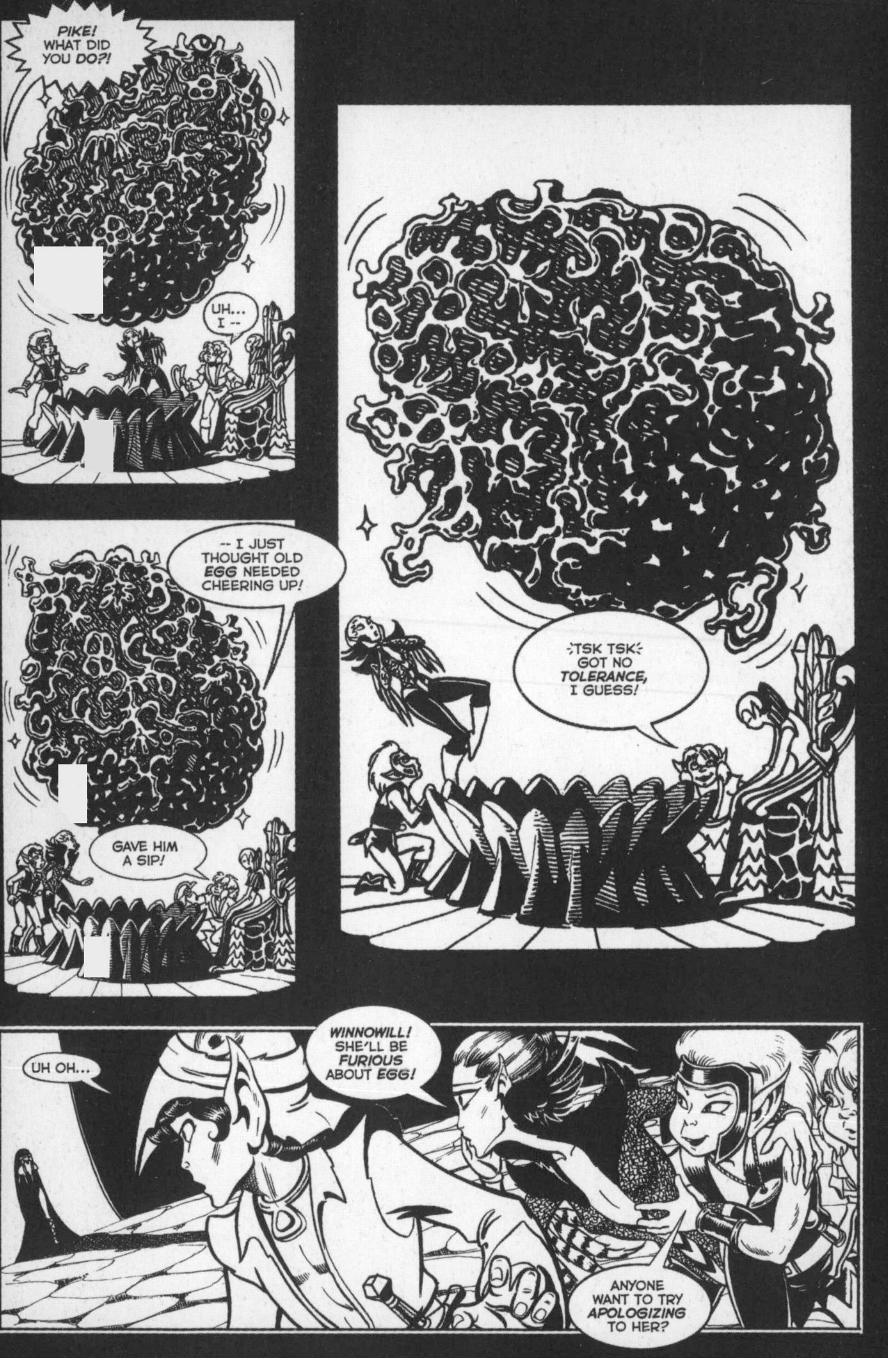
PIKE! WHAT DID YOU DO?!
UH... I --
-- I JUST THOUGHT OLD EGG NEEDED CHEERING UP!
GAVE HIM A SIP!
TSK TSK GOT NO TOLERANCE, I GUESS!
UH OH...
WINNOWILL! SHE'LL BE FURIOUS ABOUT EGG!
ANYONE WANT TO TRY APOLOGIZING TO HER?

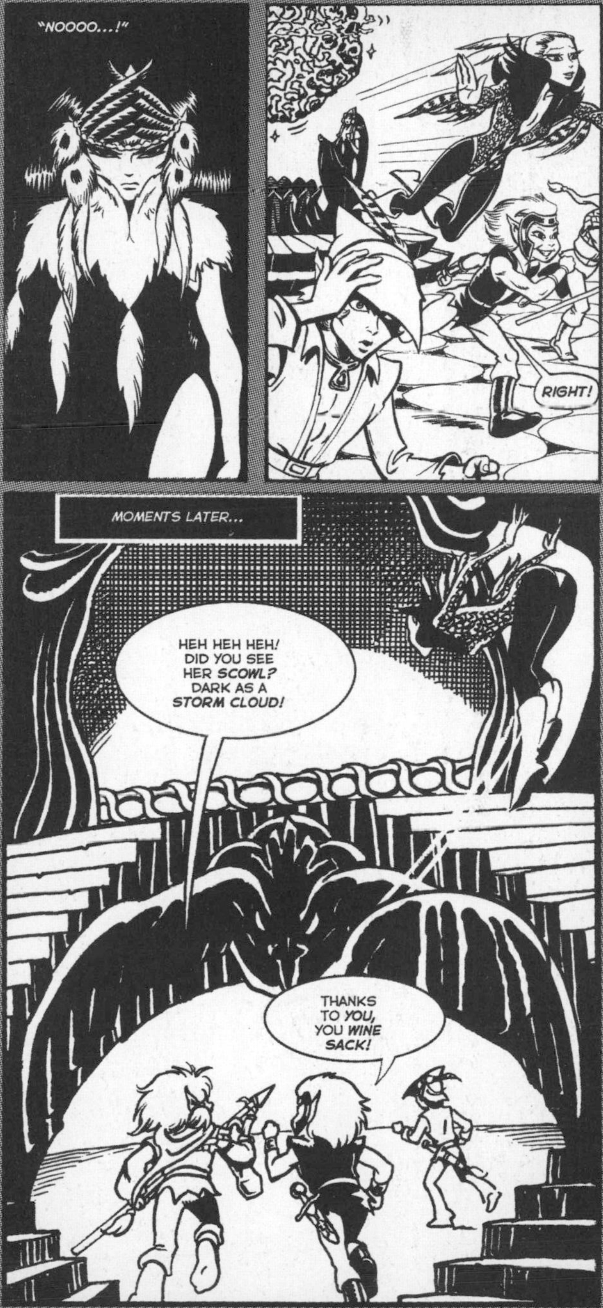
"NOOOO...!"
RIGHT!
MOMENTS LATER...
HEH HEH HEH! DID YOU SEE HER SCOWL? DARK AS A STORM CLOUD!
THANKS TO YOU, YOU WINE SACK!

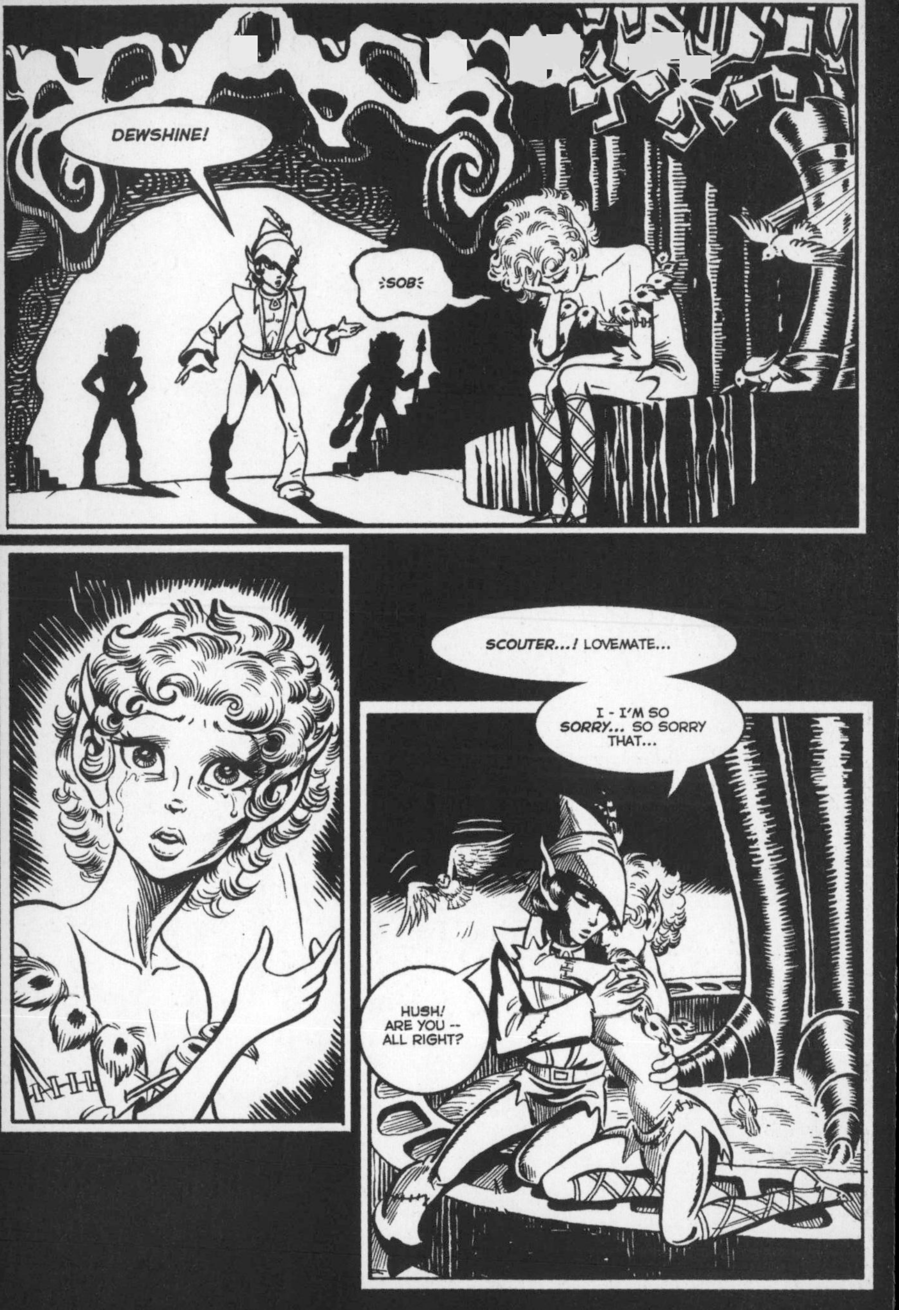
DEWSHINE!
SOB
SCOUTER...! LOVEMATE...
I - I'M SO SORRY... SO SORRY THAT...
HUSH! ARE YOU -- ALL RIGHT?

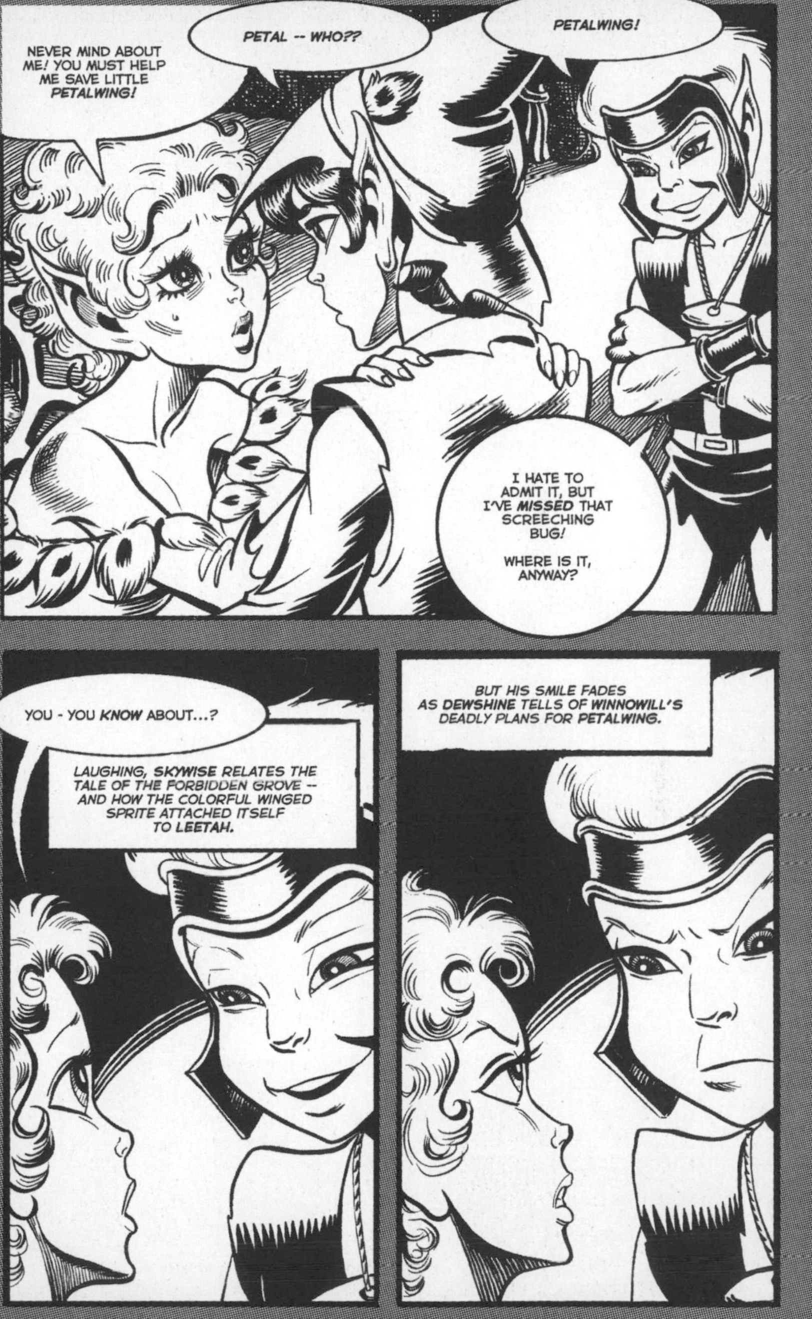
NEVER MIND ABOUT ME! YOU MUST HELP ME SAVE LITTLE PETALWING!
PETAL -- WHO??
PETALWING!
I HATE TO ADMIT IT, BUT I'VE MISSED THAT SCREECHING BUG!
WHERE IS IT, ANYWAY?
YOU - YOU KNOW ABOUT...?
LAUGHING, SKYWISE RELATES THE TALE OF THE FORBIDDEN GROVE -- AND HOW THE COLORFUL WINGED SPRITE ATTACHED ITSELF TO LEETAH.
BUT HIS SMILE FADES AS DEWSHINE TELLS OF WINNOWILL'S DEADLY PLANS FOR PETALWING.

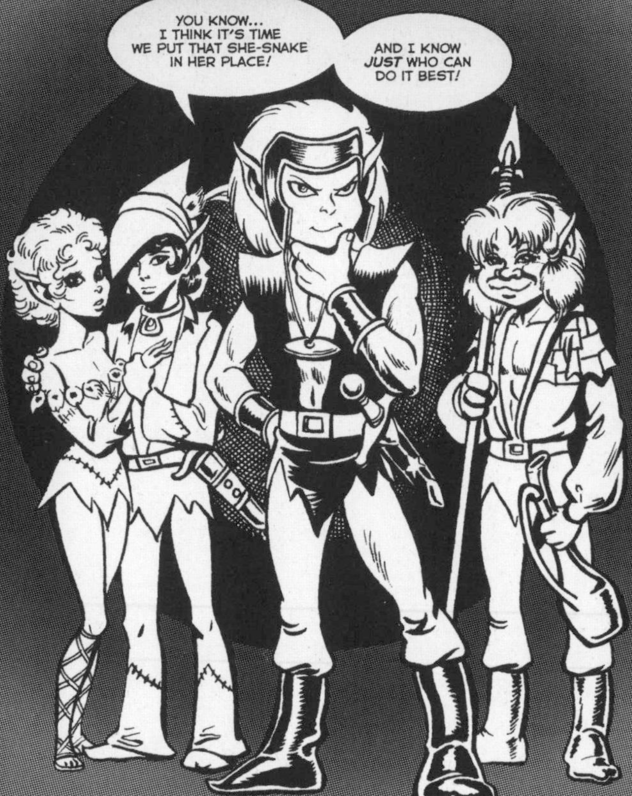
YOU KNOW... I THINK IT'S TIME WE PUT THAT SHE-SNAKE IN HER PLACE!
AND I KNOW *JUST* WHO CAN DO IT BEST!

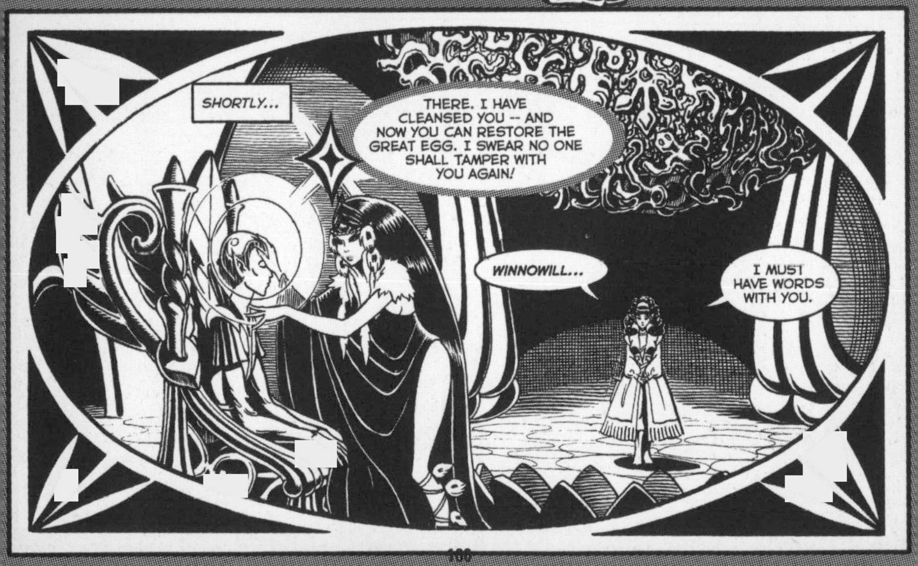
SHORTLY...
THERE. I HAVE CLEANSED YOU -- AND NOW YOU CAN RESTORE THE GREAT EGG. I SWEAR NO ONE SHALL TAMPER WITH YOU AGAIN!
WINNOWILL...
I MUST HAVE WORDS WITH YOU.

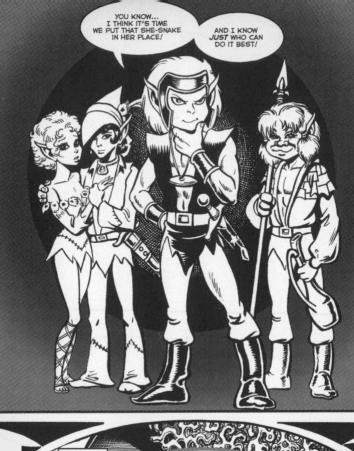

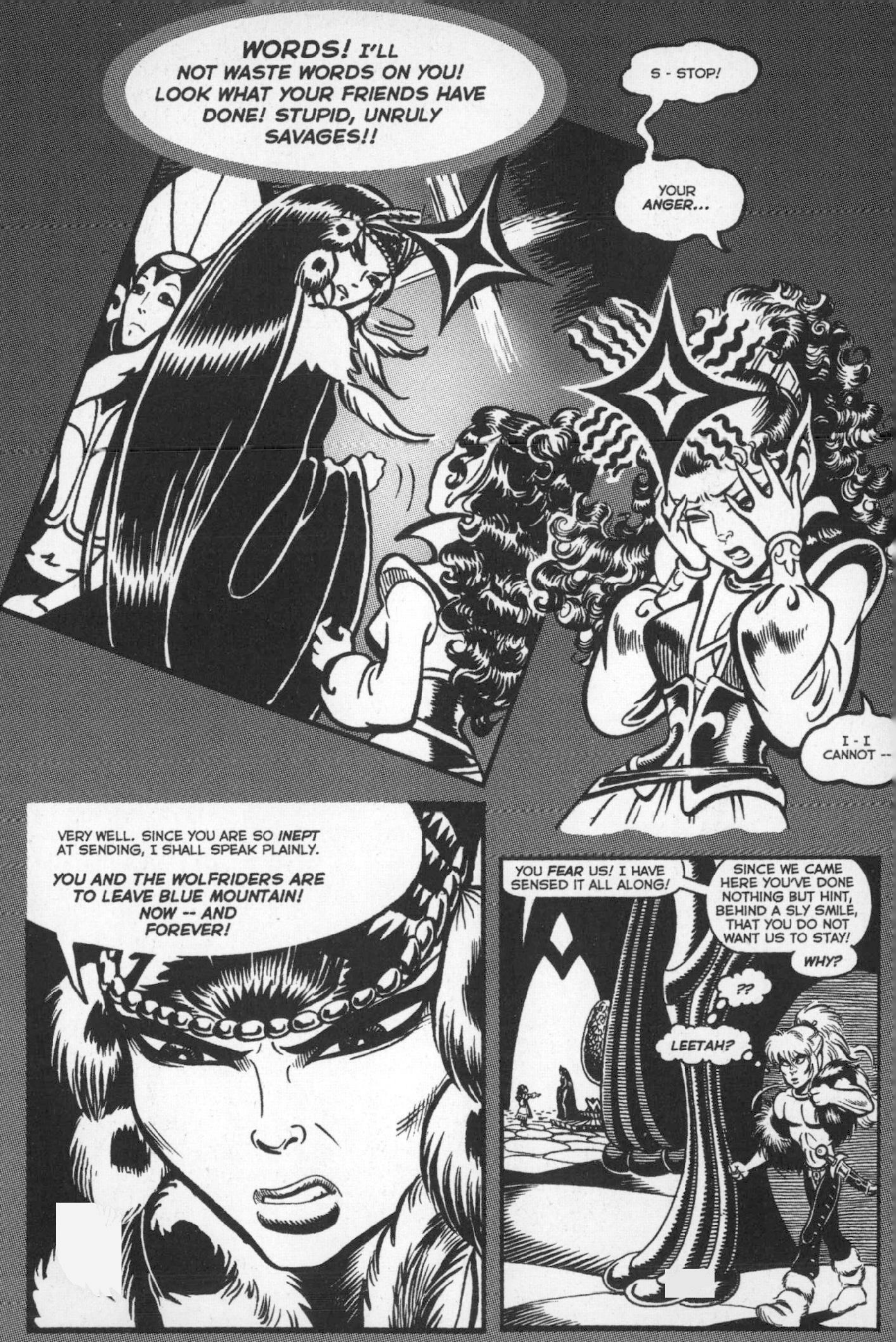
WORDS! I'LL NOT WASTE WORDS ON YOU! LOOK WHAT YOUR FRIENDS HAVE DONE! STUPID, UNRULY SAVAGES!!
S - STOP!
YOUR ANGER...
I - I CANNOT --
VERY WELL. SINCE YOU ARE SO INEPT AT SENDING, I SHALL SPEAK PLAINLY.
YOU AND THE WOLFRIDERS ARE TO LEAVE BLUE MOUNTAIN! NOW -- AND FOREVER!
YOU FEAR US! I HAVE SENSED IT ALL ALONG!
SINCE WE CAME HERE YOU'VE DONE NOTHING BUT HINT, BEHIND A SLY SMILE, THAT YOU DO NOT WANT US TO STAY!
WHY?
??
LEETAH?

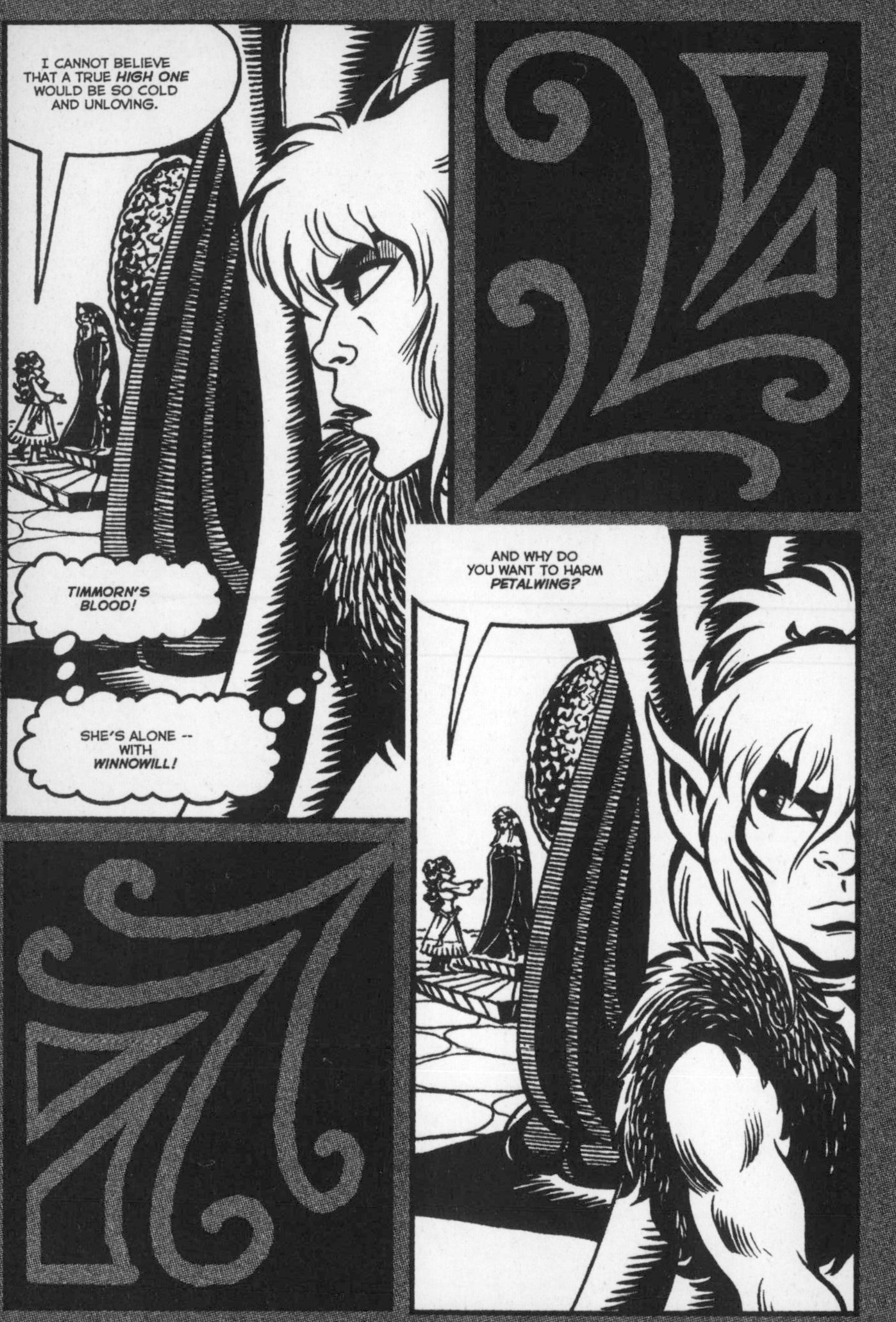
I CANNOT BELIEVE THAT A TRUE *HIGH ONE* WOULD BE SO COLD AND UNLOVING.
TIMMORN'S BLOOD!
SHE'S ALONE -- WITH *WINNOWILL!*
AND WHY DO YOU WANT TO HARM *PETALWING?*

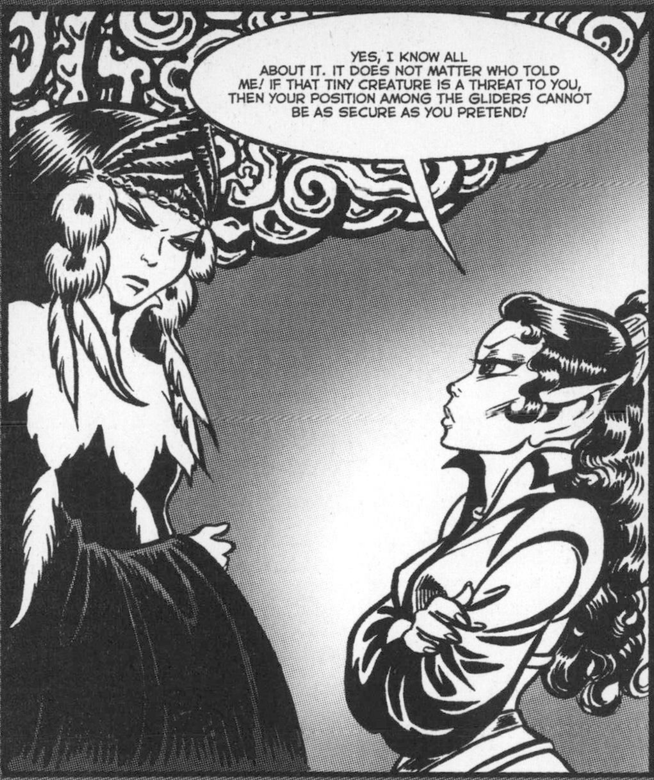
YES, I KNOW ALL ABOUT IT. IT DOES NOT MATTER WHO TOLD ME! IF THAT TINY CREATURE IS A THREAT TO YOU, THEN YOUR POSITION AMONG THE GLIDERS CANNOT BE AS SECURE AS YOU PRETEND!

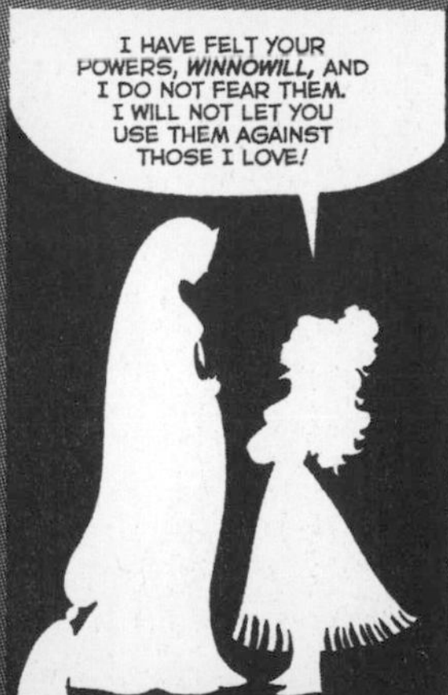
I HAVE FELT YOUR POWERS, WINNOWILL, AND I DO NOT FEAR THEM. I WILL NOT LET YOU USE THEM AGAINST THOSE I LOVE!

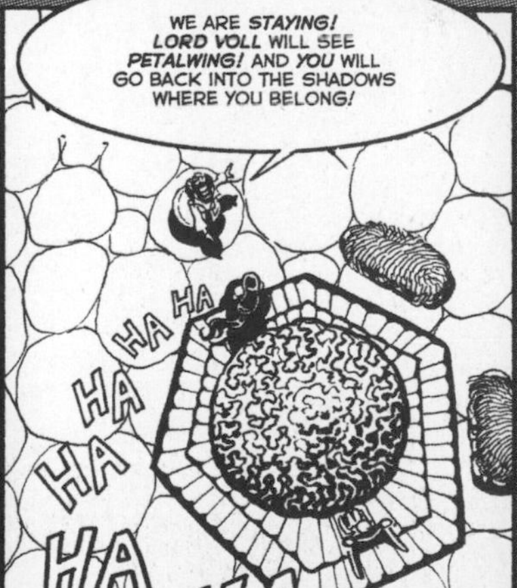
WE ARE STAYING! LORD VOLL WILL SEE PETALWING! AND YOU WILL GO BACK INTO THE SHADOWS WHERE YOU BELONG!
HA HA HA HA HA HA HA

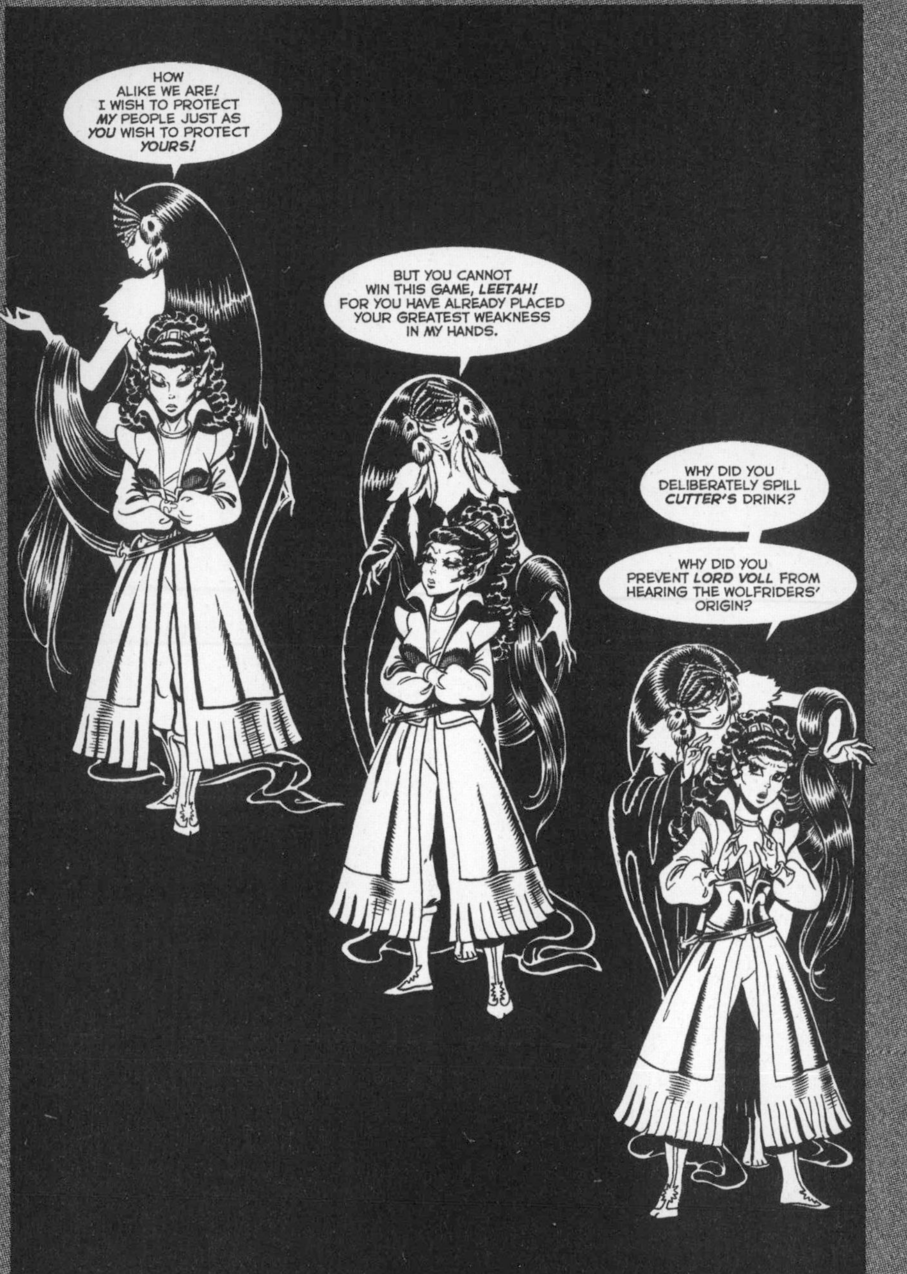
HOW ALIKE WE ARE! I WISH TO PROTECT MY PEOPLE JUST AS YOU WISH TO PROTECT YOURS!
BUT YOU CANNOT WIN THIS GAME, LEETAH! FOR YOU HAVE ALREADY PLACED YOUR GREATEST WEAKNESS IN MY HANDS.
WHY DID YOU DELIBERATELY SPILL CUTTER'S DRINK?
WHY DID YOU PREVENT LORD VOLL FROM HEARING THE WOLFRIDERS' ORIGIN?

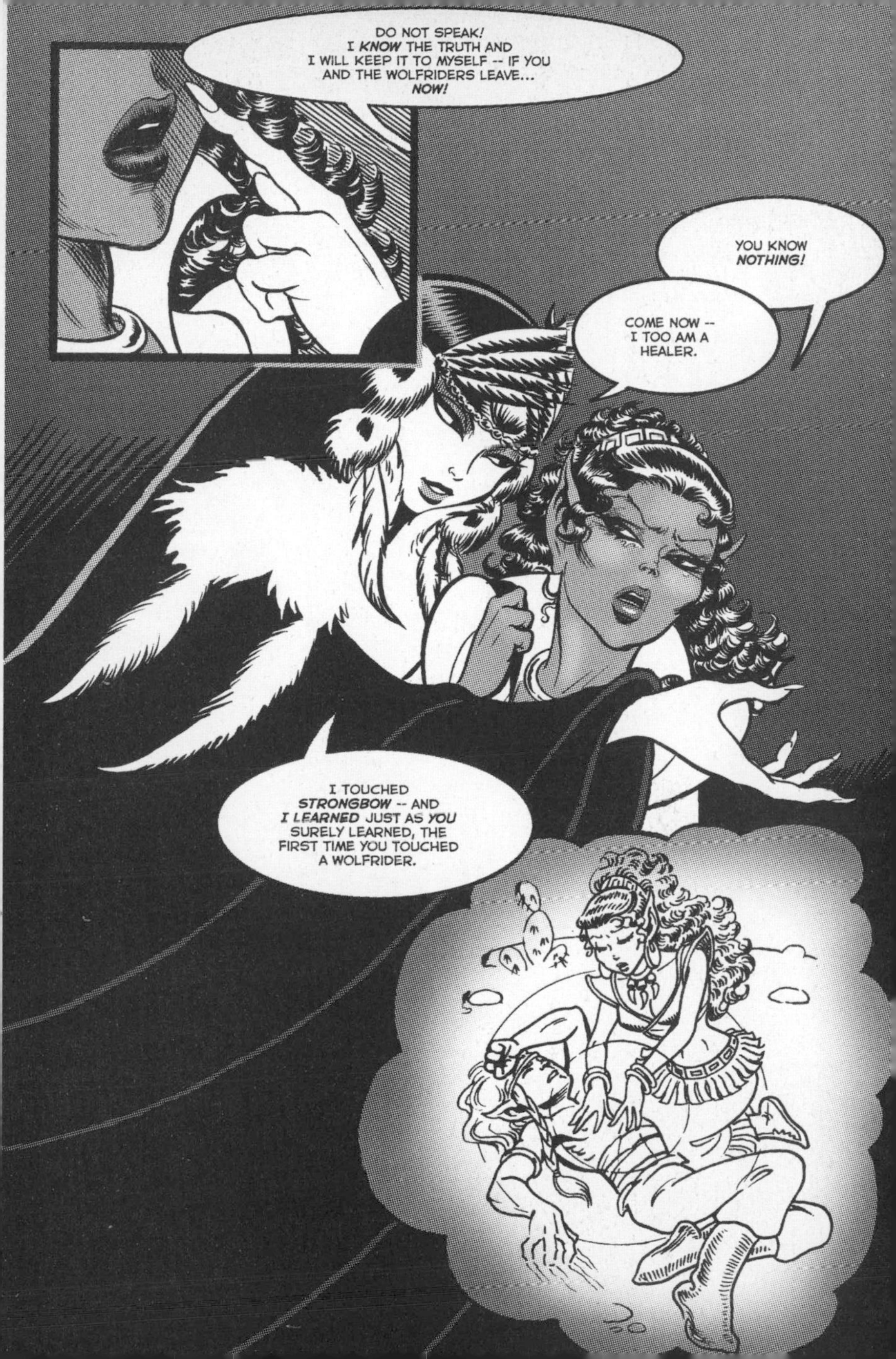
DO NOT SPEAK! I *KNOW* THE TRUTH AND I WILL KEEP IT TO *MYSELF* -- IF YOU AND THE WOLFRIDERS LEAVE... *NOW!*
YOU KNOW *NOTHING!*
COME NOW -- I TOO AM A HEALER.
I TOUCHED *STRONGBOW* -- AND *I LEARNED* JUST AS *YOU* SURELY LEARNED, THE FIRST TIME YOU TOUCHED A WOLFRIDER.

TELL ME, DARK SISTER... HOW DID YOU RECONCILE YOURSELF --

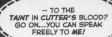

-- TO THE *TAINT* IN *CUTTER'S* BLOOD? GO ON...YOU CAN SPEAK FREELY TO *ME!*

DID IT *THRILL* YOU -- THE MINGLING OF HIS BLOOD WITH YOURS?

IT IS EXCITING TO FLIRT WITH *DEATH*, IS IT NOT?

STOP!

THE WOLFRIDERS ARE INDEED BROTHERS TO THEIR SHORT-LIVED WOLVES. I WONDER HOW THEY BECAME SO, AND WHEN? LONG AGO, I SHOULD THINK...

CUTTER SPOKE OF LIVING AS LONG AS *LORD VOLL.*

HOW PATHETIC!

OR DO THEY CONTINUE TO RENEW THEIR BLOOD KIN-SHIP EVEN NOW?

BE SILENT!

OBVIOUSLY THE WOLFRIDERS ARE IGNORANT OF THE *PRICE* THEY MUST PAY FOR THEIR ANCESTORS' FOLLY!

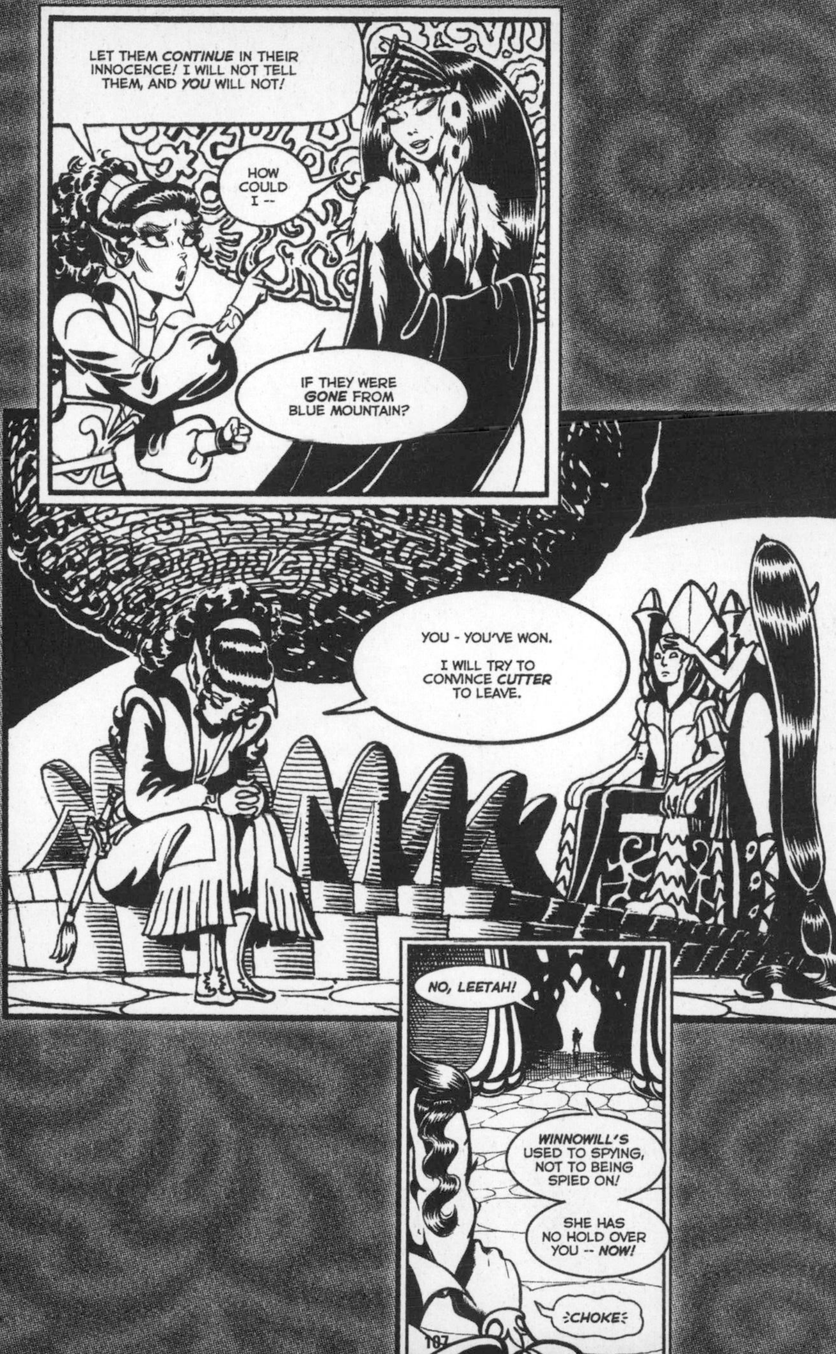
LET THEM CONTINUE IN THEIR INNOCENCE! I WILL NOT TELL THEM, AND YOU WILL NOT!
HOW COULD I --
IF THEY WERE GONE FROM BLUE MOUNTAIN?
YOU - YOU'VE WON.
I WILL TRY TO CONVINCE CUTTER TO LEAVE.
NO, LEETAH!
WINNOWILL'S USED TO SPYING, NOT TO BEING SPIED ON!
SHE HAS NO HOLD OVER YOU -- NOW!
CHOKE

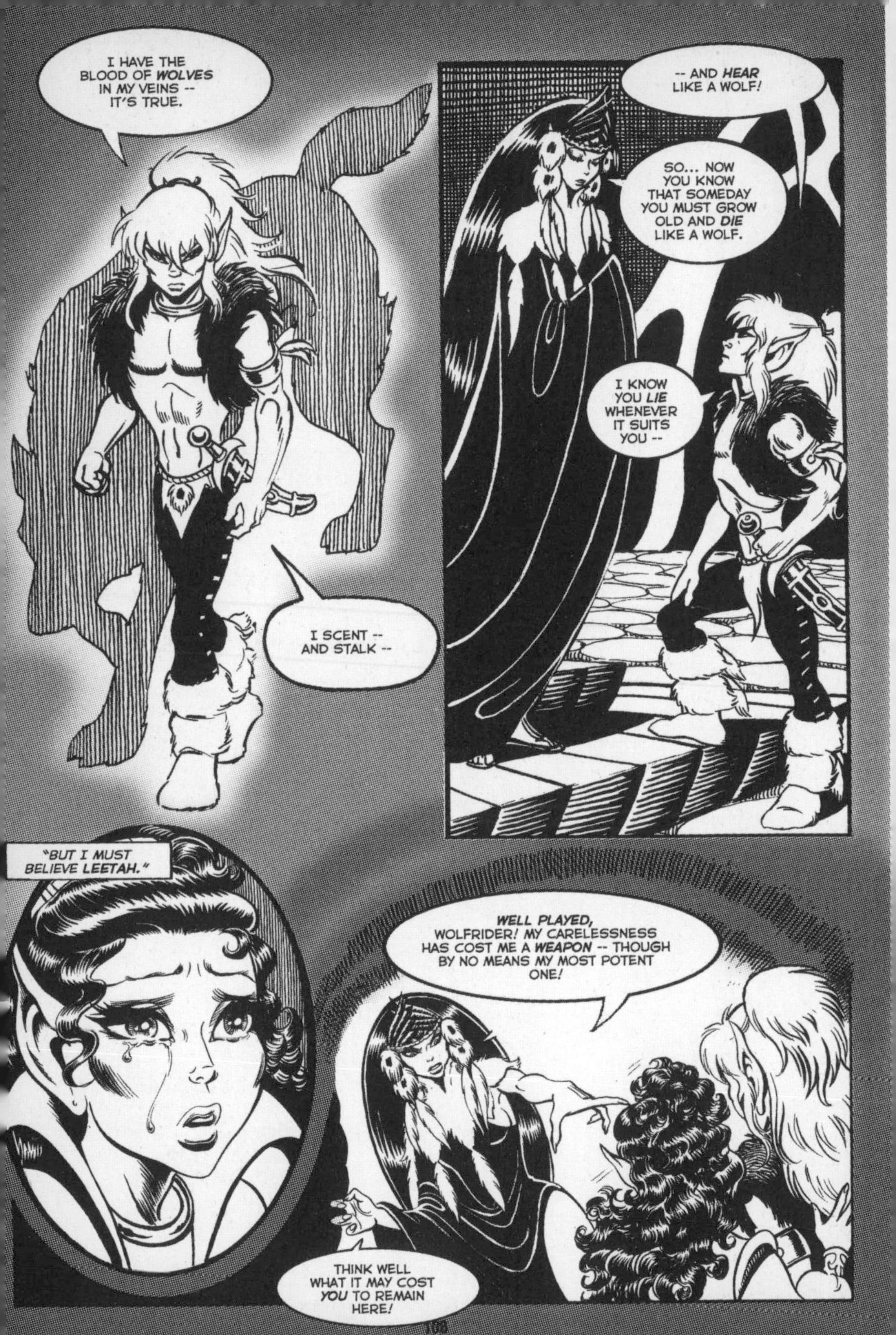
I HAVE THE BLOOD OF *WOLVES* IN *MY* VEINS -- IT'S TRUE.
I SCENT -- AND STALK --
-- AND *HEAR* LIKE A WOLF!
SO... NOW YOU KNOW THAT SOMEDAY YOU *MUST* GROW OLD AND *DIE* LIKE A WOLF.
I KNOW YOU *LIE* WHENEVER IT SUITS YOU --
"BUT I MUST BELIEVE **LEETAH**."
WELL PLAYED, WOLFRIDER! *MY* CARELESSNESS HAS COST ME A *WEAPON* -- THOUGH BY NO MEANS MY MOST POTENT ONE!
THINK WELL WHAT IT MAY COST *YOU* TO REMAIN HERE!

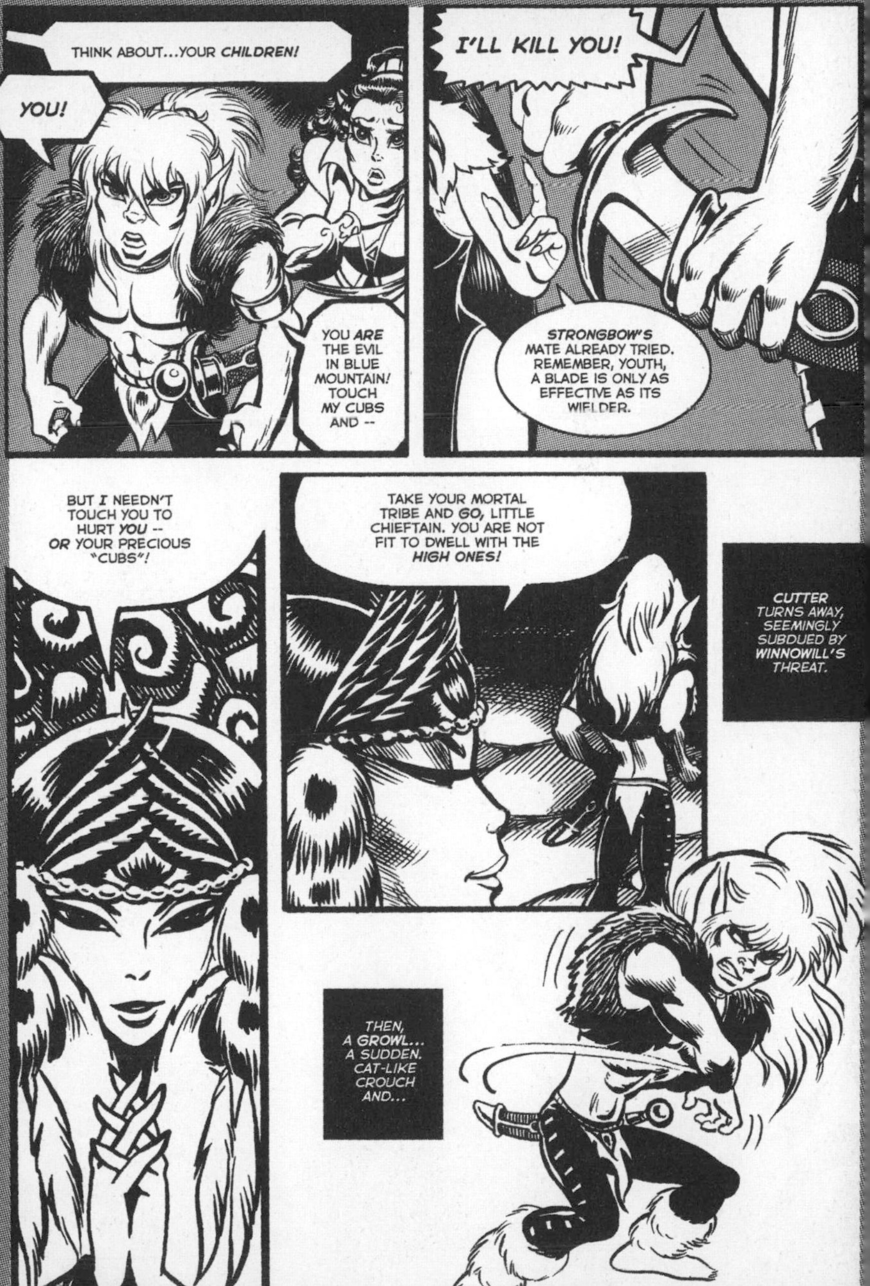
THINK ABOUT...YOUR CHILDREN!
YOU!
YOU ARE THE EVIL IN BLUE MOUNTAIN! TOUCH MY CUBS AND --
I'LL KILL YOU!
STRONGBOW'S MATE ALREADY TRIED. REMEMBER, YOUTH, A BLADE IS ONLY AS EFFECTIVE AS ITS WIELDER.
BUT I NEEDN'T TOUCH YOU TO HURT YOU -- OR YOUR PRECIOUS "CUBS"!
TAKE YOUR MORTAL TRIBE AND GO, LITTLE CHIEFTAIN. YOU ARE NOT FIT TO DWELL WITH THE HIGH ONES!
CUTTER TURNS AWAY, SEEMINGLY SUBDUED BY WINNOWILL'S THREAT.
THEN, A GROWL... A SUDDEN. CAT-LIKE CROUCH AND...

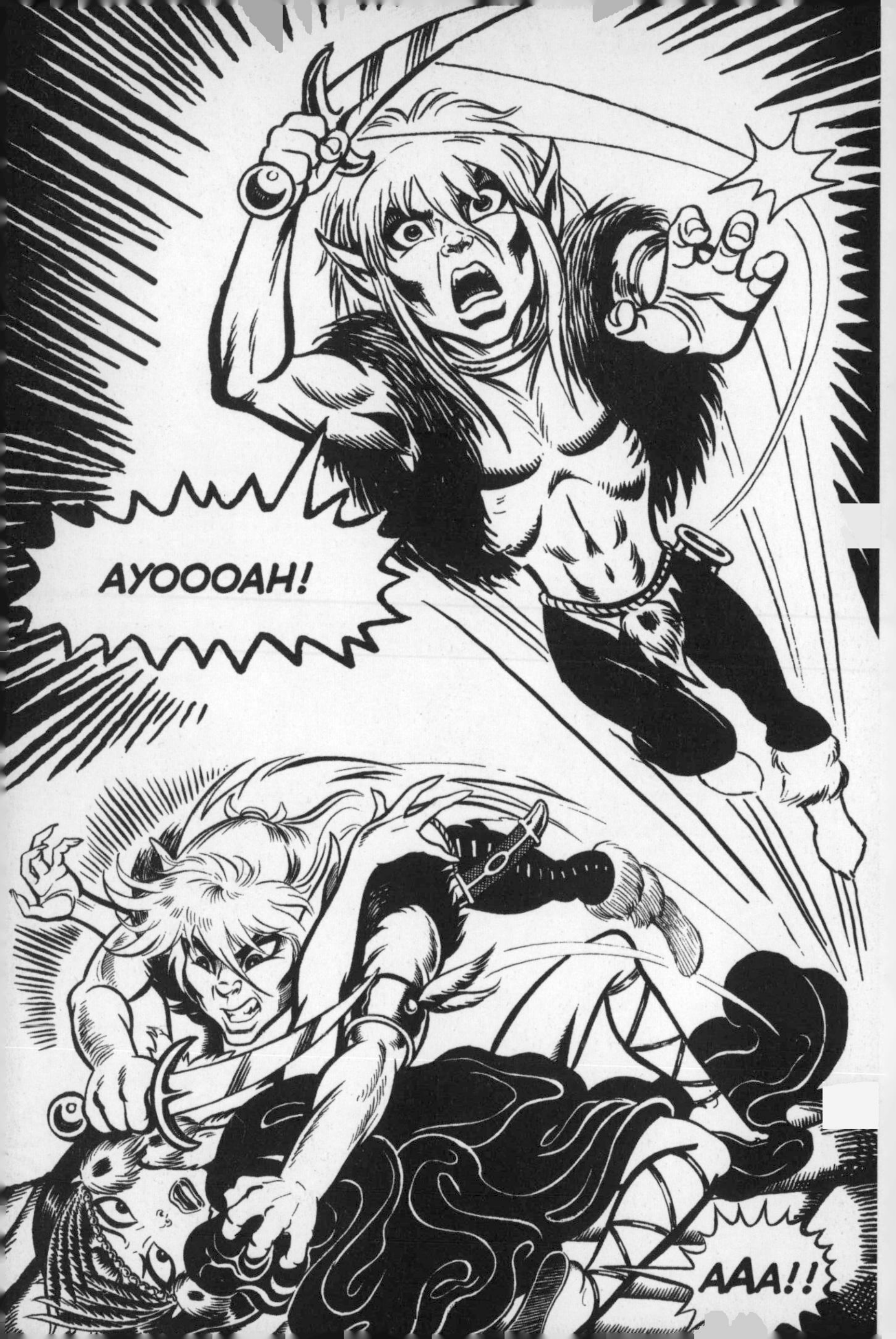
AYOOOAH!
AAA!!

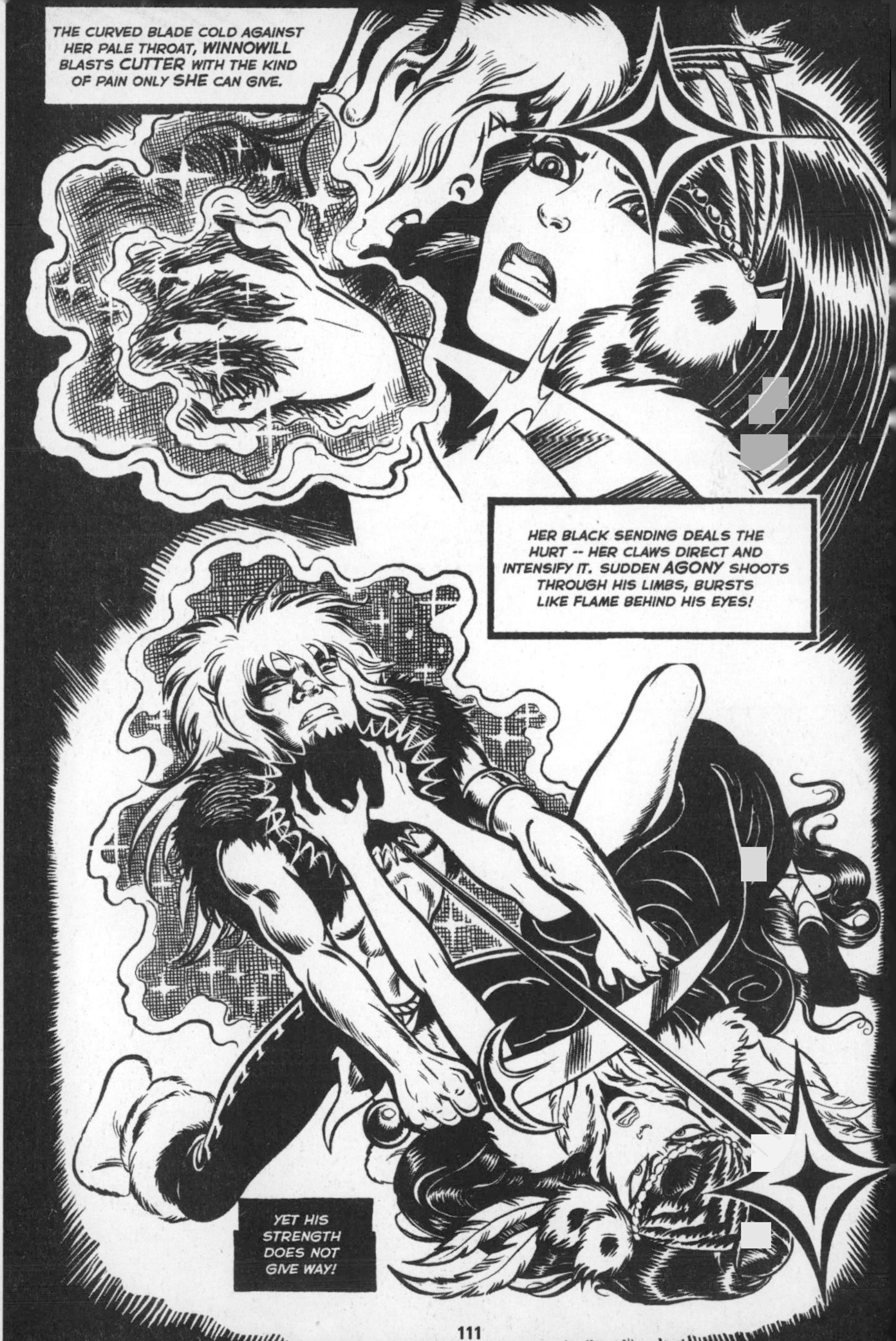
THE CURVED BLADE COLD AGAINST HER PALE THROAT, WINNOWILL BLASTS CUTTER WITH THE KIND OF PAIN ONLY SHE CAN GIVE.
HER BLACK SENDING DEALS THE HURT -- HER CLAWS DIRECT AND INTENSIFY IT. SUDDEN AGONY SHOOTS THROUGH HIS LIMBS, BURSTS LIKE FLAME BEHIND HIS EYES!
YET HIS STRENGTH DOES NOT GIVE WAY!

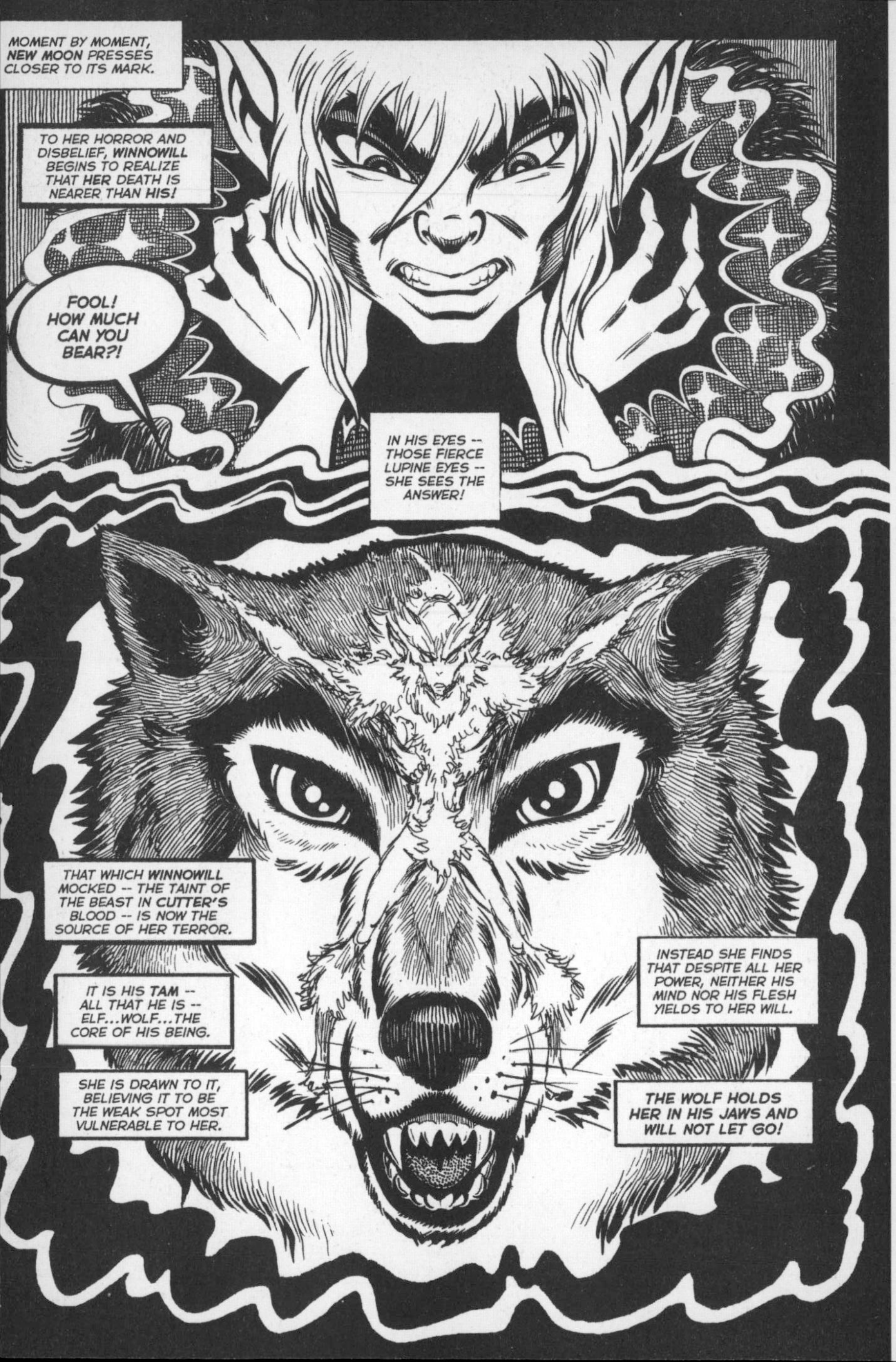
MOMENT BY MOMENT, NEW MOON PRESSES CLOSER TO ITS MARK.
TO HER HORROR AND DISBELIEF, WINNOWILL BEGINS TO REALIZE THAT HER DEATH IS NEARER THAN HIS!
FOOL! HOW MUCH CAN YOU BEAR?!
IN HIS EYES -- THOSE FIERCE LUPINE EYES -- SHE SEES THE ANSWER!
THAT WHICH WINNOWILL MOCKED -- THE TAINT OF THE BEAST IN CUTTER'S BLOOD -- IS NOW THE SOURCE OF HER TERROR.
IT IS HIS TAM -- ALL THAT HE IS -- ELF...WOLF...THE CORE OF HIS BEING.
SHE IS DRAWN TO IT, BELIEVING IT TO BE THE WEAK SPOT MOST VULNERABLE TO HER.
INSTEAD SHE FINDS THAT DESPITE ALL HER POWER, NEITHER HIS MIND NOR HIS FLESH YIELDS TO HER WILL.
THE WOLF HOLDS HER IN HIS JAWS AND WILL NOT LET GO!

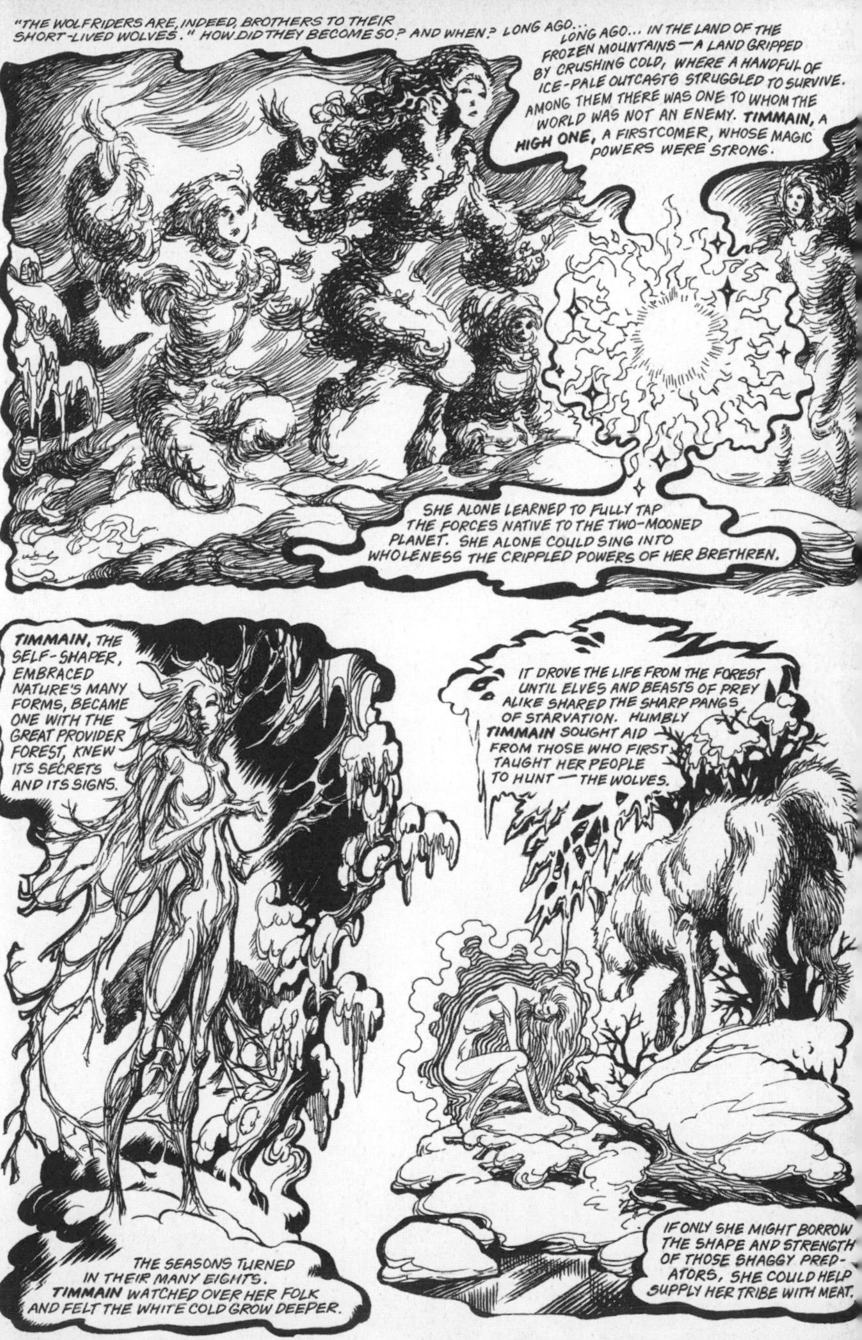
"THE WOLFRIDERS ARE, INDEED, BROTHERS TO THEIR SHORT-LIVED WOLVES." HOW DID THEY BECOME SO? AND WHEN? LONG AGO...
LONG AGO... IN THE LAND OF THE FROZEN MOUNTAINS — A LAND GRIPPED BY CRUSHING COLD, WHERE A HANDFUL OF ICE-PALE OUTCASTS STRUGGLED TO SURVIVE. AMONG THEM THERE WAS ONE TO WHOM THE WORLD WAS NOT AN ENEMY. TIMMAIN, A HIGH ONE, A FIRSTCOMER, WHOSE MAGIC POWERS WERE STRONG.
SHE ALONE LEARNED TO FULLY TAP THE FORCES NATIVE TO THE TWO-MOONED PLANET. SHE ALONE COULD SING INTO WHOLENESS THE CRIPPLED POWERS OF HER BRETHREN.
TIMMAIN, THE SELF-SHAPER, EMBRACED NATURE'S MANY FORMS, BECAME ONE WITH THE GREAT PROVIDER FOREST, KNEW ITS SECRETS AND ITS SIGNS.
THE SEASONS TURNED IN THEIR MANY EIGHTS. TIMMAIN WATCHED OVER HER FOLK AND FELT THE WHITE COLD GROW DEEPER.
IT DROVE THE LIFE FROM THE FOREST UNTIL ELVES AND BEASTS OF PREY ALIKE SHARED THE SHARP PANGS OF STARVATION. HUMBLY TIMMAIN SOUGHT AID FROM THOSE WHO FIRST TAUGHT HER PEOPLE TO HUNT — THE WOLVES.
IF ONLY SHE MIGHT BORROW THE SHAPE AND STRENGTH OF THOSE SHAGGY PREDATORS, SHE COULD HELP SUPPLY HER TRIBE WITH MEAT.

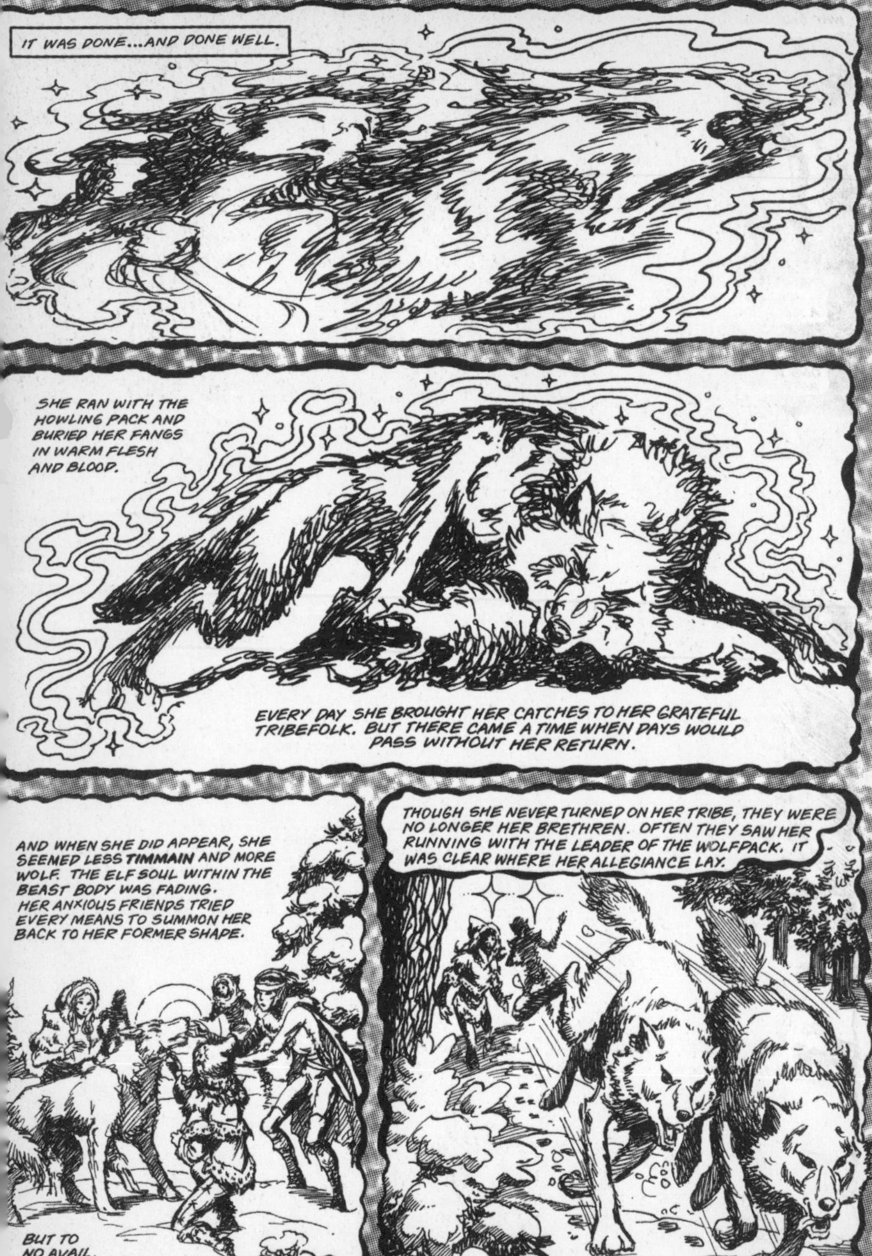
IT WAS DONE...AND DONE WELL.
SHE RAN WITH THE HOWLING PACK AND BURIED HER FANGS IN WARM FLESH AND BLOOD.
EVERY DAY SHE BROUGHT HER CATCHES TO HER GRATEFUL TRIBEFOLK. BUT THERE CAME A TIME WHEN DAYS WOULD PASS WITHOUT HER RETURN.
AND WHEN SHE DID APPEAR, SHE SEEMED LESS **TIMMAIN** AND MORE WOLF. THE ELF SOUL WITHIN THE BEAST BODY WAS FADING.
HER ANXIOUS FRIENDS TRIED EVERY MEANS TO SUMMON HER BACK TO HER FORMER SHAPE.
BUT TO NO AVAIL.
THE TRANSFORMATION WAS TOO COMPLETE.
THOUGH SHE NEVER TURNED ON HER TRIBE, THEY WERE NO LONGER HER BRETHREN. OFTEN THEY SAW HER RUNNING WITH THE LEADER OF THE WOLFPACK. IT WAS CLEAR WHERE HER ALLEGIANCE LAY.

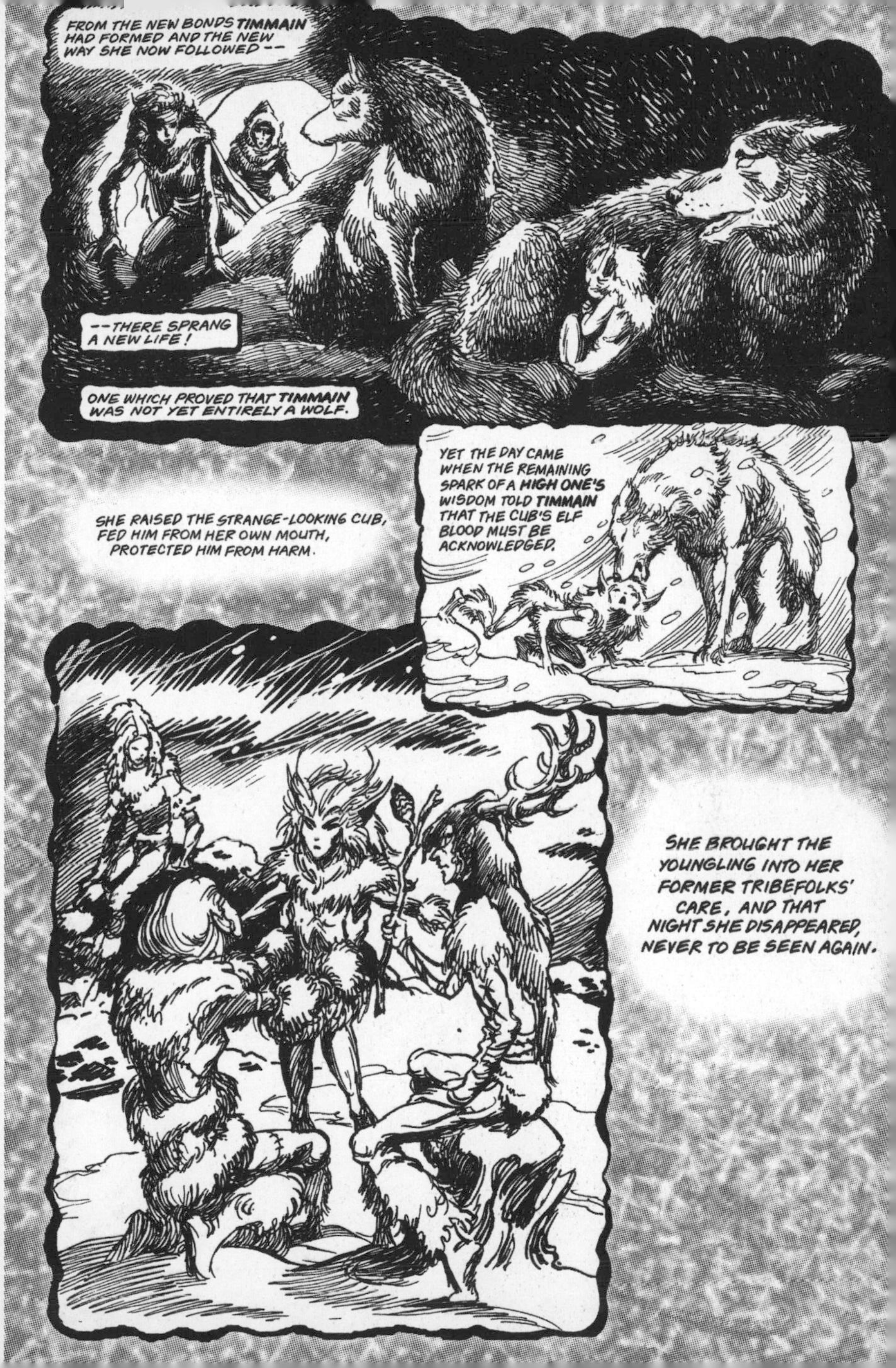
FROM THE NEW BONDS TIMMAIN HAD FORMED AND THE NEW WAY SHE NOW FOLLOWED --
--THERE SPRANG A NEW LIFE!
ONE WHICH PROVED THAT TIMMAIN WAS NOT YET ENTIRELY A WOLF.
SHE RAISED THE STRANGE-LOOKING CUB, FED HIM FROM HER OWN MOUTH, PROTECTED HIM FROM HARM.
YET THE DAY CAME WHEN THE REMAINING SPARK OF A HIGH ONE'S WISDOM TOLD TIMMAIN THAT THE CUB'S ELF BLOOD MUST BE ACKNOWLEDGED.
SHE BROUGHT THE YOUNGLING INTO HER FORMER TRIBEFOLKS' CARE, AND THAT NIGHT SHE DISAPPEARED, NEVER TO BE SEEN AGAIN.

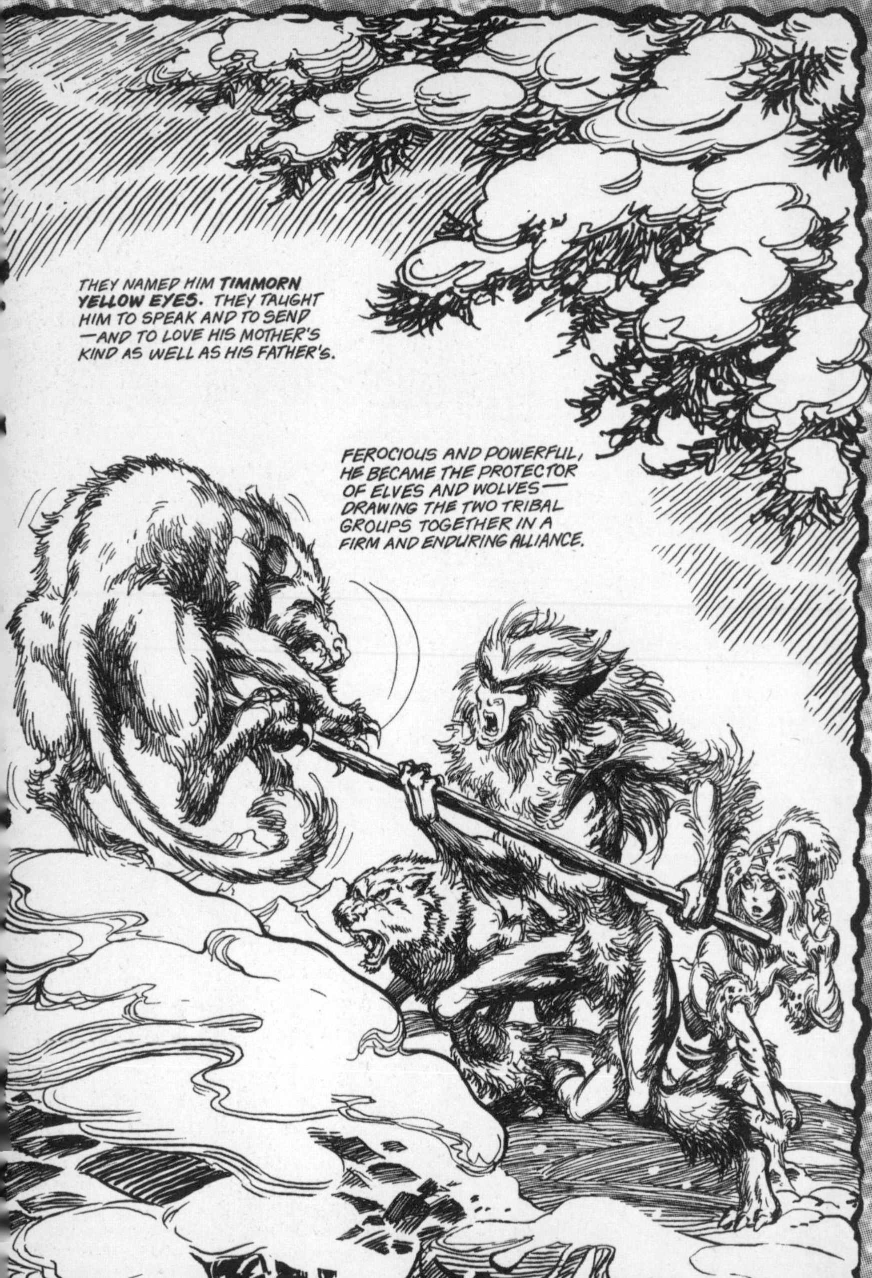
THEY NAMED HIM **TIMMORN YELLOW EYES.** THEY TAUGHT HIM TO SPEAK AND TO SEND —AND TO LOVE HIS MOTHER'S KIND AS WELL AS HIS FATHER'S.
FEROCIOUS AND POWERFUL, HE BECAME THE PROTECTOR OF ELVES AND WOLVES— DRAWING THE TWO TRIBAL GROUPS TOGETHER IN A FIRM AND ENDURING ALLIANCE.

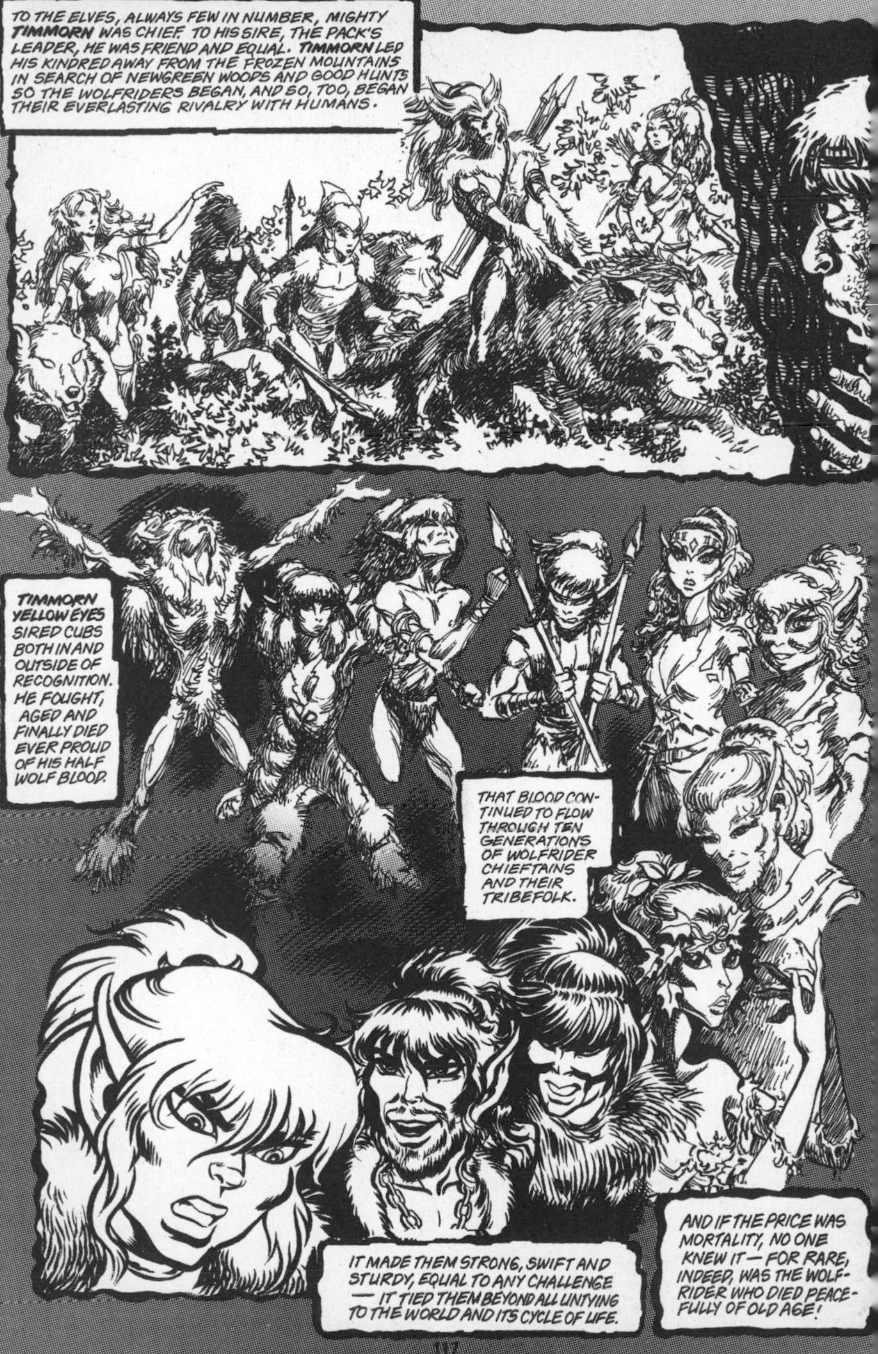

TO THE ELVES, ALWAYS FEW IN NUMBER, MIGHTY TIMMORN WAS CHIEF. TO HIS SIRE, THE PACK'S LEADER, HE WAS FRIEND AND EQUAL. TIMMORN LED HIS KINDRED AWAY FROM THE FROZEN MOUNTAINS IN SEARCH OF NEWGREEN WOODS AND GOOD HUNTS. SO THE WOLFRIDERS BEGAN, AND SO, TOO, BEGAN THEIR EVERLASTING RIVALRY WITH HUMANS.
TIMMORN YELLOW EYES SIRED CUBS BOTH IN AND OUTSIDE OF RECOGNITION. HE FOUGHT, AGED AND FINALLY DIED EVER PROUD OF HIS HALF WOLF BLOOD.
THAT BLOOD CONTINUED TO FLOW THROUGH TEN GENERATIONS OF WOLFRIDER CHIEFTAINS AND THEIR TRIBEFOLK.
IT MADE THEM STRONG, SWIFT AND STURDY, EQUAL TO ANY CHALLENGE — IT TIED THEM BEYOND ALL UNTYING TO THE WORLD AND ITS CYCLE OF LIFE.
AND IF THE PRICE WAS MORTALITY, NO ONE KNEW IT — FOR RARE, INDEED, WAS THE WOLFRIDER WHO DIED PEACEFULLY OF OLD AGE!

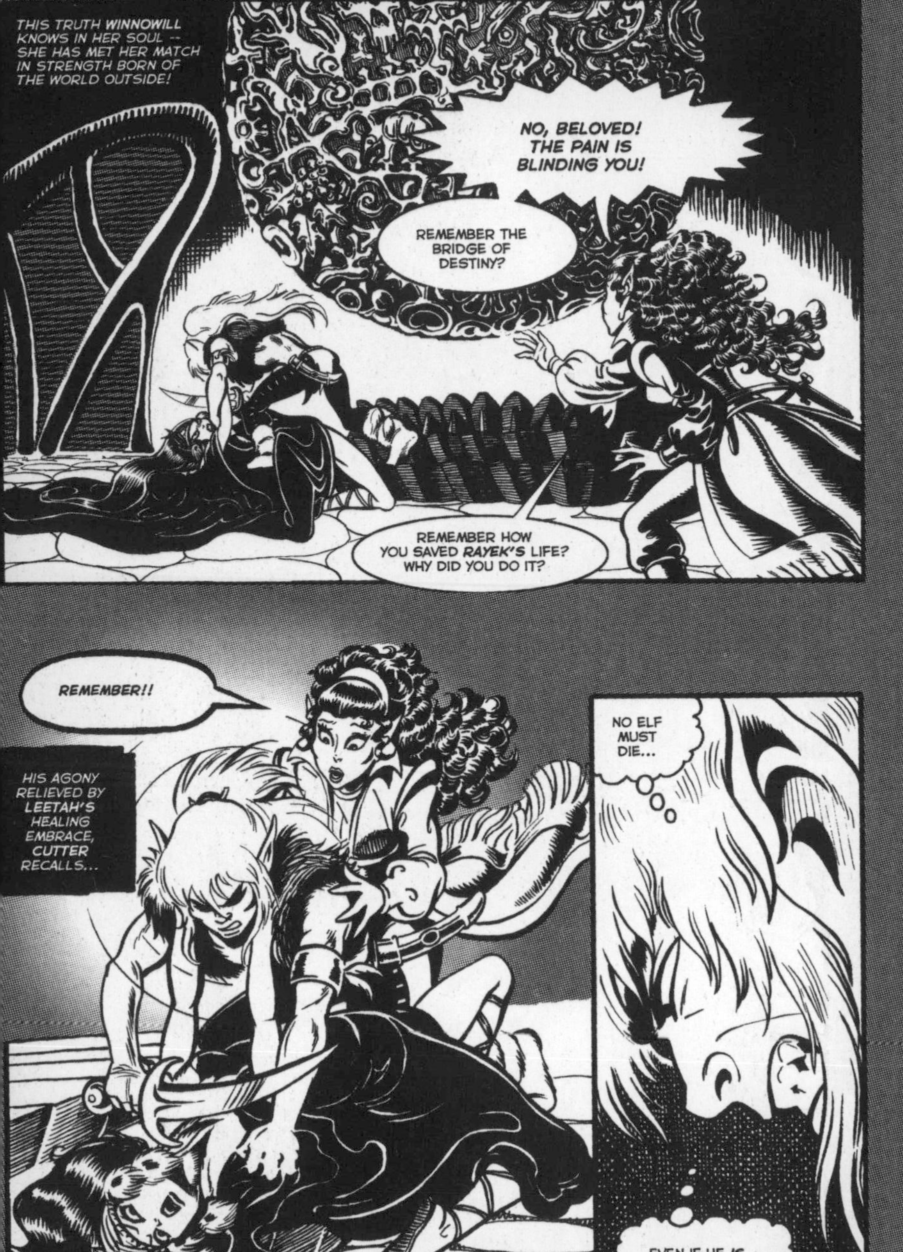

THIS TRUTH WINNOWILL KNOWS IN HER SOUL -- SHE HAS MET HER MATCH IN STRENGTH BORN OF THE WORLD OUTSIDE!
NO, BELOVED! THE PAIN IS BLINDING YOU!
REMEMBER THE BRIDGE OF DESTINY?
REMEMBER HOW YOU SAVED RAYEK'S LIFE? WHY DID YOU DO IT?
REMEMBER!!
HIS AGONY RELIEVED BY LEETAH'S HEALING EMBRACE, CUTTER RECALLS...
NO ELF MUST DIE...
EVEN IF HE IS MY ENEMY!

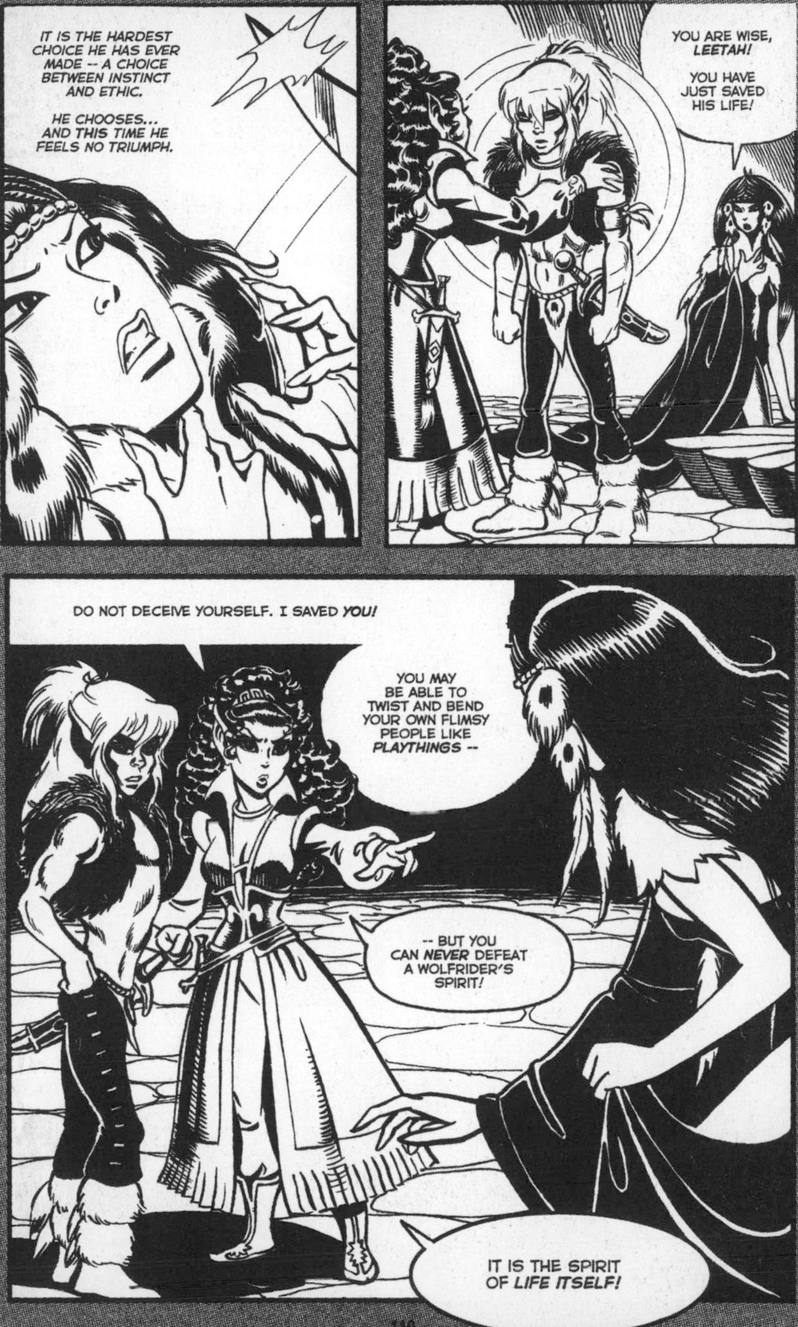
IT IS THE HARDEST CHOICE HE HAS EVER MADE -- A CHOICE BETWEEN INSTINCT AND ETHIC.
HE CHOOSES... AND THIS TIME HE FEELS NO TRIUMPH.
YOU ARE WISE, LEETAH!
YOU HAVE JUST SAVED HIS LIFE!
DO NOT DECEIVE YOURSELF. I SAVED YOU!
YOU MAY BE ABLE TO TWIST AND BEND YOUR OWN FLIMSY PEOPLE LIKE PLAYTHINGS --
-- BUT YOU CAN NEVER DEFEAT A WOLFRIDER'S SPIRIT!
IT IS THE SPIRIT OF LIFE ITSELF!

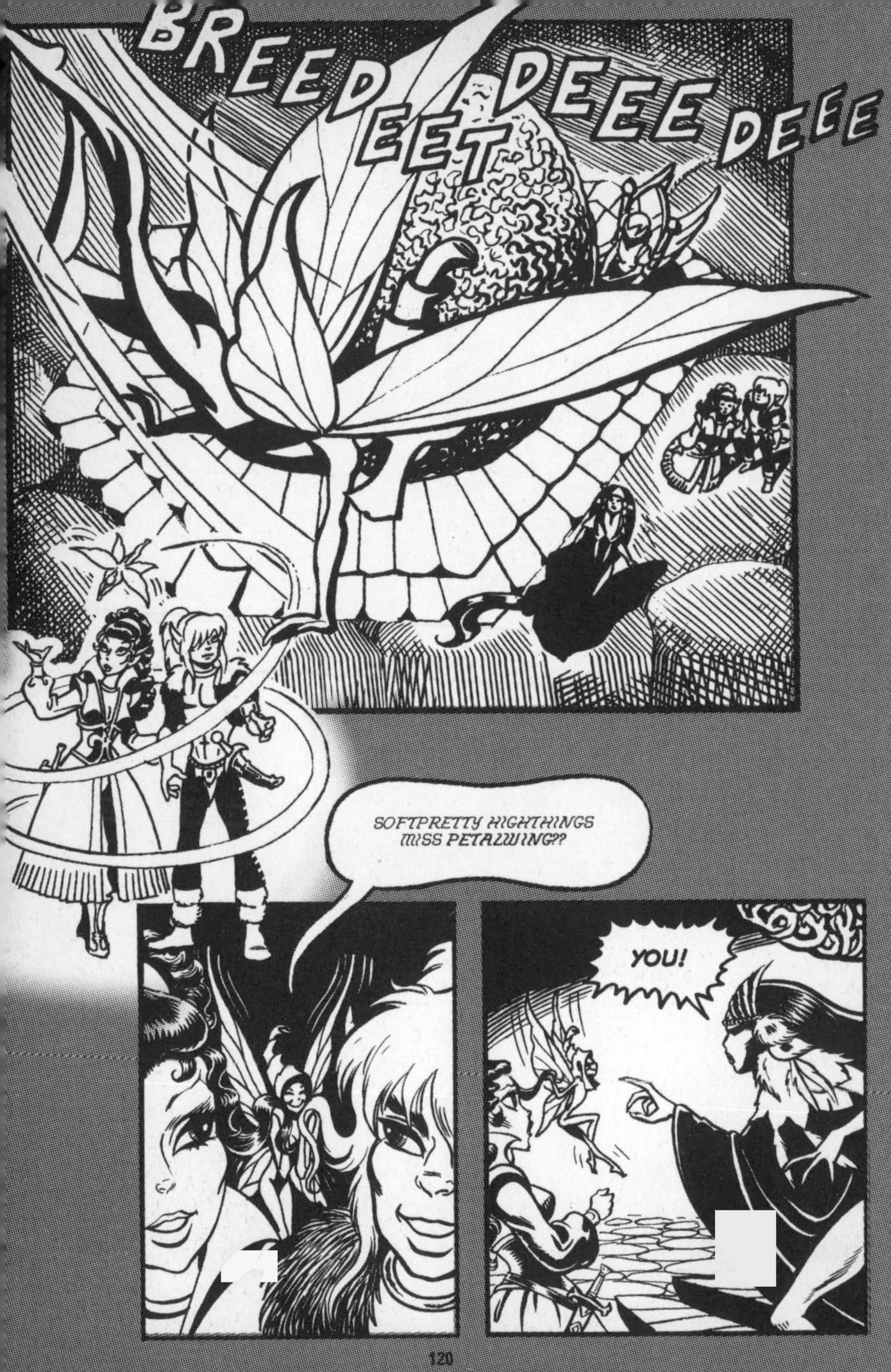
BREEDEEET DEEEE DEEE
SOFTPRETTY HIGHTHINGS MISS PETALWING??
YOU!

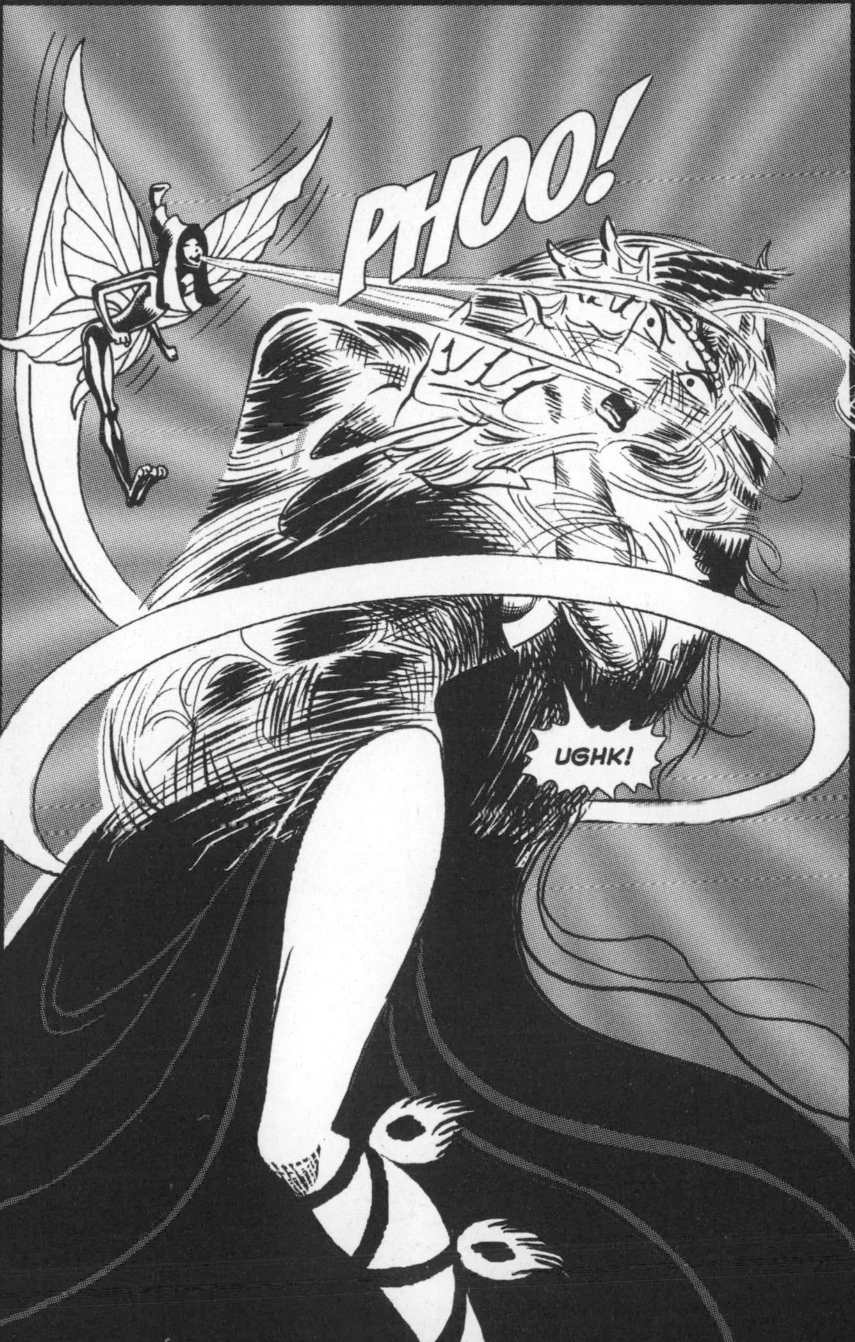
PHOO!
UGHK!

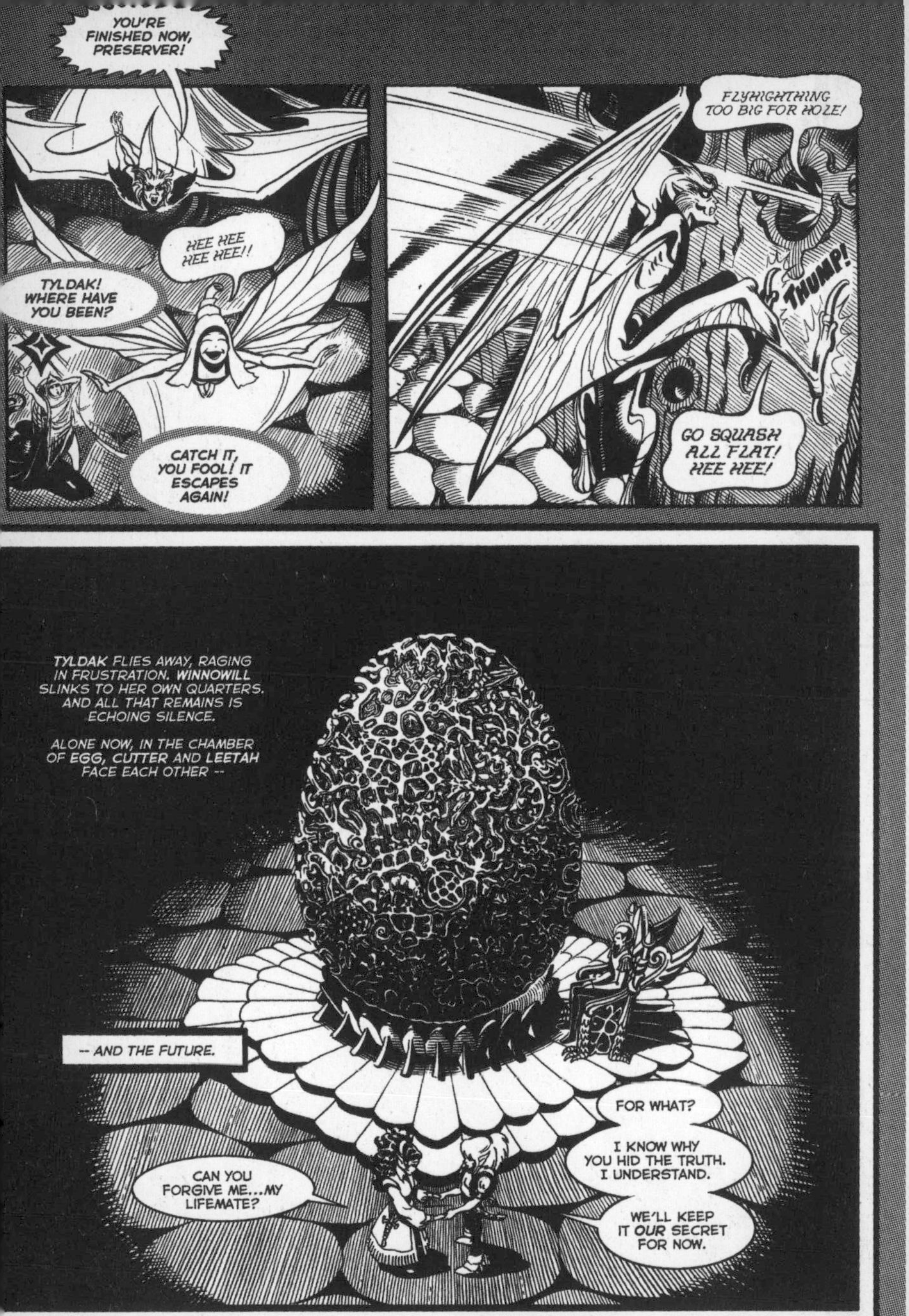

YOU'RE FINISHED NOW, PRESERVER!
HEE HEE HEE HEE!!
TYLDAK! WHERE HAVE YOU BEEN?
CATCH IT, YOU FOOL! IT ESCAPES AGAIN!
FLYHIGHTHING TOO BIG FOR HOZE!
THUMP!
GO SQUASH ALL FLAT! HEE HEE!
TYLDAK FLIES AWAY, RAGING IN FRUSTRATION. WINNOWILL SLINKS TO HER OWN QUARTERS. AND ALL THAT REMAINS IS ECHOING SILENCE.
ALONE NOW, IN THE CHAMBER OF EGG, CUTTER AND LEETAH FACE EACH OTHER --
-- AND THE FUTURE.
CAN YOU FORGIVE ME...MY LIFEMATE?
FOR WHAT?
I KNOW WHY YOU HID THE TRUTH. I UNDERSTAND.
WE'LL KEEP IT OUR SECRET FOR NOW.

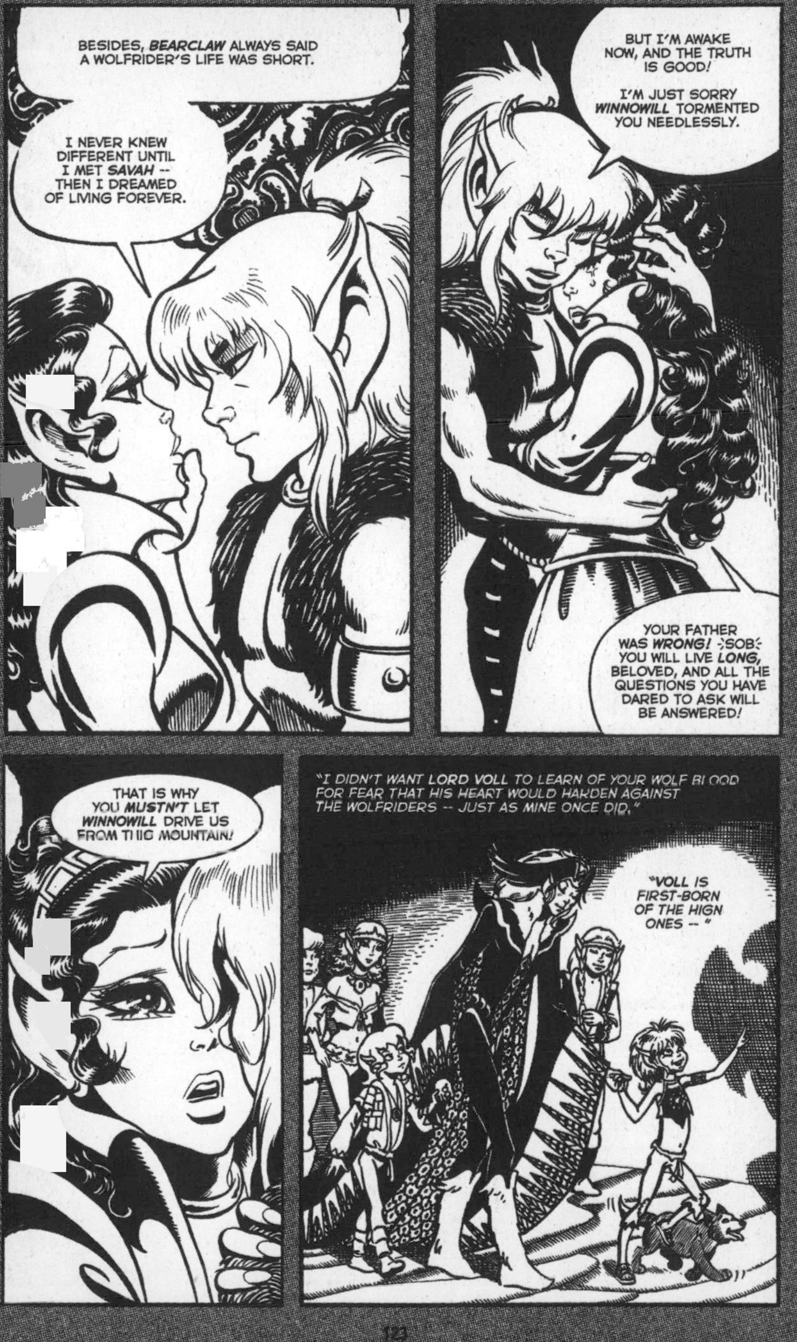
BESIDES, BEARCLAW ALWAYS SAID A WOLFRIDER'S LIFE WAS SHORT.
I NEVER KNEW DIFFERENT UNTIL I MET SAVAH -- THEN I DREAMED OF LIVING FOREVER.
BUT I'M AWAKE NOW, AND THE TRUTH IS GOOD!
I'M JUST SORRY WINNOWILL TORMENTED YOU NEEDLESSLY.
YOUR FATHER WAS WRONG! SOB YOU WILL LIVE LONG, BELOVED, AND ALL THE QUESTIONS YOU HAVE DARED TO ASK WILL BE ANSWERED!
THAT IS WHY YOU MUSTN'T LET WINNOWILL DRIVE US FROM THIS MOUNTAIN!
"I DIDN'T WANT LORD VOLL TO LEARN OF YOUR WOLF BLOOD FOR FEAR THAT HIS HEART WOULD HARDEN AGAINST THE WOLFRIDERS -- JUST AS MINE ONCE DID."
"VOLL IS FIRST-BORN OF THE HIGN ONES -- "

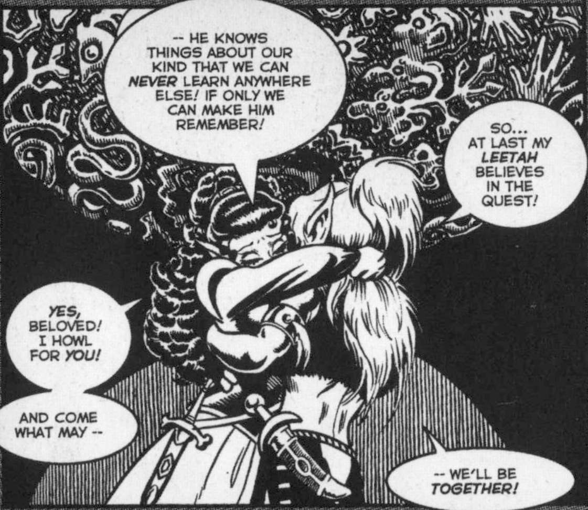
-- HE KNOWS THINGS ABOUT OUR KIND THAT WE CAN NEVER LEARN ANYWHERE ELSE! IF ONLY WE CAN MAKE HIM REMEMBER!
SO... AT LAST MY LEETAH BELIEVES IN THE QUEST!
YES, BELOVED! I HOWL FOR YOU!
AND COME WHAT MAY --
-- WE'LL BE TOGETHER!

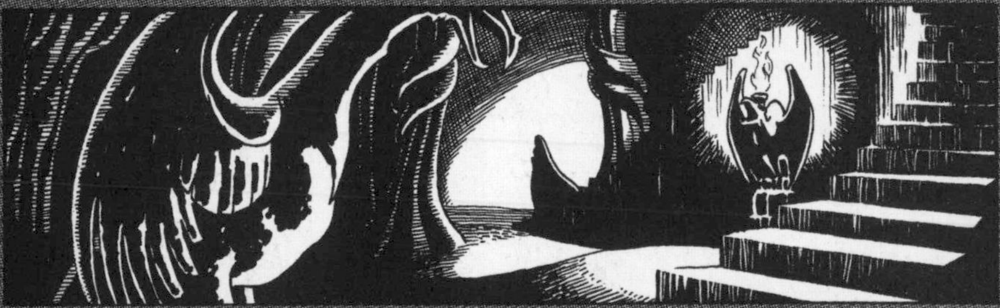

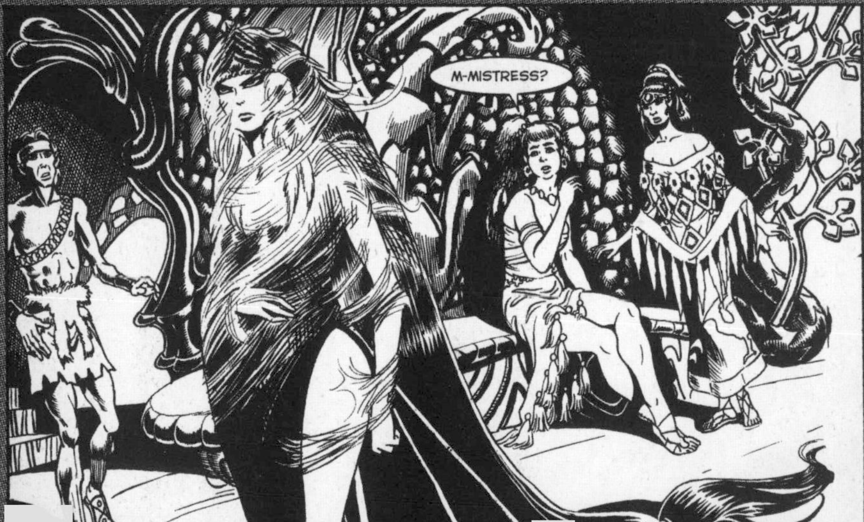
M-MISTRESS?

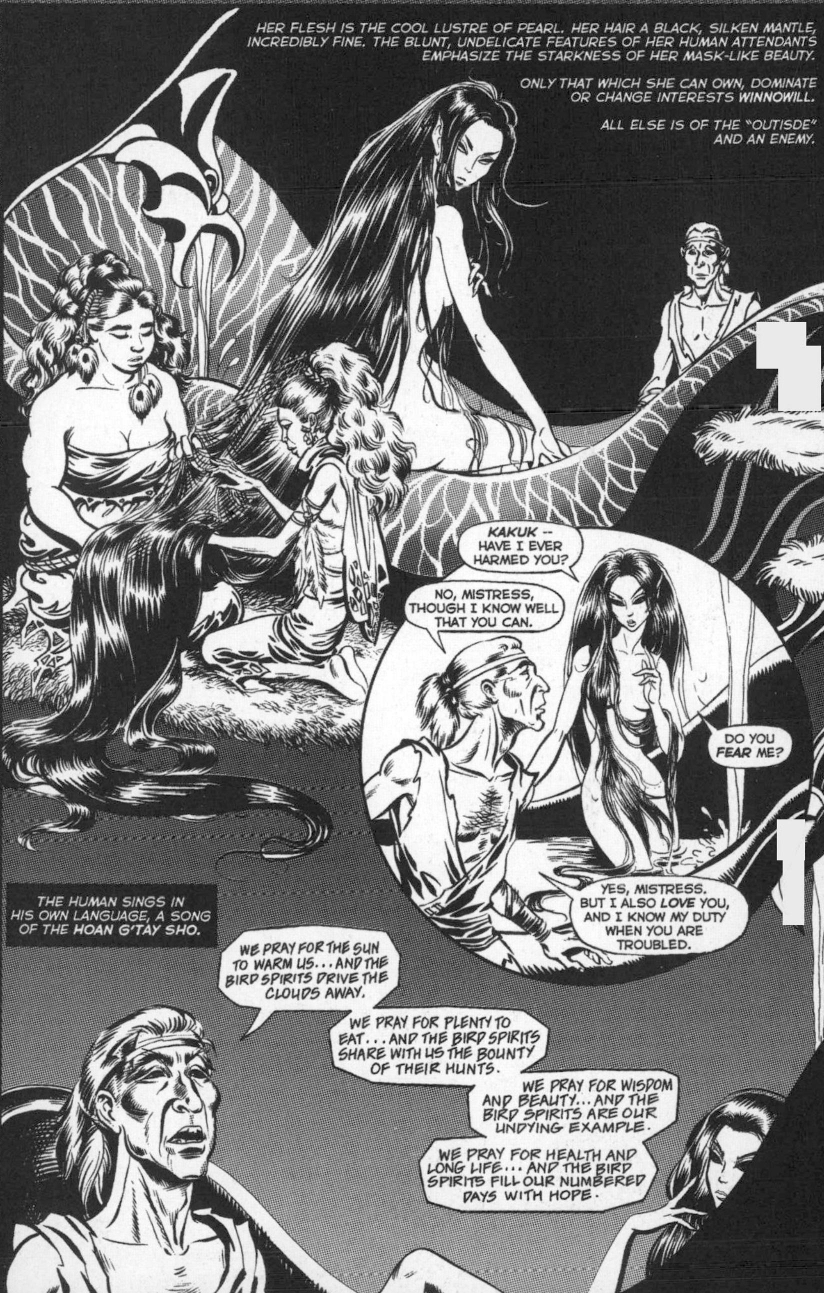
HER FLESH IS THE COOL LUSTRE OF PEARL. HER HAIR A BLACK, SILKEN MANTLE, INCREDIBLY FINE. THE BLUNT, UNDELICATE FEATURES OF HER HUMAN ATTENDANTS EMPHASIZE THE STARKNESS OF HER MASK-LIKE BEAUTY.
ONLY THAT WHICH SHE CAN OWN, DOMINATE OR CHANGE INTERESTS WINNOWILL.
ALL ELSE IS OF THE "OUTISDE" AND AN ENEMY.
KAKUK -- HAVE I EVER HARMED YOU?
NO, MISTRESS, THOUGH I KNOW WELL THAT YOU CAN.
DO YOU FEAR ME?
YES, MISTRESS. BUT I ALSO LOVE YOU, AND I KNOW MY DUTY WHEN YOU ARE TROUBLED.
THE HUMAN SINGS IN HIS OWN LANGUAGE, A SONG OF THE HOAN G'TAY SHO.
WE PRAY FOR THE SUN TO WARM US... AND THE BIRD SPIRITS DRIVE THE CLOUDS AWAY.
WE PRAY FOR PLENTY TO EAT... AND THE BIRD SPIRITS SHARE WITH US THE BOUNTY OF THEIR HUNTS.
WE PRAY FOR WISDOM AND BEAUTY... AND THE BIRD SPIRITS ARE OUR UNDYING EXAMPLE.
WE PRAY FOR HEALTH AND LONG LIFE... AND THE BIRD SPIRITS FILL OUR NUMBERED DAYS WITH HOPE.

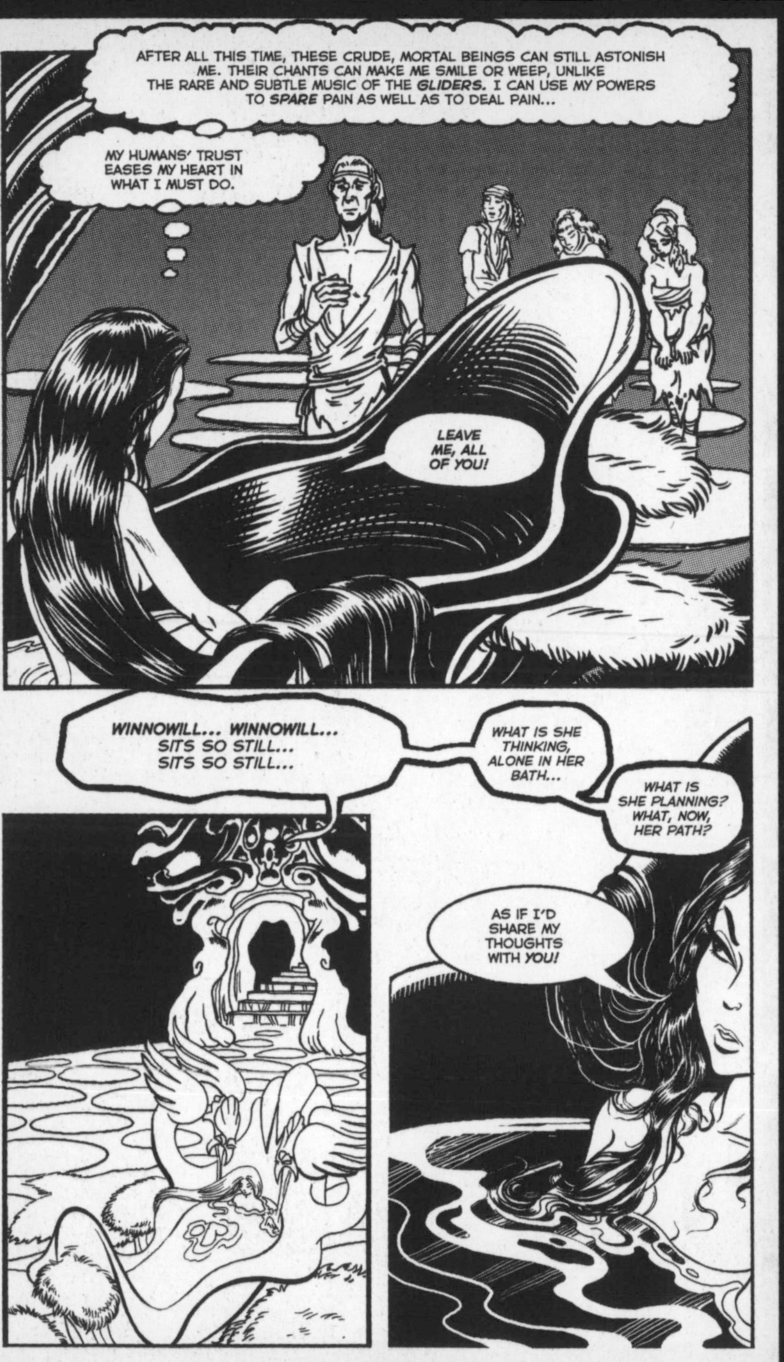
AFTER ALL THIS TIME, THESE CRUDE, MORTAL BEINGS CAN STILL ASTONISH ME. THEIR CHANTS CAN MAKE ME SMILE OR WEEP, UNLIKE THE RARE AND SUBTLE MUSIC OF THE *GLIDERS.* I CAN USE MY POWERS TO *SPARE* PAIN AS WELL AS TO DEAL PAIN...
MY HUMANS' TRUST EASES MY HEART IN WHAT I MUST DO.
LEAVE ME, ALL OF YOU!
WINNOWILL... WINNOWILL... SITS SO STILL... SITS SO STILL...
WHAT IS SHE THINKING, ALONE IN HER BATH...
WHAT IS SHE PLANNING? WHAT, NOW, HER PATH?
AS IF I'D SHARE MY THOUGHTS WITH *YOU!*

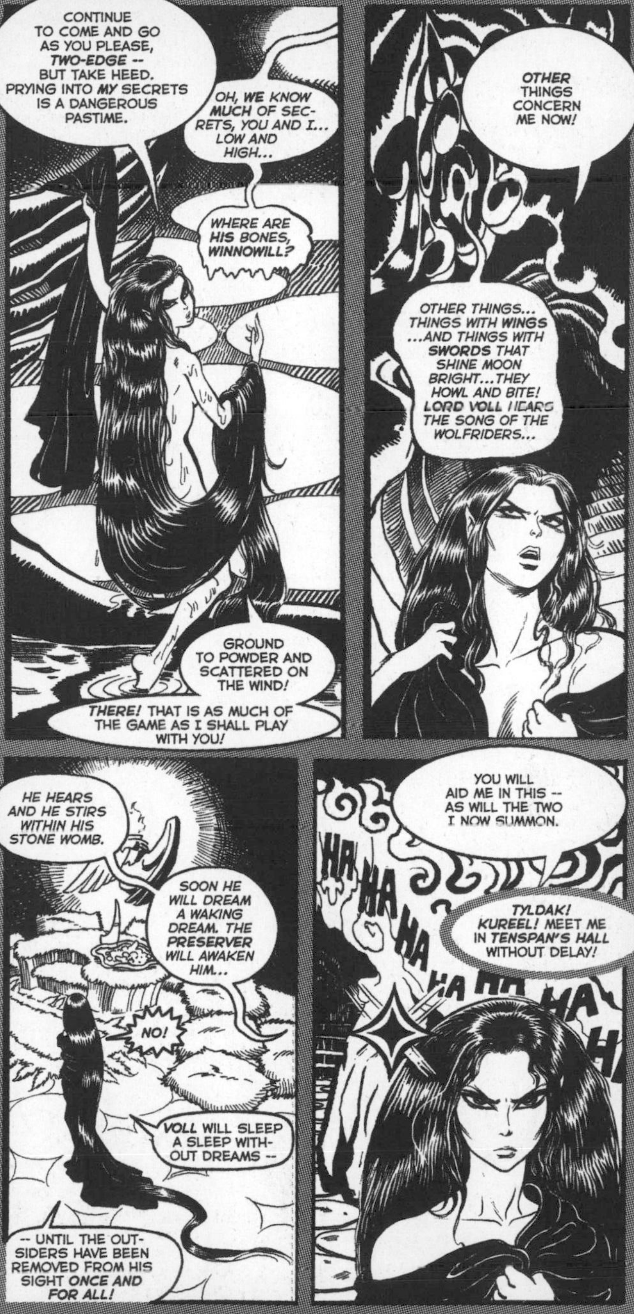

CONTINUE TO COME AND GO AS YOU PLEASE, TWO-EDGE -- BUT TAKE HEED. PRYING INTO MY SECRETS IS A DANGEROUS PASTIME.
OH, WE KNOW MUCH OF SECRETS, YOU AND I... LOW AND HIGH...
WHERE ARE HIS BONES, WINNOWILL?
GROUND TO POWDER AND SCATTERED ON THE WIND!
THERE! THAT IS AS MUCH OF THE GAME AS I SHALL PLAY WITH YOU!
OTHER THINGS CONCERN ME NOW!
OTHER THINGS... THINGS WITH WINGS ...AND THINGS WITH SWORDS THAT SHINE MOON BRIGHT... THEY HOWL AND BITE! LORD VOLL HEARS THE SONG OF THE WOLFRIDERS...
HE HEARS AND HE STIRS WITHIN HIS STONE WOMB.
SOON HE WILL DREAM A WAKING DREAM. THE PRESERVER WILL AWAKEN HIM...
NO!
VOLL WILL SLEEP A SLEEP WITHOUT DREAMS --
-- UNTIL THE OUTSIDERS HAVE BEEN REMOVED FROM HIS SIGHT ONCE AND FOR ALL!
YOU WILL AID ME IN THIS -- AS WILL THE TWO I NOW SUMMON.
HA HA HA HA HA HA HA HA HA HA
TYLDAK! KUREEL! MEET ME IN TENSPAN'S HALL WITHOUT DELAY!

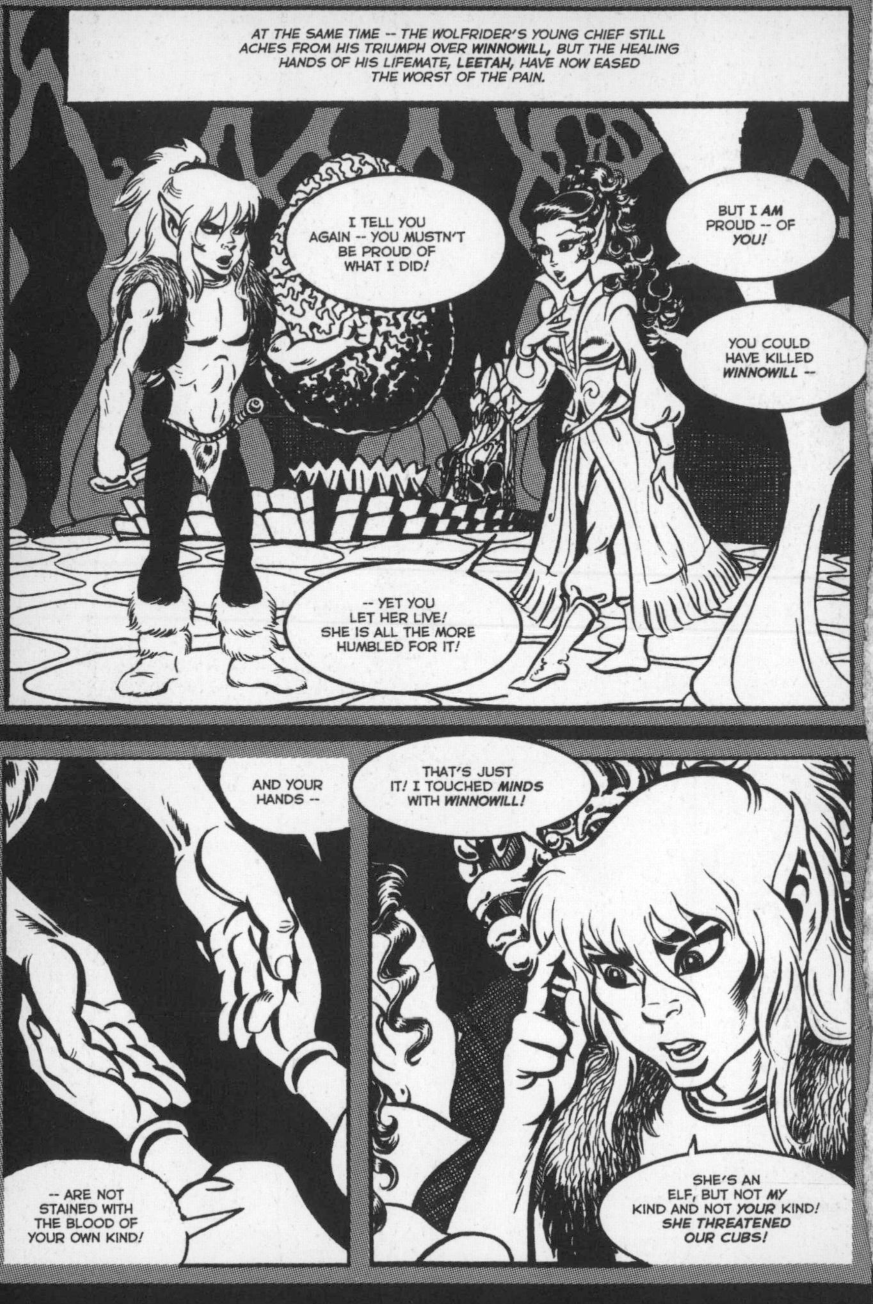
AT THE SAME TIME -- THE WOLFRIDER'S YOUNG CHIEF STILL ACHES FROM HIS TRIUMPH OVER WINNOWILL, BUT THE HEALING HANDS OF HIS LIFEMATE, LEETAH, HAVE NOW EASED THE WORST OF THE PAIN.
I TELL YOU AGAIN -- YOU MUSTN'T BE PROUD OF WHAT I DID!
BUT I AM PROUD -- OF YOU!
YOU COULD HAVE KILLED WINNOWILL --
-- YET YOU LET HER LIVE! SHE IS ALL THE MORE HUMBLED FOR IT!
AND YOUR HANDS --
-- ARE NOT STAINED WITH THE BLOOD OF YOUR OWN KIND!
THAT'S JUST IT! I TOUCHED MINDS WITH WINNOWILL!
SHE'S AN ELF, BUT NOT MY KIND AND NOT YOUR KIND! SHE THREATENED OUR CUBS!

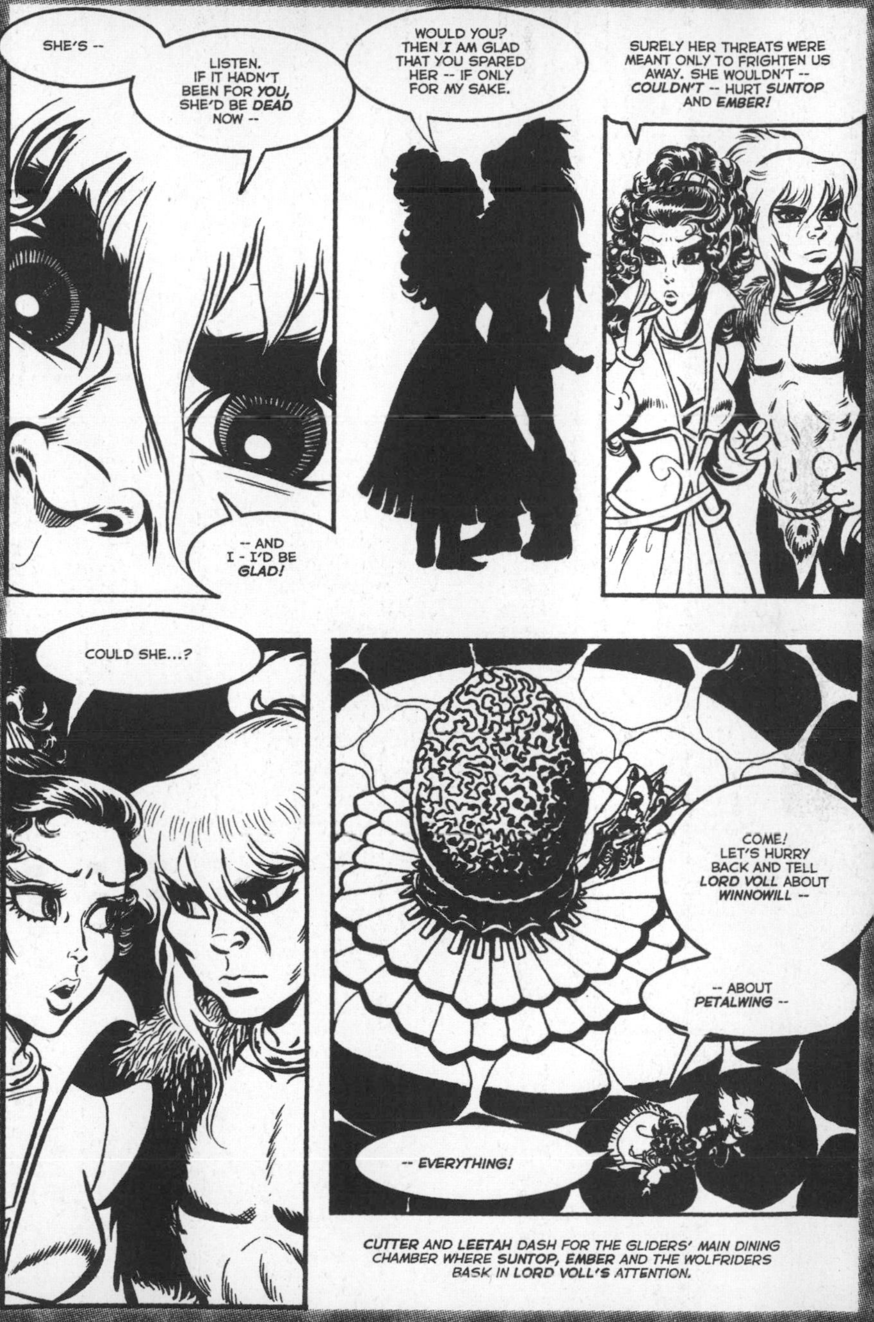
SHE'S --
LISTEN. IF IT HADN'T BEEN FOR YOU, SHE'D BE DEAD NOW --
-- AND I - I'D BE GLAD!
WOULD YOU? THEN I AM GLAD THAT YOU SPARED HER -- IF ONLY FOR MY SAKE.
SURELY HER THREATS WERE MEANT ONLY TO FRIGHTEN US AWAY. SHE WOULDN'T -- COULDN'T -- HURT SUNTOP AND EMBER!
COULD SHE...?
COME! LET'S HURRY BACK AND TELL LORD VOLL ABOUT WINNOWILL --
-- ABOUT PETALWING --
-- EVERYTHING!
CUTTER AND LEETAH DASH FOR THE GLIDERS' MAIN DINING CHAMBER WHERE SUNTOP, EMBER AND THE WOLFRIDERS BASK IN LORD VOLL'S ATTENTION.

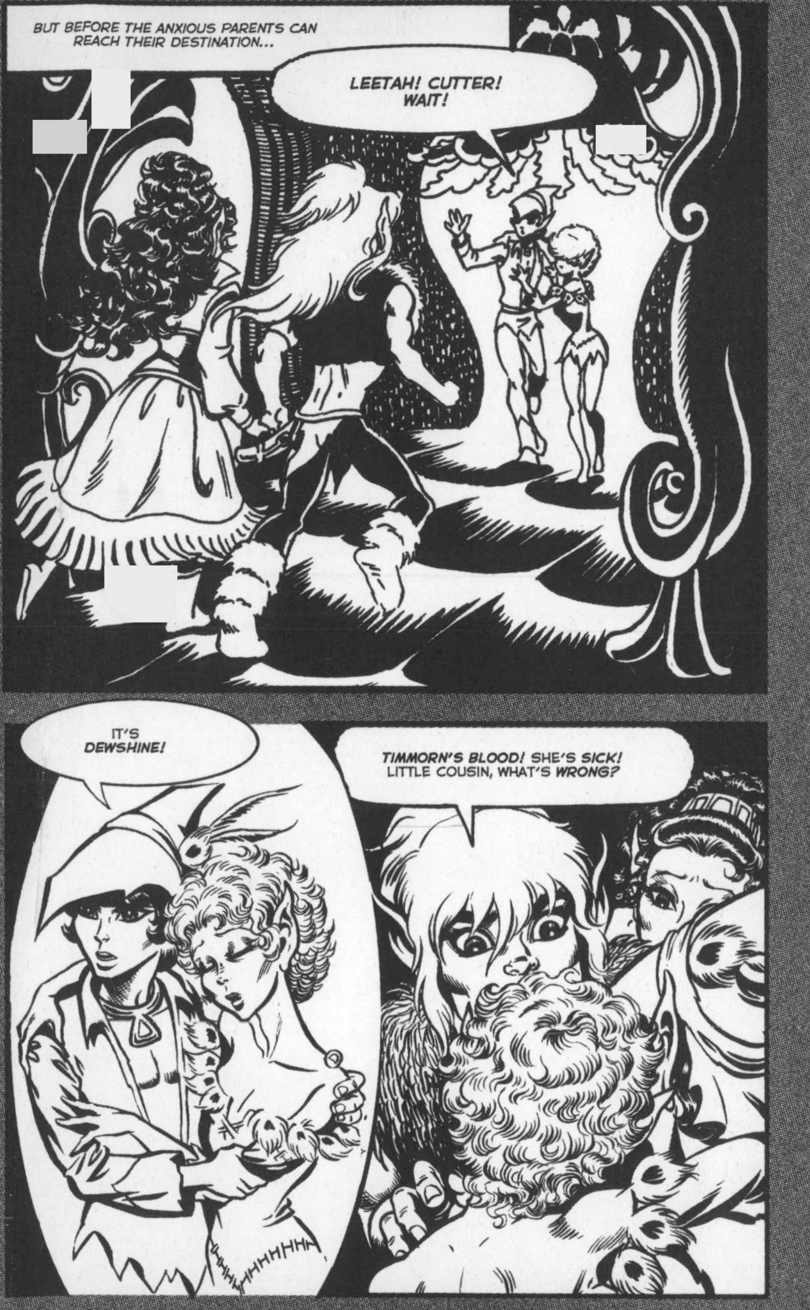
BUT BEFORE THE ANXIOUS PARENTS CAN REACH THEIR DESTINATION...
LEETAH! CUTTER! WAIT!
IT'S *DEWSHINE!*
TIMMORN'S BLOOD! SHE'S *SICK!* LITTLE COUSIN, WHAT'S *WRONG?*

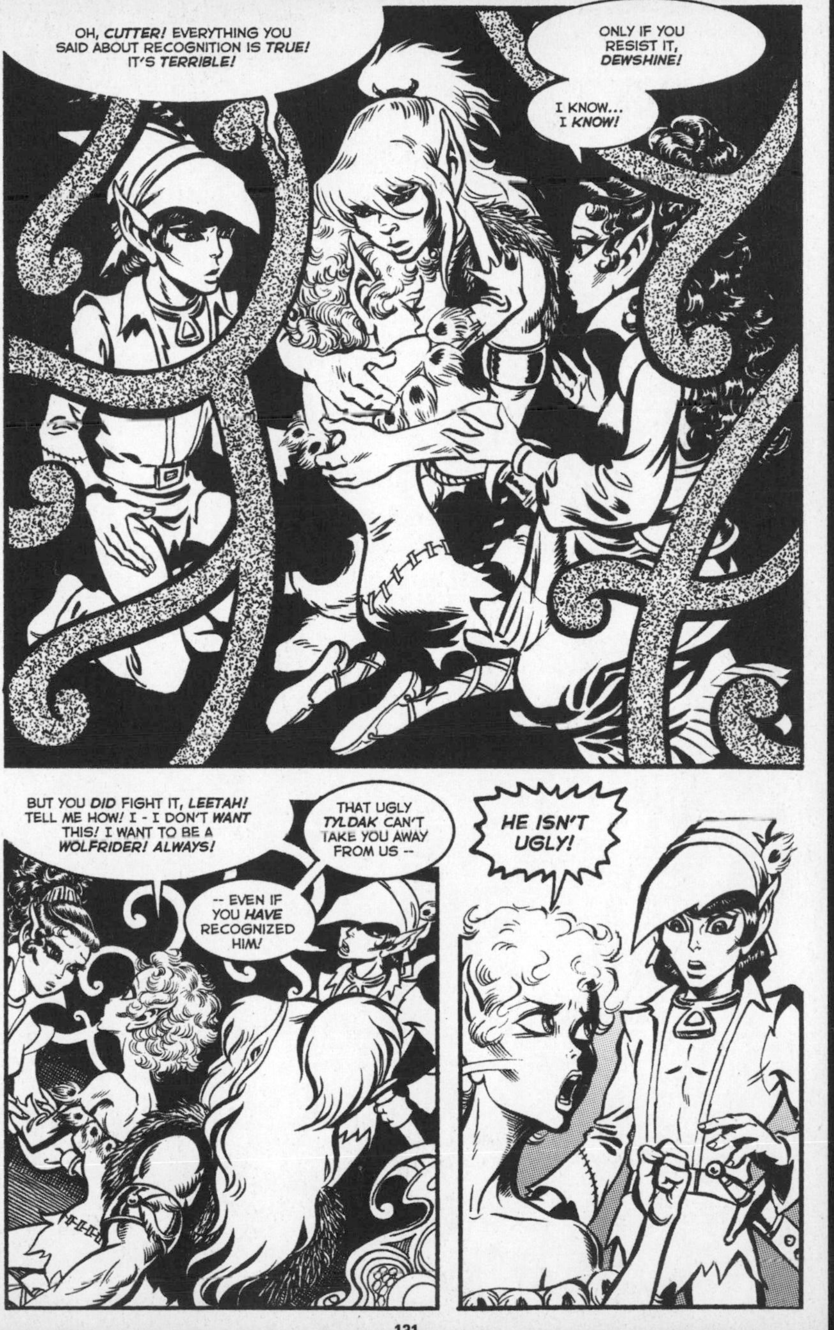
OH, CUTTER! EVERYTHING YOU SAID ABOUT RECOGNITION IS TRUE! IT'S TERRIBLE!
ONLY IF YOU RESIST IT, DEWSHINE!
I KNOW... I KNOW!
BUT YOU DID FIGHT IT, LEETAH! TELL ME HOW! I - I DON'T WANT THIS! I WANT TO BE A WOLFRIDER! ALWAYS!
THAT UGLY TYLDAK CAN'T TAKE YOU AWAY FROM US --
-- EVEN IF YOU HAVE RECOGNIZED HIM!
HE ISN'T UGLY!

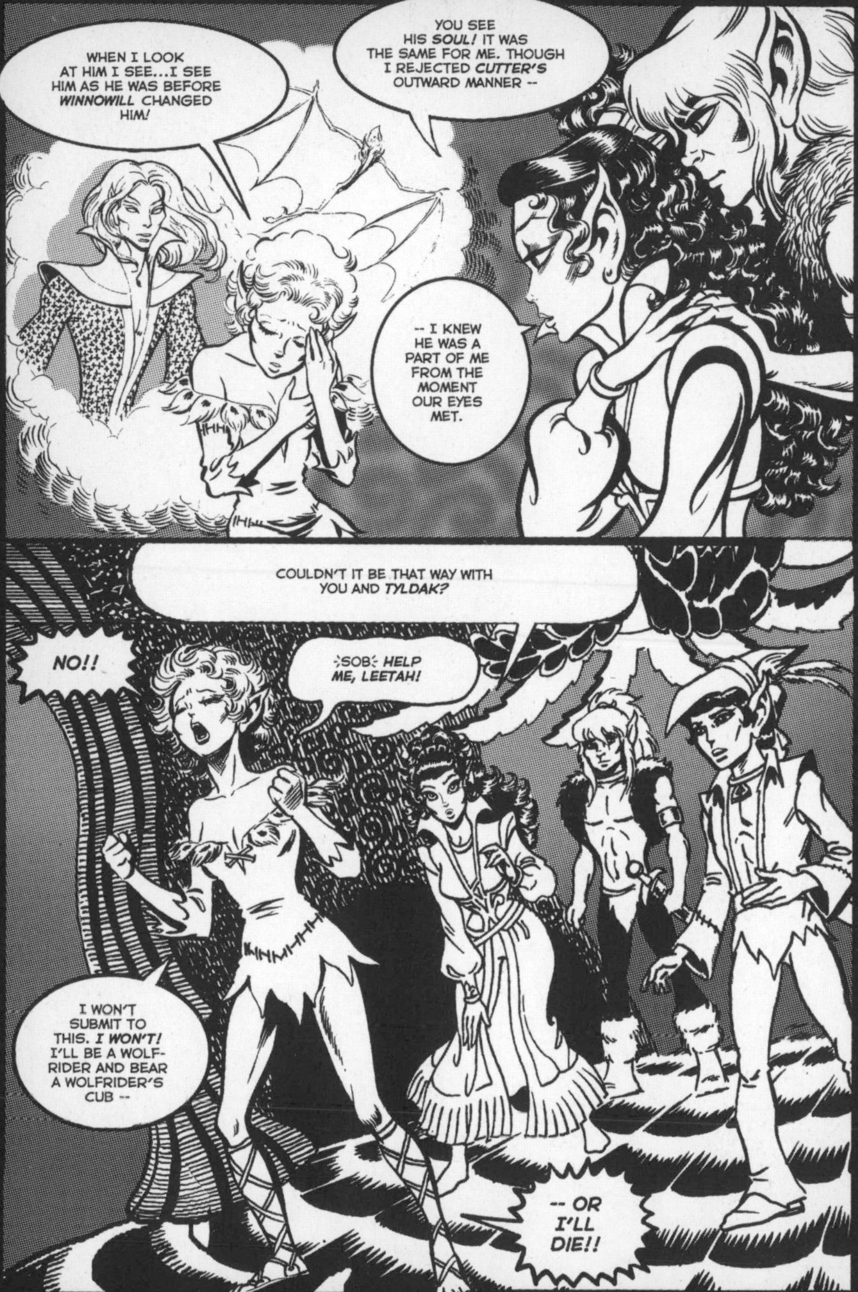

WHEN I LOOK AT HIM I SEE...I SEE HIM AS HE WAS BEFORE *WINNOWILL* CHANGED HIM!
YOU SEE HIS *SOUL!* IT WAS THE SAME FOR ME. THOUGH I REJECTED *CUTTER'S* OUTWARD MANNER --
-- I KNEW HE WAS A PART OF ME FROM THE MOMENT OUR EYES MET.
COULDN'T IT BE THAT WAY WITH YOU AND *TYLDAK?*
NO!!
-SOB- HELP ME, LEETAH!
I WON'T SUBMIT TO THIS. *I WON'T!* I'LL BE A WOLF-RIDER AND BEAR A WOLFRIDER'S CUB --
-- OR I'LL DIE!!

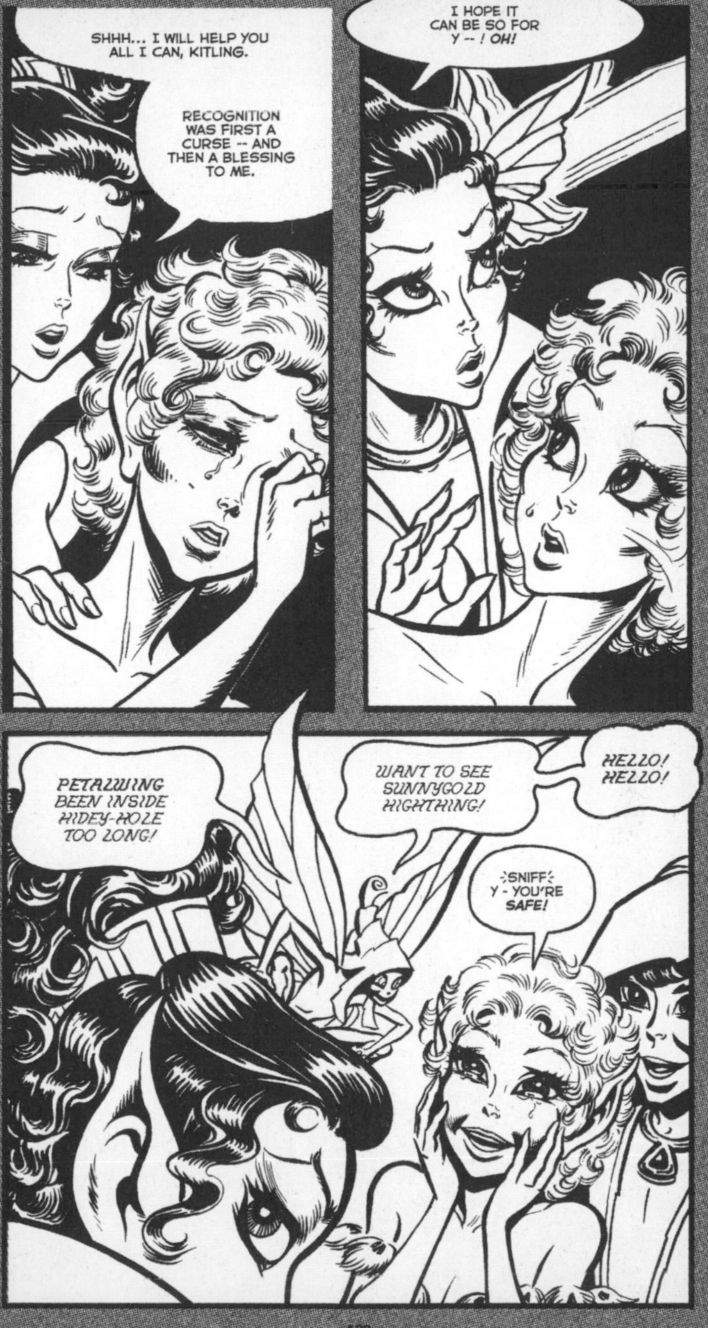
SHHH... I WILL HELP YOU ALL I CAN, KITLING.
RECOGNITION WAS FIRST A CURSE -- AND THEN A BLESSING TO ME.
I HOPE IT CAN BE SO FOR Y -- ! OH!
PETALWING BEEN INSIDE HIDEY-HOLE TOO LONG!
WANT TO SEE SUNNYGOLD HIGHTHING!
HELLO! HELLO!
SNIFF Y - YOU'RE SAFE!

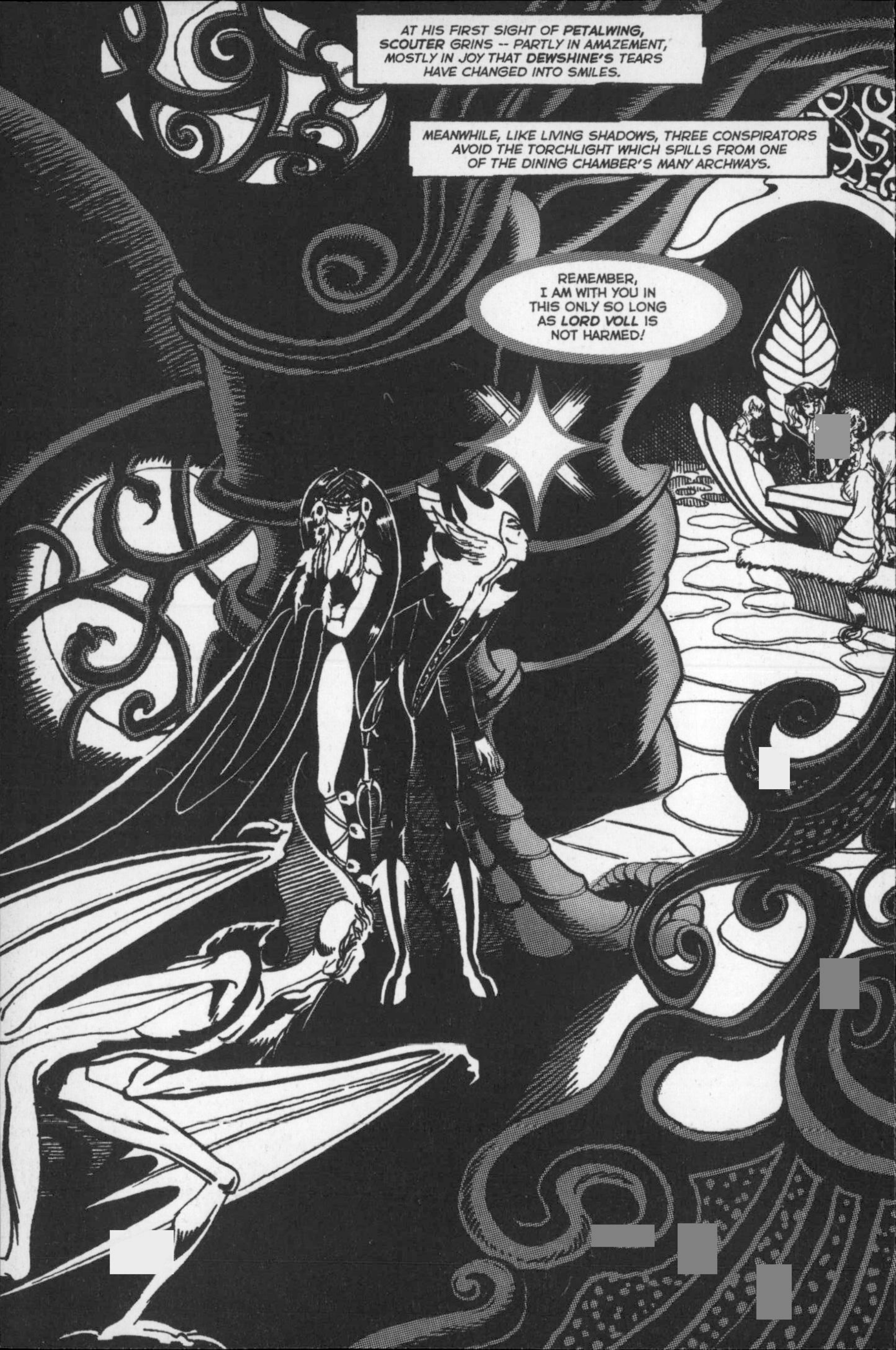
AT HIS FIRST SIGHT OF PETALWING, SCOUTER GRINS -- PARTLY IN AMAZEMENT, MOSTLY IN JOY THAT DEWSHINE'S TEARS HAVE CHANGED INTO SMILES.
MEANWHILE, LIKE LIVING SHADOWS, THREE CONSPIRATORS AVOID THE TORCHLIGHT WHICH SPILLS FROM ONE OF THE DINING CHAMBER'S MANY ARCHWAYS.
REMEMBER, I AM WITH YOU IN THIS ONLY SO LONG AS LORD VOLL IS NOT HARMED!

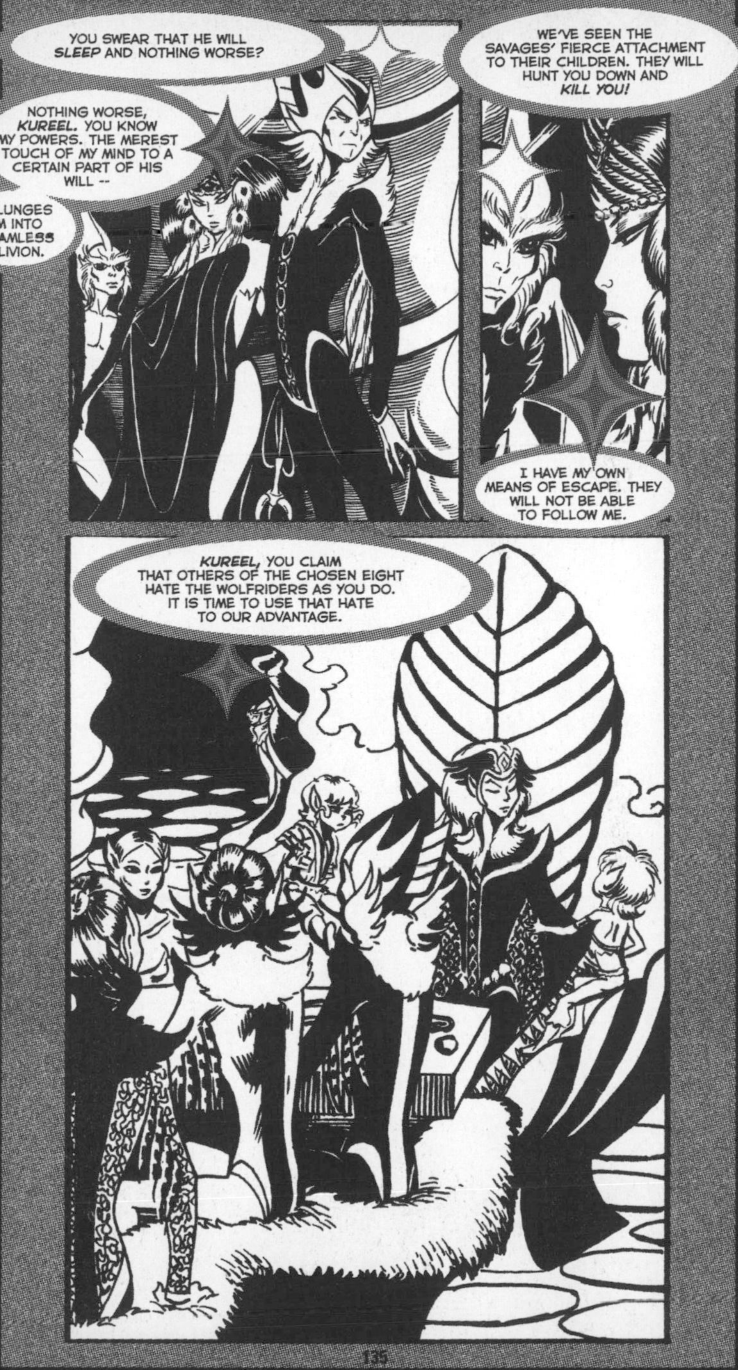
YOU SWEAR THAT HE WILL SLEEP AND NOTHING WORSE?
NOTHING WORSE, KUREEL. YOU KNOW MY POWERS. THE MEREST TOUCH OF MY MIND TO A CERTAIN PART OF HIS WILL --
-- PLUNGES HIM INTO DREAMLESS OBLIVION.
WE'VE SEEN THE SAVAGES' FIERCE ATTACHMENT TO THEIR CHILDREN. THEY WILL HUNT YOU DOWN AND KILL YOU!
I HAVE MY OWN MEANS OF ESCAPE. THEY WILL NOT BE ABLE TO FOLLOW ME.
KUREEL, YOU CLAIM THAT OTHERS OF THE CHOSEN EIGHT HATE THE WOLFRIDERS AS YOU DO. IT IS TIME TO USE THAT HATE TO OUR ADVANTAGE.

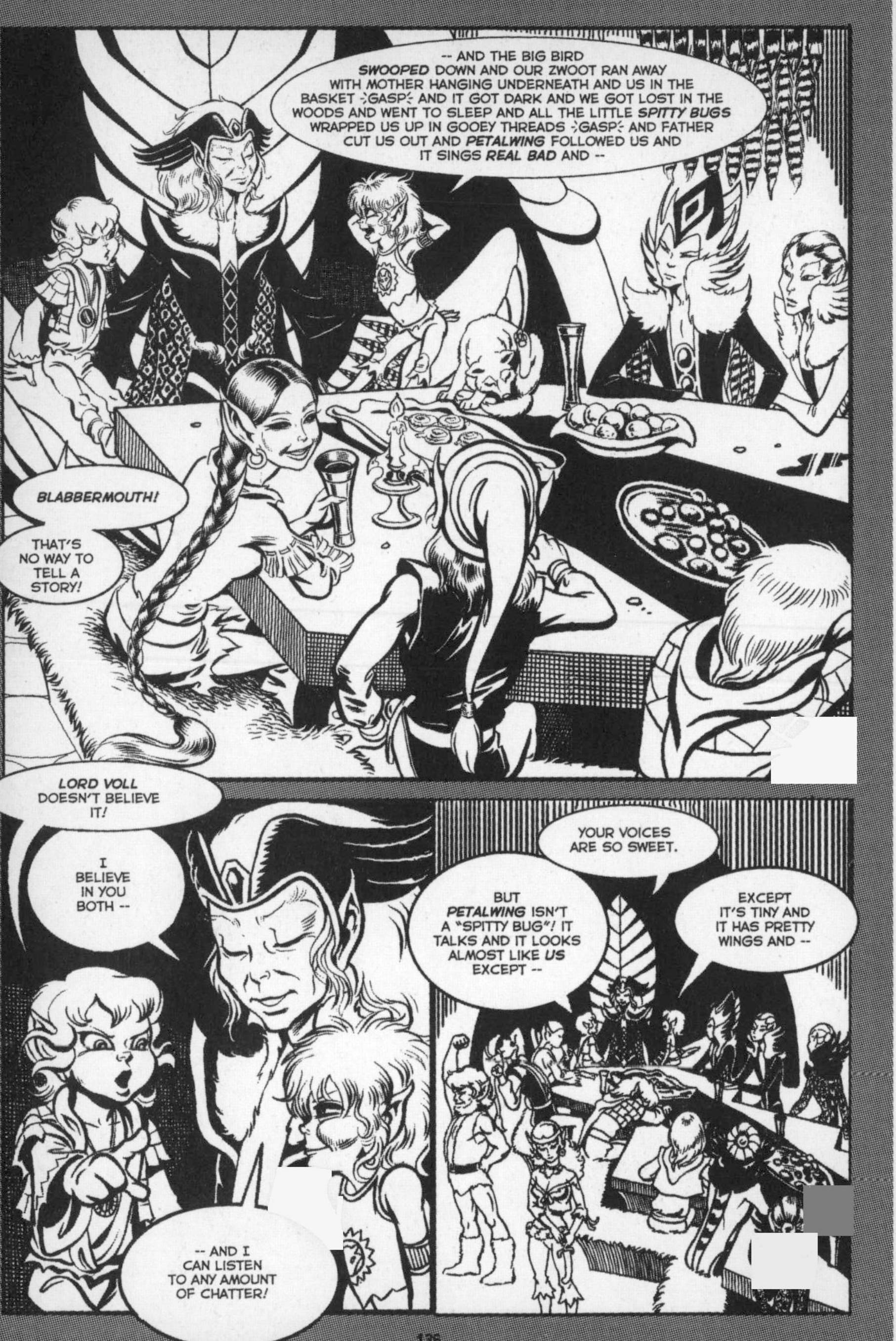
-- AND THE BIG BIRD SWOOPED DOWN AND OUR ZWOOT RAN AWAY WITH MOTHER HANGING UNDERNEATH AND US IN THE BASKET -GASP- AND IT GOT DARK AND WE GOT LOST IN THE WOODS AND WENT TO SLEEP AND ALL THE LITTLE SPITTY BUGS WRAPPED US UP IN GOOEY THREADS -GASP- AND FATHER CUT US OUT AND PETALWING FOLLOWED US AND IT SINGS REAL BAD AND --
BLABBERMOUTH!
THAT'S NO WAY TO TELL A STORY!
LORD VOLL DOESN'T BELIEVE IT!
I BELIEVE IN YOU BOTH --
-- AND I CAN LISTEN TO ANY AMOUNT OF CHATTER!
YOUR VOICES ARE SO SWEET.
BUT PETALWING ISN'T A "SPITTY BUG"! IT TALKS AND IT LOOKS ALMOST LIKE US EXCEPT --
EXCEPT IT'S TINY AND IT HAS PRETTY WINGS AND --

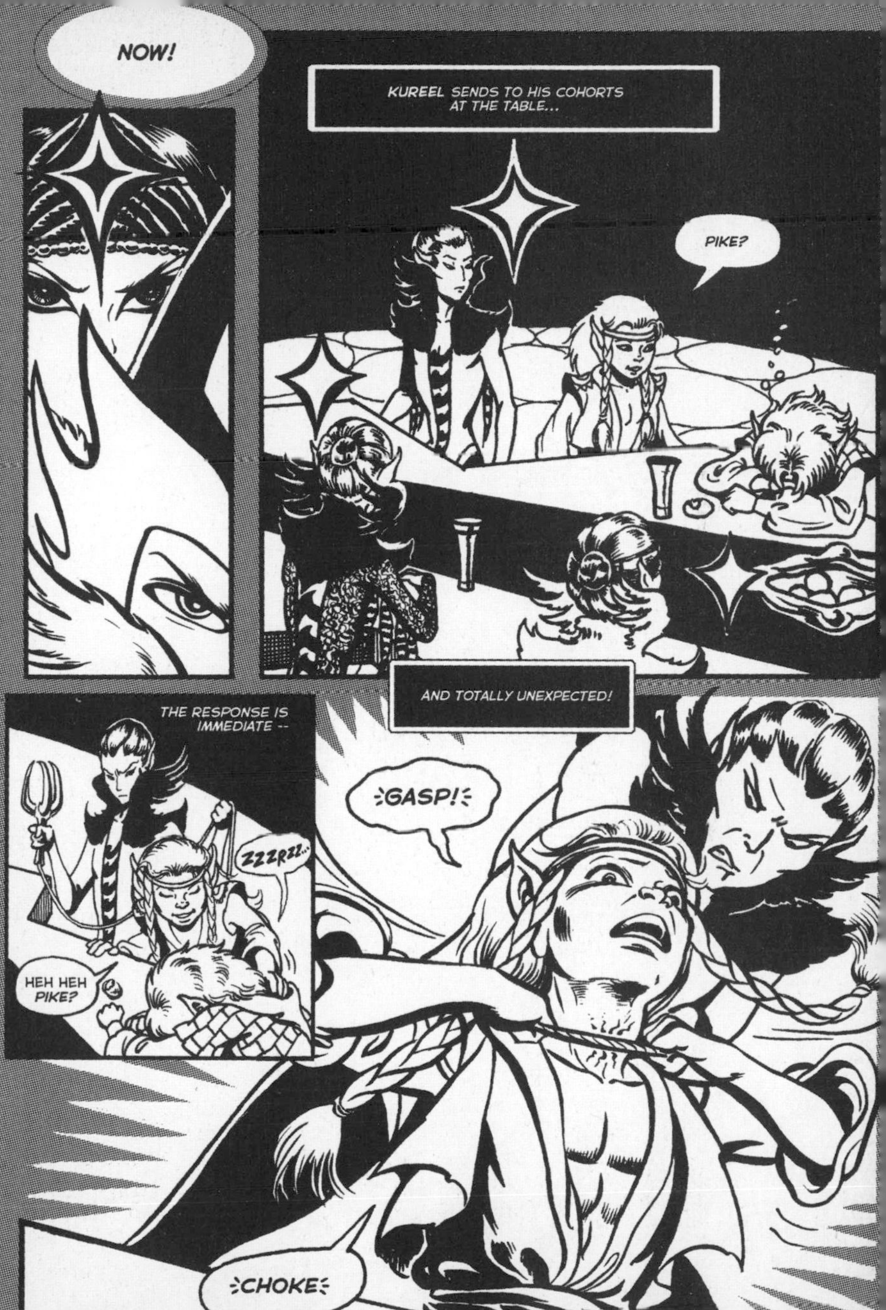
NOW!
KUREEL SENDS TO HIS COHORTS AT THE TABLE...
PIKE?
THE RESPONSE IS IMMEDIATE --
ZZZRZZ...
HEH HEH PIKE?
AND TOTALLY UNEXPECTED!
GASP!
CHOKE

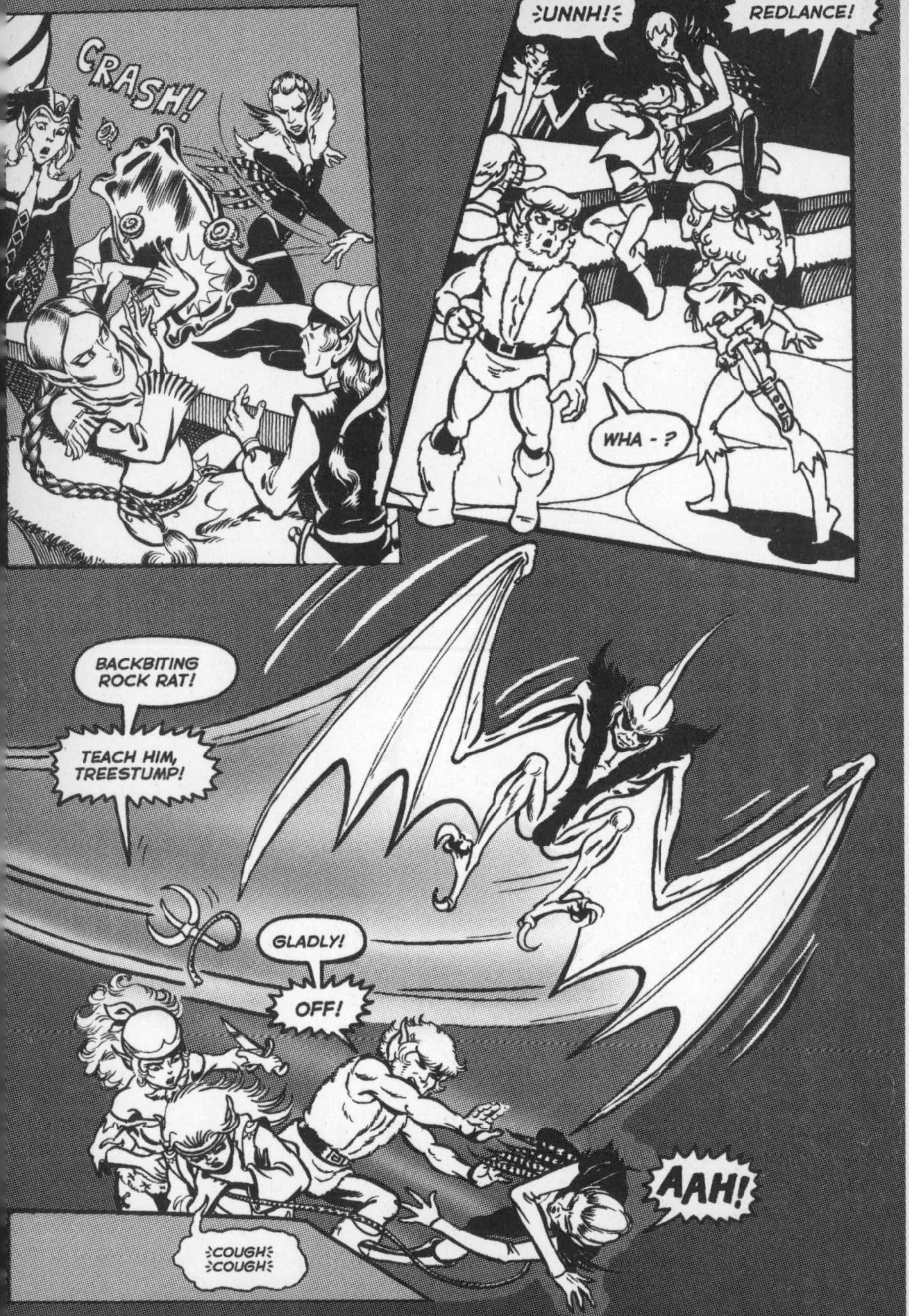
CRASH!
UNNH!
REDLANCE!
WHA - ?
BACKBITING ROCK RAT!
TEACH HIM, TREESTUMP!
GLADLY!
OFF!
AAH!
COUGH COUGH

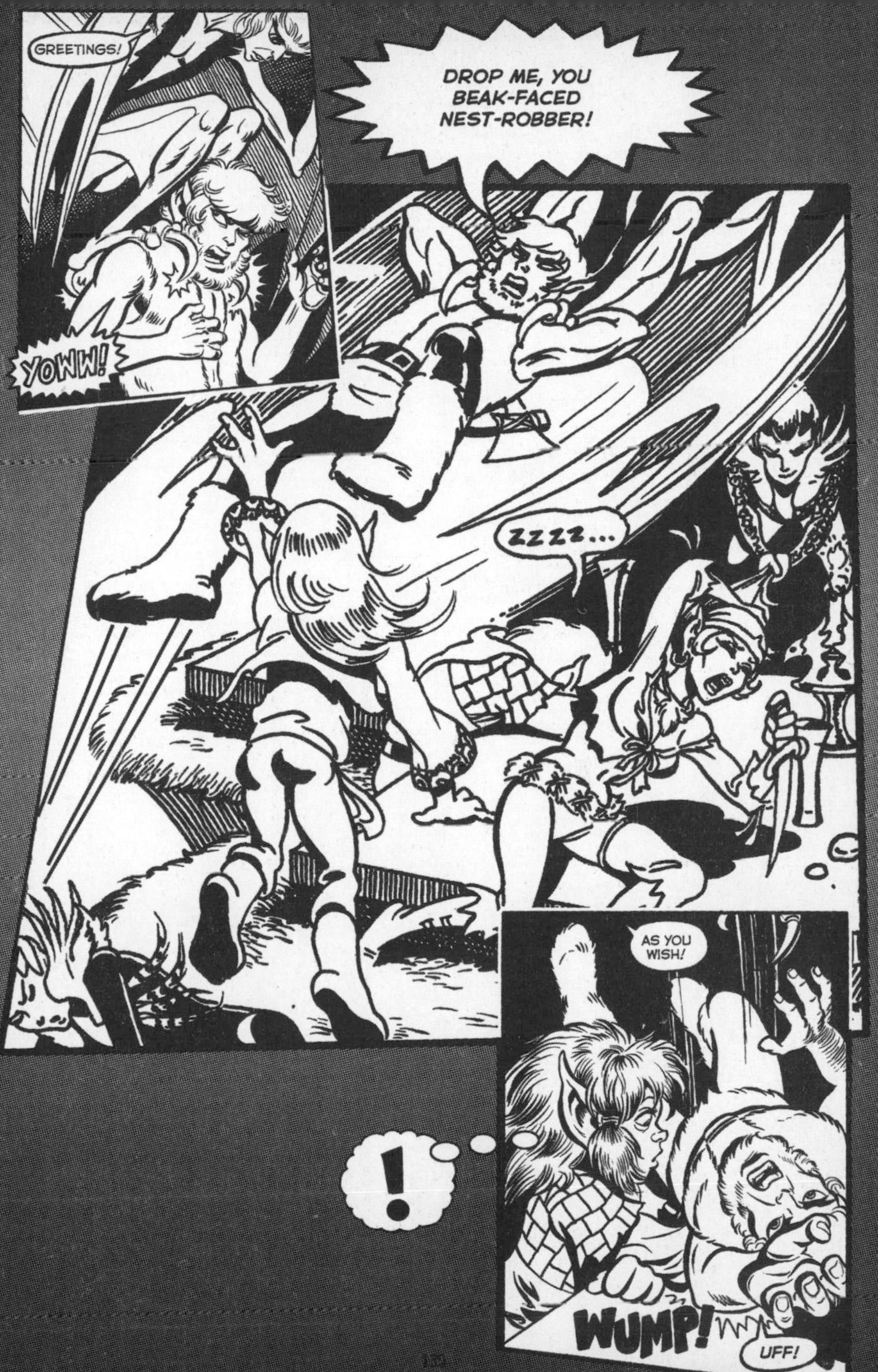
GREETINGS!
YOWW!
DROP ME, YOU BEAK-FACED NEST-ROBBER!
ZZZZ...
AS YOU WISH!
!
WUMP!
UFF!

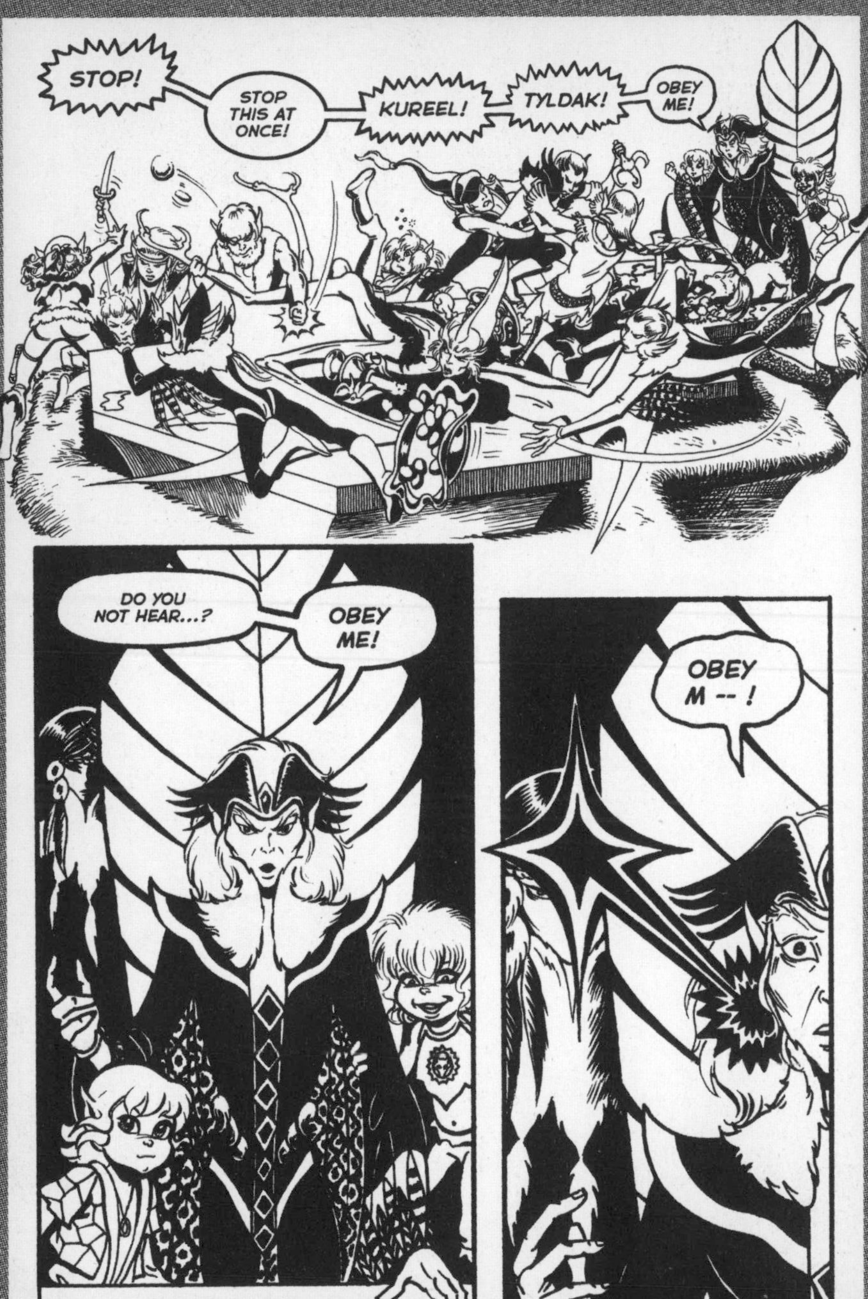
STOP!
STOP THIS AT ONCE!
KUREEL!
TYLDAK!
OBEY ME!
DO YOU NOT HEAR...?
OBEY ME!
OBEY M -- !

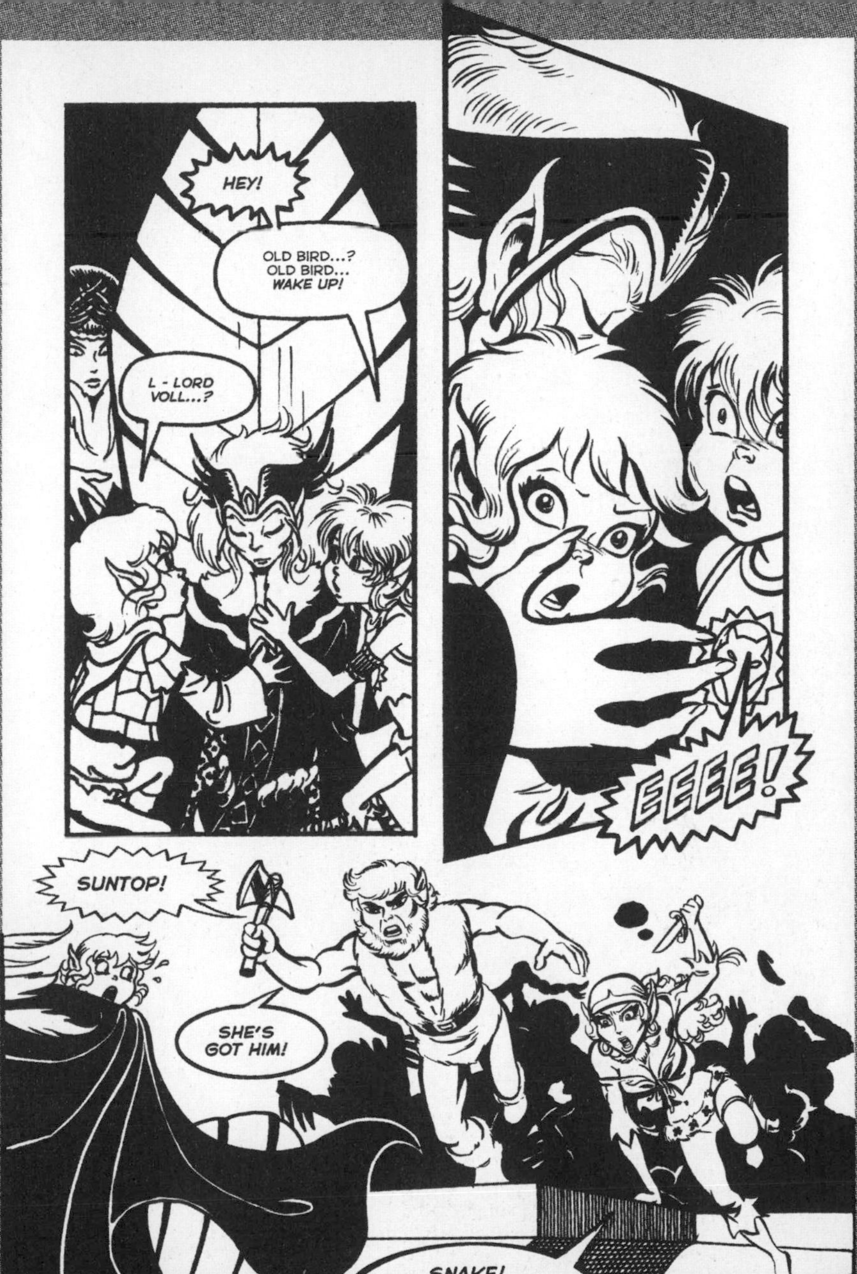
HEY!
OLD BIRD...? OLD BIRD... WAKE UP!
L - LORD VOLL...?
EEEE!
SUNTOP!
SHE'S GOT HIM!
SNAKE! DROP HIM OR DIE!

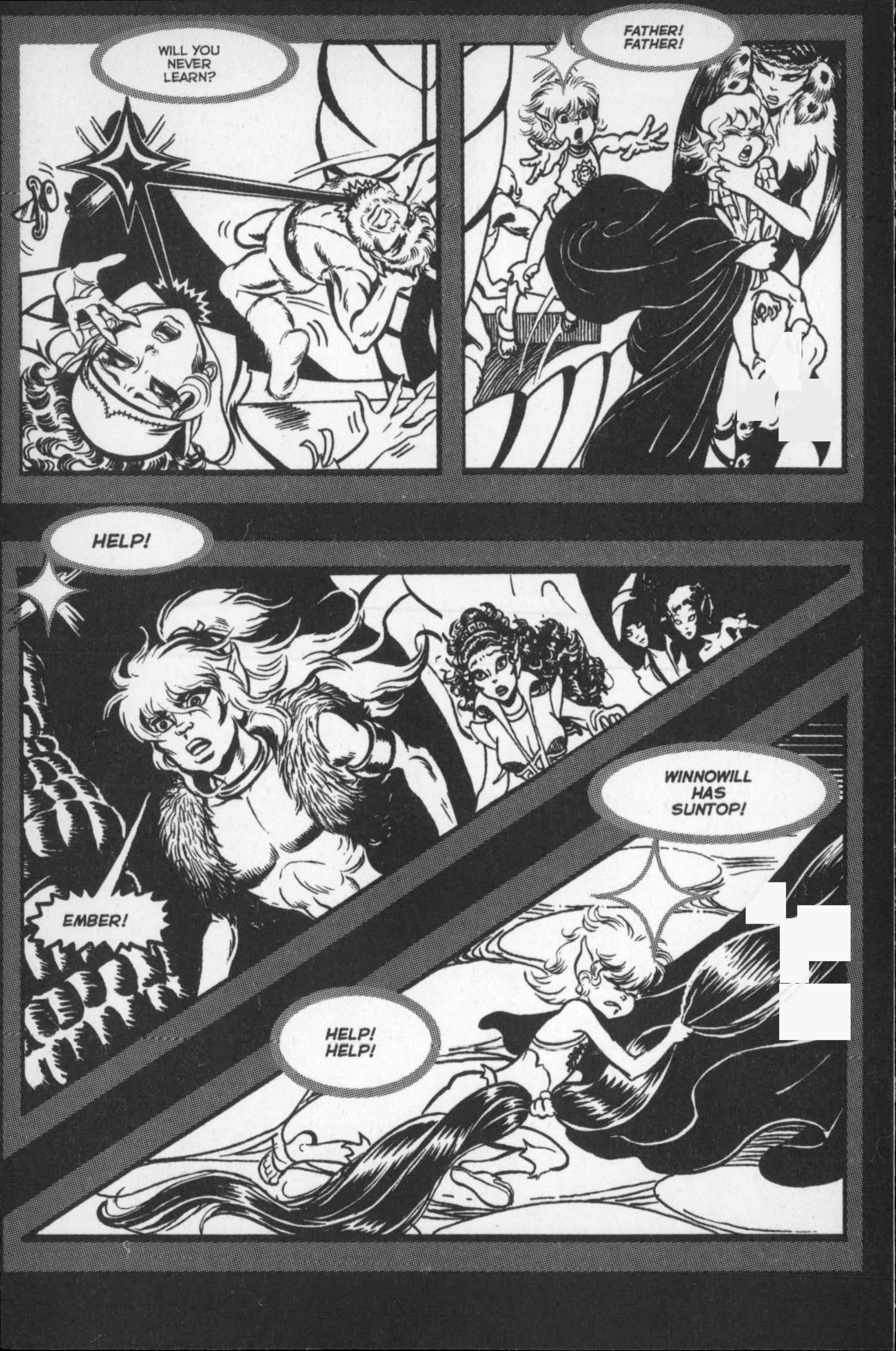

WILL YOU NEVER LEARN?
FATHER! FATHER!
HELP!
EMBER!
WINNOWILL HAS SUNTOP!
HELP! HELP!

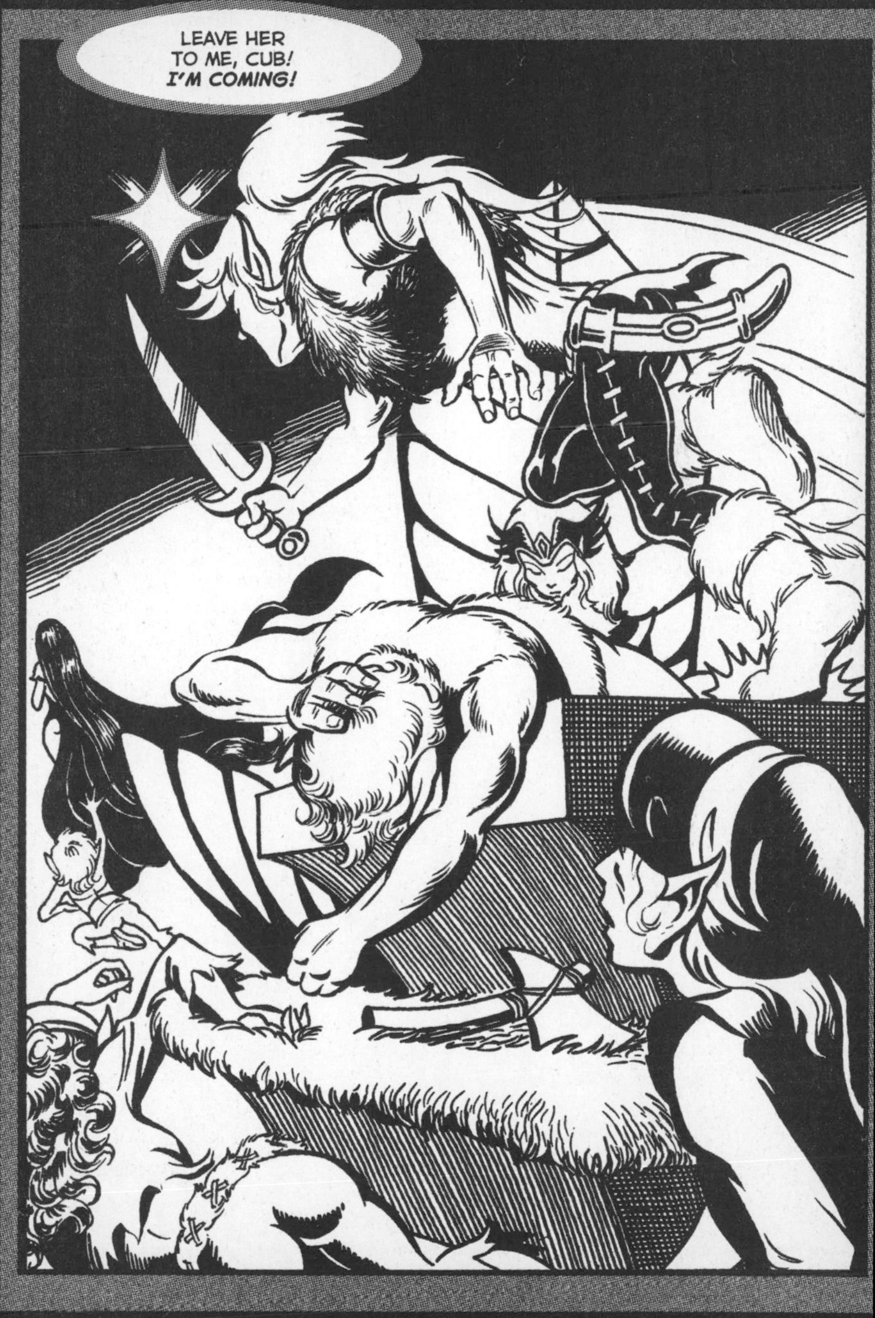
LEAVE HER TO ME, CUB! *I'M COMING!*

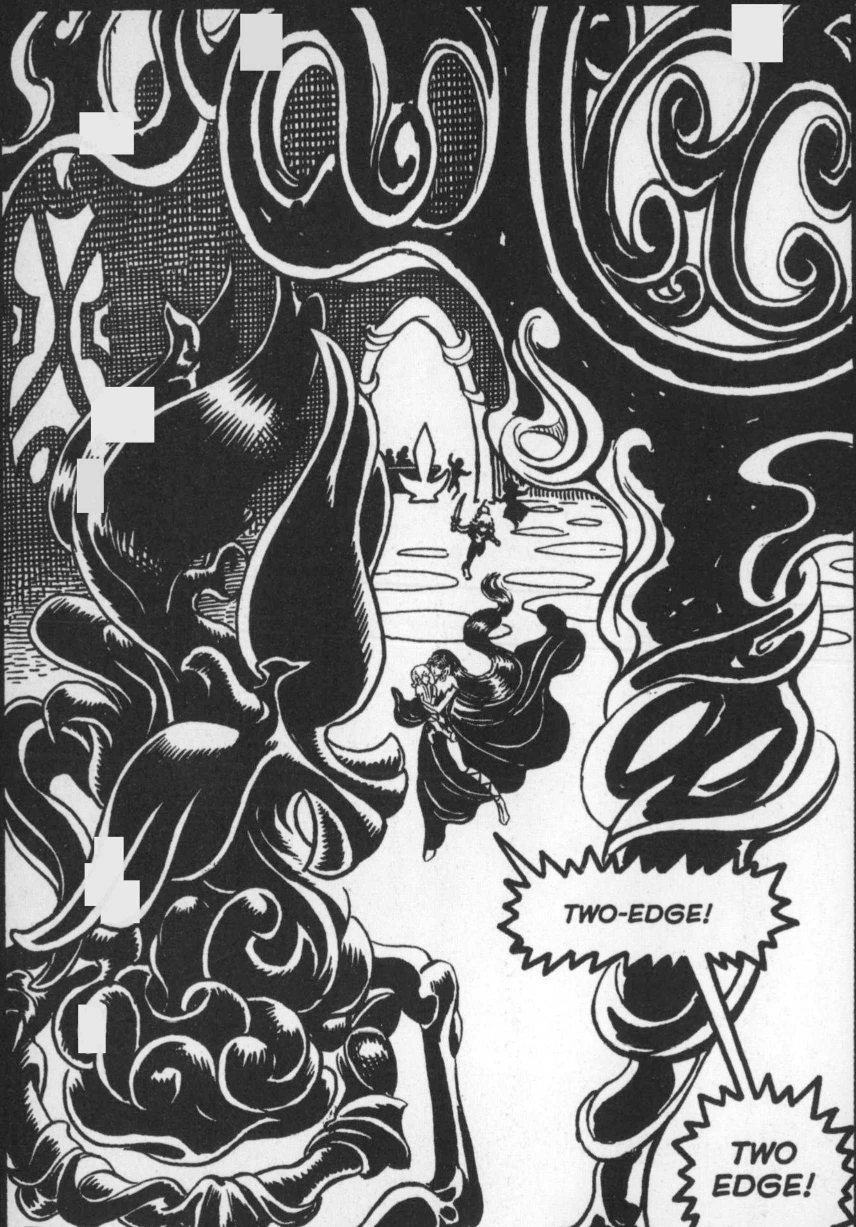
TWO-EDGE!
TWO EDGE!

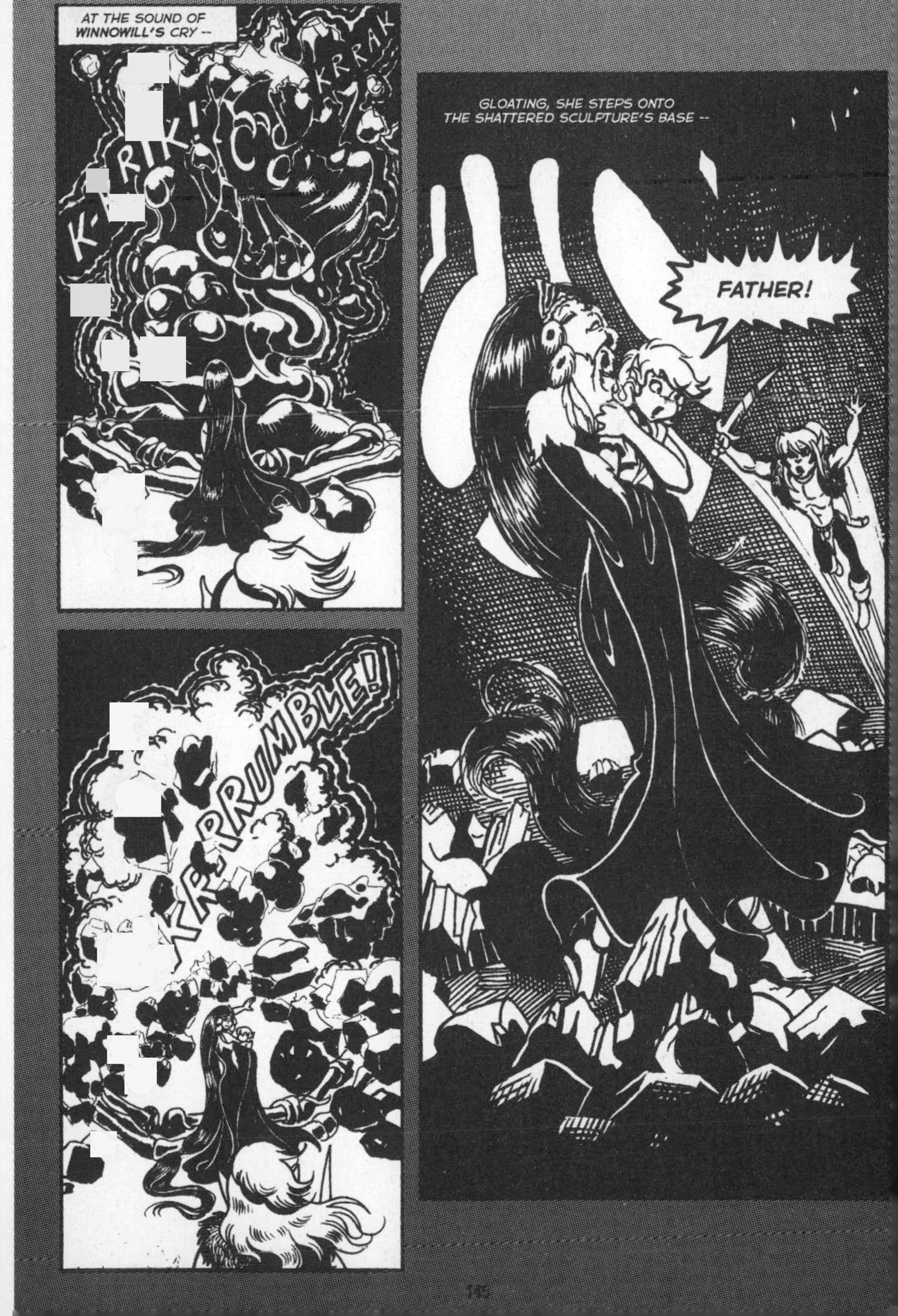
AT THE SOUND OF WINNOWILL'S CRY --
KRRAK
K-RIIK!
KRRUMBLE!
GLOATING, SHE STEPS ONTO THE SHATTERED SCULPTURE'S BASE --
FATHER!

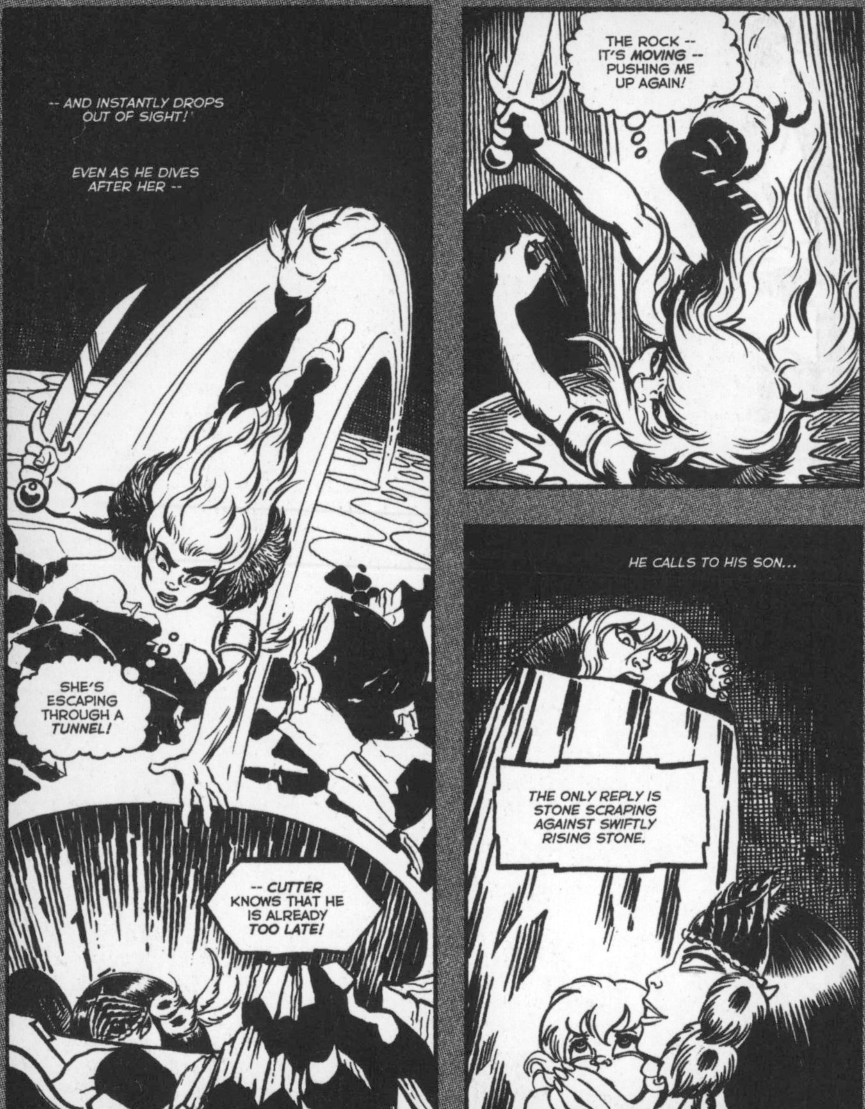
-- AND INSTANTLY DROPS OUT OF SIGHT!
EVEN AS HE DIVES AFTER HER --
SHE'S ESCAPING THROUGH A *TUNNEL!*
-- *CUTTER* KNOWS THAT HE IS ALREADY *TOO LATE!*
THE ROCK -- IT'S *MOVING* -- PUSHING ME UP AGAIN!
HE CALLS TO HIS SON...
THE ONLY REPLY IS STONE SCRAPING AGAINST SWIFTLY RISING STONE.

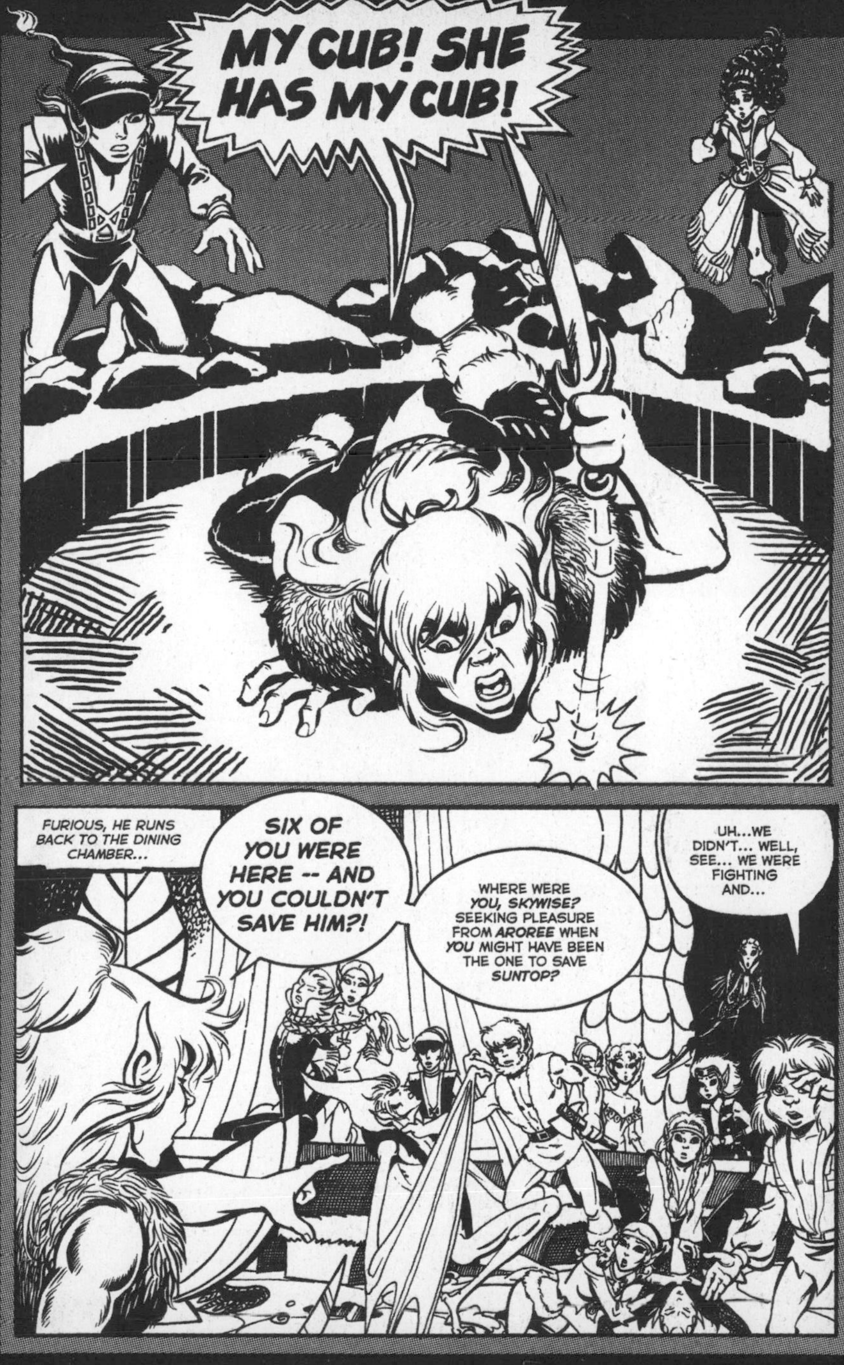
MY CUB! SHE HAS MY CUB!
FURIOUS, HE RUNS BACK TO THE DINING CHAMBER...
SIX OF YOU WERE HERE -- AND YOU COULDN'T SAVE HIM?!
WHERE WERE YOU, SKYWISE? SEEKING PLEASURE FROM AROREE WHEN YOU MIGHT HAVE BEEN THE ONE TO SAVE SUNTOP?
UH...WE DIDN'T... WELL, SEE... WE WERE FIGHTING AND...

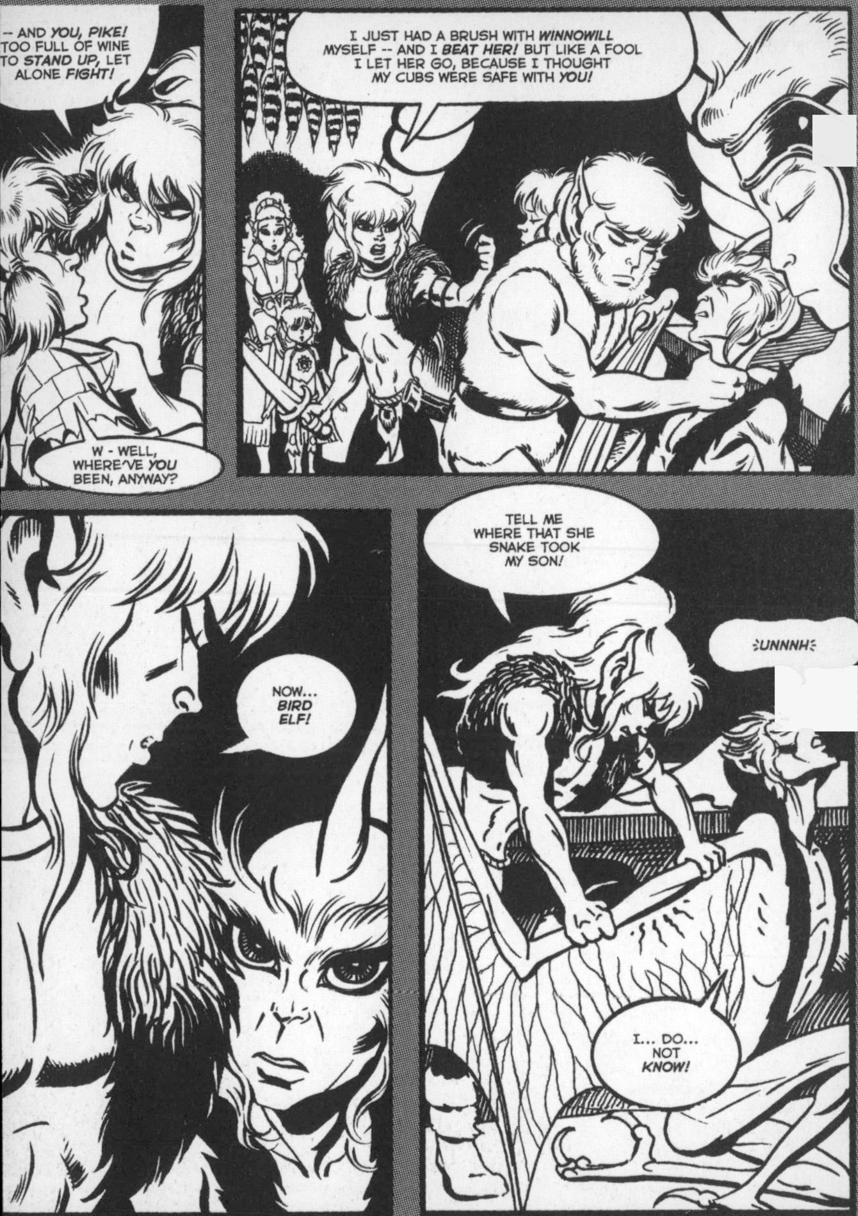
-- AND YOU, PIKE! TOO FULL OF WINE TO STAND UP, LET ALONE FIGHT!
W - WELL, WHERE'VE YOU BEEN, ANYWAY?
I JUST HAD A BRUSH WITH WINNOWILL MYSELF -- AND I BEAT HER! BUT LIKE A FOOL I LET HER GO, BECAUSE I THOUGHT MY CUBS WERE SAFE WITH YOU!
NOW... BIRD ELF!
TELL ME WHERE THAT SHE SNAKE TOOK MY SON!
UNNNH
I... DO... NOT KNOW!

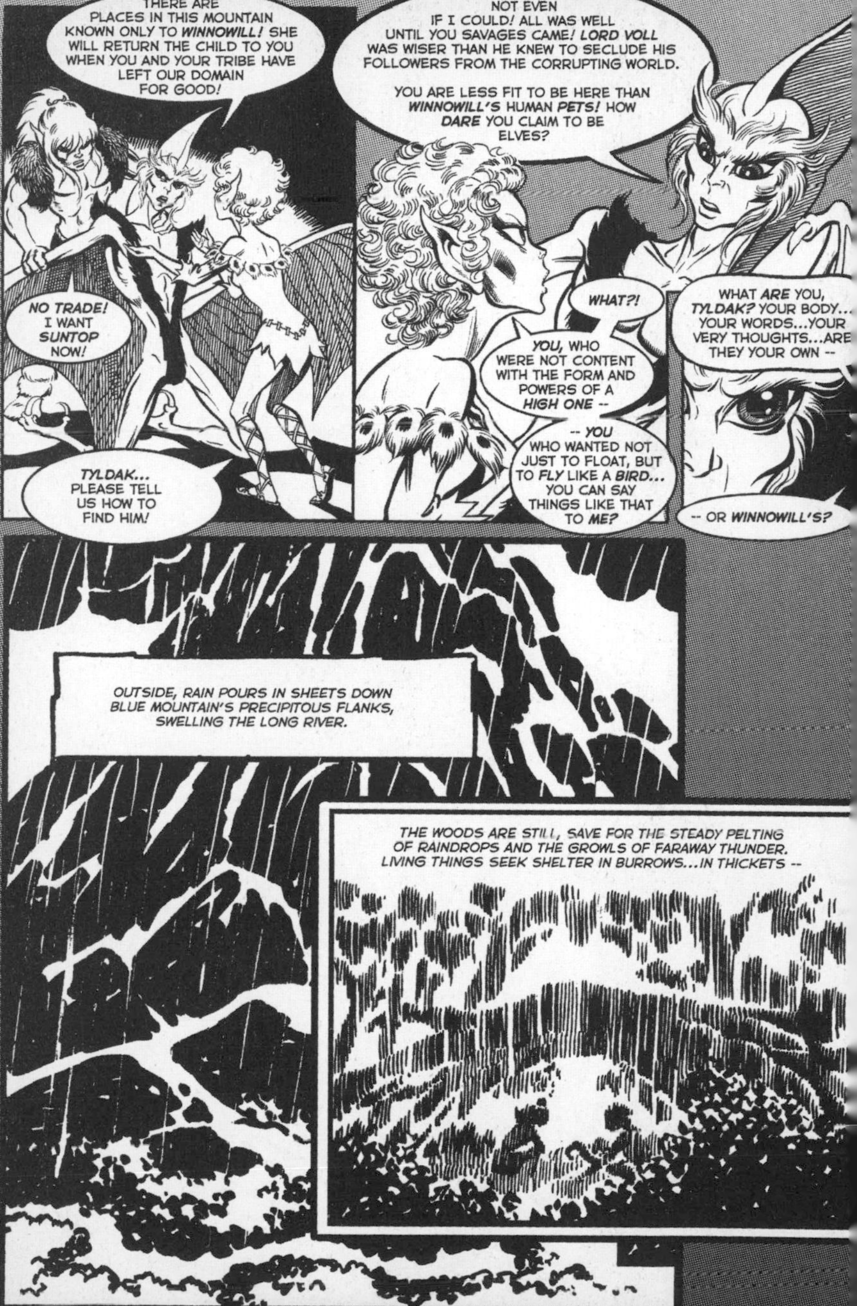
THERE ARE PLACES IN THIS MOUNTAIN KNOWN ONLY TO WINNOWILL! SHE WILL RETURN THE CHILD TO YOU WHEN YOU AND YOUR TRIBE HAVE LEFT OUR DOMAIN FOR GOOD!
NO TRADE! I WANT SUNTOP NOW!
TYLDAK... PLEASE TELL US HOW TO FIND HIM!
NOT EVEN IF I COULD! ALL WAS WELL UNTIL YOU SAVAGES CAME! LORD VOLL WAS WISER THAN HE KNEW TO SECLUDE HIS FOLLOWERS FROM THE CORRUPTING WORLD.
YOU ARE LESS FIT TO BE HERE THAN WINNOWILL'S HUMAN PETS! HOW DARE YOU CLAIM TO BE ELVES?
WHAT?!
YOU, WHO WERE NOT CONTENT WITH THE FORM AND POWERS OF A HIGH ONE --
-- YOU WHO WANTED NOT JUST TO FLOAT, BUT TO FLY LIKE A BIRD... YOU CAN SAY THINGS LIKE THAT TO ME?
WHAT ARE YOU, TYLDAK? YOUR BODY... YOUR WORDS...YOUR VERY THOUGHTS...ARE THEY YOUR OWN --
-- OR WINNOWILL'S?
OUTSIDE, RAIN POURS IN SHEETS DOWN BLUE MOUNTAIN'S PRECIPITOUS FLANKS, SWELLING THE LONG RIVER.
THE WOODS ARE STILL, SAVE FOR THE STEADY PELTING OF RAINDROPS AND THE GROWLS OF FARAWAY THUNDER. LIVING THINGS SEEK SHELTER IN BURROWS...IN THICKETS --

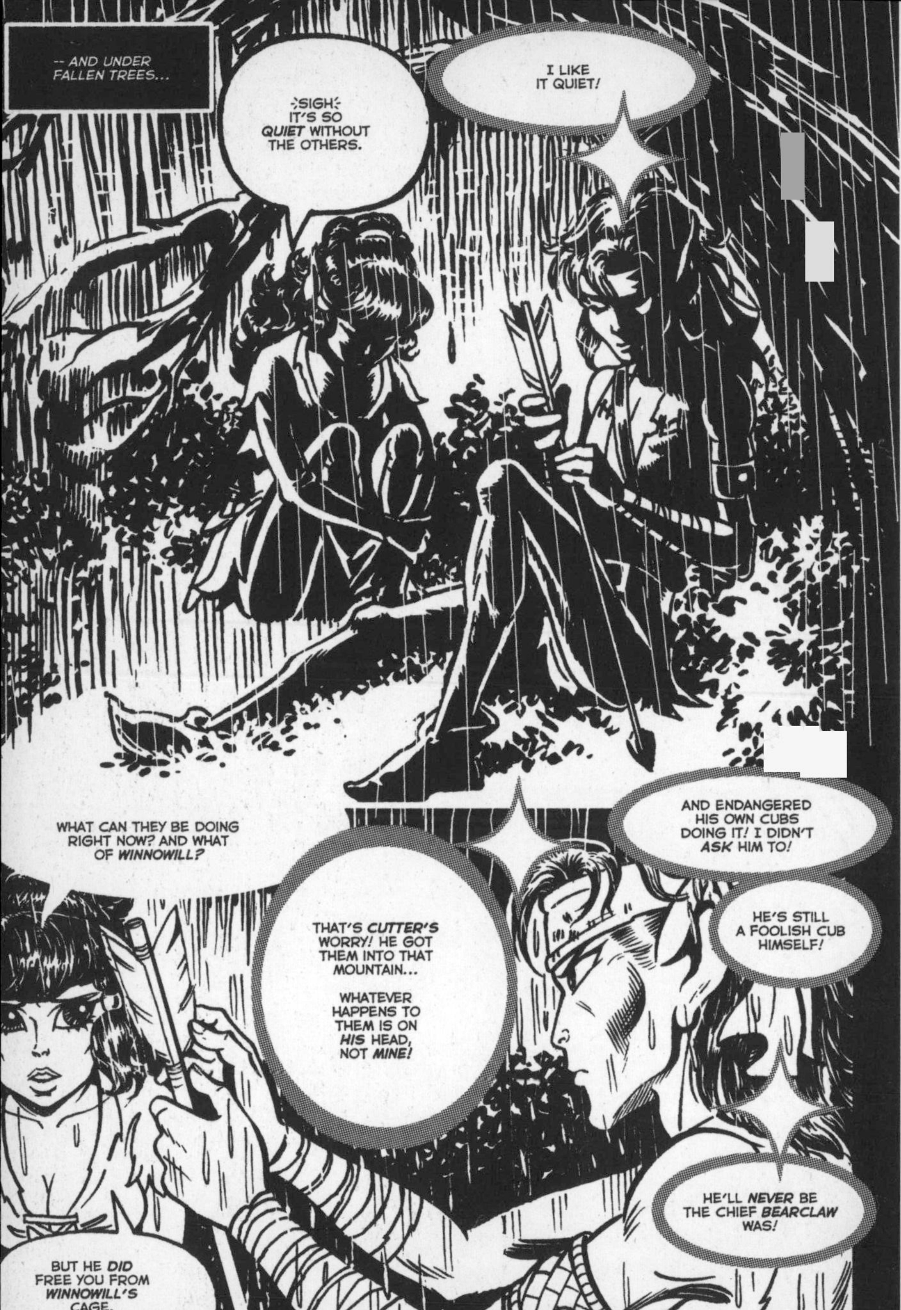
-- AND UNDER FALLEN TREES...
SIGH IT'S SO QUIET WITHOUT THE OTHERS.
I LIKE IT QUIET!
WHAT CAN THEY BE DOING RIGHT NOW? AND WHAT OF WINNOWILL?
THAT'S CUTTER'S WORRY! HE GOT THEM INTO THAT MOUNTAIN... WHATEVER HAPPENS TO THEM IS ON HIS HEAD, NOT MINE!
AND ENDANGERED HIS OWN CUBS DOING IT! I DIDN'T ASK HIM TO!
HE'S STILL A FOOLISH CUB HIMSELF!
BUT HE DID FREE YOU FROM WINNOWILL'S CAGE.
HE'LL NEVER BE THE CHIEF BEARCLAW WAS!

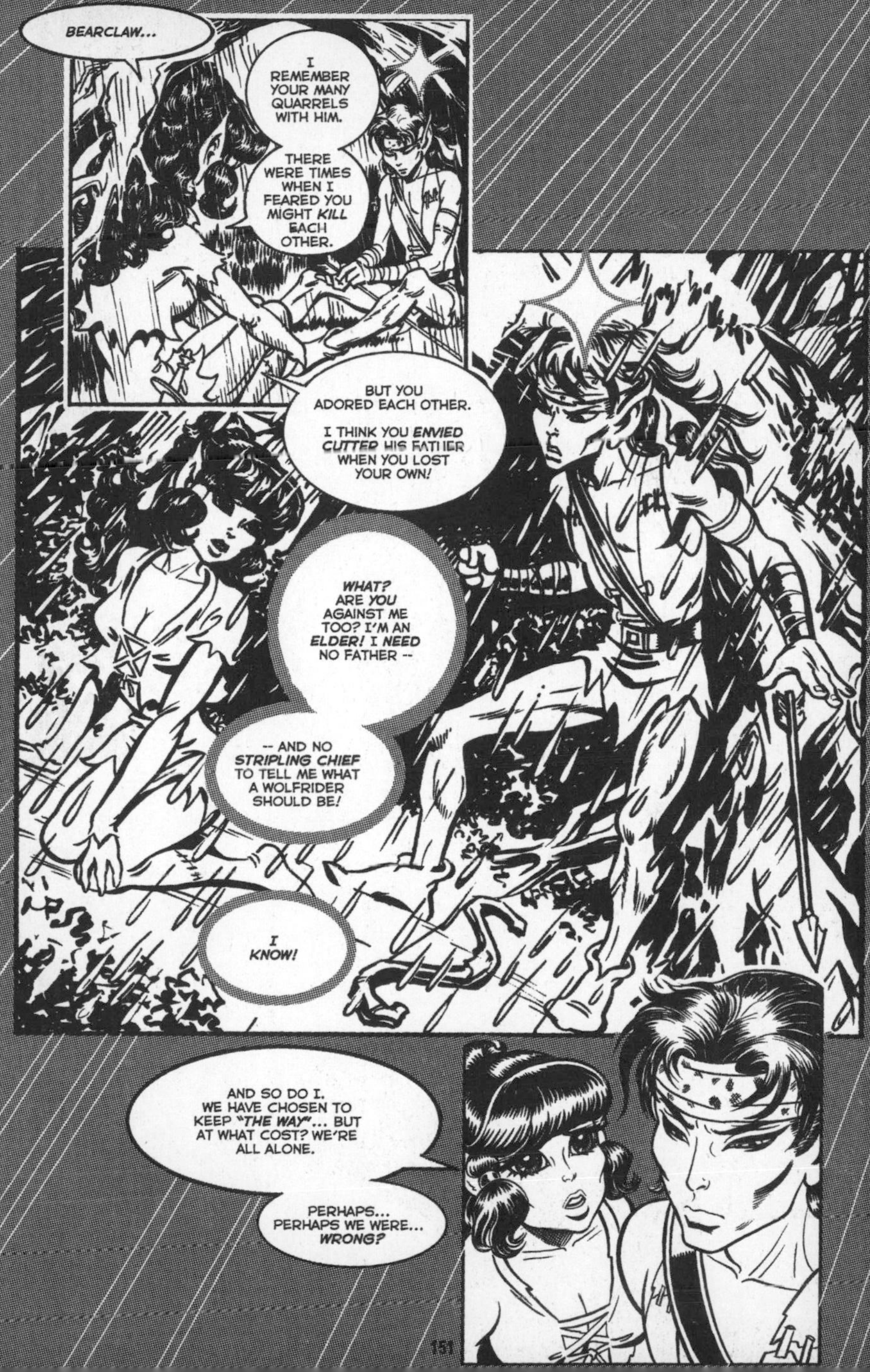
BEARCLAW...
I REMEMBER YOUR MANY QUARRELS WITH HIM.
THERE WERE TIMES WHEN I FEARED YOU MIGHT KILL EACH OTHER.
BUT YOU ADORED EACH OTHER.
I THINK YOU ENVIED CUTTER HIS FATHER WHEN YOU LOST YOUR OWN!
WHAT? ARE YOU AGAINST ME TOO? I'M AN ELDER! I NEED NO FATHER --
-- AND NO STRIPLING CHIEF TO TELL ME WHAT A WOLFRIDER SHOULD BE!
I KNOW!
AND SO DO I. WE HAVE CHOSEN TO KEEP "THE WAY"... BUT AT WHAT COST? WE'RE ALL ALONE.
PERHAPS... PERHAPS WE WERE... WRONG?

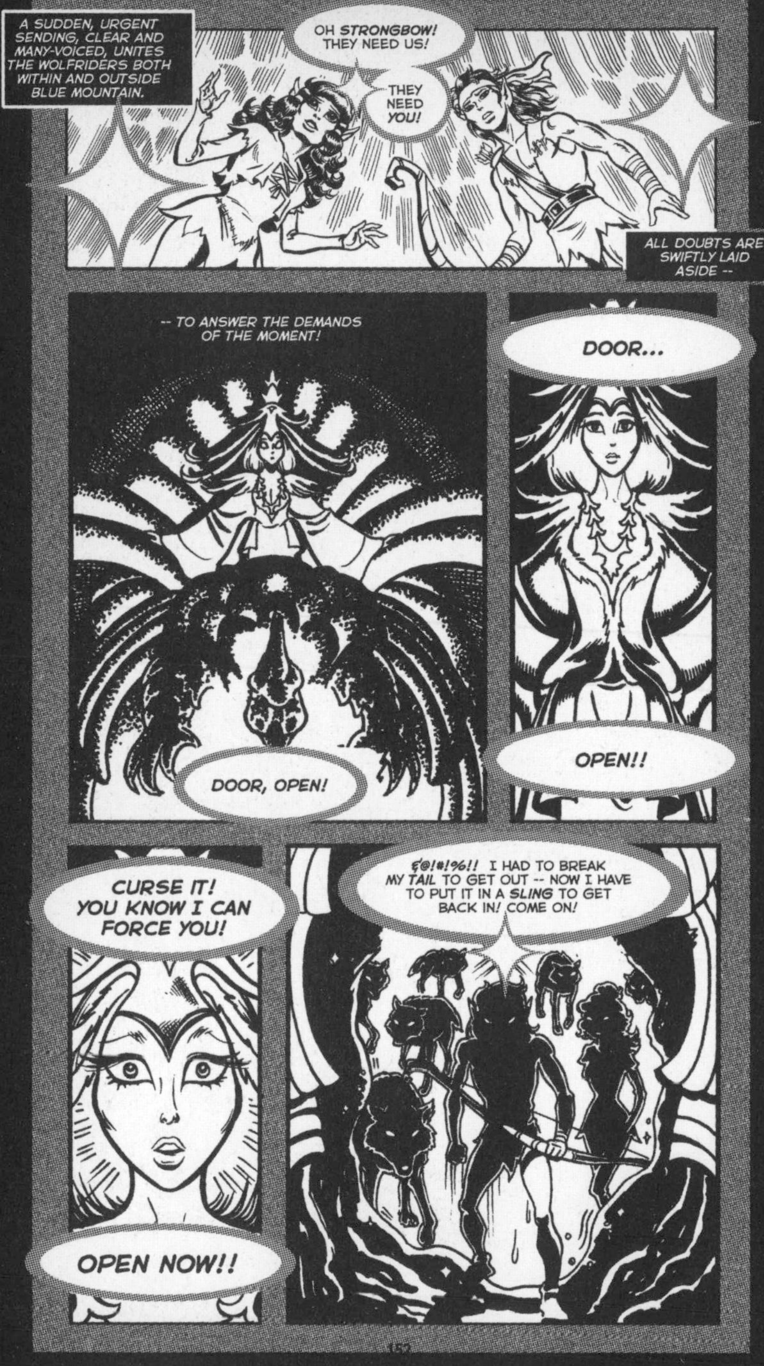
A SUDDEN, URGENT SENDING, CLEAR AND MANY-VOICED, UNITES THE WOLFRIDERS BOTH WITHIN AND OUTSIDE BLUE MOUNTAIN.
OH STRONGBOW! THEY NEED US!
THEY NEED YOU!
ALL DOUBTS ARE SWIFTLY LAID ASIDE --
-- TO ANSWER THE DEMANDS OF THE MOMENT!
DOOR, OPEN!
DOOR...
OPEN!!
CURSE IT! YOU KNOW I CAN FORCE YOU!
OPEN NOW!!
¢@!#!%!! I HAD TO BREAK MY TAIL TO GET OUT -- NOW I HAVE TO PUT IT IN A SLING TO GET BACK IN! COME ON!

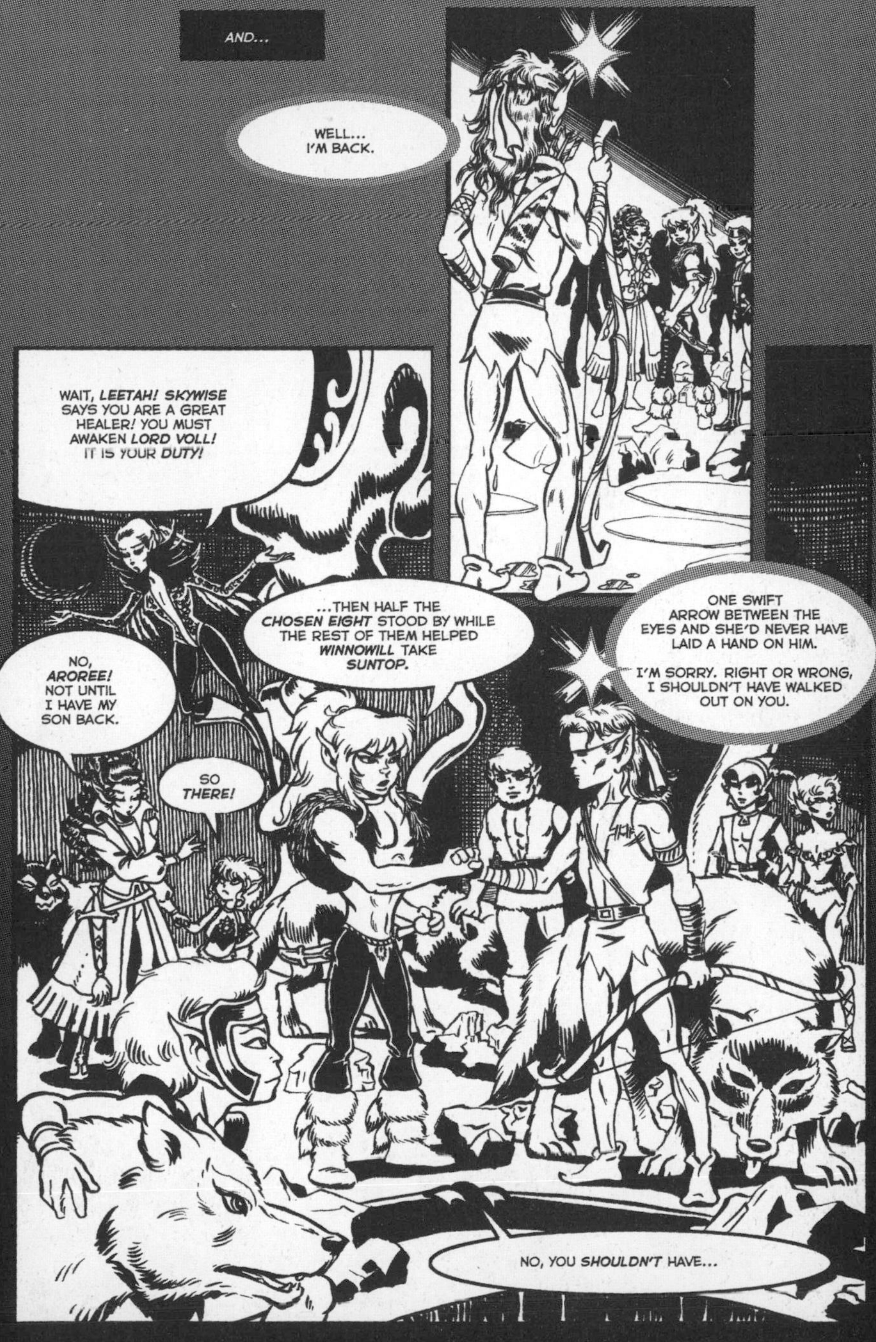
AND...
WELL... I'M BACK.
WAIT, LEETAH! SKYWISE SAYS YOU ARE A GREAT HEALER! YOU MUST AWAKEN LORD VOLL! IT IS YOUR DUTY!
NO, AROREE! NOT UNTIL I HAVE MY SON BACK.
SO THERE!
...THEN HALF THE CHOSEN EIGHT STOOD BY WHILE THE REST OF THEM HELPED WINNOWILL TAKE SUNTOP.
ONE SWIFT ARROW BETWEEN THE EYES AND SHE'D NEVER HAVE LAID A HAND ON HIM.
I'M SORRY. RIGHT OR WRONG, I SHOULDN'T HAVE WALKED OUT ON YOU.
NO, YOU SHOULDN'T HAVE...

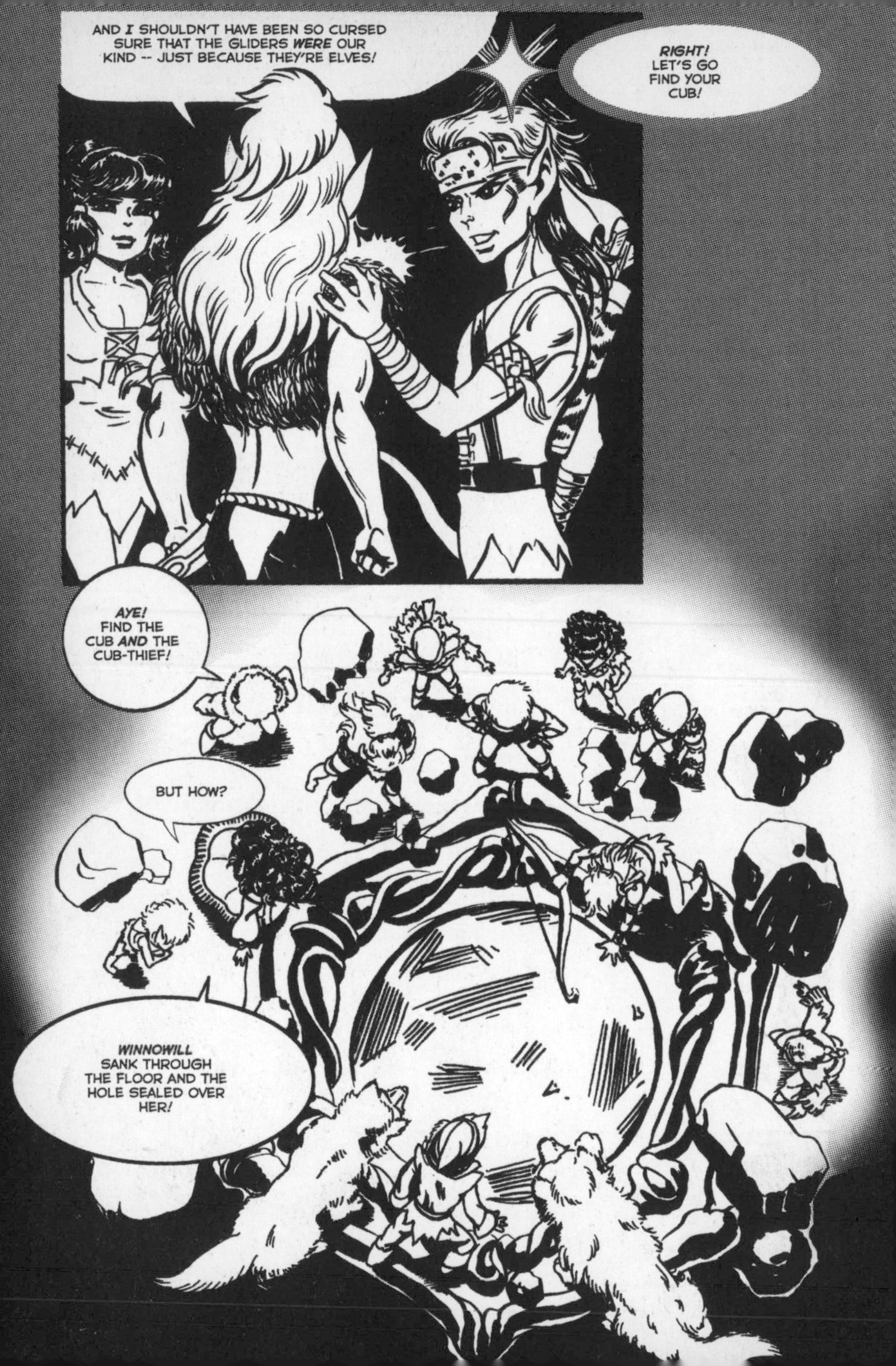
AND I SHOULDN'T HAVE BEEN SO CURSED SURE THAT THE GLIDERS WERE OUR KIND -- JUST BECAUSE THEY'RE ELVES!
RIGHT! LET'S GO FIND YOUR CUB!
AYE! FIND THE CUB AND THE CUB-THIEF!
BUT HOW?
WINNOWILL SANK THROUGH THE FLOOR AND THE HOLE SEALED OVER HER!

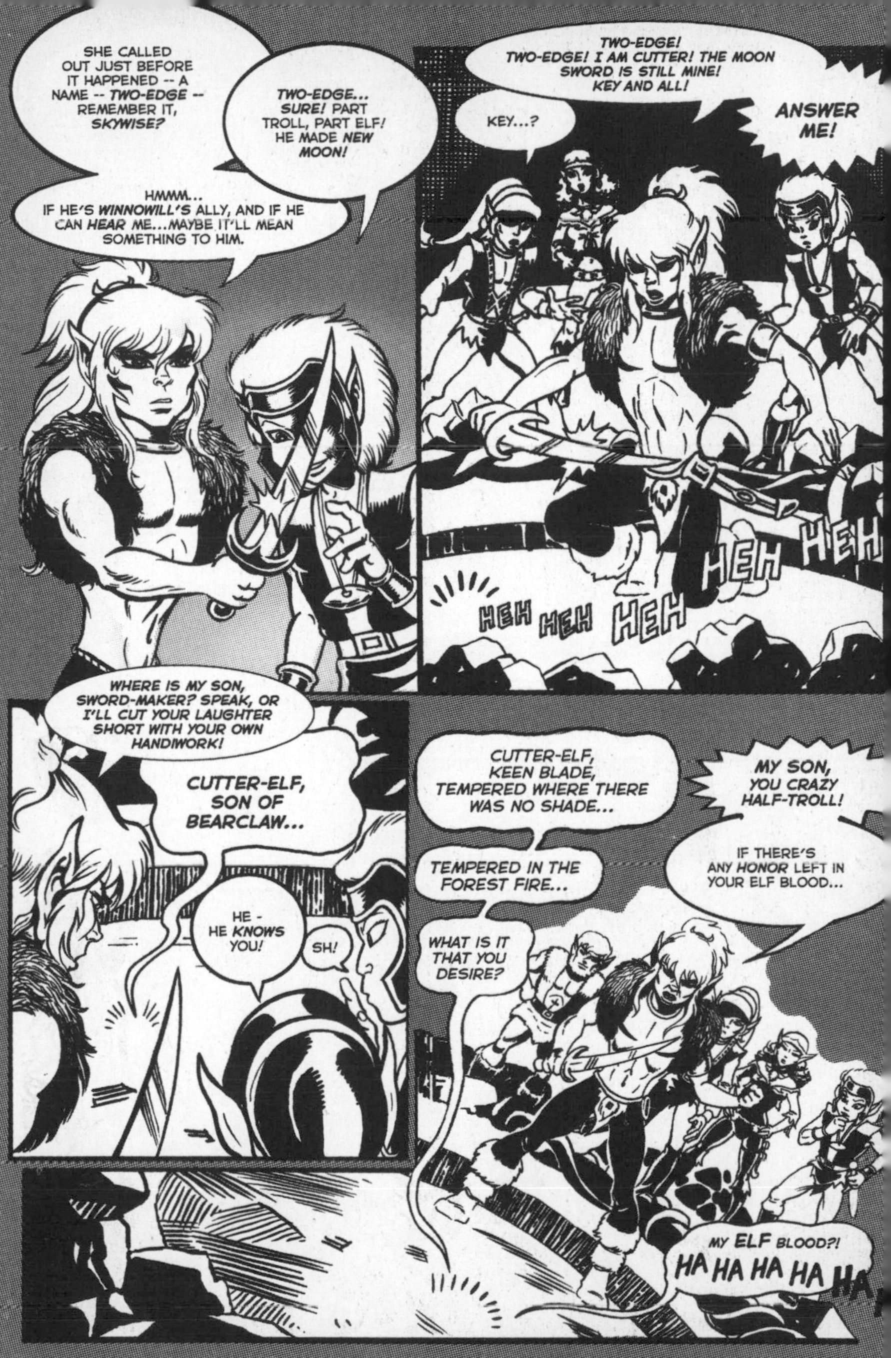
SHE CALLED OUT JUST BEFORE IT HAPPENED -- A NAME -- TWO-EDGE -- REMEMBER IT, SKYWISE?
TWO-EDGE... SURE! PART TROLL, PART ELF! HE MADE NEW MOON!
HMMM... IF HE'S WINNOWILL'S ALLY, AND IF HE CAN HEAR ME...MAYBE IT'LL MEAN SOMETHING TO HIM.
TWO-EDGE! TWO-EDGE! I AM CUTTER! THE MOON SWORD IS STILL MINE! KEY AND ALL!
KEY...?
ANSWER ME!
HEH HEH HEH HEH HEH
WHERE IS MY SON, SWORD-MAKER? SPEAK, OR I'LL CUT YOUR LAUGHTER SHORT WITH YOUR OWN HANDIWORK!
CUTTER-ELF, SON OF BEARCLAW...
HE - HE KNOWS YOU!
SH!
CUTTER-ELF, KEEN BLADE, TEMPERED WHERE THERE WAS NO SHADE...
TEMPERED IN THE FOREST FIRE...
WHAT IS IT THAT YOU DESIRE?
MY SON, YOU CRAZY HALF-TROLL!
IF THERE'S ANY HONOR LEFT IN YOUR ELF BLOOD...
MY ELF BLOOD?!
HA HA HA HA HA HA

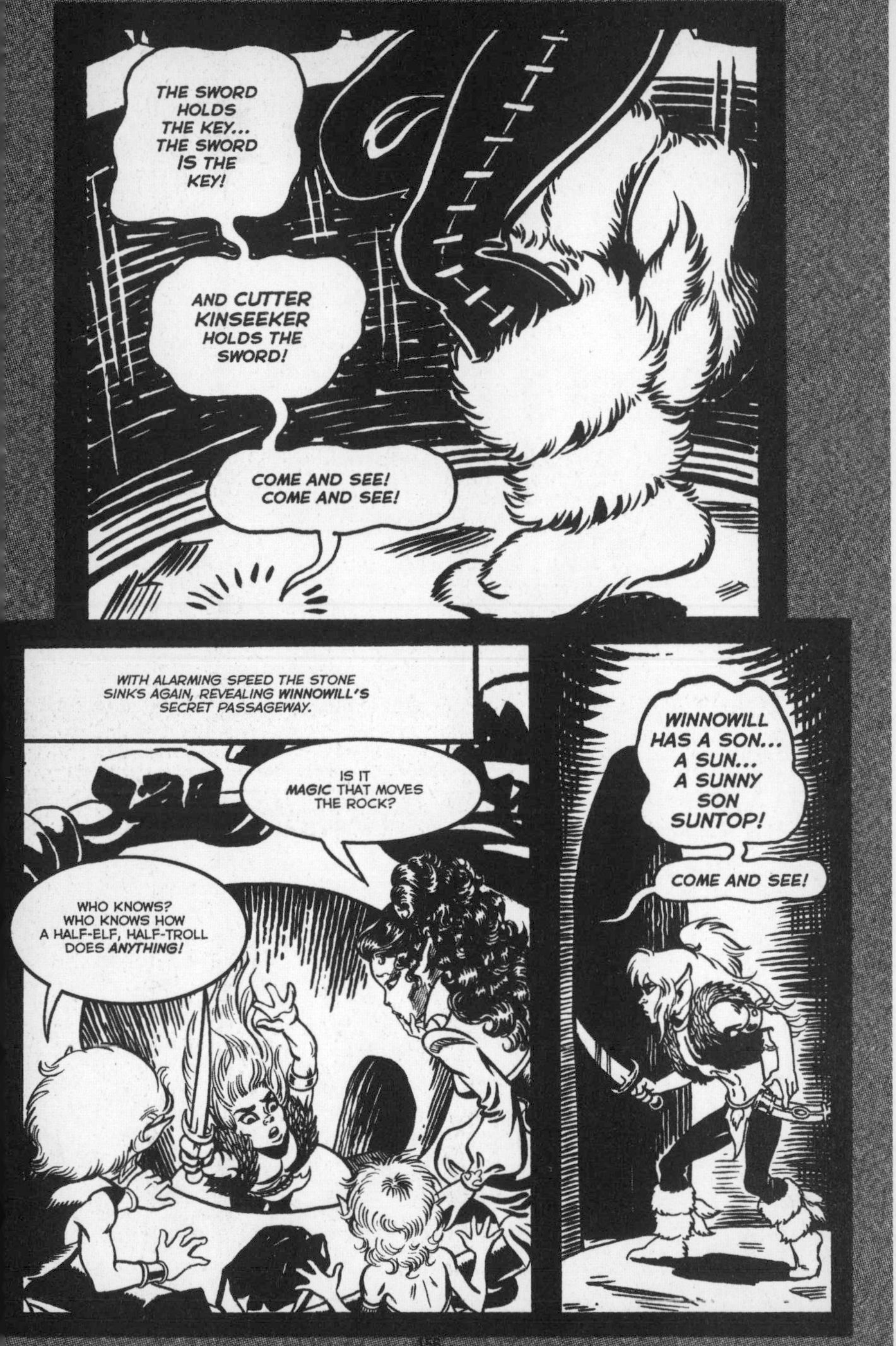
THE SWORD HOLDS THE KEY... THE SWORD IS THE KEY!
AND CUTTER KINSEEKER HOLDS THE SWORD!
COME AND SEE! COME AND SEE!
WITH ALARMING SPEED THE STONE SINKS AGAIN, REVEALING WINNOWILL'S SECRET PASSAGEWAY.
IS IT MAGIC THAT MOVES THE ROCK?
WHO KNOWS? WHO KNOWS HOW A HALF-ELF, HALF-TROLL DOES ANYTHING!
WINNOWILL HAS A SON... A SUN... A SUNNY SON SUNTOP!
COME AND SEE!

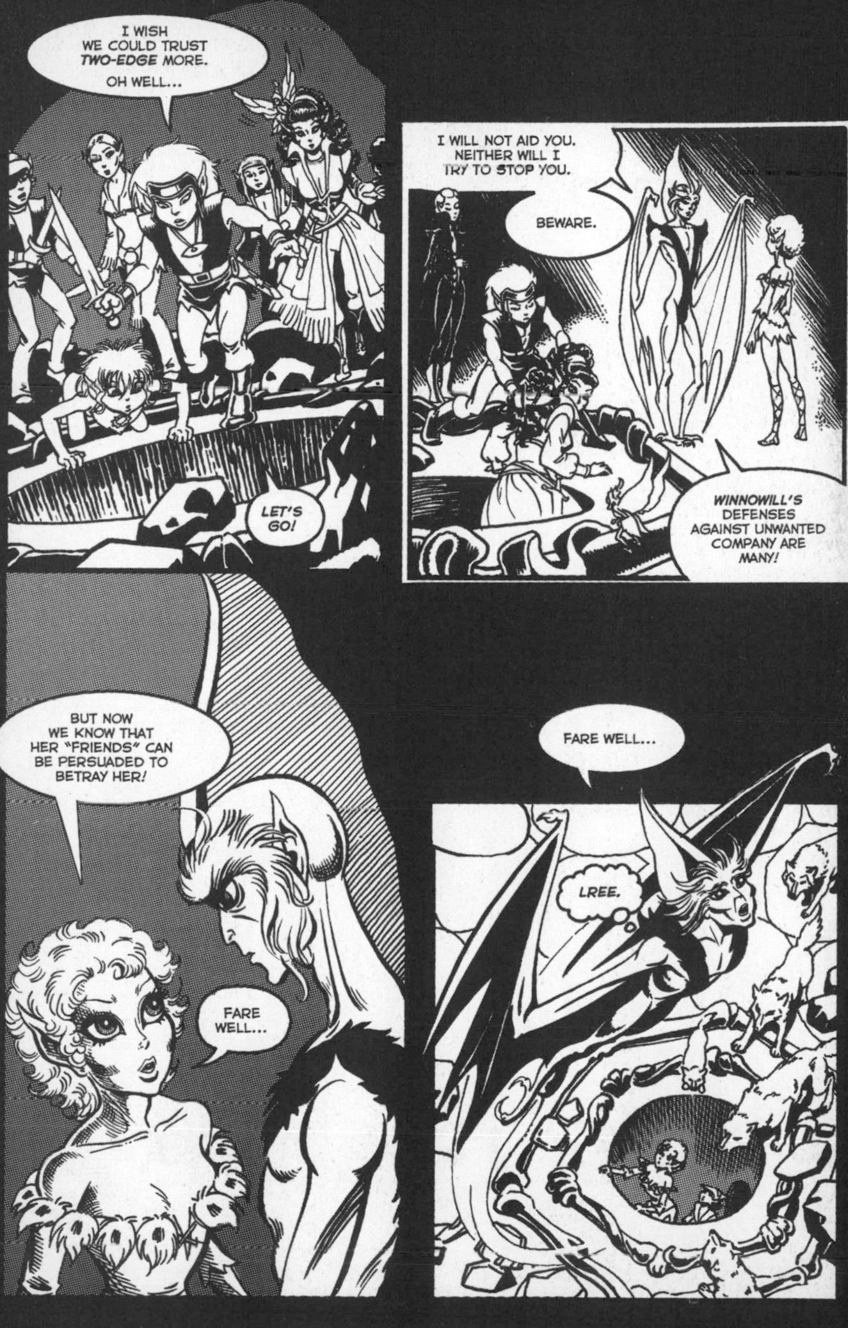
I WISH WE COULD TRUST *TWO-EDGE* MORE.
OH WELL...
LET'S GO!
I WILL NOT AID YOU. NEITHER WILL I TRY TO STOP YOU.
BEWARE.
WINNOWILL'S DEFENSES AGAINST UNWANTED COMPANY ARE MANY!
BUT NOW WE KNOW THAT HER "FRIENDS" CAN BE PERSUADED TO BETRAY HER!
FARE WELL...
FARE WELL...
LREE.

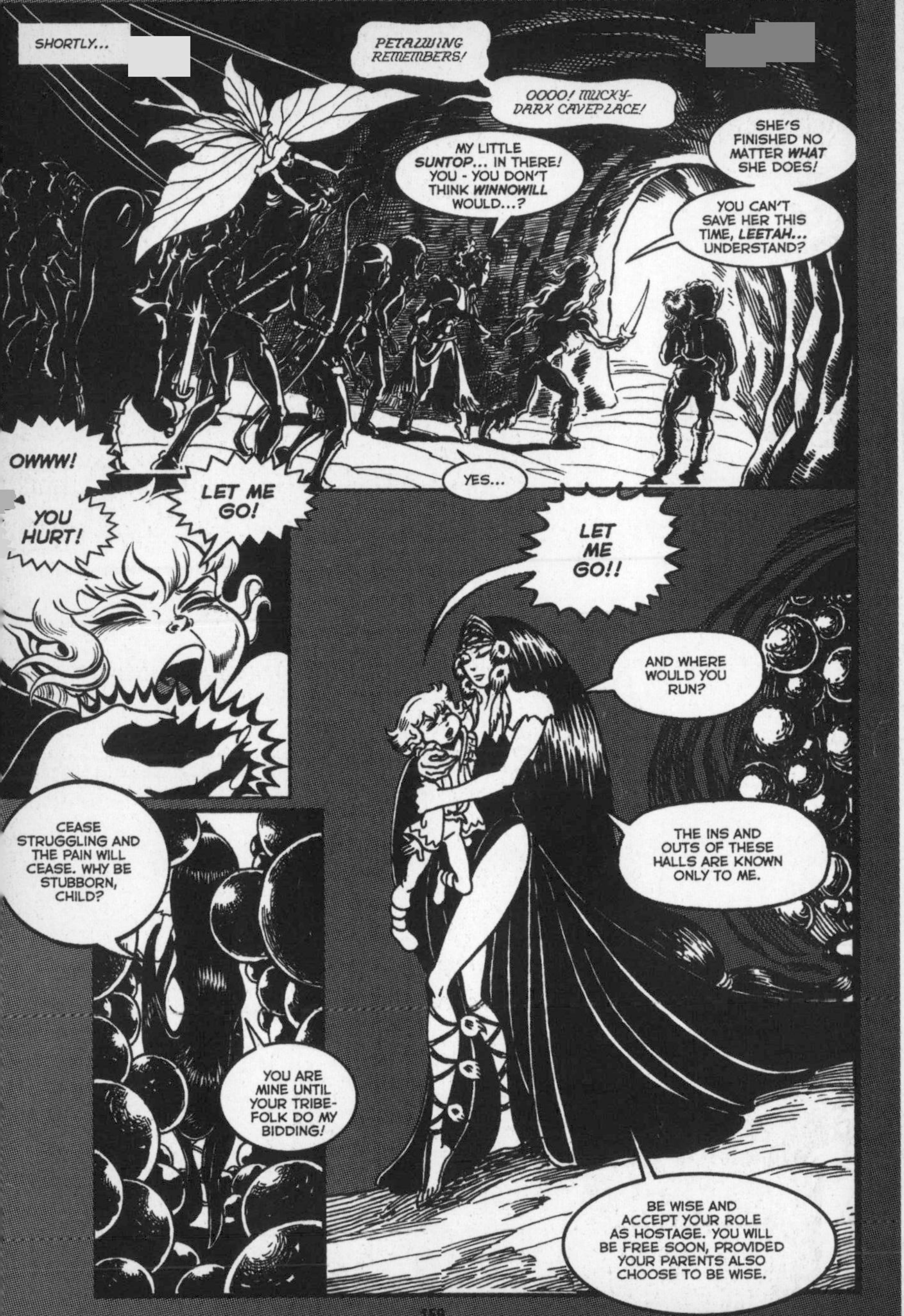
SHORTLY...
PETALWING REMEMBERS!
OOOO! MUCKY-DARK CAVEPLACE!
MY LITTLE SUNTOP... IN THERE! YOU - YOU DON'T THINK WINNOWILL WOULD...?
SHE'S FINISHED NO MATTER WHAT SHE DOES!
YOU CAN'T SAVE HER THIS TIME, LEETAH... UNDERSTAND?
YES...
OWWW!
YOU HURT!
LET ME GO!
LET ME GO!!
AND WHERE WOULD YOU RUN?
CEASE STRUGGLING AND THE PAIN WILL CEASE. WHY BE STUBBORN, CHILD?
THE INS AND OUTS OF THESE HALLS ARE KNOWN ONLY TO ME.
YOU ARE MINE UNTIL YOUR TRIBE-FOLK DO MY BIDDING!
BE WISE AND ACCEPT YOUR ROLE AS HOSTAGE. YOU WILL BE FREE SOON, PROVIDED YOUR PARENTS ALSO CHOOSE TO BE WISE.

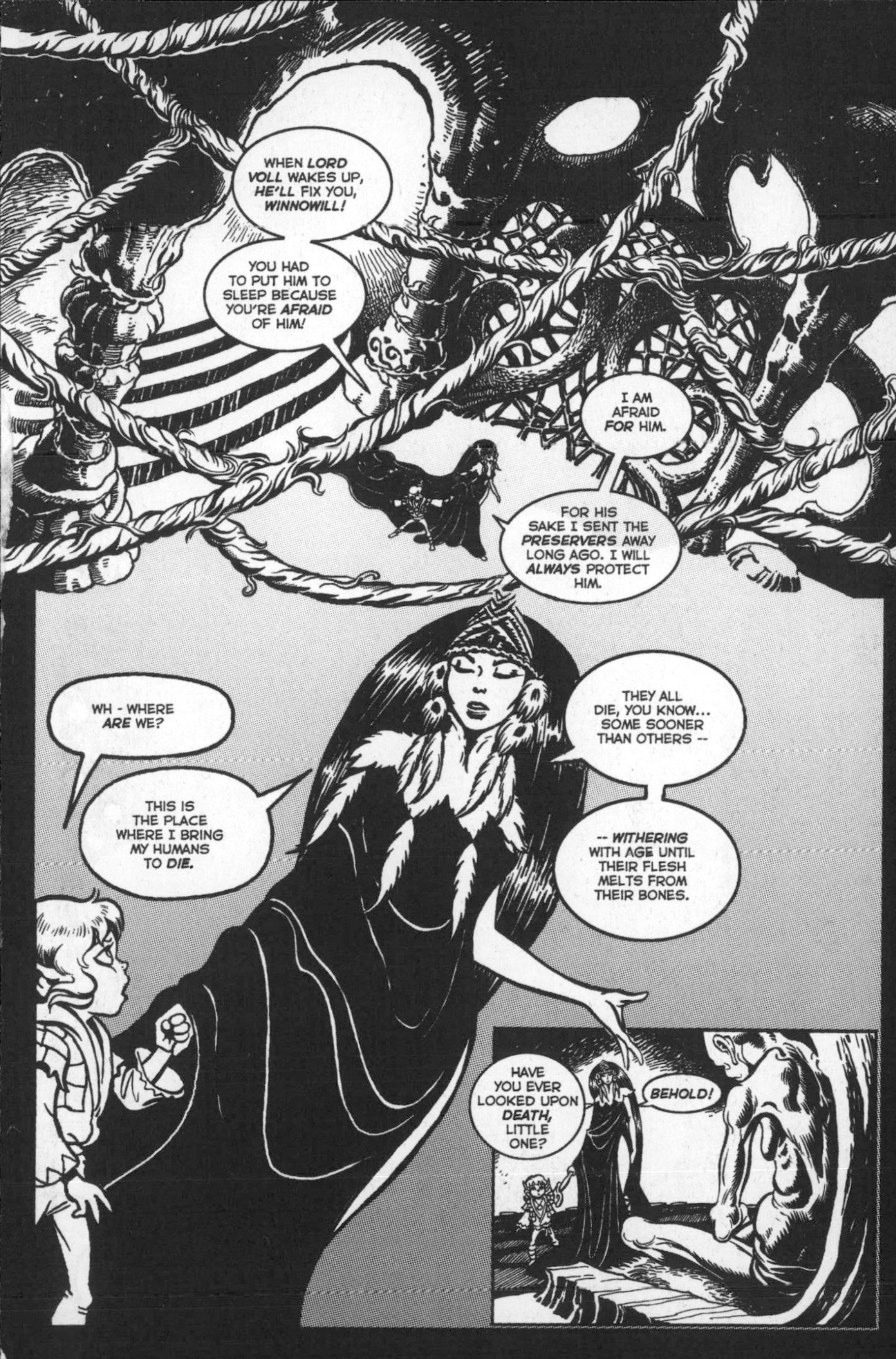
WHEN *LORD VOLL* WAKES UP, *HE'LL* FIX YOU, *WINNOWILL!*
YOU HAD TO PUT HIM TO SLEEP BECAUSE YOU'RE *AFRAID* OF HIM!
I AM AFRAID *FOR* HIM.
FOR HIS SAKE I SENT THE *PRESERVERS* AWAY LONG AGO. I WILL *ALWAYS* PROTECT HIM.
WH - WHERE *ARE* WE?
THIS IS THE PLACE WHERE I BRING MY HUMANS TO *DIE.*
THEY ALL DIE, YOU KNOW... SOME SOONER THAN OTHERS --
-- *WITHERING* WITH AGE UNTIL THEIR FLESH MELTS FROM THEIR BONES.
HAVE YOU EVER LOOKED UPON *DEATH,* LITTLE ONE?
BEHOLD!

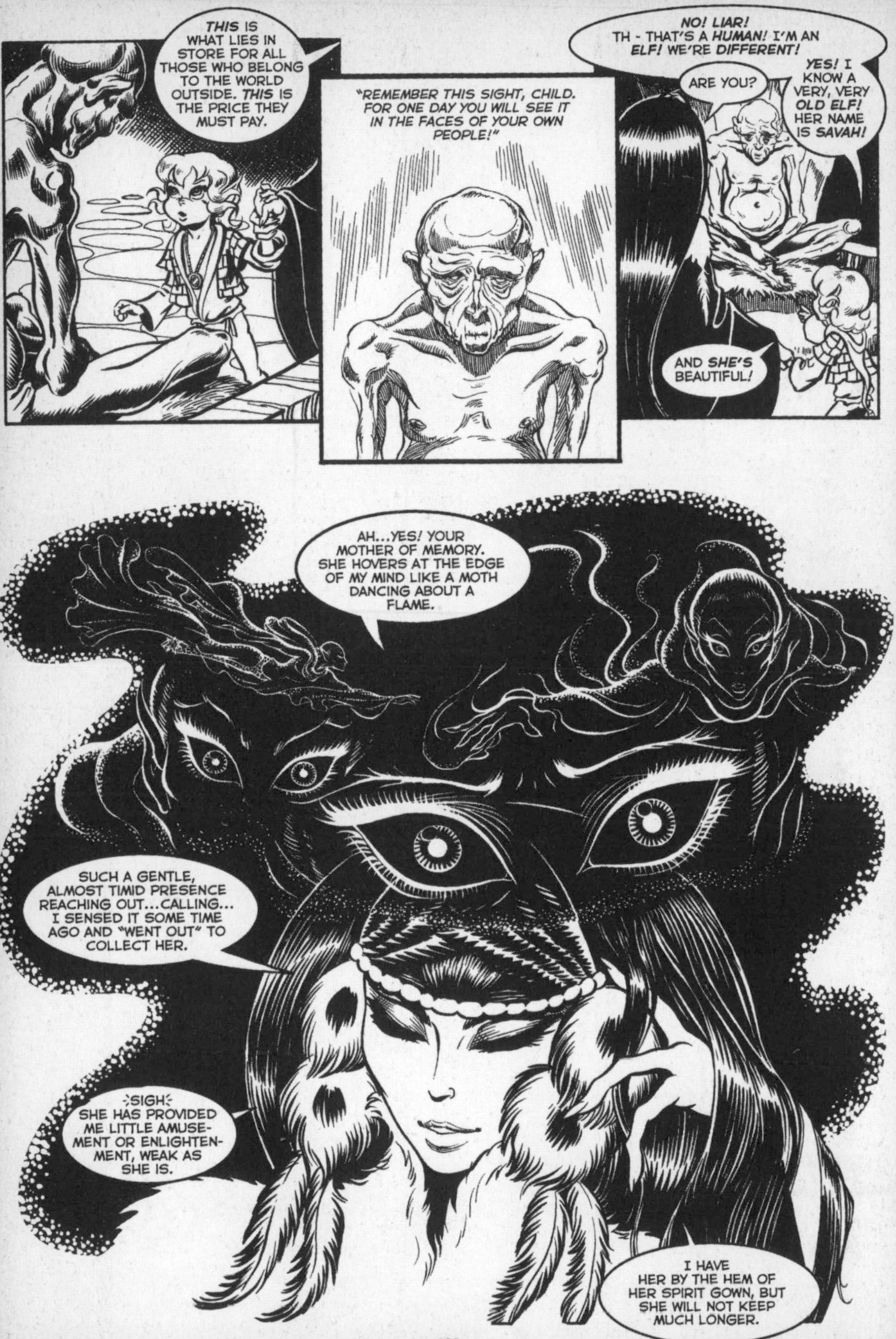
THIS IS WHAT LIES IN STORE FOR ALL THOSE WHO BELONG TO THE WORLD OUTSIDE. THIS IS THE PRICE THEY MUST PAY.
"REMEMBER THIS SIGHT, CHILD. FOR ONE DAY YOU WILL SEE IT IN THE FACES OF YOUR OWN PEOPLE!"
NO! LIAR! TH - THAT'S A HUMAN! I'M AN ELF! WE'RE DIFFERENT!
ARE YOU?
YES! I KNOW A VERY, VERY OLD ELF! HER NAME IS SAVAH!
AND SHE'S BEAUTIFUL!
AH...YES! YOUR MOTHER OF MEMORY. SHE HOVERS AT THE EDGE OF MY MIND LIKE A MOTH DANCING ABOUT A FLAME.
SUCH A GENTLE, ALMOST TIMID PRESENCE REACHING OUT...CALLING... I SENSED IT SOME TIME AGO AND "WENT OUT" TO COLLECT HER.
SIGH
SHE HAS PROVIDED ME LITTLE AMUSEMENT OR ENLIGHTENMENT, WEAK AS SHE IS.
I HAVE HER BY THE HEM OF HER SPIRIT GOWN, BUT SHE WILL NOT KEEP MUCH LONGER.

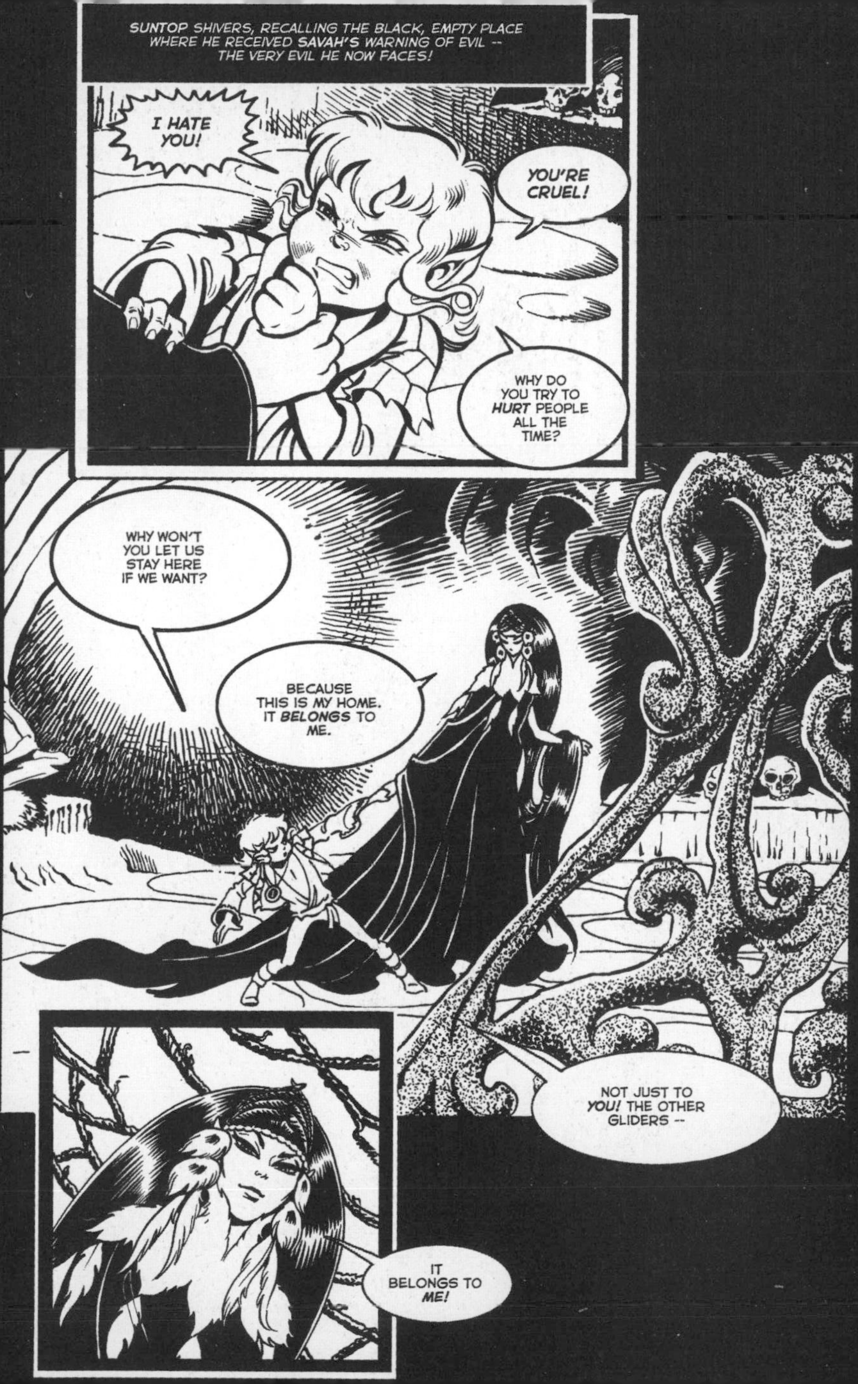
SUNTOP SHIVERS, RECALLING THE BLACK, EMPTY PLACE WHERE HE RECEIVED SAVAH'S WARNING OF EVIL -- THE VERY EVIL HE NOW FACES!
I HATE YOU!
YOU'RE CRUEL!
WHY DO YOU TRY TO HURT PEOPLE ALL THE TIME?
WHY WON'T YOU LET US STAY HERE IF WE WANT?
BECAUSE THIS IS MY HOME. IT BELONGS TO ME.
NOT JUST TO YOU! THE OTHER GLIDERS --
IT BELONGS TO ME!

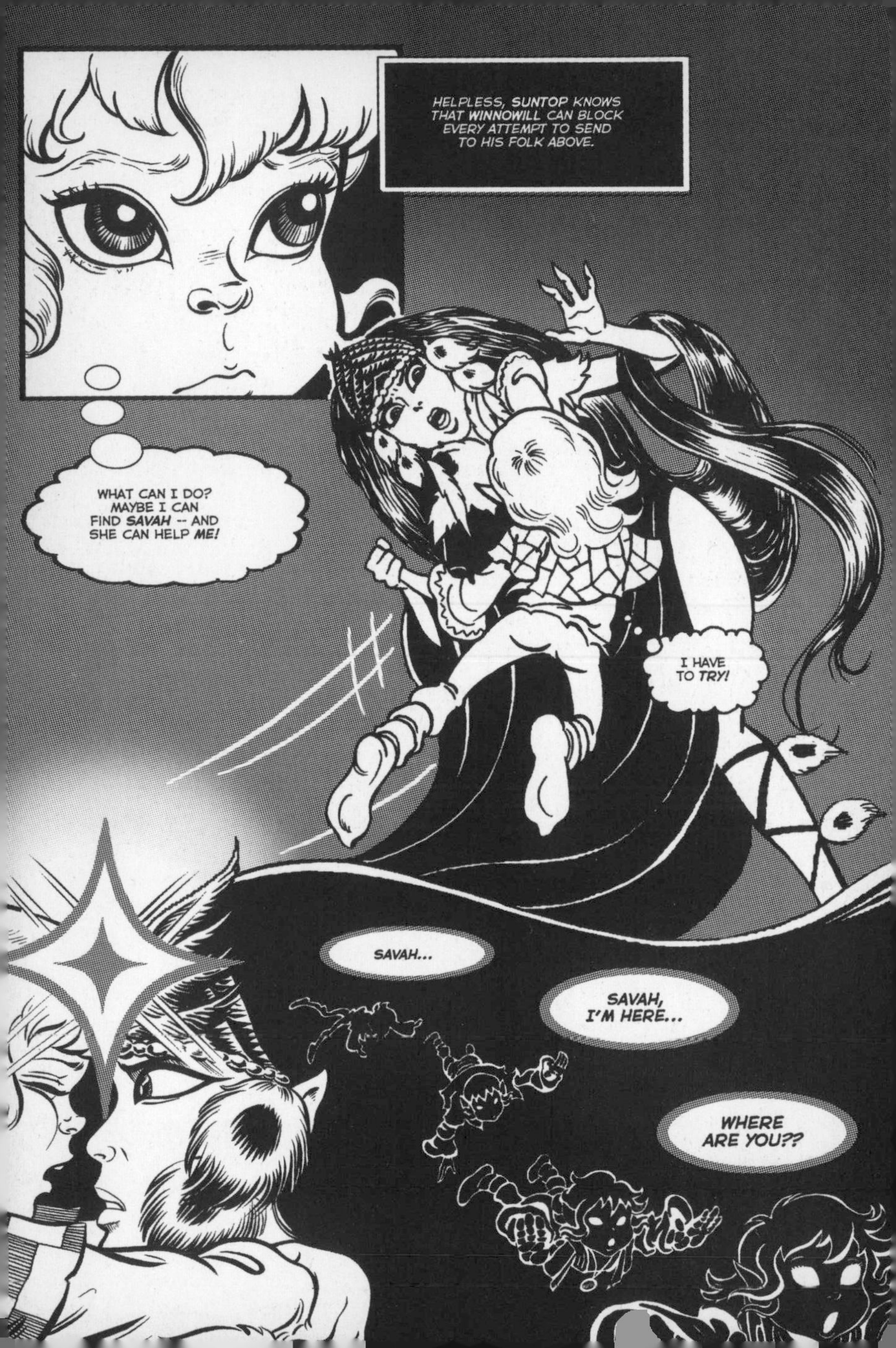
HELPLESS, SUNTOP KNOWS THAT WINNOWILL CAN BLOCK EVERY ATTEMPT TO SEND TO HIS FOLK ABOVE.
WHAT CAN I DO? MAYBE I CAN FIND SAVAH -- AND SHE CAN HELP ME!
I HAVE TO TRY!
SAVAH...
SAVAH, I'M HERE...
WHERE ARE YOU??

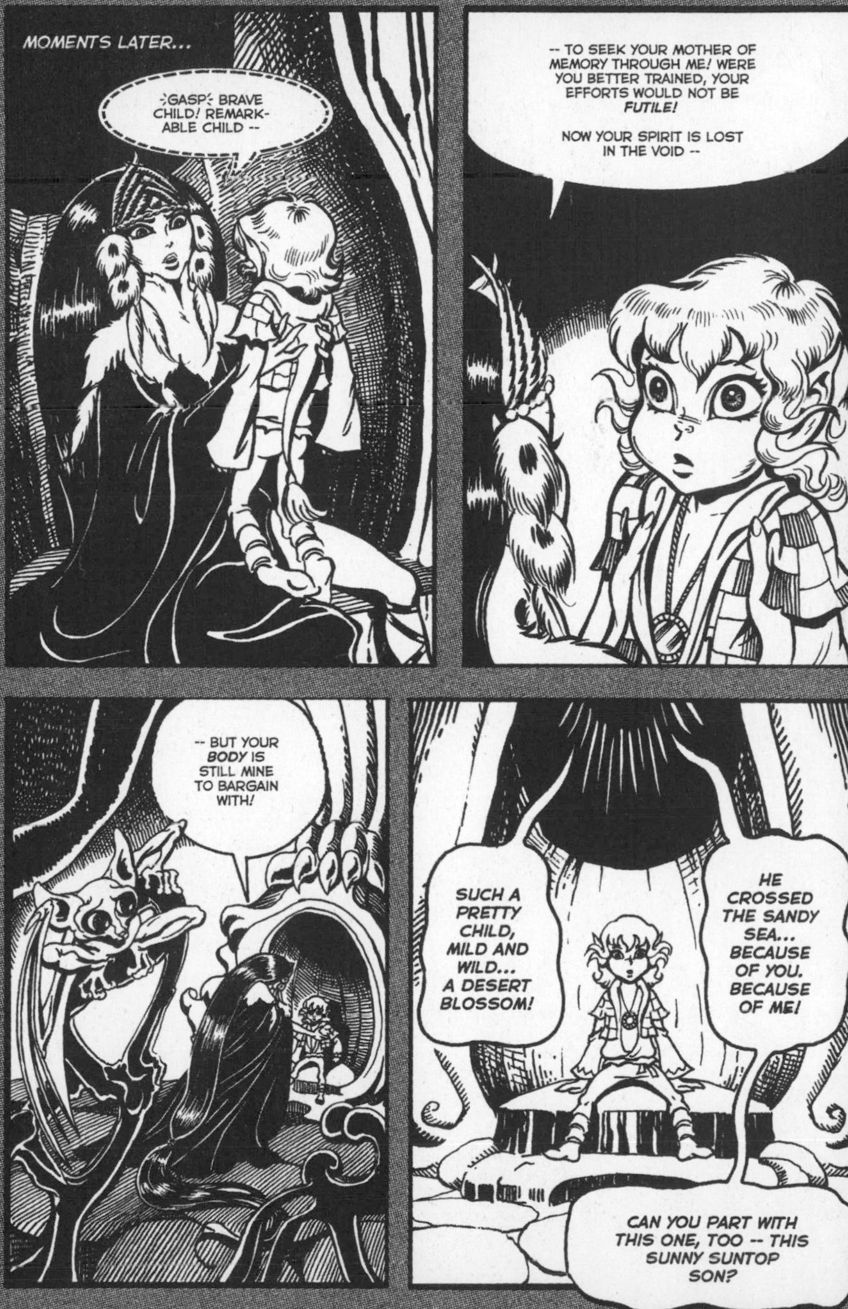
MOMENTS LATER...
:GASP: BRAVE CHILD! REMARKABLE CHILD --
-- TO SEEK YOUR MOTHER OF MEMORY THROUGH ME! WERE YOU BETTER TRAINED, YOUR EFFORTS WOULD NOT BE FUTILE!
NOW YOUR SPIRIT IS LOST IN THE VOID --
-- BUT YOUR BODY IS STILL MINE TO BARGAIN WITH!
SUCH A PRETTY CHILD, MILD AND WILD... A DESERT BLOSSOM!
HE CROSSED THE SANDY SEA... BECAUSE OF YOU. BECAUSE OF ME!
CAN YOU PART WITH THIS ONE, TOO -- THIS SUNNY SUNTOP SON?

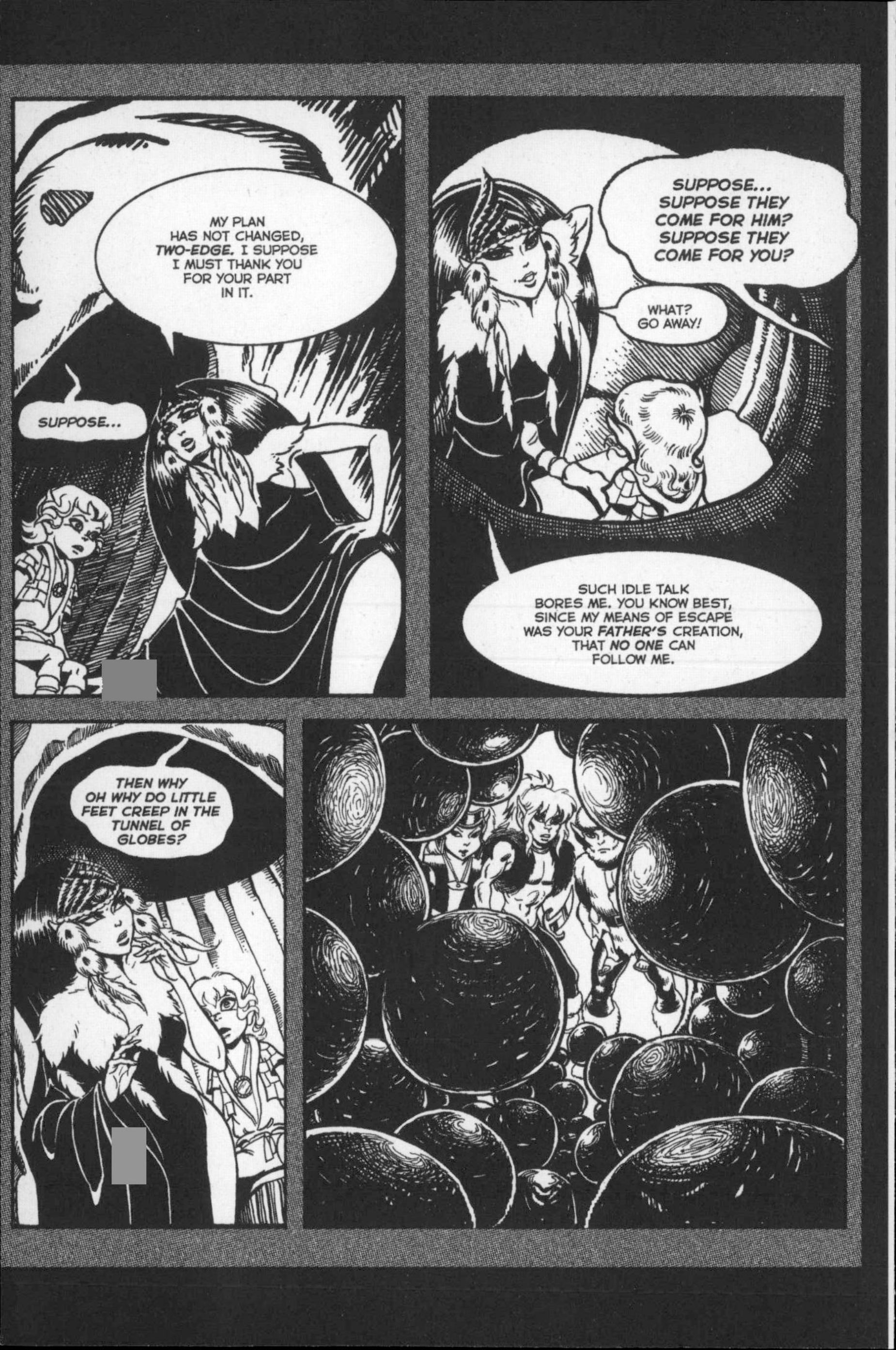
MY PLAN HAS NOT CHANGED, *TWO-EDGE.* I SUPPOSE I MUST THANK YOU FOR YOUR PART IN IT.
SUPPOSE...
SUPPOSE... SUPPOSE THEY COME FOR HIM? SUPPOSE THEY COME FOR YOU?
WHAT? GO AWAY!
SUCH IDLE TALK BORES ME. YOU KNOW BEST, SINCE MY MEANS OF ESCAPE WAS YOUR *FATHER'S* CREATION, THAT *NO ONE* CAN FOLLOW ME.
THEN WHY OH WHY DO LITTLE FEET CREEP IN THE TUNNEL OF GLOBES?

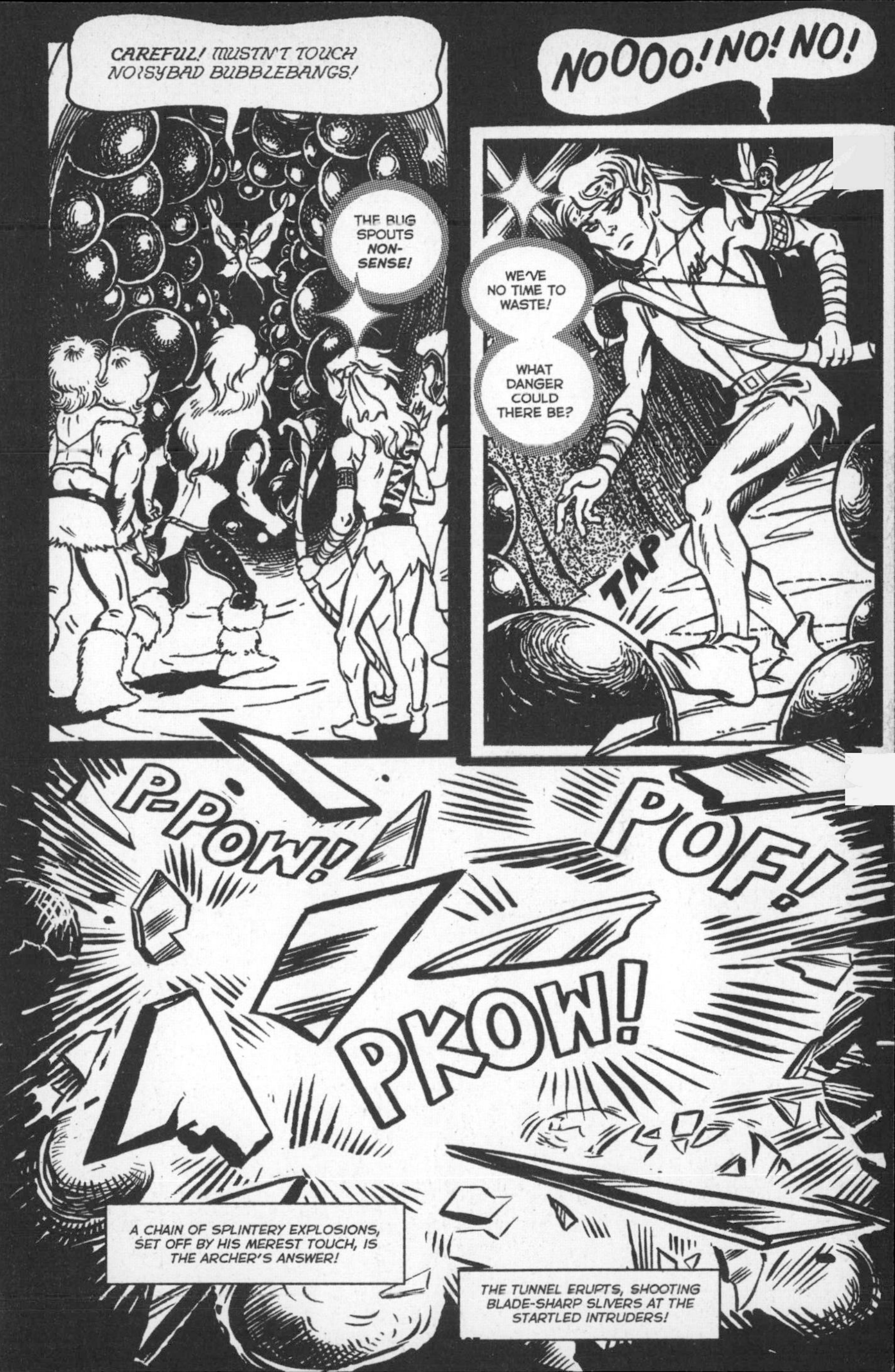
CAREFUL! MUSTN'T TOUCH NOISYBAD BUBBLEBANGS!
THE BUG SPOUTS NON-SENSE!
NOOOOO! NO! NO!
WE'VE NO TIME TO WASTE!
WHAT DANGER COULD THERE BE?
TAP
P-POW!
POF!
PKOW!
A CHAIN OF SPLINTERY EXPLOSIONS, SET OFF BY HIS MEREST TOUCH, IS THE ARCHER'S ANSWER!
THE TUNNEL ERUPTS, SHOOTING BLADE-SHARP SLIVERS AT THE STARTLED INTRUDERS!

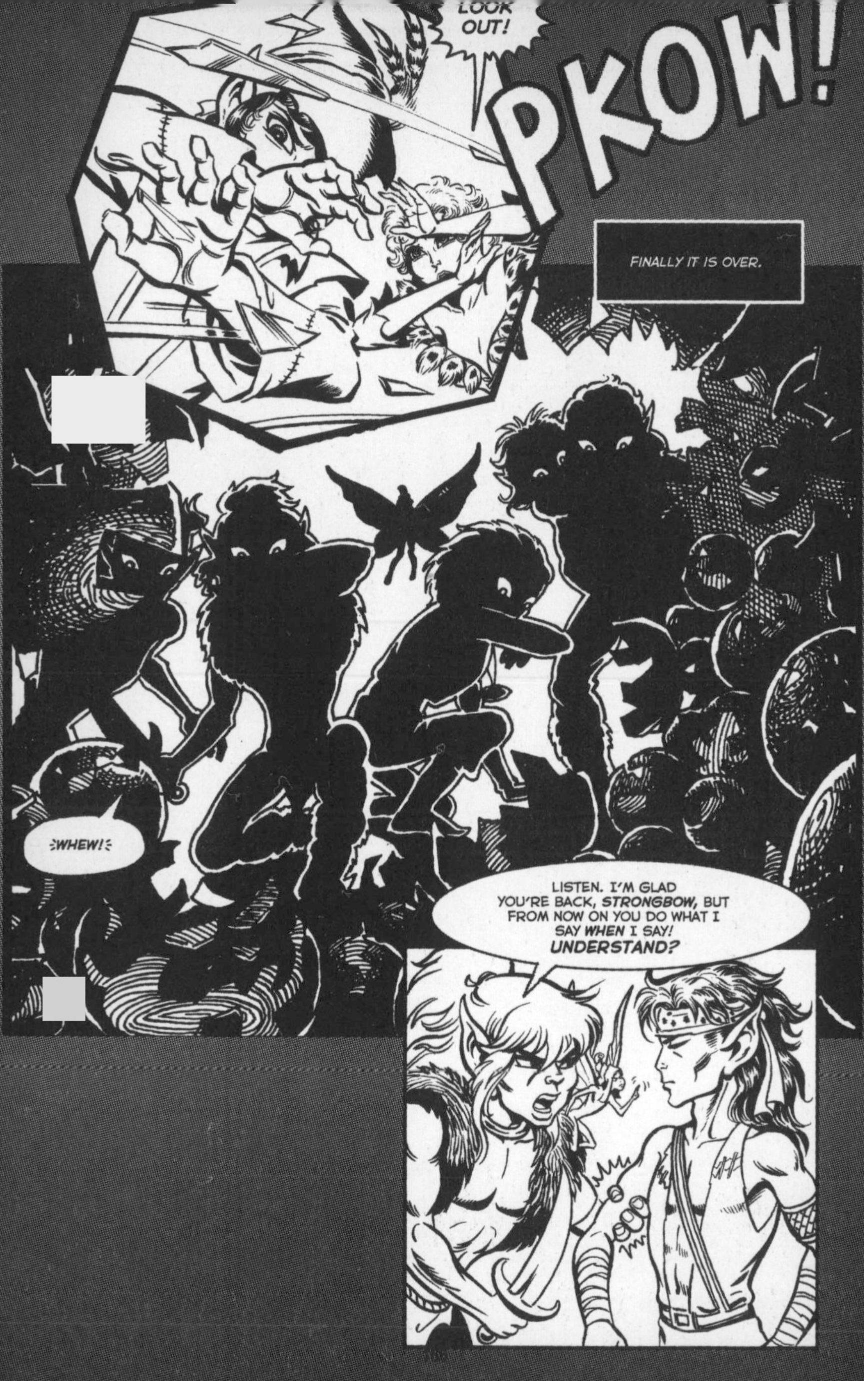
LOOK OUT!
PKOW!
FINALLY IT IS OVER.
WHEW!
LISTEN. I'M GLAD YOU'RE BACK, STRONGBOW, BUT FROM NOW ON YOU DO WHAT I SAY WHEN I SAY! UNDERSTAND?

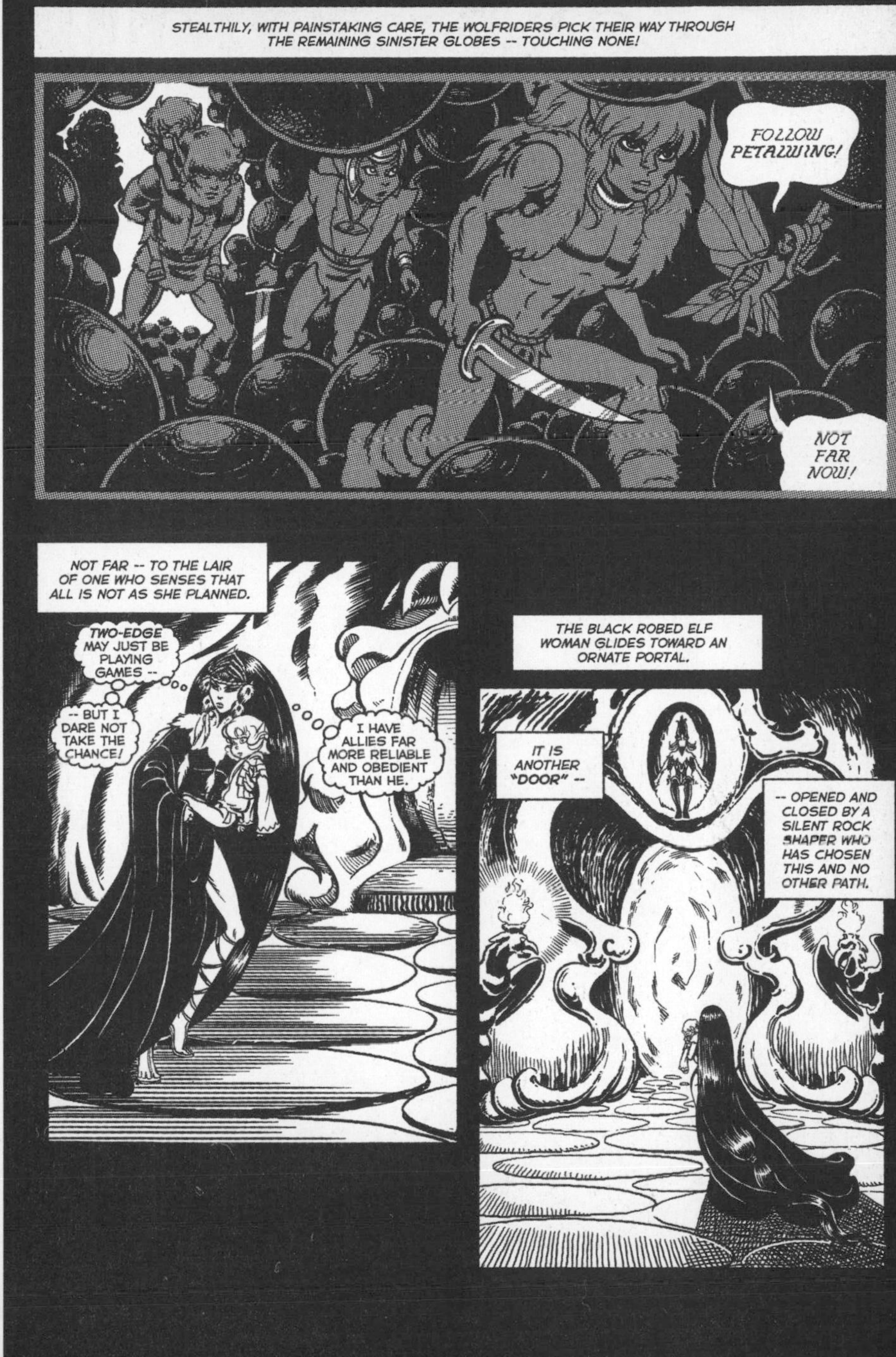
STEALTHILY, WITH PAINSTAKING CARE, THE WOLFRIDERS PICK THEIR WAY THROUGH THE REMAINING SINISTER GLOBES -- TOUCHING NONE!
FOLLOW PETALWING!
NOT FAR NOW!
NOT FAR -- TO THE LAIR OF ONE WHO SENSES THAT ALL IS NOT AS SHE PLANNED.
TWO-EDGE MAY JUST BE PLAYING GAMES --
-- BUT I DARE NOT TAKE THE CHANCE!
I HAVE ALLIES FAR MORE RELIABLE AND OBEDIENT THAN HE.
THE BLACK ROBED ELF WOMAN GLIDES TOWARD AN ORNATE PORTAL.
IT IS ANOTHER "DOOR" --
-- OPENED AND CLOSED BY A SILENT ROCK SHAPER WHO HAS CHOSEN THIS AND NO OTHER PATH.

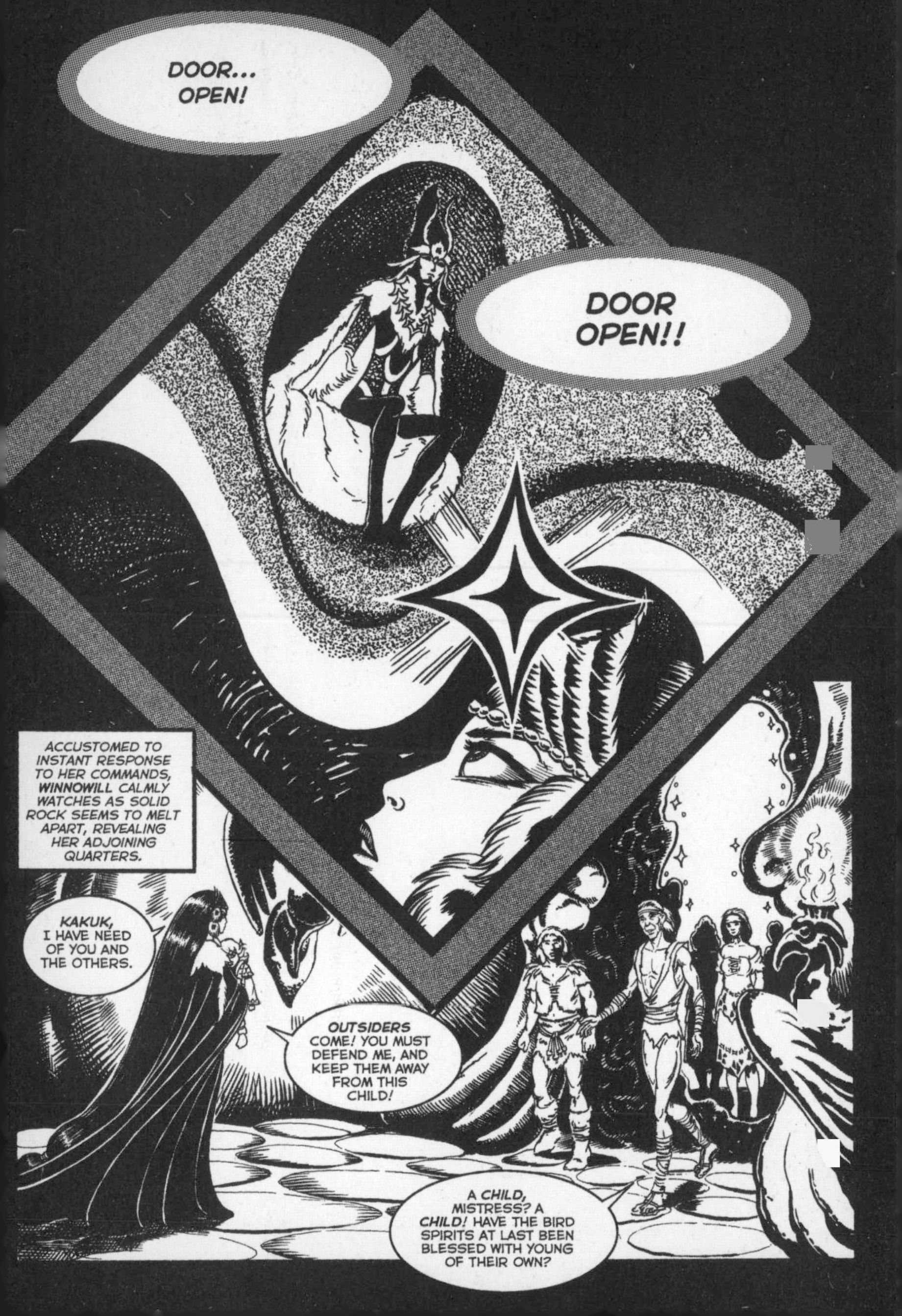
DOOR... OPEN!
DOOR OPEN!!
ACCUSTOMED TO INSTANT RESPONSE TO HER COMMANDS, WINNOWILL CALMLY WATCHES AS SOLID ROCK SEEMS TO MELT APART, REVEALING HER ADJOINING QUARTERS.
KAKUK, I HAVE NEED OF YOU AND THE OTHERS.
OUTSIDERS COME! YOU MUST DEFEND ME, AND KEEP THEM AWAY FROM THIS CHILD!
A CHILD, MISTRESS? A CHILD! HAVE THE BIRD SPIRITS AT LAST BEEN BLESSED WITH YOUNG OF THEIR OWN?

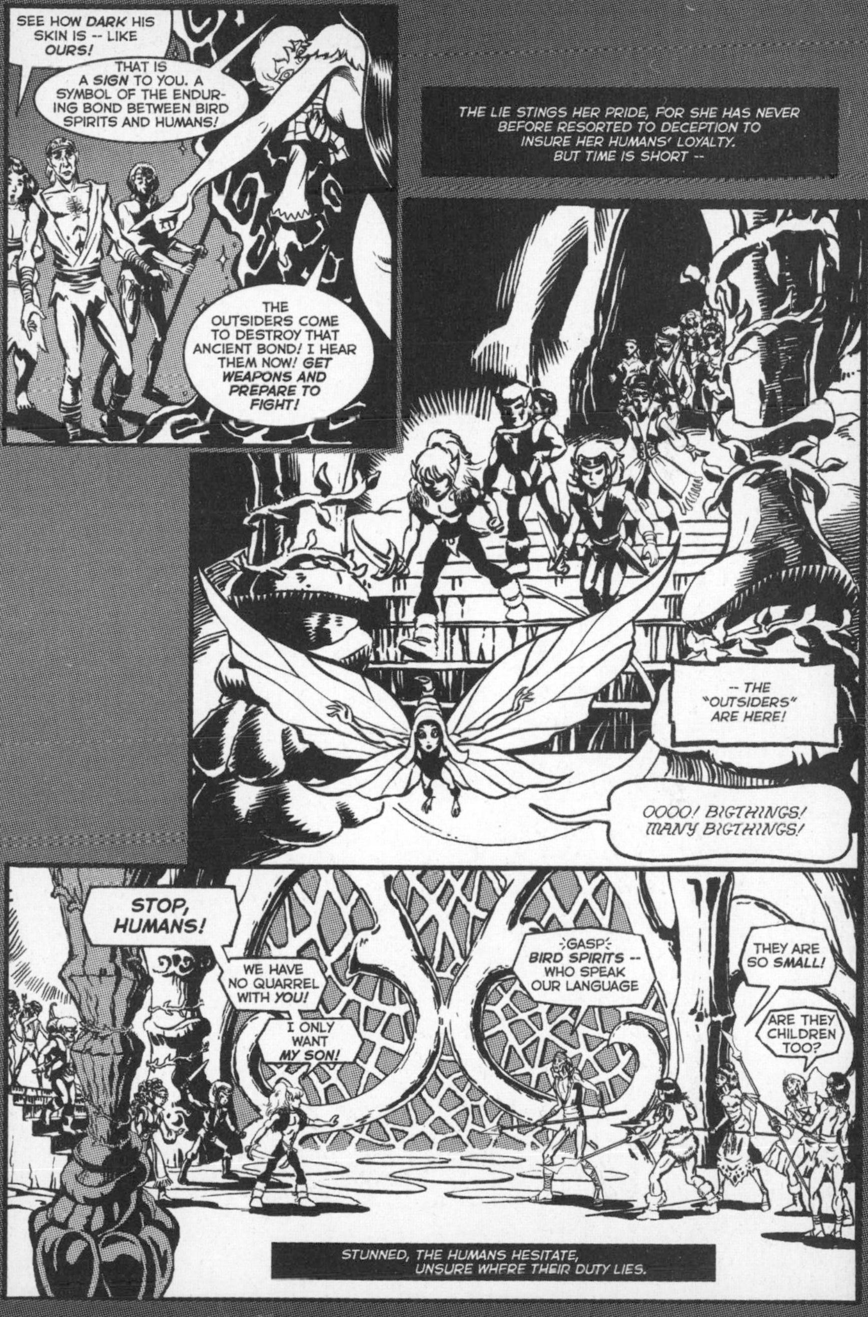
SEE HOW DARK HIS SKIN IS -- LIKE OURS!
THAT IS A SIGN TO YOU. A SYMBOL OF THE ENDURING BOND BETWEEN BIRD SPIRITS AND HUMANS!
THE OUTSIDERS COME TO DESTROY THAT ANCIENT BOND! I HEAR THEM NOW! GET WEAPONS AND PREPARE TO FIGHT!
THE LIE STINGS HER PRIDE, FOR SHE HAS NEVER BEFORE RESORTED TO DECEPTION TO INSURE HER HUMANS' LOYALTY. BUT TIME IS SHORT --
-- THE "OUTSIDERS" ARE HERE!
OOOO! BIGTHINGS! MANY BIGTHINGS!
STOP, HUMANS!
WE HAVE NO QUARREL WITH YOU!
I ONLY WANT MY SON!
GASP BIRD SPIRITS -- WHO SPEAK OUR LANGUAGE
THEY ARE SO SMALL!
ARE THEY CHILDREN TOO?
STUNNED, THE HUMANS HESITATE, UNSURE WHFRE THEIR DUTY LIES.

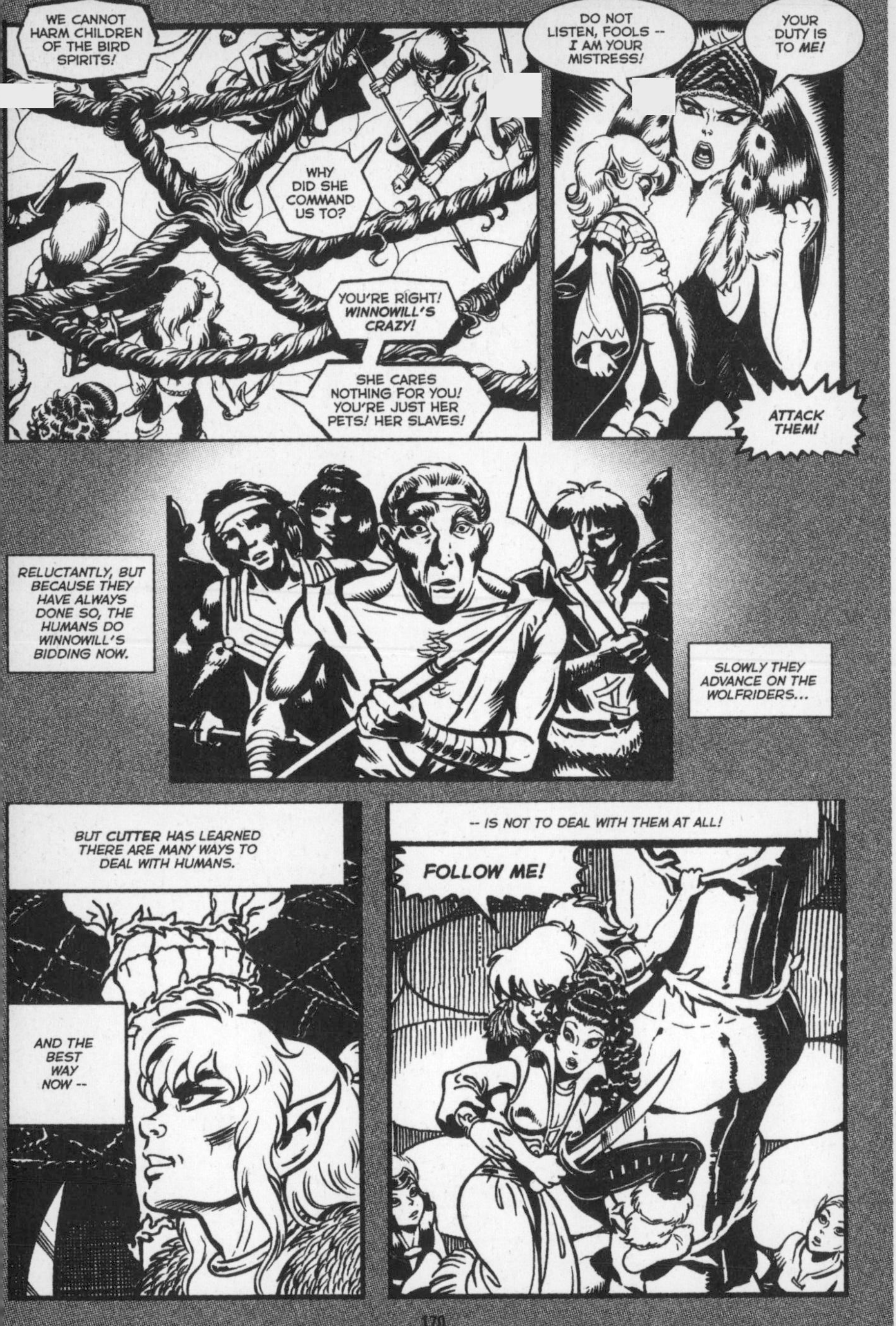
WE CANNOT HARM CHILDREN OF THE BIRD SPIRITS!
WHY DID SHE COMMAND US TO?
YOU'RE RIGHT! WINNOWILL'S CRAZY!
SHE CARES NOTHING FOR YOU! YOU'RE JUST HER PETS! HER SLAVES!
DO NOT LISTEN, FOOLS -- I AM YOUR MISTRESS!
YOUR DUTY IS TO ME!
ATTACK THEM!
RELUCTANTLY, BUT BECAUSE THEY HAVE ALWAYS DONE SO, THE HUMANS DO WINNOWILL'S BIDDING NOW.
SLOWLY THEY ADVANCE ON THE WOLFRIDERS...
BUT CUTTER HAS LEARNED THERE ARE MANY WAYS TO DEAL WITH HUMANS.
AND THE BEST WAY NOW --
-- IS NOT TO DEAL WITH THEM AT ALL!
FOLLOW ME!

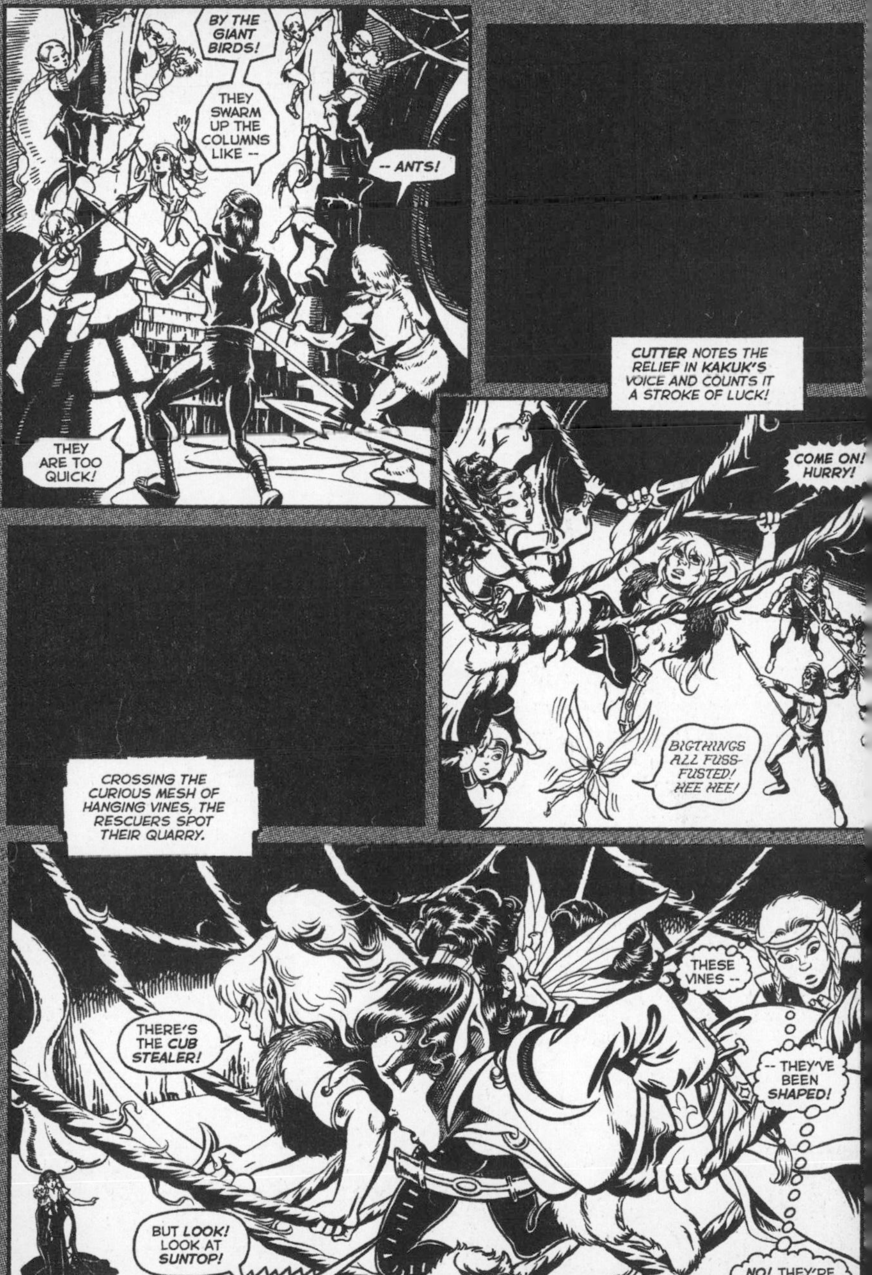
BY THE GIANT BIRDS!
THEY SWARM UP THE COLUMNS LIKE --
-- ANTS!
THEY ARE TOO QUICK!
CUTTER NOTES THE RELIEF IN KAKUK'S VOICE AND COUNTS IT A STROKE OF LUCK!
COME ON! HURRY!
BIGTHINGS ALL FUSS-FUSTED! HEE HEE!
CROSSING THE CURIOUS MESH OF HANGING VINES, THE RESCUERS SPOT THEIR QUARRY.
THERE'S THE CUB STEALER!
BUT LOOK! LOOK AT SUNTOP!
WHAT HAS SHE DONE TO HIM?!
THESE VINES --
-- THEY'VE BEEN SHAPED!
NO! THEY'RE NOT VINES AT ALL! THEY'RE...

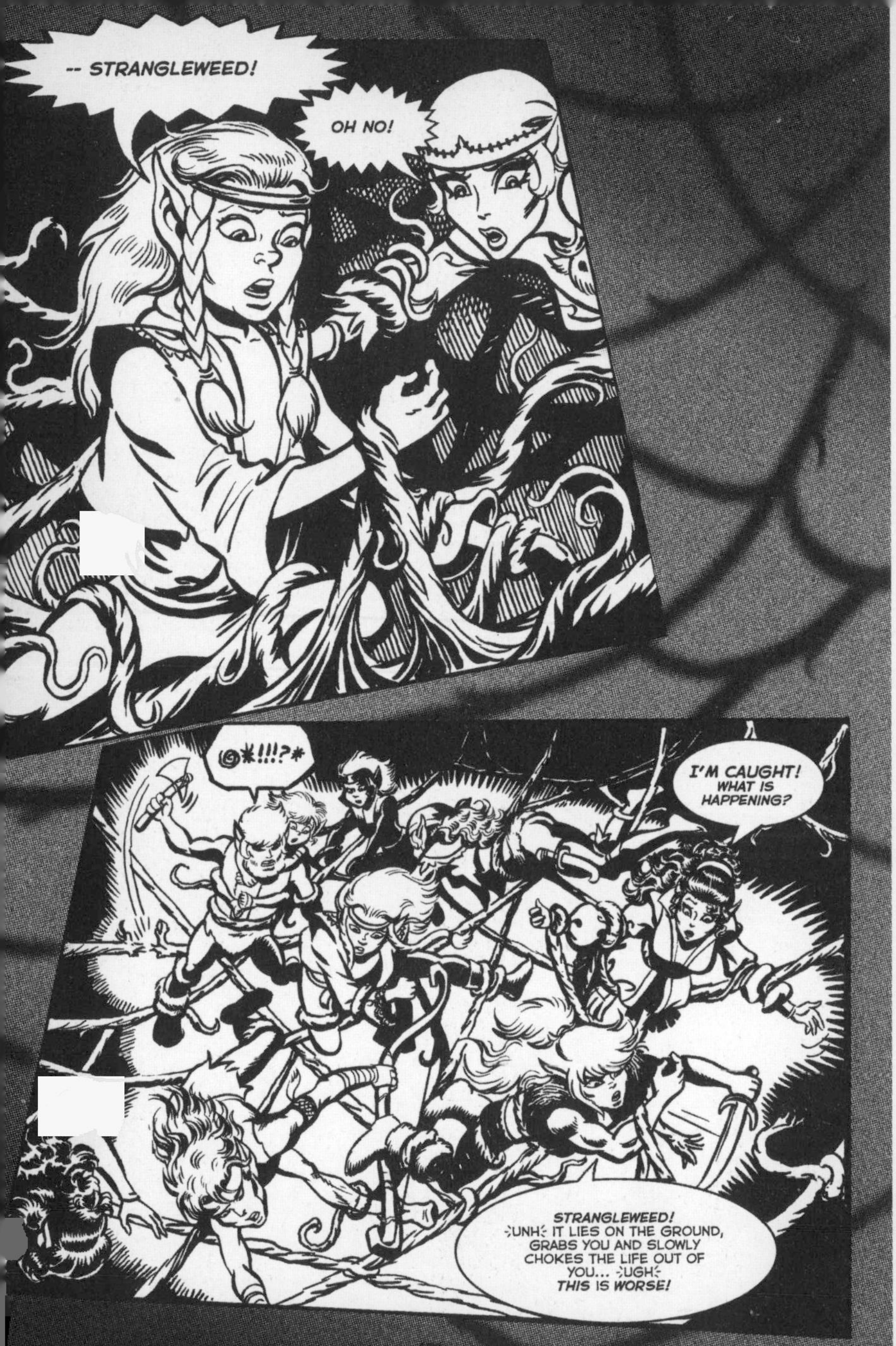

-- STRANGLEWEED!
OH NO!
@*!!!?*
I'M CAUGHT! WHAT IS HAPPENING?
STRANGLEWEED! *UNH* IT LIES ON THE GROUND, GRABS YOU AND SLOWLY CHOKES THE LIFE OUT OF YOU... *UGH* THIS IS WORSE!

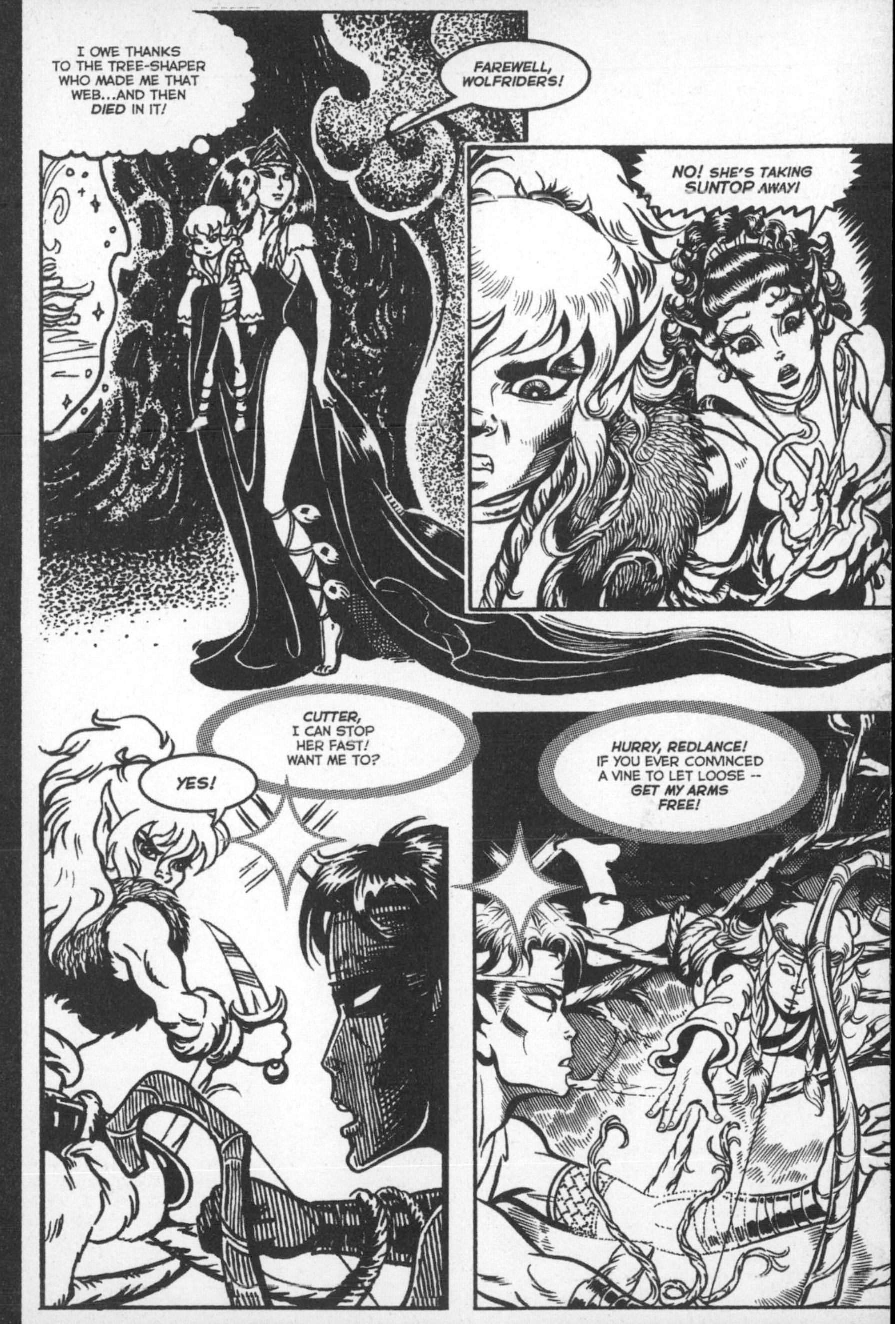

I OWE THANKS TO THE TREE-SHAPER WHO MADE ME THAT WEB...AND THEN DIED IN IT!
FAREWELL, WOLFRIDERS!
NO! SHE'S TAKING SUNTOP AWAY!
CUTTER, I CAN STOP HER FAST! WANT ME TO?
YES!
HURRY, REDLANCE! IF YOU EVER CONVINCED A VINE TO LET LOOSE -- GET MY ARMS FREE!

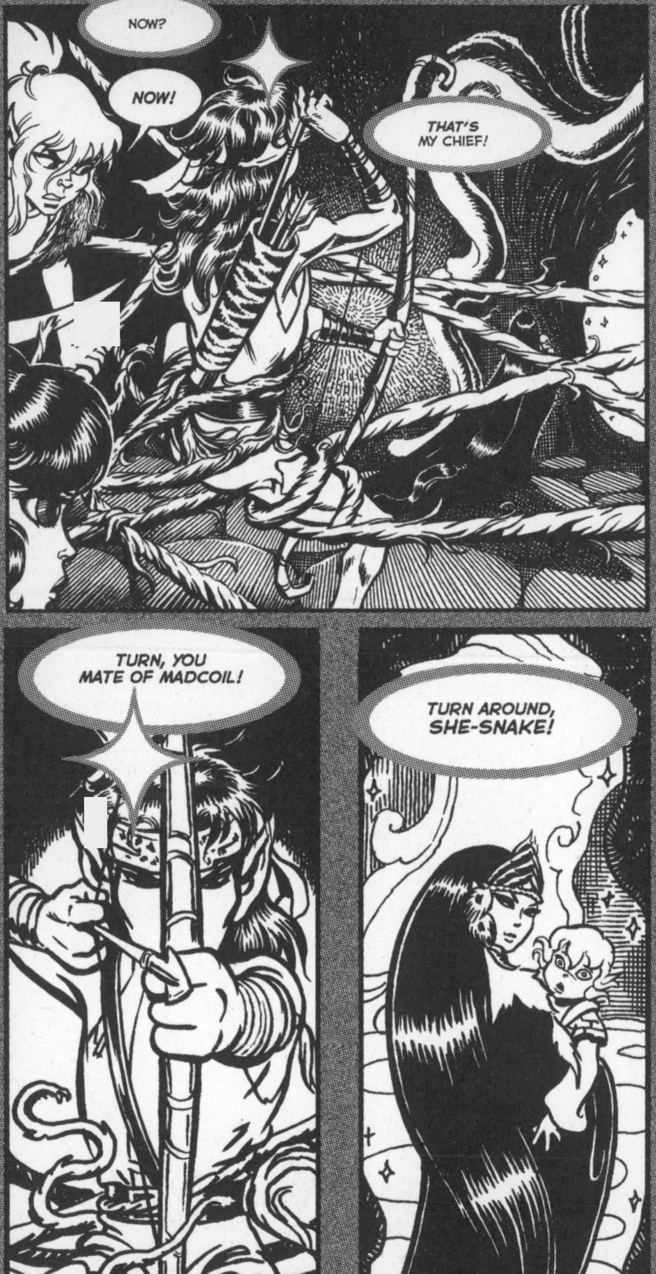
NOW?
NOW!
THAT'S MY CHIEF!
TURN, YOU MATE OF MADCOIL!
TURN AROUND, SHE-SNAKE!

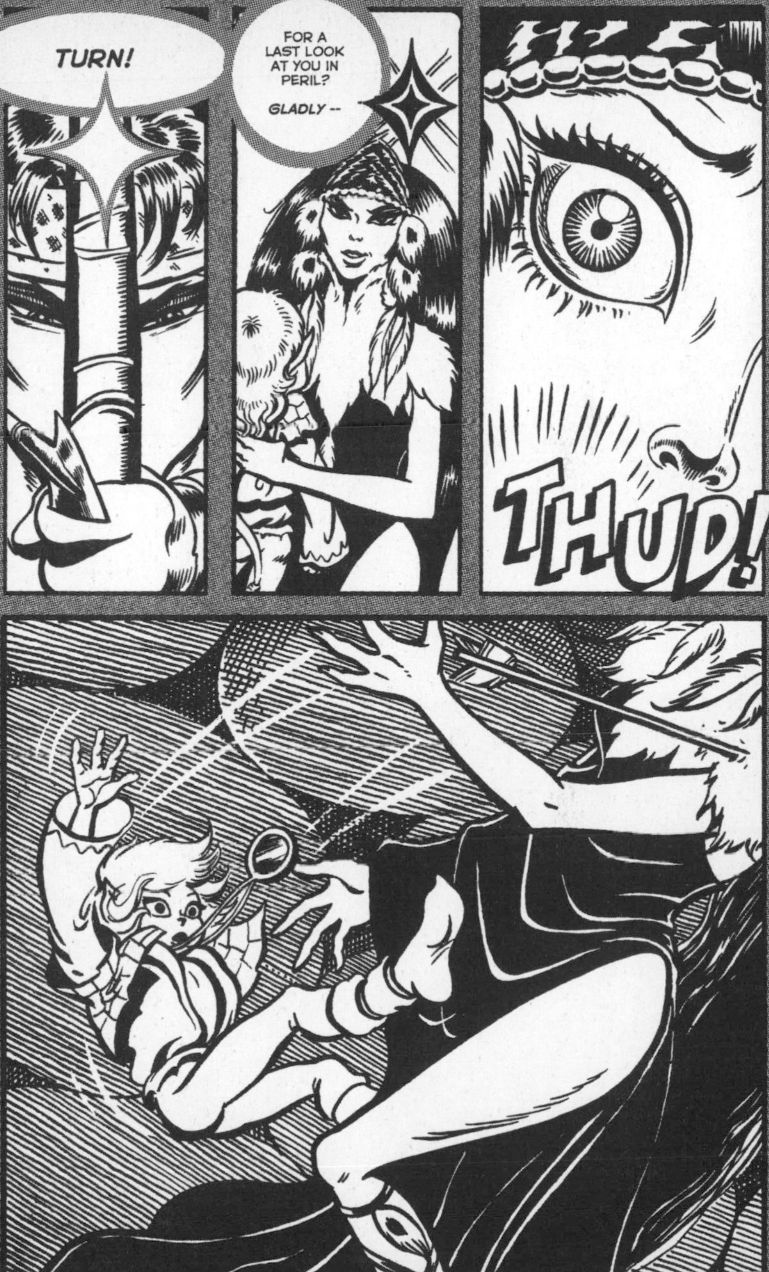
TURN!
FOR A LAST LOOK AT YOU IN PERIL?
GLADLY --
THUD!

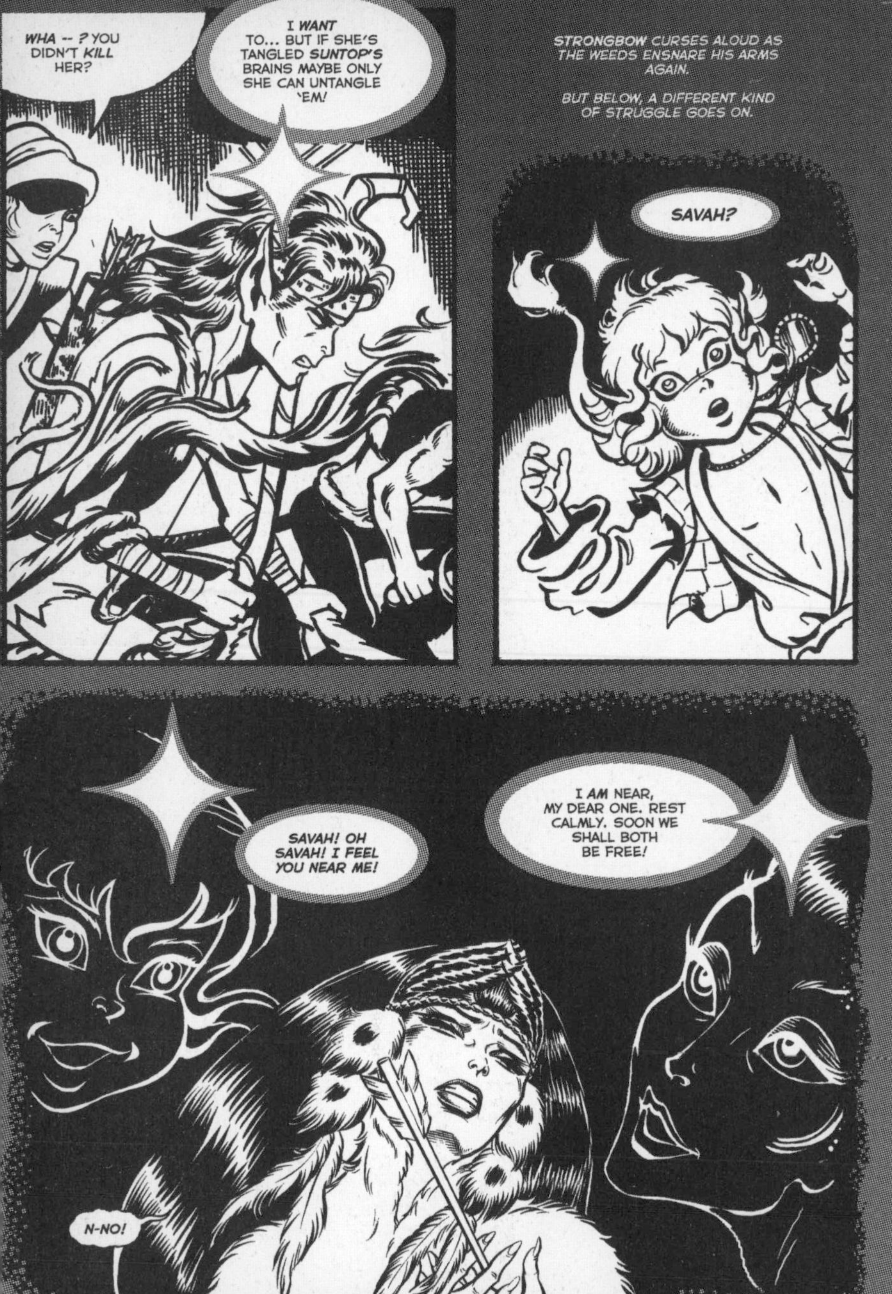
WHA -- ? YOU DIDN'T KILL HER?
I WANT TO... BUT IF SHE'S TANGLED SUNTOP'S BRAINS MAYBE ONLY SHE CAN UNTANGLE 'EM!
STRONGBOW CURSES ALOUD AS THE WEEDS ENSNARE HIS ARMS AGAIN.
BUT BELOW, A DIFFERENT KIND OF STRUGGLE GOES ON.
SAVAH?
SAVAH! OH SAVAH! I FEEL YOU NEAR ME!
I AM NEAR, MY DEAR ONE. REST CALMLY. SOON WE SHALL BOTH BE FREE!
N-NO!

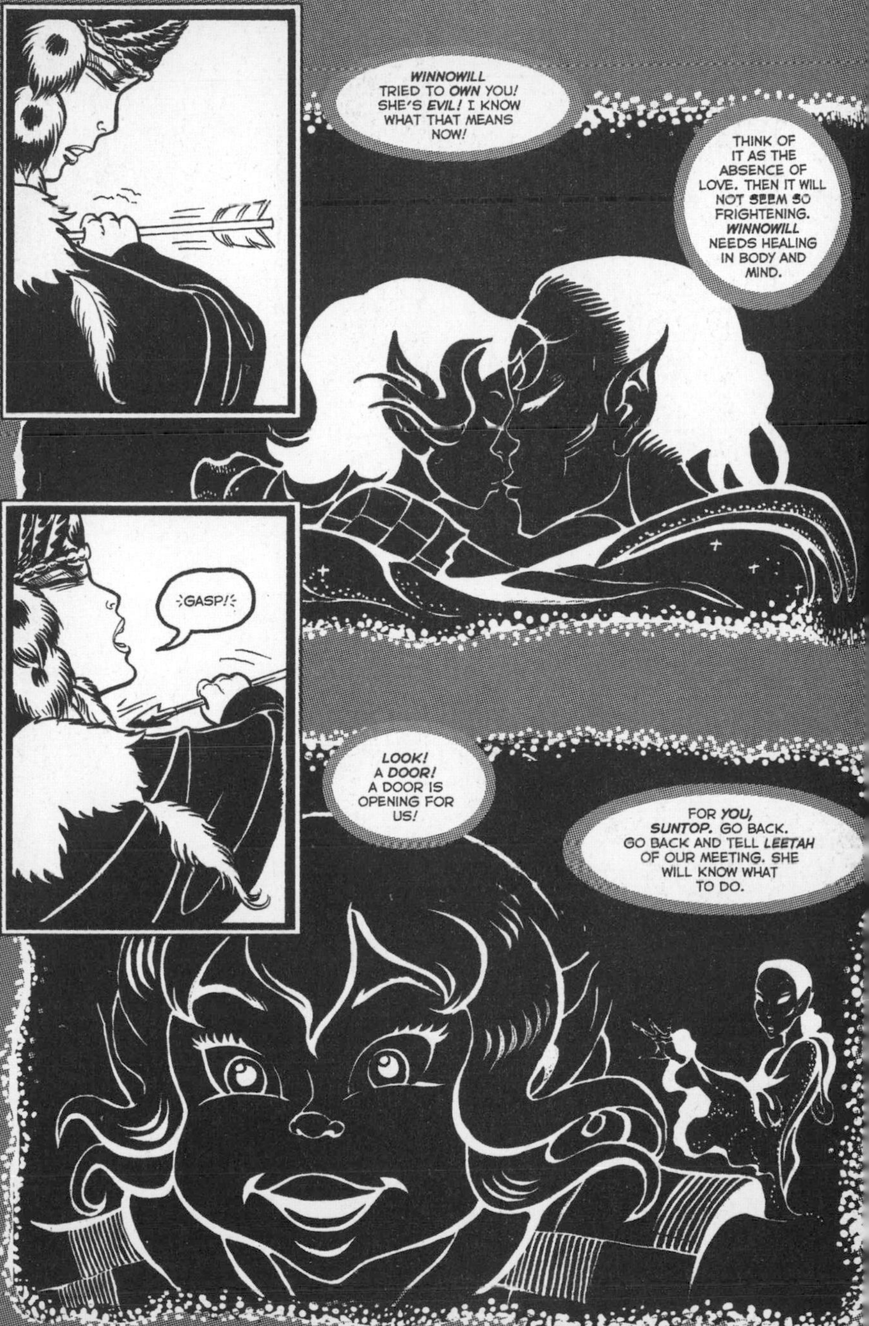
WINNOWILL TRIED TO OWN YOU! SHE'S EVIL! I KNOW WHAT THAT MEANS NOW!
THINK OF IT AS THE ABSENCE OF LOVE. THEN IT WILL NOT SEEM SO FRIGHTENING. WINNOWILL NEEDS HEALING IN BODY AND MIND.
GASP!
LOOK! A DOOR! A DOOR IS OPENING FOR US!
FOR YOU, SUNTOP. GO BACK. GO BACK AND TELL LEETAH OF OUR MEETING. SHE WILL KNOW WHAT TO DO.

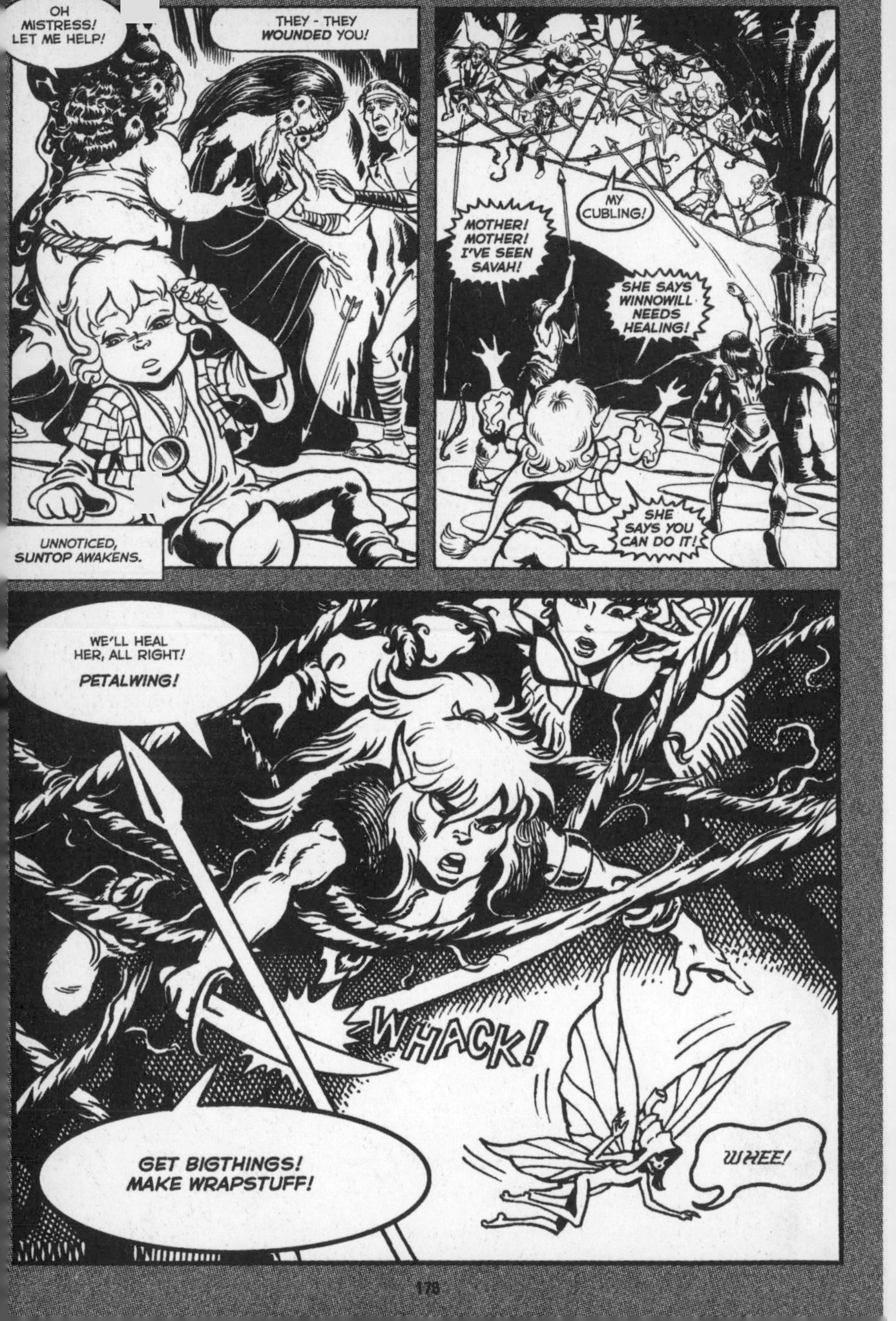
OH MISTRESS! LET ME HELP!
THEY - THEY WOUNDED YOU!
UNNOTICED, SUNTOP AWAKENS.
MOTHER! MOTHER! I'VE SEEN SAVAH!
MY CUBLING!
SHE SAYS WINNOWILL NEEDS HEALING!
SHE SAYS YOU CAN DO IT!
WE'LL HEAL HER, ALL RIGHT! PETALWING!
WHACK!
GET BIGTHINGS! MAKE WRAPSTUFF!
WHEE!

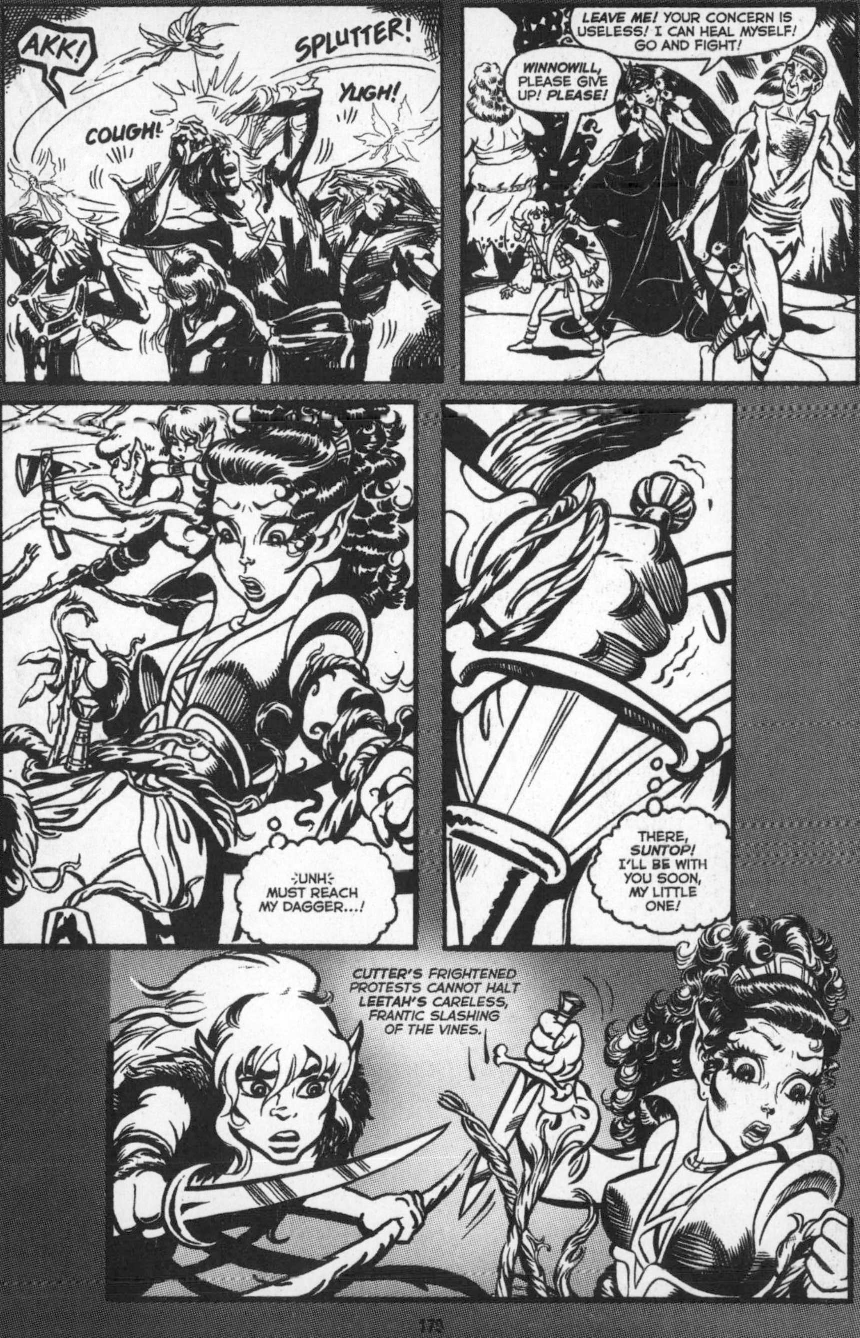
AKK!
SPLUTTER!
YUGH!
COUGH!
LEAVE ME! YOUR CONCERN IS USELESS! I CAN HEAL MYSELF! GO AND FIGHT!
WINNOWILL, PLEASE GIVE UP! PLEASE!
UNH MUST REACH MY DAGGER...!
THERE, SUNTOP! I'LL BE WITH YOU SOON, MY LITTLE ONE!
CUTTER'S FRIGHTENED PROTESTS CANNOT HALT LEETAH'S CARELESS, FRANTIC SLASHING OF THE VINES.

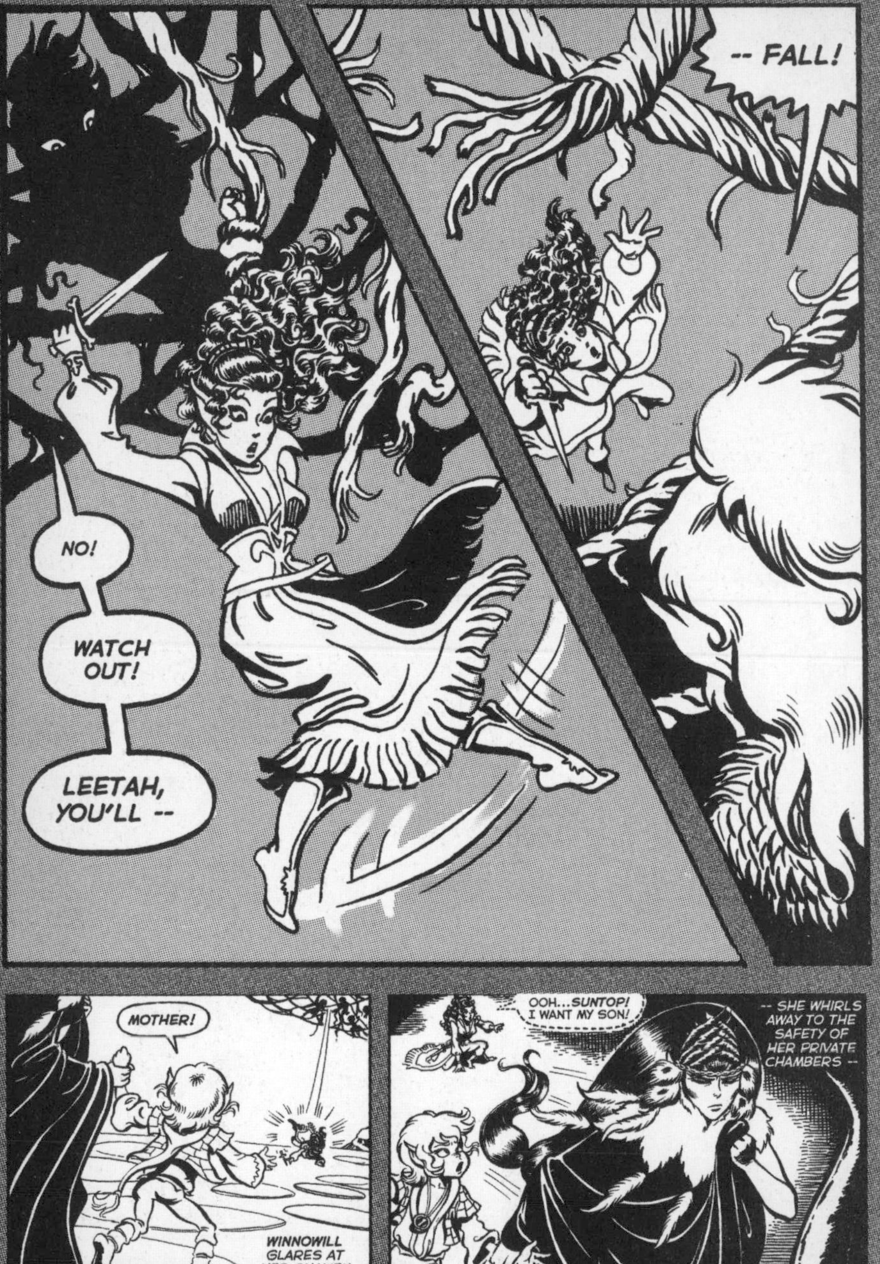

NO!
WATCH OUT!
LEETAH, YOU'LL --
-- FALL!
MOTHER!
WINNOWILL GLARES AT HER SHAKEN OPPONENT... AND THEN --
OOH...SUNTOP! I WANT MY SON!
-- SHE WHIRLS AWAY TO THE SAFETY OF HER PRIVATE CHAMBERS --

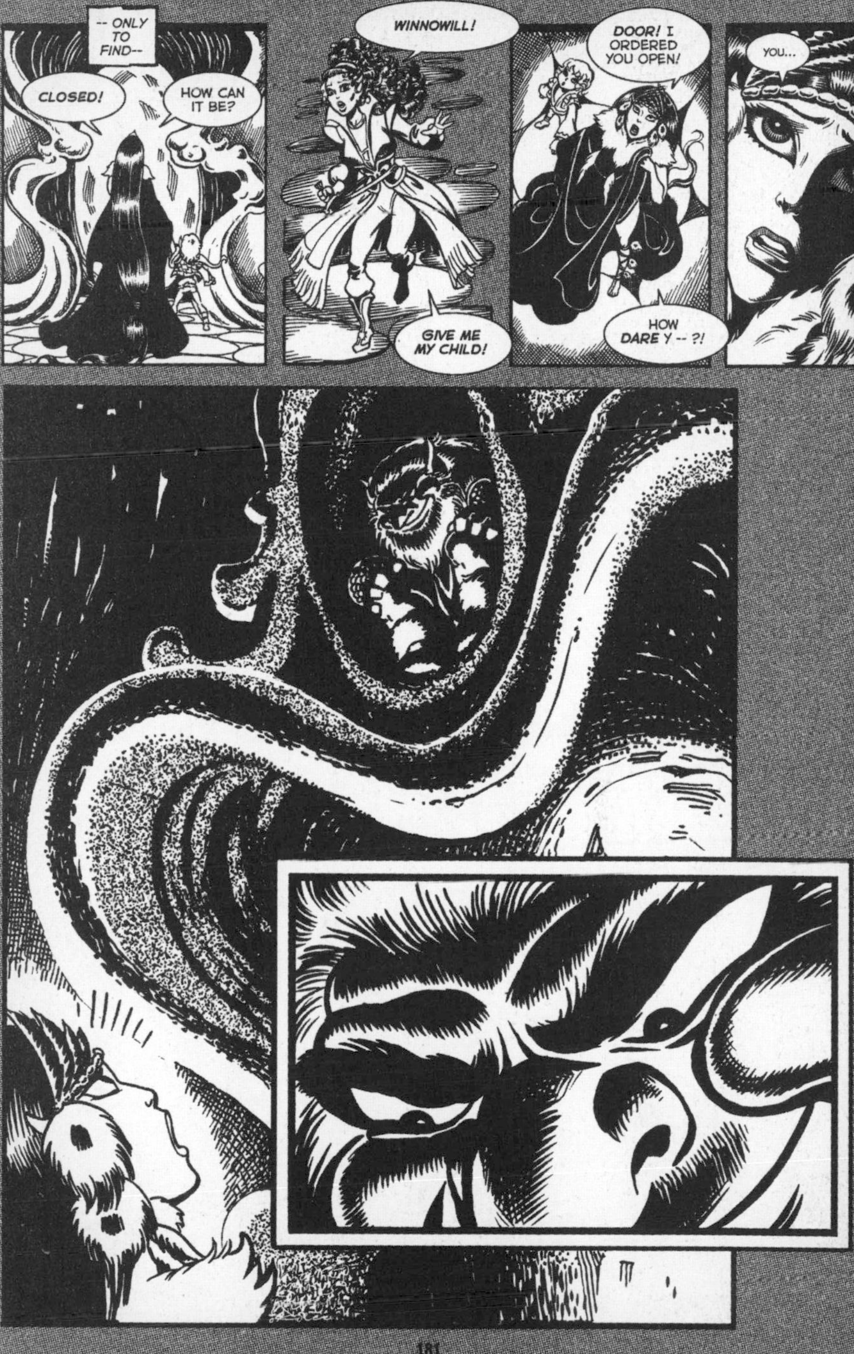
-- ONLY TO FIND--
CLOSED!
HOW CAN IT BE?
WINNOWILL!
GIVE ME MY CHILD!
DOOR! I ORDERED YOU OPEN!
HOW DARE Y -- ?!
YOU...

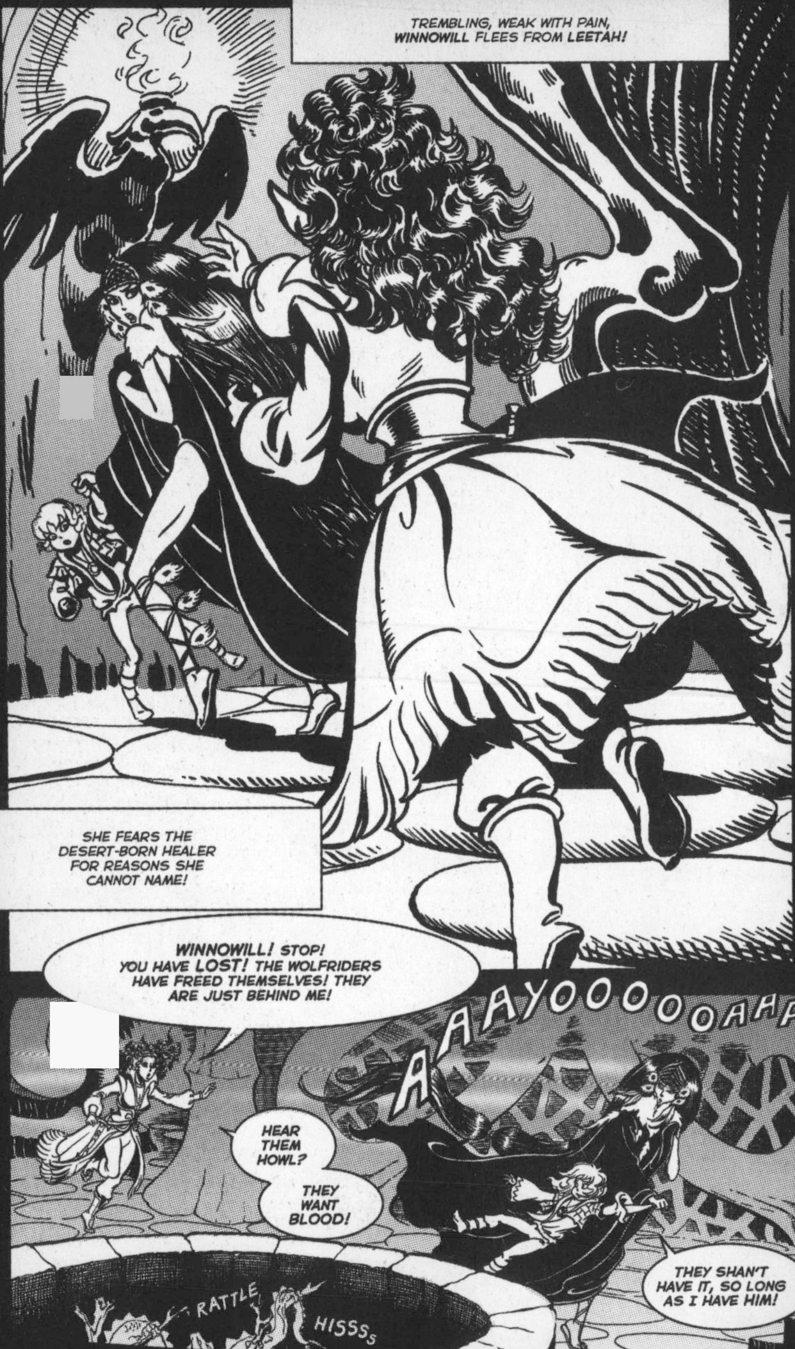
TREMBLING, WEAK WITH PAIN, WINNOWILL FLEES FROM LEETAH!
SHE FEARS THE DESERT-BORN HEALER FOR REASONS SHE CANNOT NAME!
WINNOWILL! STOP! YOU HAVE LOST! THE WOLFRIDERS HAVE FREED THEMSELVES! THEY ARE JUST BEHIND ME!
AAAAYOOOOOOOAHHA
HEAR THEM HOWL?
THEY WANT BLOOD!
THEY SHAN'T HAVE IT, SO LONG AS I HAVE HIM!
RATTLE
HISSSs

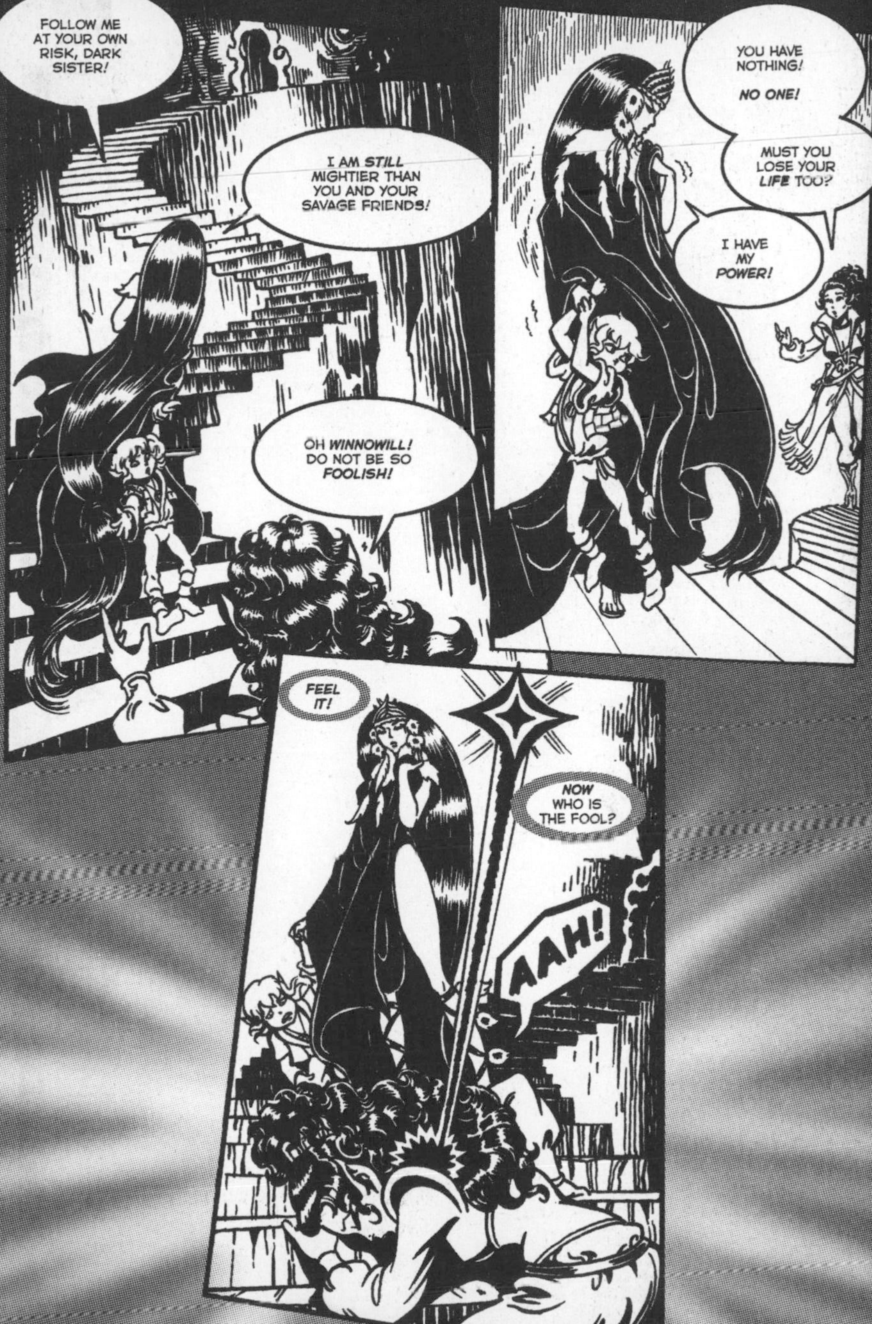
FOLLOW ME AT YOUR OWN RISK, DARK SISTER!
I AM STILL MIGHTIER THAN YOU AND YOUR SAVAGE FRIENDS!
OH WINNOWILL! DO NOT BE SO FOOLISH!
YOU HAVE NOTHING!
NO ONE!
MUST YOU LOSE YOUR LIFE TOO?
I HAVE MY POWER!
FEEL IT!
NOW WHO IS THE FOOL?
AAH!

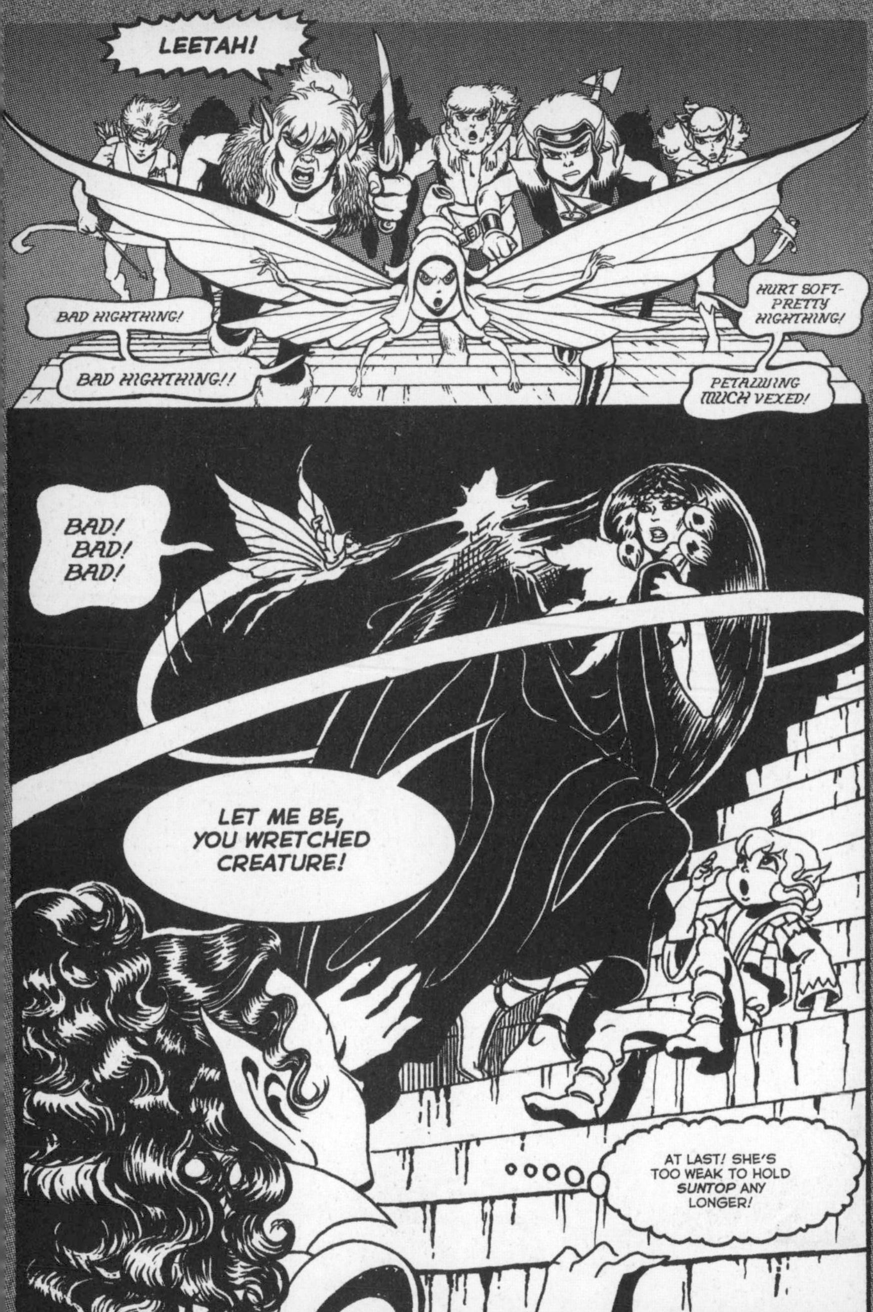
LEETAH!
BAD HIGHTHING!
BAD HIGHTHING!!
HURT SOFT-PRETTY HIGHTHING!
PETALWING MUCH VEXED!
BAD! BAD! BAD!
LET ME BE, YOU WRETCHED CREATURE!
AT LAST! SHE'S TOO WEAK TO HOLD SUNTOP ANY LONGER!

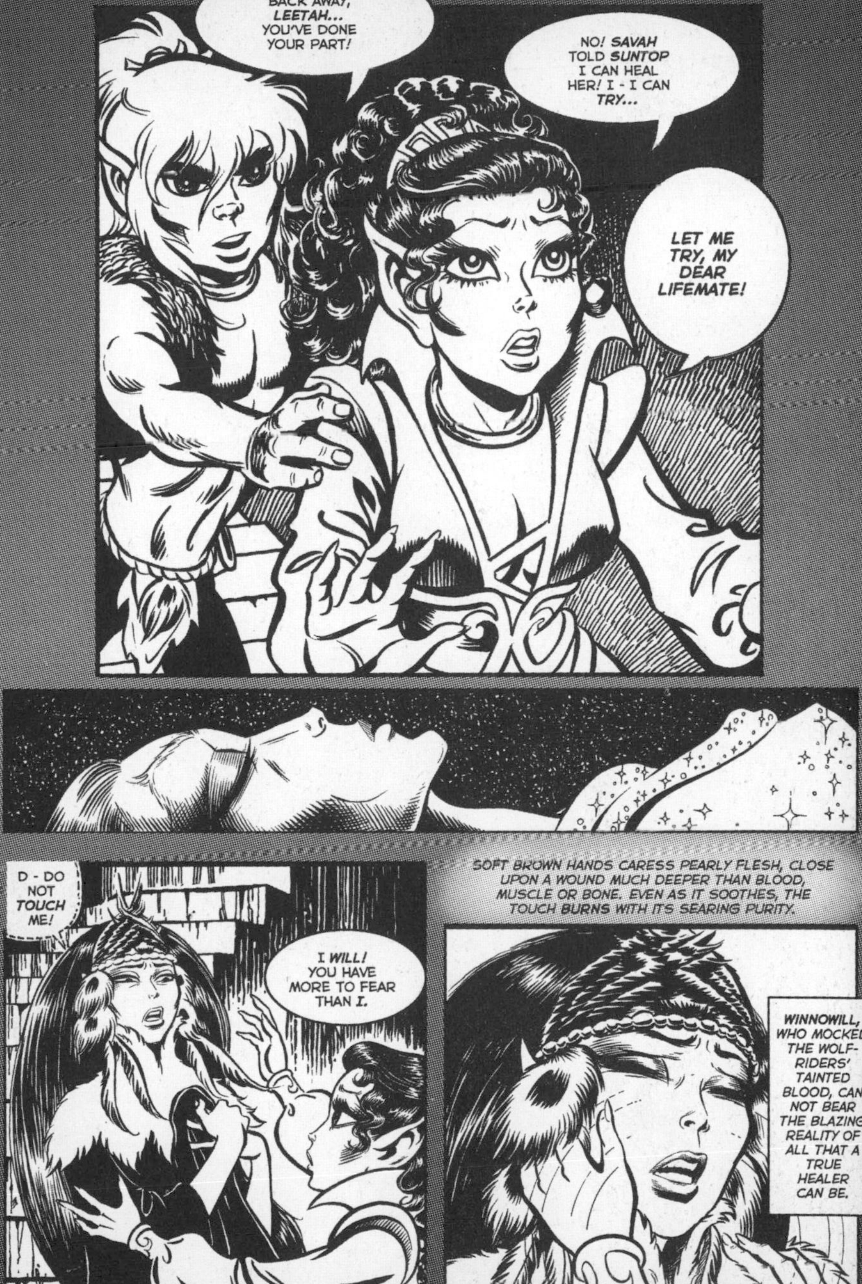
BACK AWAY, LEETAH... YOU'VE DONE YOUR PART!
NO! SAVAH TOLD SUNTOP I CAN HEAL HER! I - I CAN TRY...
LET ME TRY, MY DEAR LIFEMATE!
D - DO NOT TOUCH ME!
I WILL! YOU HAVE MORE TO FEAR THAN I.
SOFT BROWN HANDS CARESS PEARLY FLESH, CLOSE UPON A WOUND MUCH DEEPER THAN BLOOD, MUSCLE OR BONE. EVEN AS IT SOOTHES, THE TOUCH BURNS WITH ITS SEARING PURITY.
WINNOWILL, WHO MOCKED THE WOLF-RIDERS' TAINTED BLOOD, CAN NOT BEAR THE BLAZING REALITY OF ALL THAT A TRUE HEALER CAN BE.

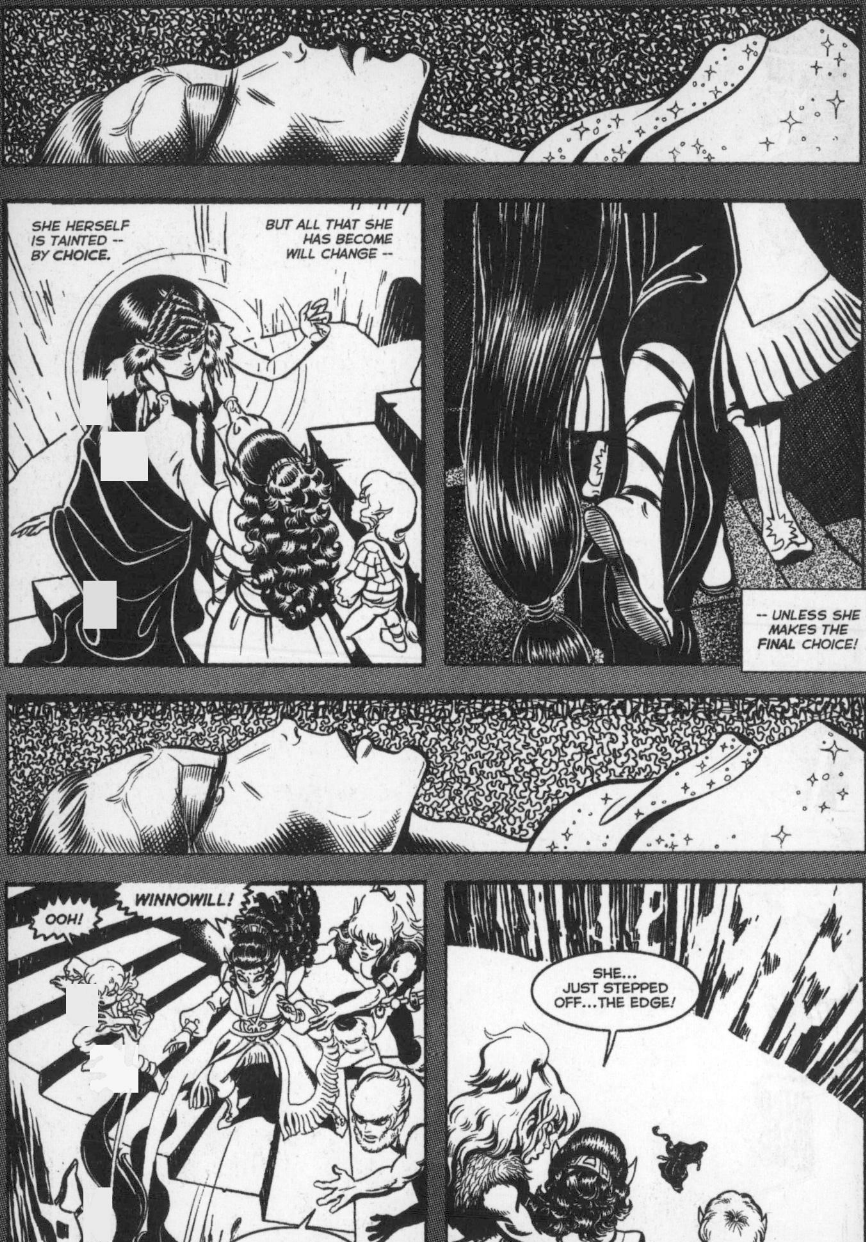
SHE HERSELF IS TAINTED -- BY CHOICE.
BUT ALL THAT SHE HAS BECOME WILL CHANGE --
-- UNLESS SHE MAKES THE FINAL CHOICE!
OOH!
WINNOWILL!
TIMMORN'S BLOOD!
SHE... JUST STEPPED OFF... THE EDGE!

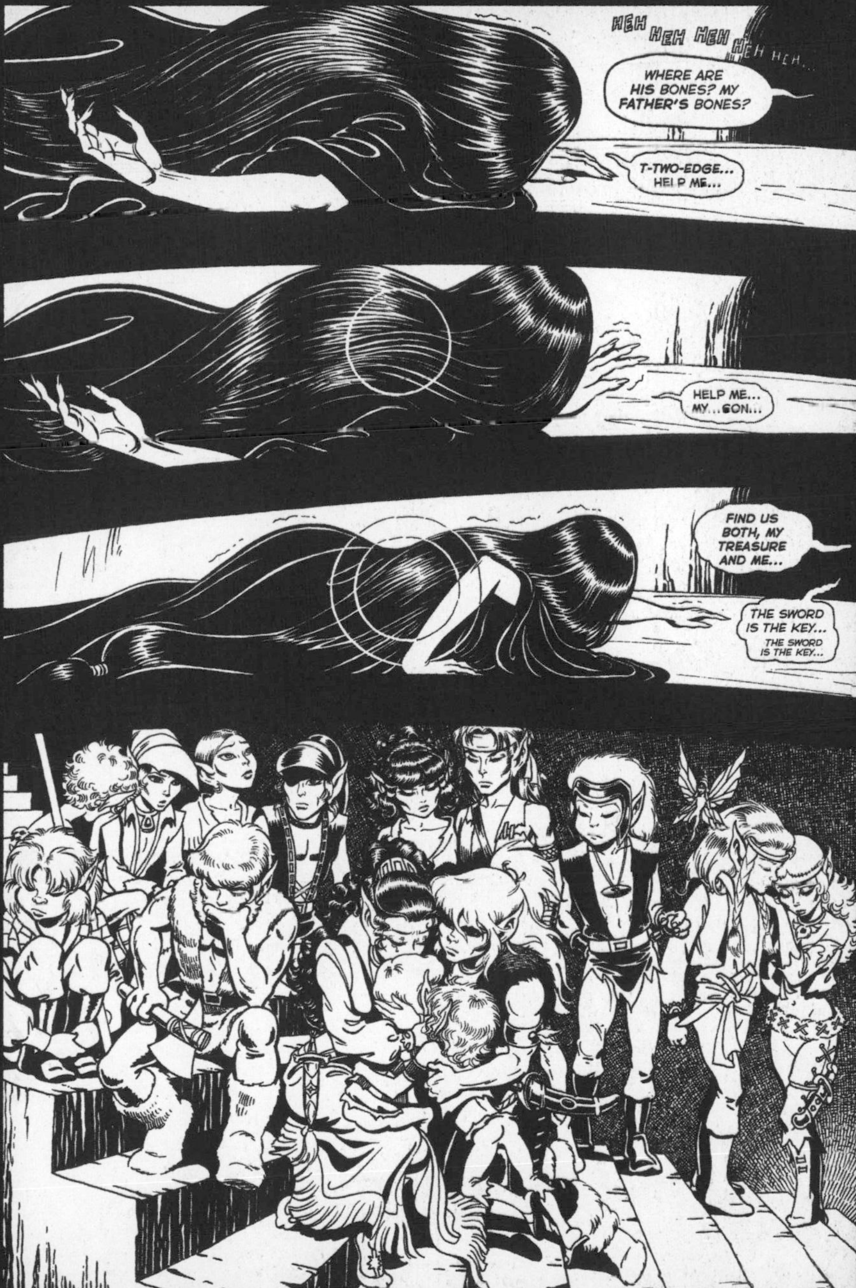
HEH HEH HEH HEH HEH...
WHERE ARE HIS BONES? MY FATHER'S BONES?
T-TWO-EDGE... HELP ME...
HELP ME... MY...SON...
FIND US BOTH, MY TREASURE AND ME...
THE SWORD IS THE KEY... THE SWORD IS THE KEY...

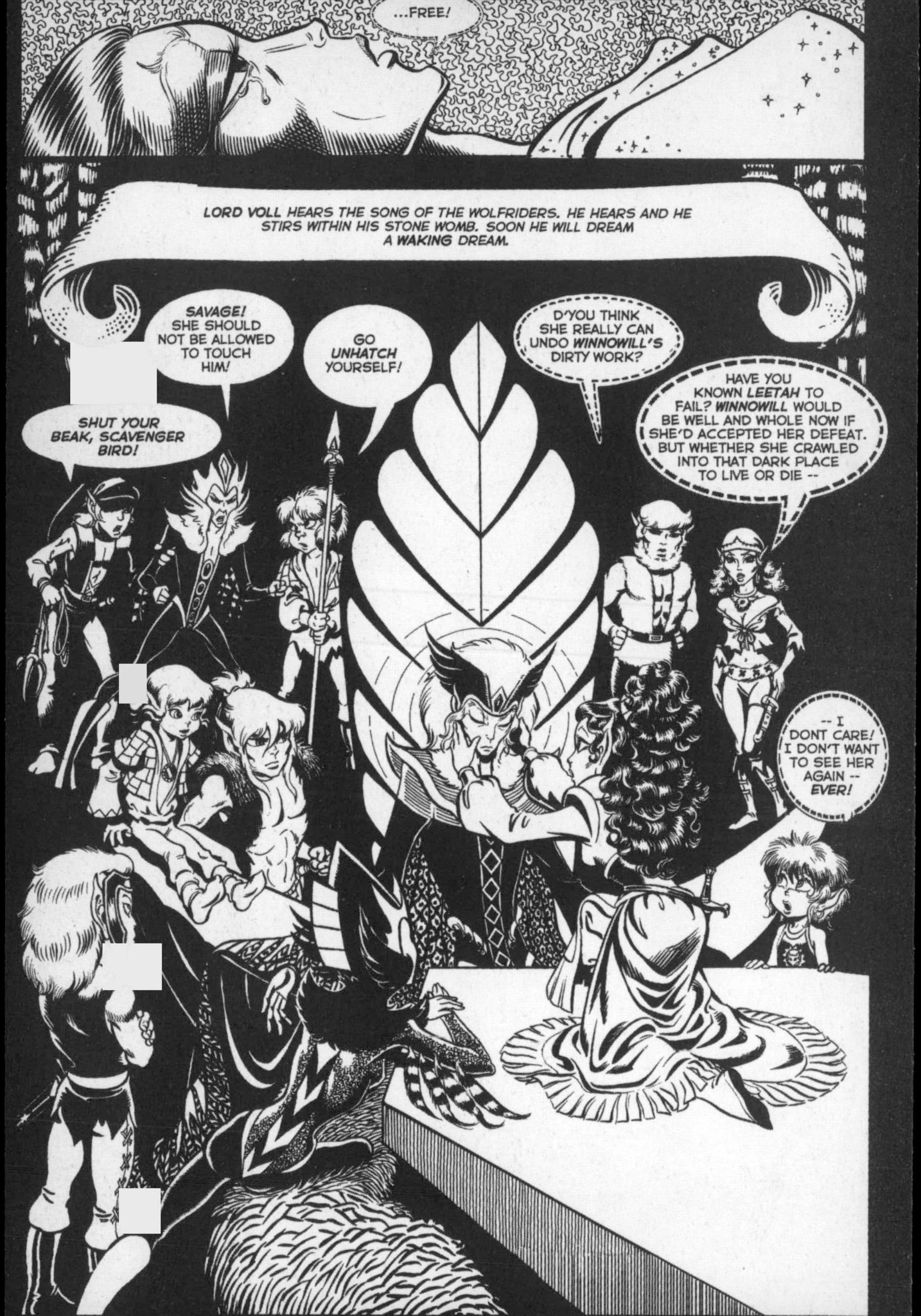
...FREE!
LORD VOLL HEARS THE SONG OF THE WOLFRIDERS. HE HEARS AND HE STIRS WITHIN HIS STONE WOMB. SOON HE WILL DREAM A WAKING DREAM.
SAVAGE! SHE SHOULD NOT BE ALLOWED TO TOUCH HIM!
SHUT YOUR BEAK, SCAVENGER BIRD!
GO UNHATCH YOURSELF!
D'YOU THINK SHE REALLY CAN UNDO WINNOWILL'S DIRTY WORK?
HAVE YOU KNOWN LEETAH TO FAIL? WINNOWILL WOULD BE WELL AND WHOLE NOW IF SHE'D ACCEPTED HER DEFEAT. BUT WHETHER SHE CRAWLED INTO THAT DARK PLACE TO LIVE OR DIE --
-- I DONT CARE! I DON'T WANT TO SEE HER AGAIN -- EVER!

NO! STOP THIS SHAMEFUL BRAWLING! *KUREEL! TYLDAK!* WHA -- ?

WH - WHAT HAS HAPPENED?

COME, GENTLE LORD... OPEN YOUR EYES!

MMM... MPH...

WINNOWILL PUT YOU TO SLEEP, *LORD VOLL,* SO THAT YOU COULD NOT INTERFERE WITH HER PLANS!

PLANS?

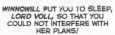

THE WOLFRIDERS NEARLY FALL OVER ONE ANOTHER IN THEIR HASTE TO TELL VOLL OF WINNOWILL'S EVERY CRUEL MANIPULATION --

--FROM THE TORTURE OF STRONGBOW TO THE KIDNAPPING OF SUNTOP!

SHE TRIED TO *FORCE* US TO LEAVE BLUE MOUNTAIN IN EXCHANGE FOR THE CUB'S RETURN!

-- SO SHE TURNED HER POWERS AGAINST ME! EVEN *ME!* BUT WHY? WHY SUCH DESPERATION TO DRIVE YOU WOLFRIDERS AWAY?

WHAT WAS HER TERRIBLE FEAR?

NOTHING MORE TERRIBLE --

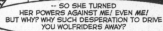

BUT SHE KNEW YOU'D NEVER LET HER GET AWAY WITH IT --

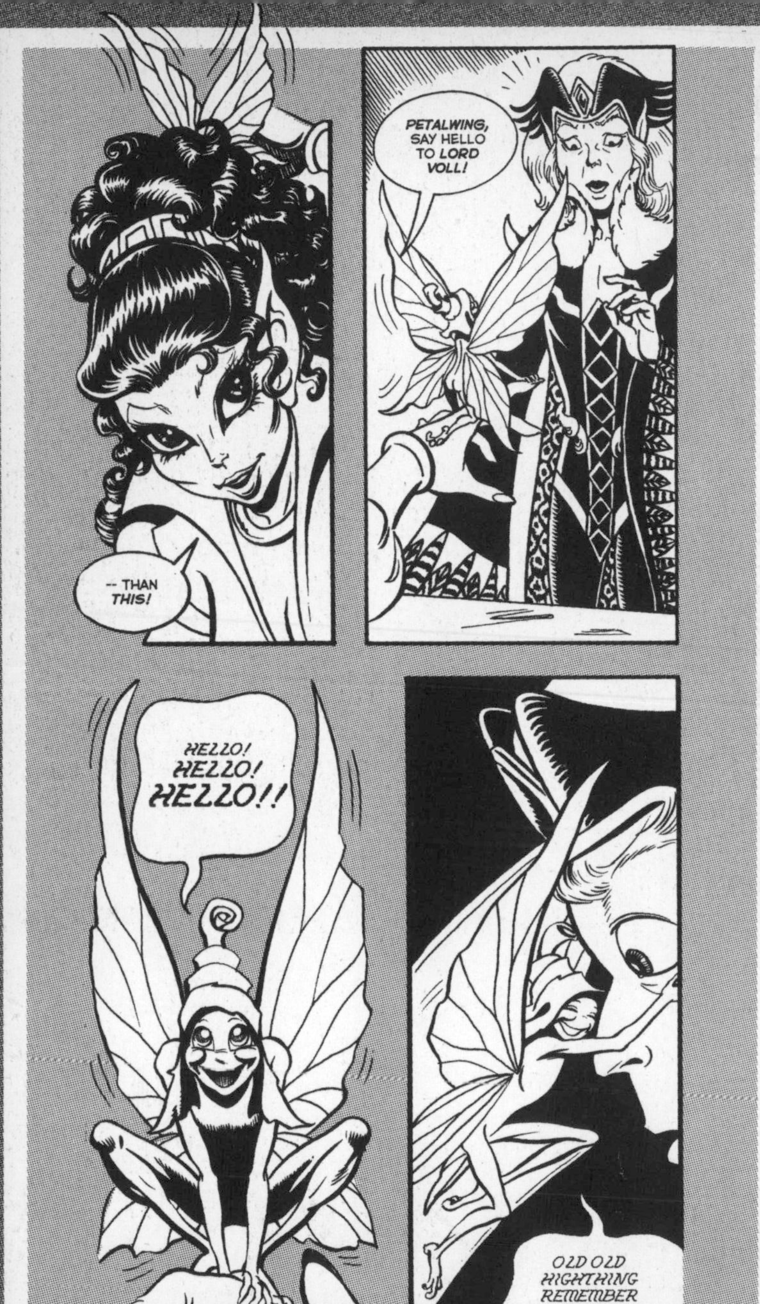
-- THAN THIS!
PETALWING, SAY HELLO TO LORD VOLL!
HELLO! HELLO! HELLO!!
OLD OLD HIGHTHING REMEMBER PETALWING?

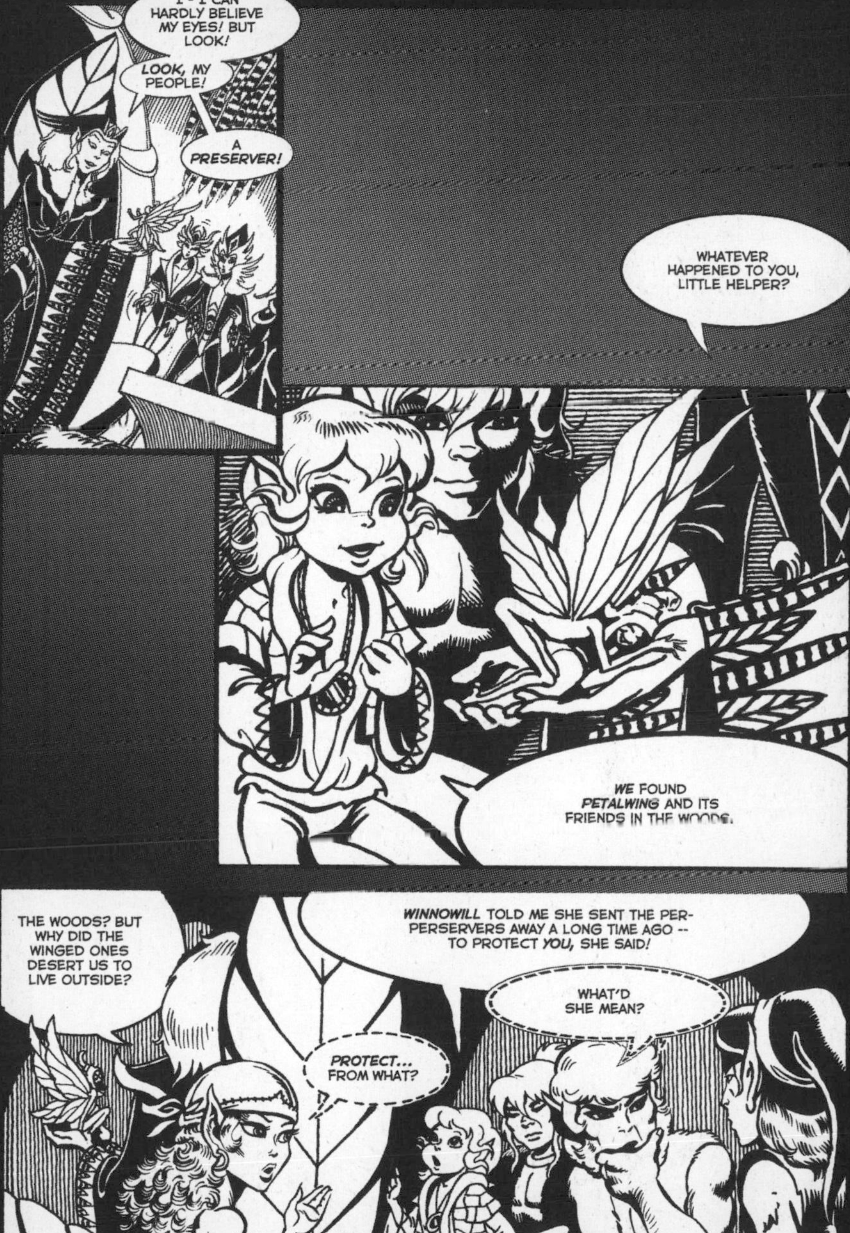
I - I CAN HARDLY BELIEVE MY EYES! BUT LOOK!
LOOK, MY PEOPLE!
A PRESERVER!
WHATEVER HAPPENED TO YOU, LITTLE HELPER?
WE FOUND PETALWING AND ITS FRIENDS IN THE WOODS.
THE WOODS? BUT WHY DID THE WINGED ONES DESERT US TO LIVE OUTSIDE?
WINNOWILL TOLD ME SHE SENT THE PER-PERSERVERS AWAY A LONG TIME AGO -- TO PROTECT YOU, SHE SAID!
WHAT'D SHE MEAN?
PROTECT... FROM WHAT?

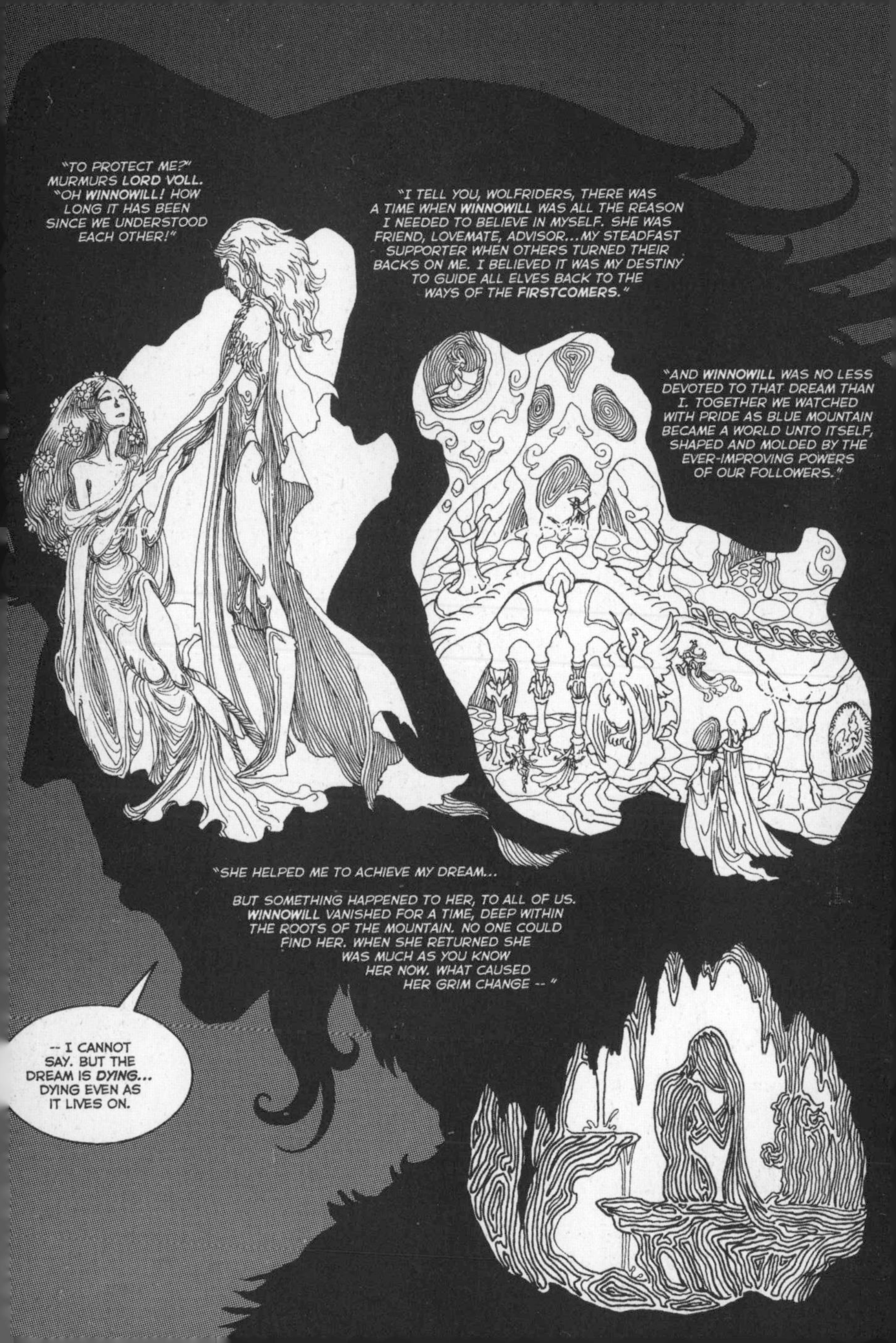
"TO PROTECT ME?" MURMURS LORD VOLL. "OH WINNOWILL! HOW LONG IT HAS BEEN SINCE WE UNDERSTOOD EACH OTHER!"
"I TELL YOU, WOLFRIDERS, THERE WAS A TIME WHEN WINNOWILL WAS ALL THE REASON I NEEDED TO BELIEVE IN MYSELF. SHE WAS FRIEND, LOVEMATE, ADVISOR... MY STEADFAST SUPPORTER WHEN OTHERS TURNED THEIR BACKS ON ME. I BELIEVED IT WAS MY DESTINY TO GUIDE ALL ELVES BACK TO THE WAYS OF THE FIRSTCOMERS."
"AND WINNOWILL WAS NO LESS DEVOTED TO THAT DREAM THAN I. TOGETHER WE WATCHED WITH PRIDE AS BLUE MOUNTAIN BECAME A WORLD UNTO ITSELF, SHAPED AND MOLDED BY THE EVER-IMPROVING POWERS OF OUR FOLLOWERS."
"SHE HELPED ME TO ACHIEVE MY DREAM...
BUT SOMETHING HAPPENED TO HER, TO ALL OF US. WINNOWILL VANISHED FOR A TIME, DEEP WITHIN THE ROOTS OF THE MOUNTAIN. NO ONE COULD FIND HER. WHEN SHE RETURNED SHE WAS MUCH AS YOU KNOW HER NOW. WHAT CAUSED HER GRIM CHANGE --"
-- I CANNOT SAY. BUT THE DREAM IS DYING... DYING EVEN AS IT LIVES ON.

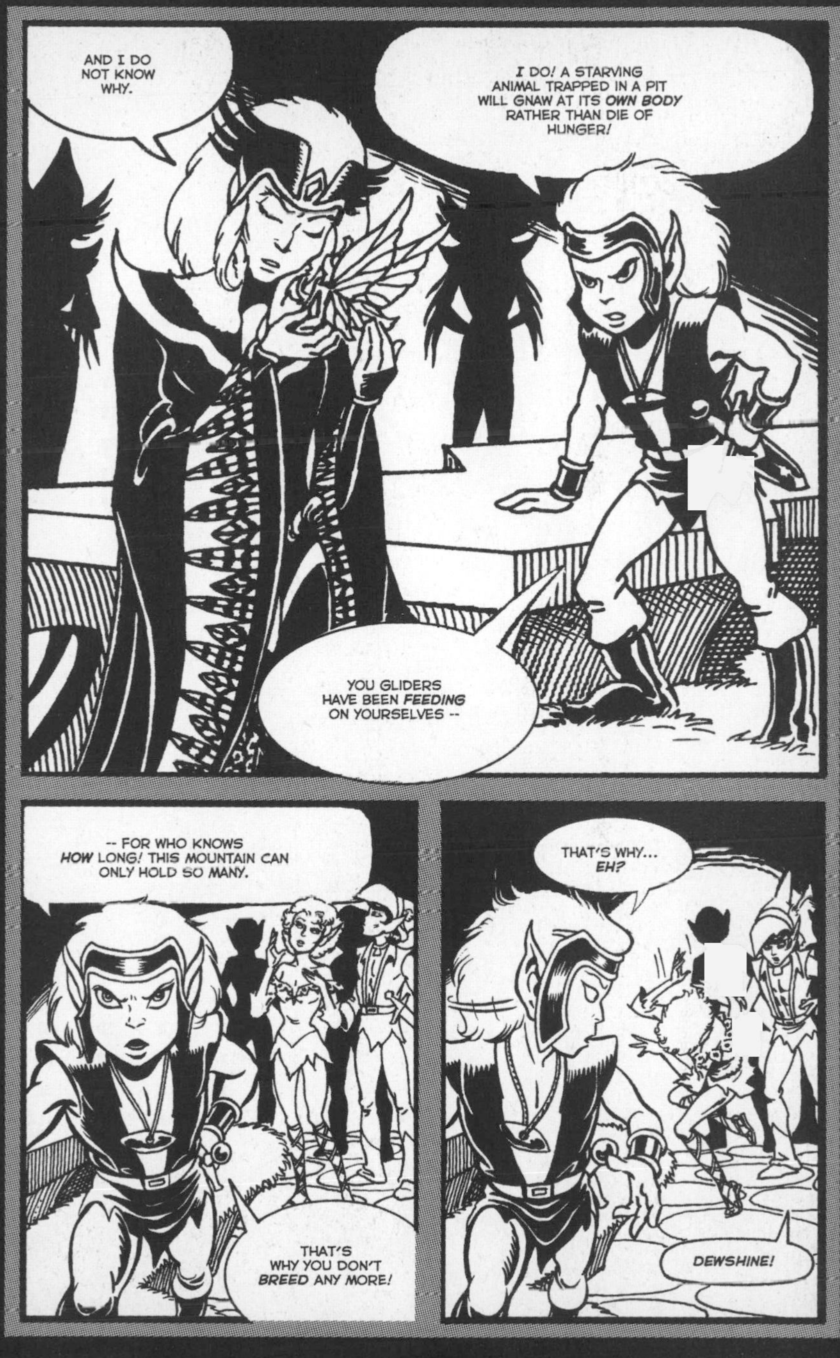
AND I DO NOT KNOW WHY.
I DO! A STARVING ANIMAL TRAPPED IN A PIT WILL GNAW AT ITS OWN BODY RATHER THAN DIE OF HUNGER!
YOU GLIDERS HAVE BEEN FEEDING ON YOURSELVES --
-- FOR WHO KNOWS HOW LONG! THIS MOUNTAIN CAN ONLY HOLD SO MANY.
THAT'S WHY YOU DON'T BREED ANY MORE!
THAT'S WHY... EH?
DEWSHINE!

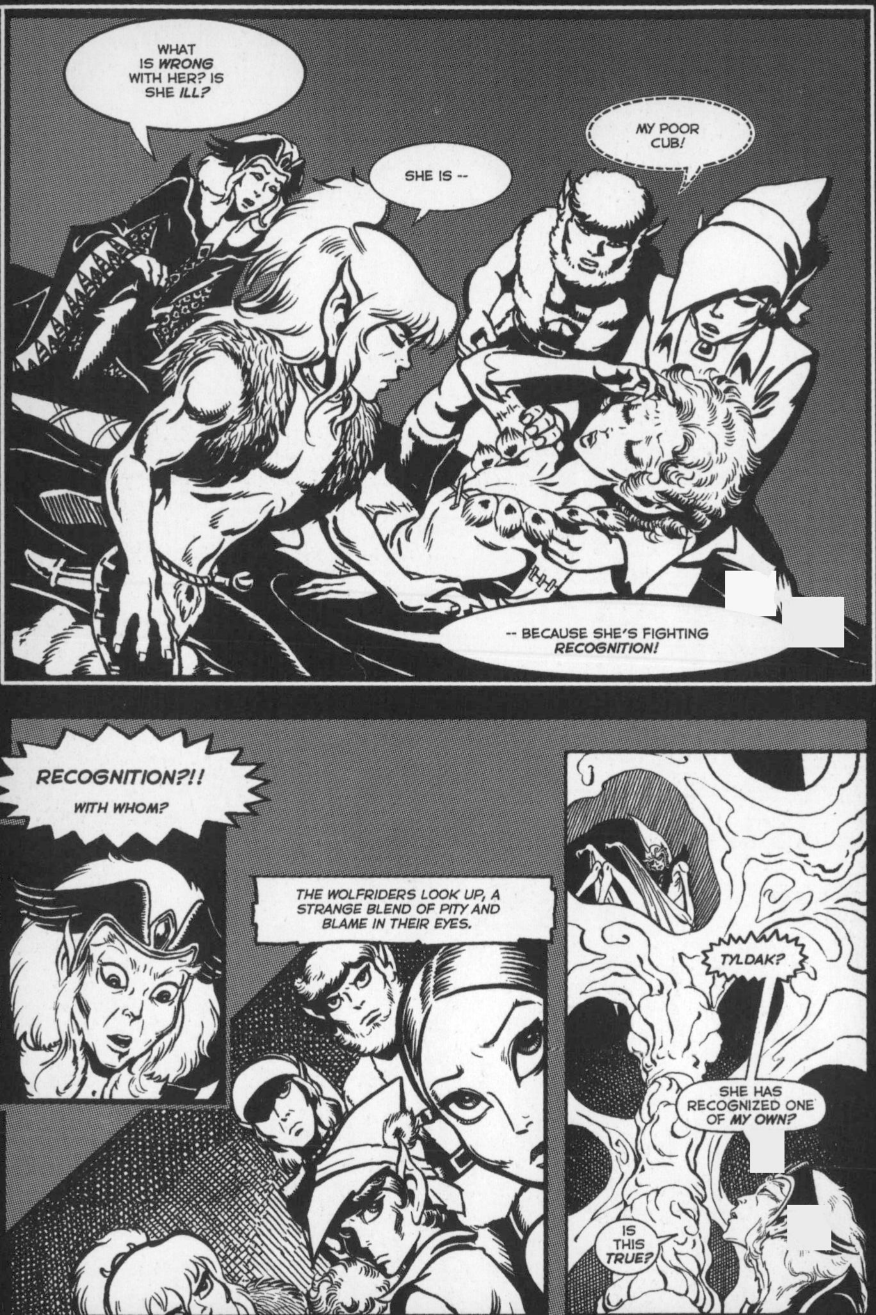
WHAT IS WRONG WITH HER? IS SHE ILL?
MY POOR CUB!
SHE IS --
-- BECAUSE SHE'S FIGHTING RECOGNITION!
RECOGNITION?!! WITH WHOM?
THE WOLFRIDERS LOOK UP, A STRANGE BLEND OF PITY AND BLAME IN THEIR EYES.
TYLDAK?
SHE HAS RECOGNIZED ONE OF MY OWN?
IS THIS TRUE?

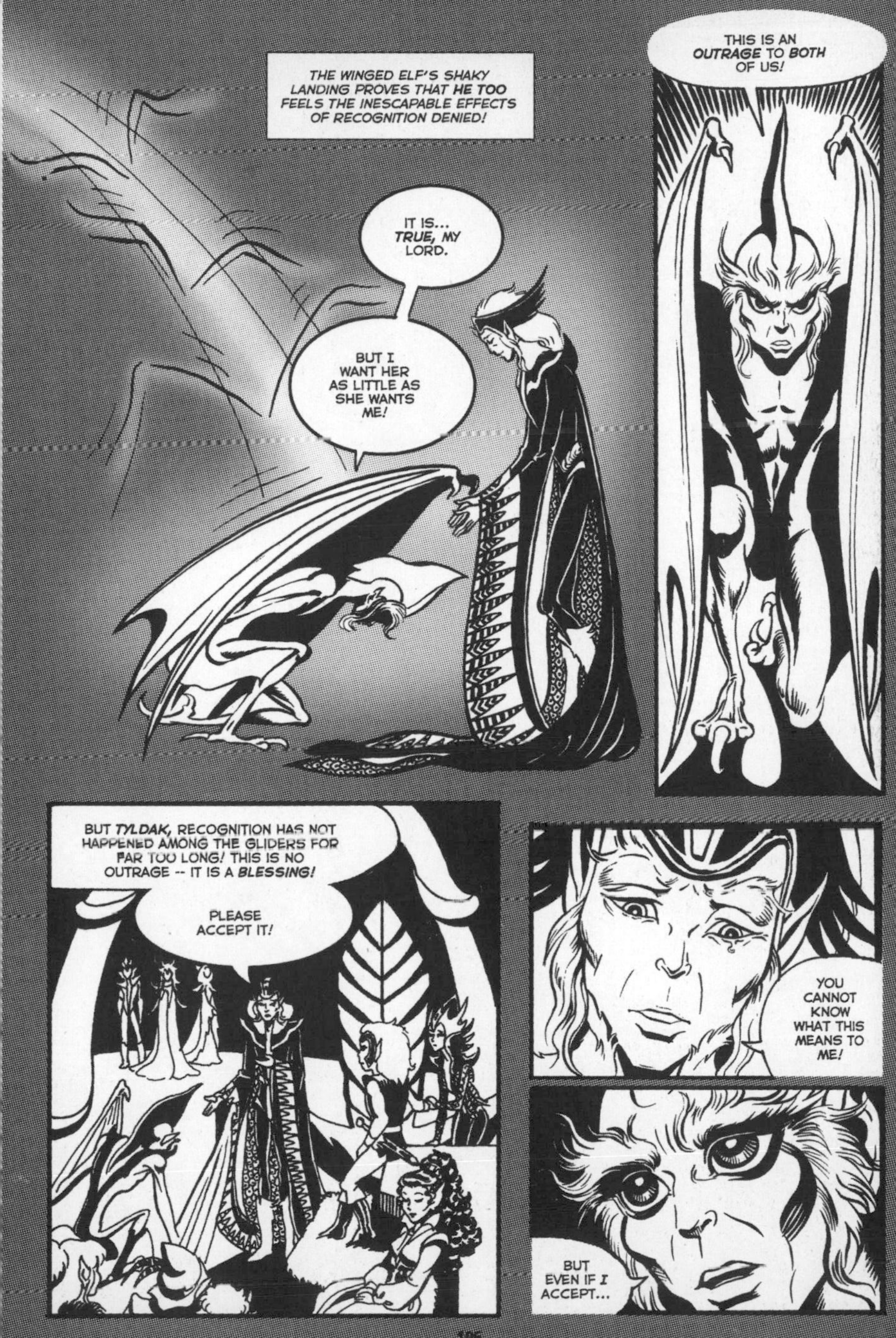
THE WINGED ELF'S SHAKY LANDING PROVES THAT HE TOO FEELS THE INESCAPABLE EFFECTS OF RECOGNITION DENIED!
IT IS... TRUE, MY LORD.
BUT I WANT HER AS LITTLE AS SHE WANTS ME!
THIS IS AN OUTRAGE TO BOTH OF US!
BUT TYLDAK, RECOGNITION HAS NOT HAPPENED AMONG THE GLIDERS FOR FAR TOO LONG! THIS IS NO OUTRAGE -- IT IS A BLESSING!
PLEASE ACCEPT IT!
YOU CANNOT KNOW WHAT THIS MEANS TO ME!
BUT EVEN IF I ACCEPT...

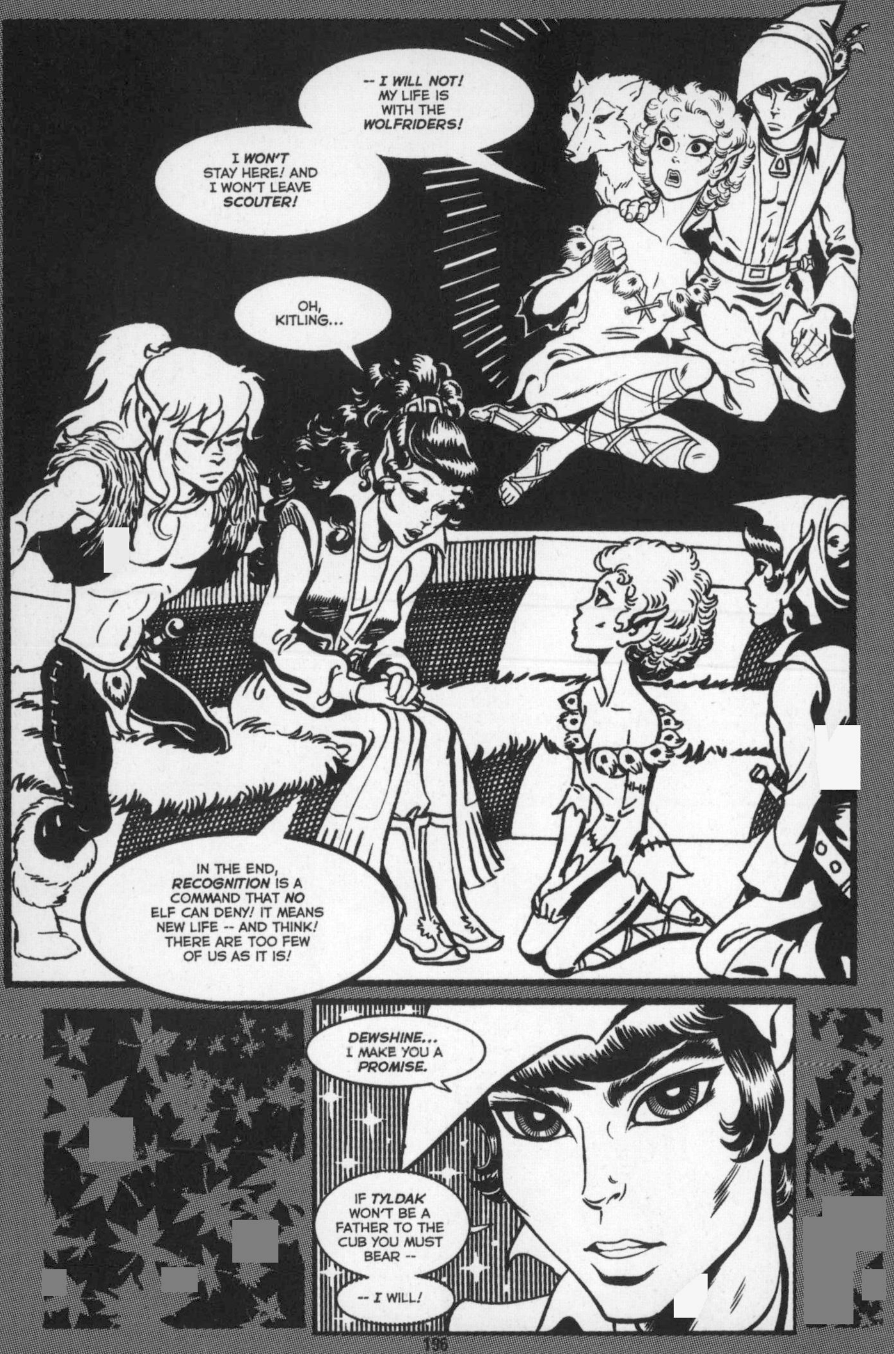
I WON'T STAY HERE! AND I WON'T LEAVE SCOUTER!
-- I WILL NOT! MY LIFE IS WITH THE WOLFRIDERS!
OH, KITLING...
IN THE END, RECOGNITION IS A COMMAND THAT NO ELF CAN DENY! IT MEANS NEW LIFE -- AND THINK! THERE ARE TOO FEW OF US AS IT IS!
DEWSHINE... I MAKE YOU A PROMISE.
IF TYLDAK WON'T BE A FATHER TO THE CUB YOU MUST BEAR --
-- I WILL!

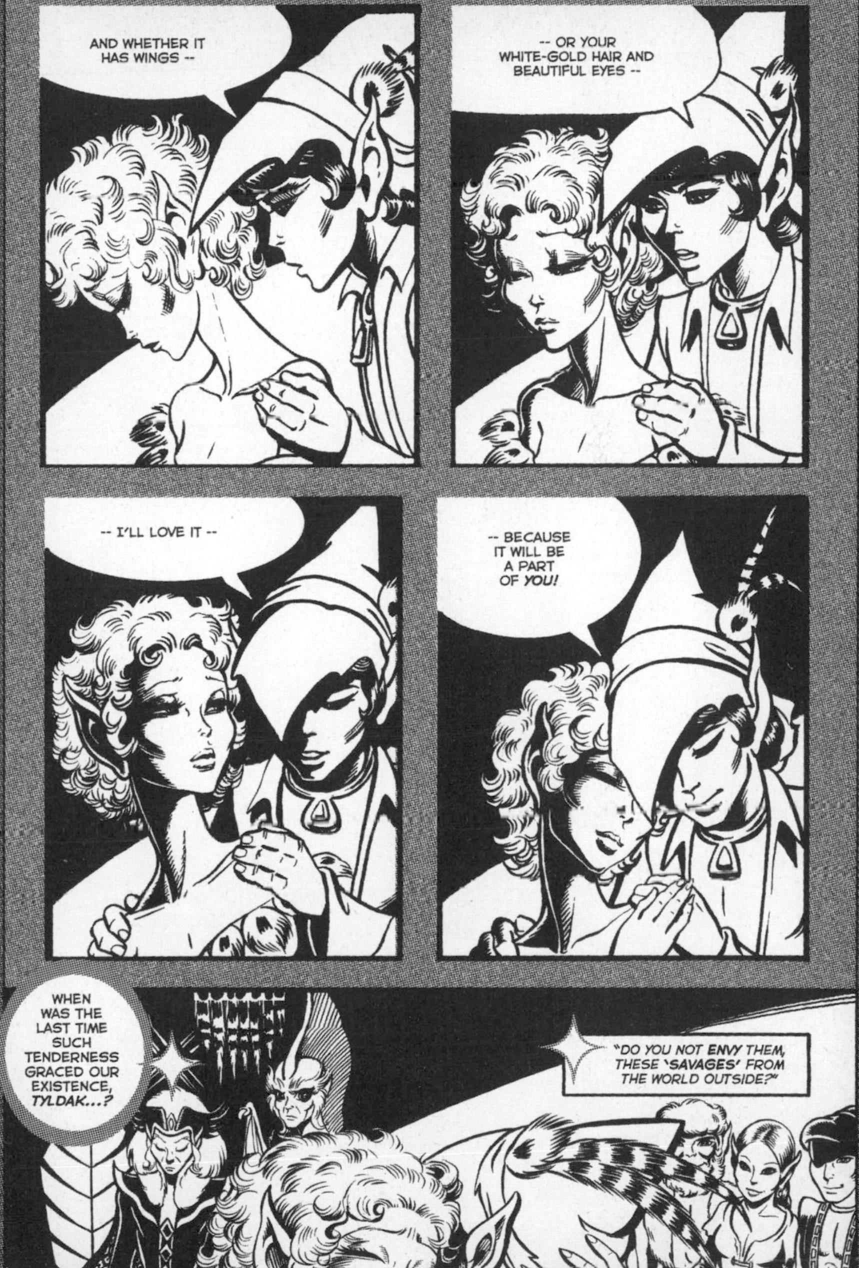
AND WHETHER IT HAS WINGS --
-- OR YOUR WHITE-GOLD HAIR AND BEAUTIFUL EYES --
-- I'LL LOVE IT --
-- BECAUSE IT WILL BE A PART OF *YOU!*
WHEN WAS THE LAST TIME SUCH TENDERNESS GRACED OUR EXISTENCE, *TYLDAK...?*
*"DO YOU NOT **ENVY** THEM, THESE **'SAVAGES'** FROM THE WORLD OUTSIDE?"*
DEWSHINE TURNS...

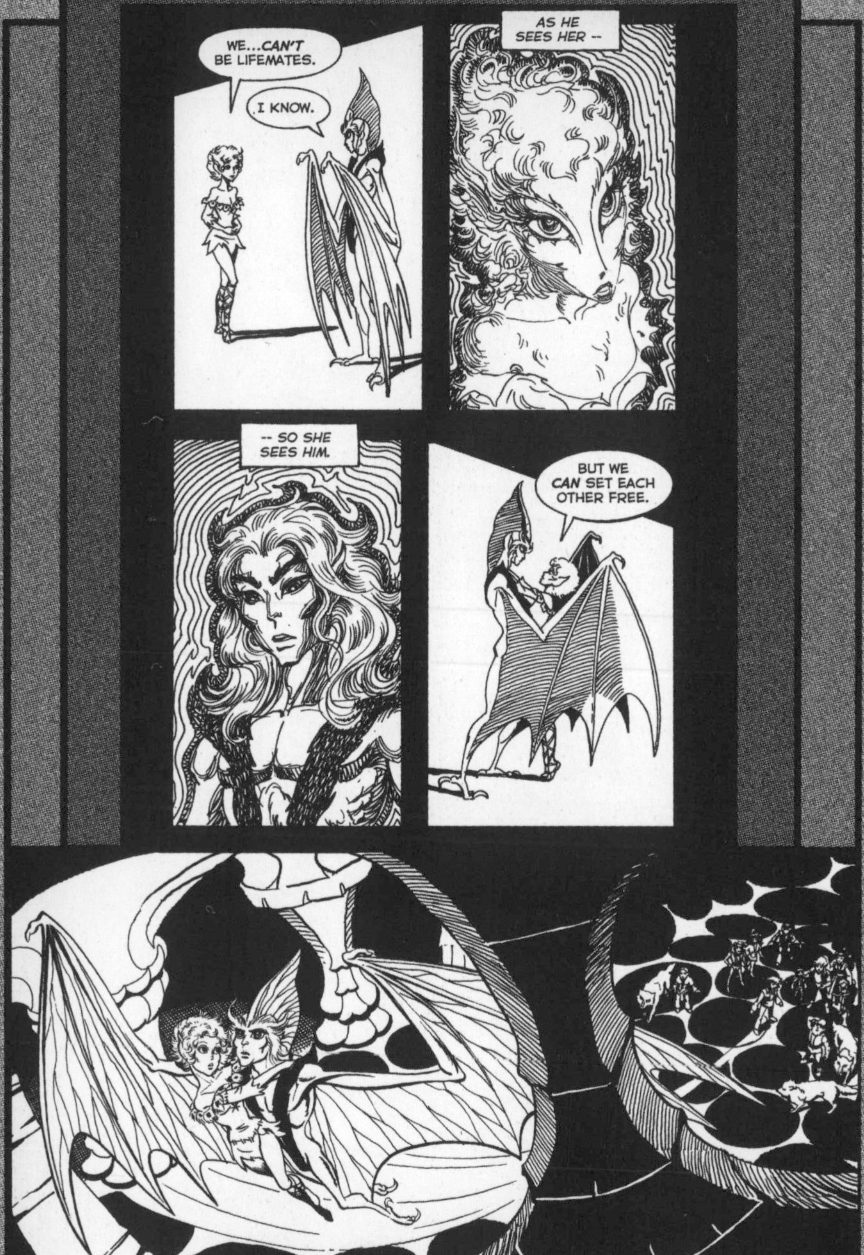
WE...CAN'T BE LIFEMATES.
I KNOW.
AS HE SEES HER --
-- SO SHE SEES HIM.
BUT WE CAN SET EACH OTHER FREE.

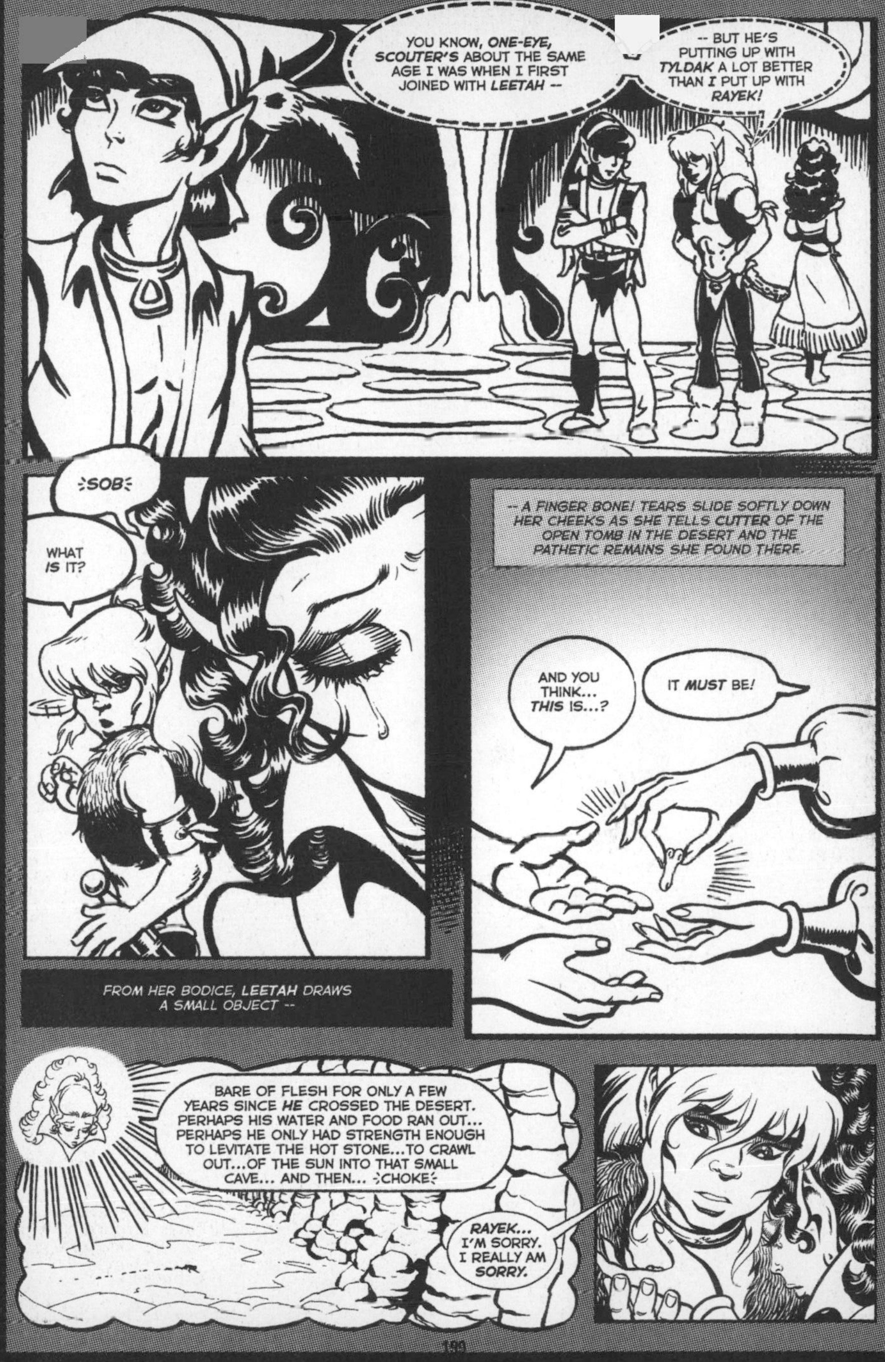
YOU KNOW, ONE-EYE, SCOUTER'S ABOUT THE SAME AGE I WAS WHEN I FIRST JOINED WITH LEETAH --
-- BUT HE'S PUTTING UP WITH TYLDAK A LOT BETTER THAN I PUT UP WITH RAYEK!
SOB
WHAT IS IT?
FROM HER BODICE, LEETAH DRAWS A SMALL OBJECT --
-- A FINGER BONE! TEARS SLIDE SOFTLY DOWN HER CHEEKS AS SHE TELLS CUTTER OF THE OPEN TOMB IN THE DESERT AND THE PATHETIC REMAINS SHE FOUND THERE.
AND YOU THINK... THIS IS...?
IT MUST BE!
BARE OF FLESH FOR ONLY A FEW YEARS SINCE HE CROSSED THE DESERT. PERHAPS HIS WATER AND FOOD RAN OUT... PERHAPS HE ONLY HAD STRENGTH ENOUGH TO LEVITATE THE HOT STONE...TO CRAWL OUT...OF THE SUN INTO THAT SMALL CAVE... AND THEN... CHOKE
RAYEK... I'M SORRY. I REALLY AM SORRY.

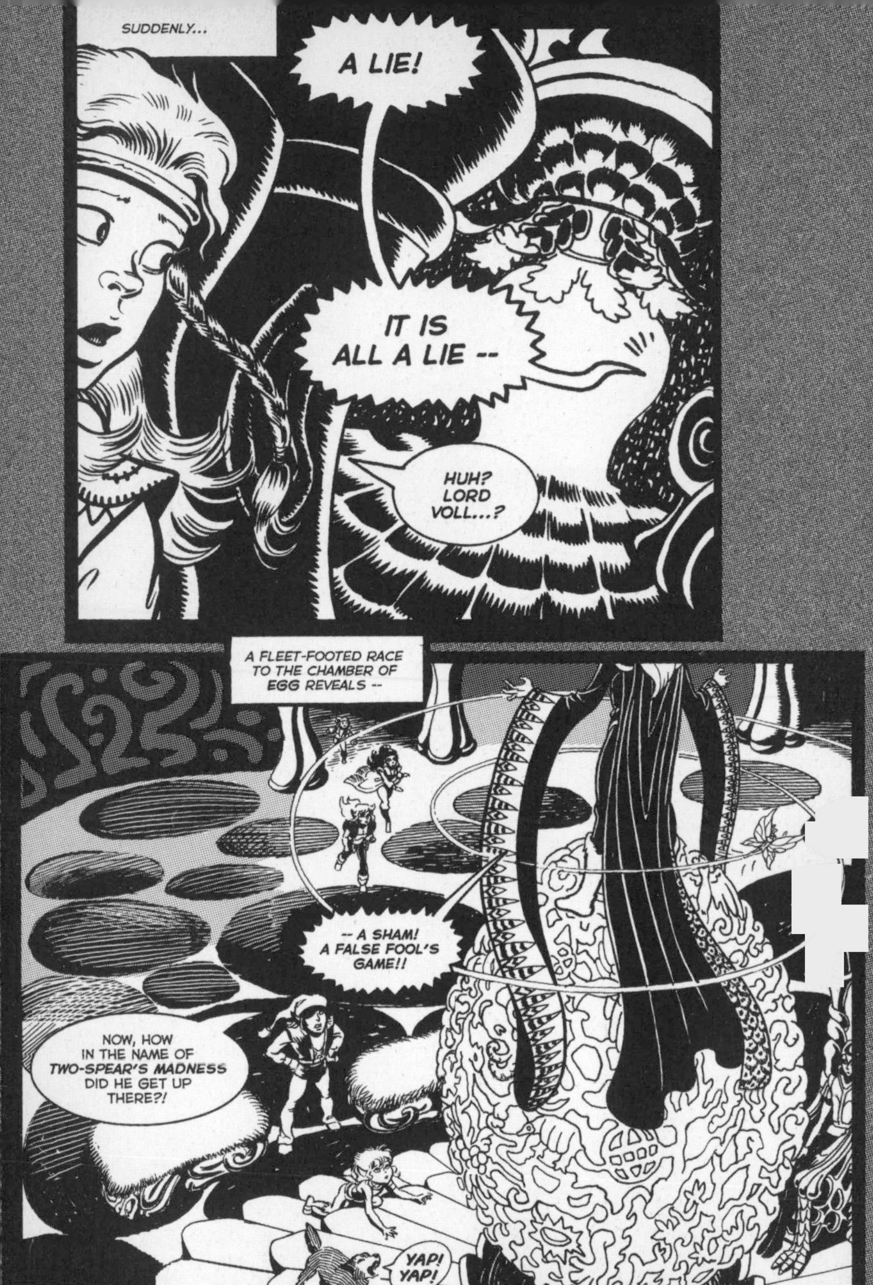
SUDDENLY...
A LIE!
IT IS ALL A LIE --
HUH? LORD VOLL...?
A FLEET-FOOTED RACE TO THE CHAMBER OF EGG REVEALS --
-- A SHAM! A FALSE FOOL'S GAME!!
NOW, HOW IN THE NAME OF TWO-SPEAR'S MADNESS DID HE GET UP THERE?!
YAP! YAP!

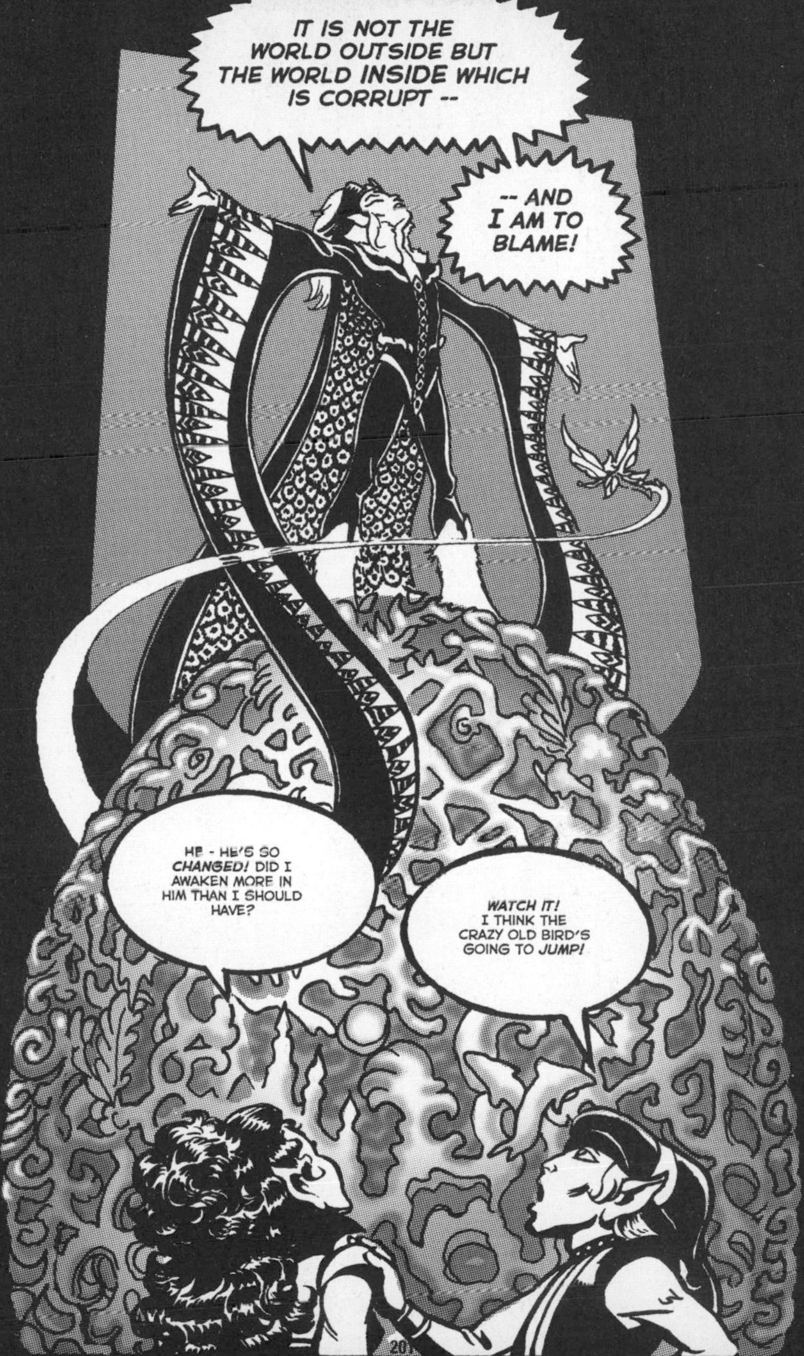
IT IS NOT THE WORLD OUTSIDE BUT THE WORLD INSIDE WHICH IS CORRUPT --
-- AND I AM TO BLAME!
HE - HE'S SO CHANGED! DID I AWAKEN MORE IN HIM THAN I SHOULD HAVE?
WATCH IT! I THINK THE CRAZY OLD BIRD'S GOING TO JUMP!

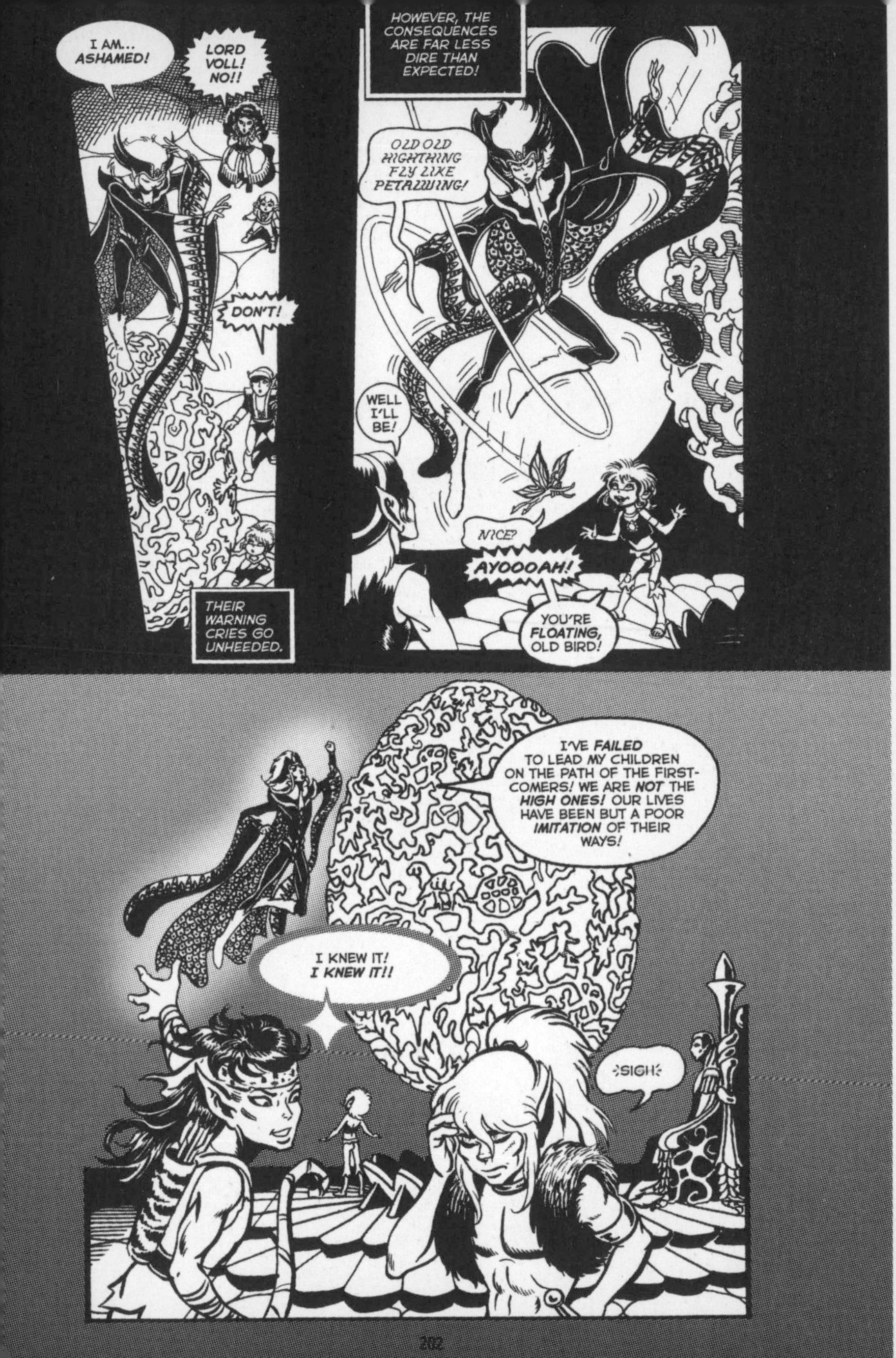
I AM... ASHAMED!
LORD VOLL! NO!!
DON'T!
THEIR WARNING CRIES GO UNHEEDED.
HOWEVER, THE CONSEQUENCES ARE FAR LESS DIRE THAN EXPECTED!
OLD OLD HIGHTHING FLY LIKE PETALWING!
WELL I'LL BE!
NICE?
AYOOOAH!
YOU'RE FLOATING, OLD BIRD!
I'VE FAILED TO LEAD MY CHILDREN ON THE PATH OF THE FIRST-COMERS! WE ARE NOT THE HIGH ONES! OUR LIVES HAVE BEEN BUT A POOR IMITATION OF THEIR WAYS!
I KNEW IT! I KNEW IT!!
SIGH

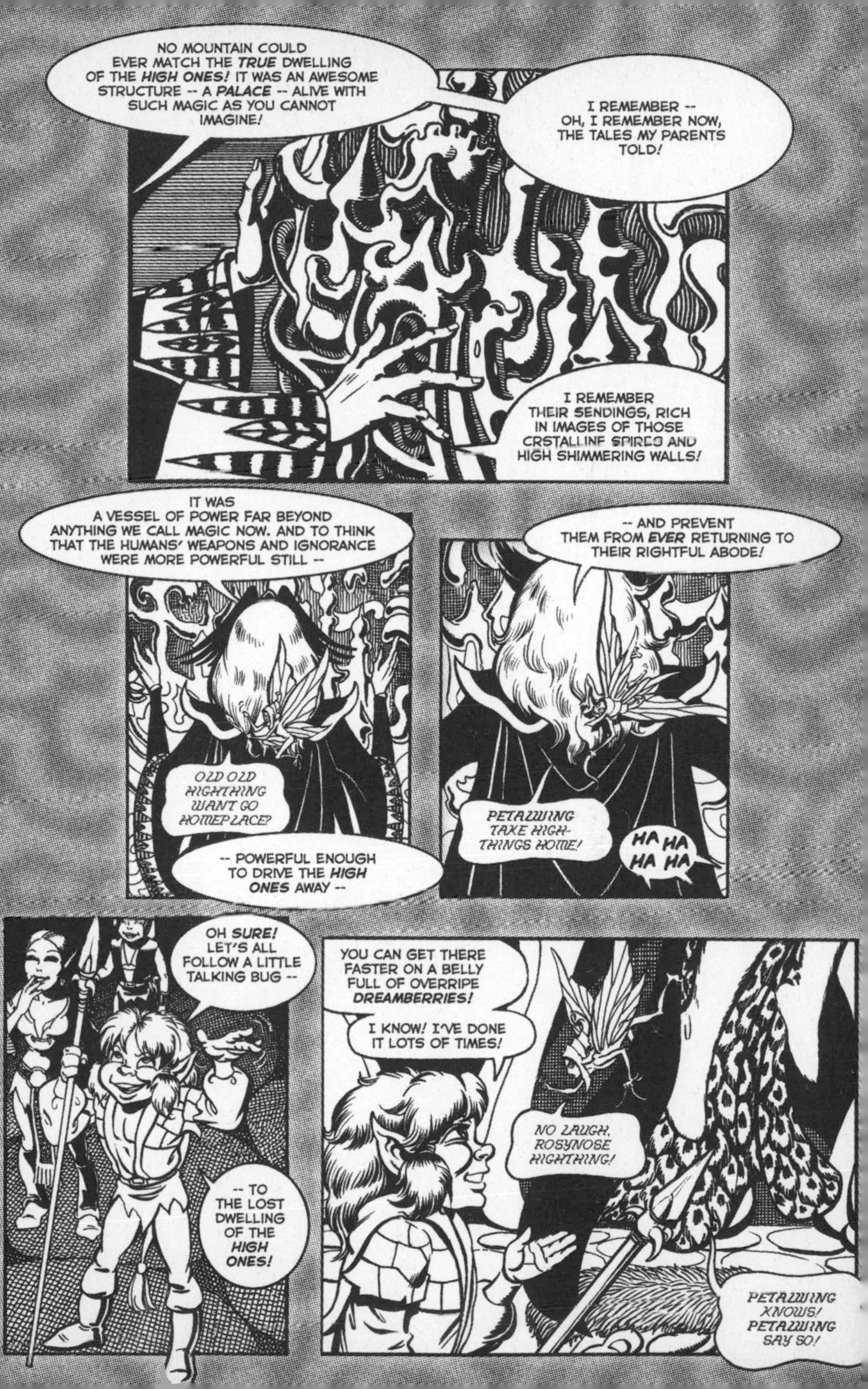
NO MOUNTAIN COULD EVER MATCH THE TRUE DWELLING OF THE HIGH ONES! IT WAS AN AWESOME STRUCTURE -- A PALACE -- ALIVE WITH SUCH MAGIC AS YOU CANNOT IMAGINE!
I REMEMBER -- OH, I REMEMBER NOW, THE TALES MY PARENTS TOLD!
I REMEMBER THEIR SENDINGS, RICH IN IMAGES OF THOSE CRSTALLINE SPIRES AND HIGH SHIMMERING WALLS!
IT WAS A VESSEL OF POWER FAR BEYOND ANYTHING WE CALL MAGIC NOW. AND TO THINK THAT THE HUMANS' WEAPONS AND IGNORANCE WERE MORE POWERFUL STILL --
OLD OLD HIGHTHING WANT GO HOMEPLACE?
-- POWERFUL ENOUGH TO DRIVE THE HIGH ONES AWAY --
-- AND PREVENT THEM FROM EVER RETURNING TO THEIR RIGHTFUL ABODE!
PETALWING TAKE HIGH-THINGS HOME!
HA HA HA HA
OH SURE! LET'S ALL FOLLOW A LITTLE TALKING BUG --
-- TO THE LOST DWELLING OF THE HIGH ONES!
YOU CAN GET THERE FASTER ON A BELLY FULL OF OVERRIPE DREAMBERRIES!
I KNOW! I'VE DONE IT LOTS OF TIMES!
NO LAUGH, ROSYNOSE HIGHTHING!
PETALWING KNOWS! PETALWING SAY SO!

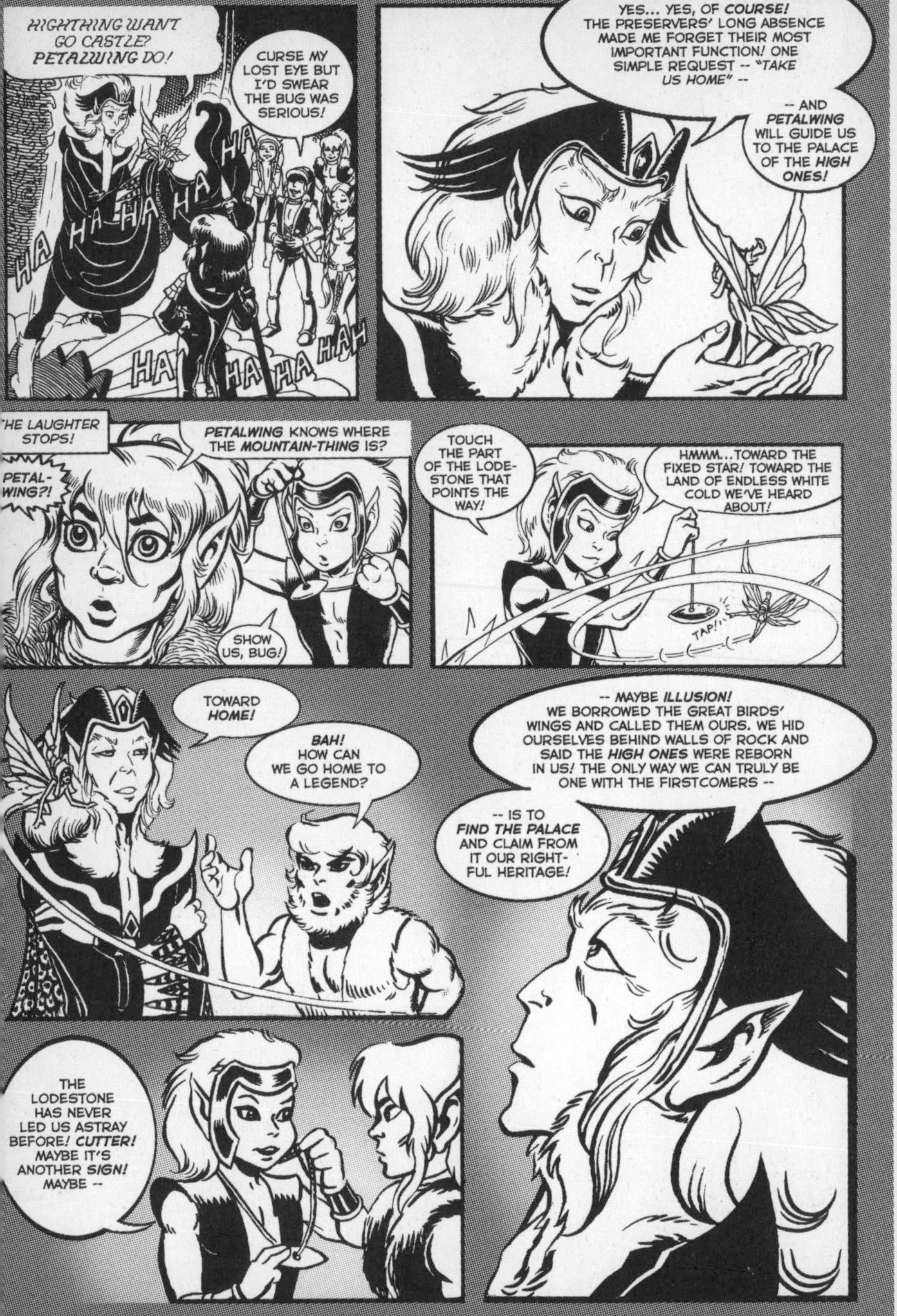
HIGHTHING WANT GO CASTLE? PETALWING DO!
CURSE MY LOST EYE BUT I'D SWEAR THE BUG WAS SERIOUS!
HA HA HA HA HA HA
HA HA HA HA HAH
YES... YES, OF COURSE! THE PRESERVERS' LONG ABSENCE MADE ME FORGET THEIR MOST IMPORTANT FUNCTION! ONE SIMPLE REQUEST -- "TAKE US HOME" --
-- AND PETALWING WILL GUIDE US TO THE PALACE OF THE HIGH ONES!
THE LAUGHTER STOPS!
PETALWING KNOWS WHERE THE MOUNTAIN-THING IS?
PETAL-WING?!
SHOW US, BUG!
TOUCH THE PART OF THE LODE-STONE THAT POINTS THE WAY!
HMMM...TOWARD THE FIXED STAR! TOWARD THE LAND OF ENDLESS WHITE COLD WE'VE HEARD ABOUT!
TAP!
TOWARD HOME!
BAH! HOW CAN WE GO HOME TO A LEGEND?
THE LODESTONE HAS NEVER LED US ASTRAY BEFORE! CUTTER! MAYBE IT'S ANOTHER SIGN! MAYBE --
-- MAYBE ILLUSION! WE BORROWED THE GREAT BIRDS' WINGS AND CALLED THEM OURS. WE HID OURSELVES BEHIND WALLS OF ROCK AND SAID THE HIGH ONES WERE REBORN IN US! THE ONLY WAY WE CAN TRULY BE ONE WITH THE FIRSTCOMERS --
-- IS TO FIND THE PALACE AND CLAIM FROM IT OUR RIGHT-FUL HERITAGE!

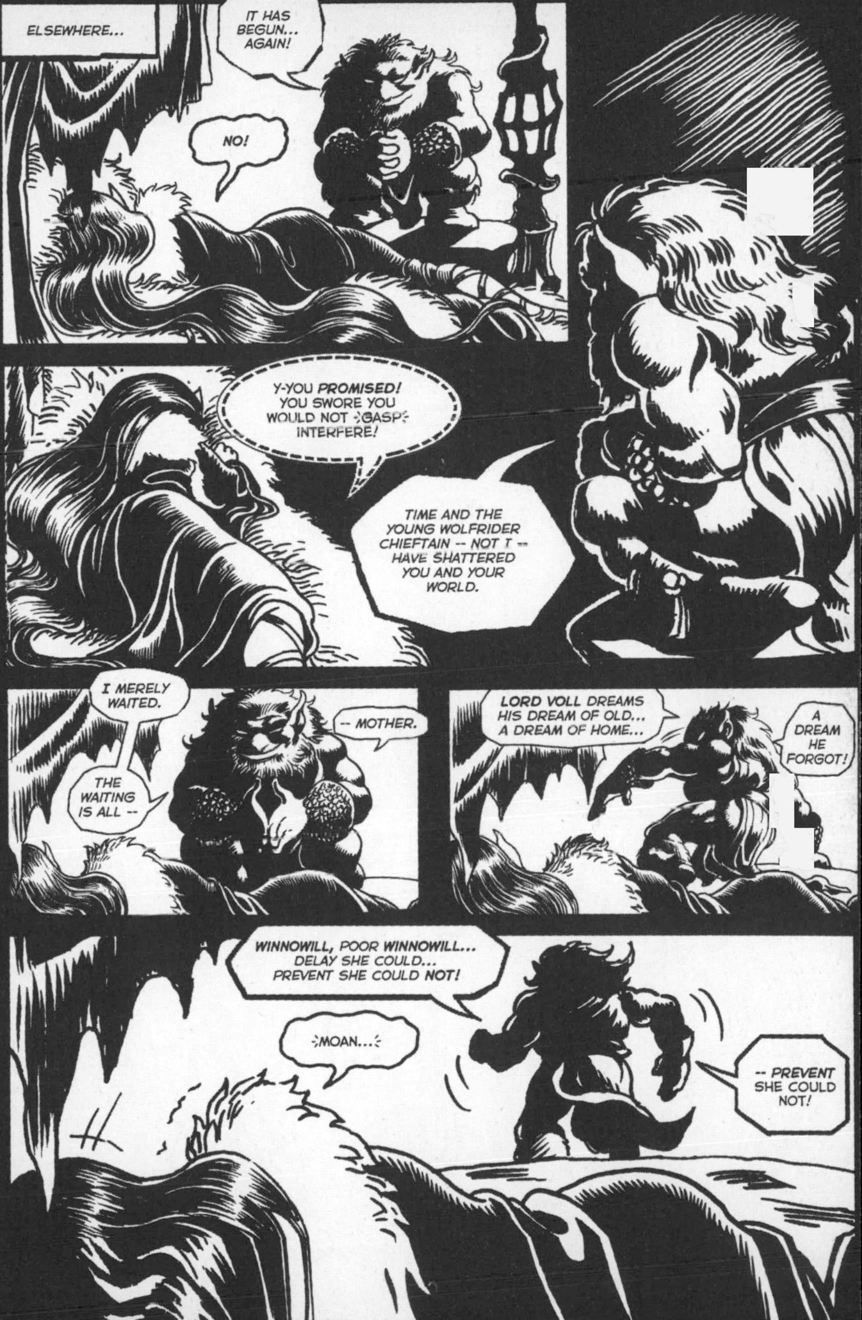
ELSEWHERE...
IT HAS BEGUN... AGAIN!
NO!
Y-YOU PROMISED! YOU SWORE YOU WOULD NOT -GASP- INTERFERE!
TIME AND THE YOUNG WOLFRIDER CHIEFTAIN -- NOT I -- HAVE SHATTERED YOU AND YOUR WORLD.
I MERELY WAITED.
THE WAITING IS ALL --
-- MOTHER.
LORD VOLL DREAMS HIS DREAM OF OLD... A DREAM OF HOME...
A DREAM HE FORGOT!
WINNOWILL, POOR WINNOWILL... DELAY SHE COULD... PREVENT SHE COULD NOT!
MOAN...
-- PREVENT SHE COULD NOT!

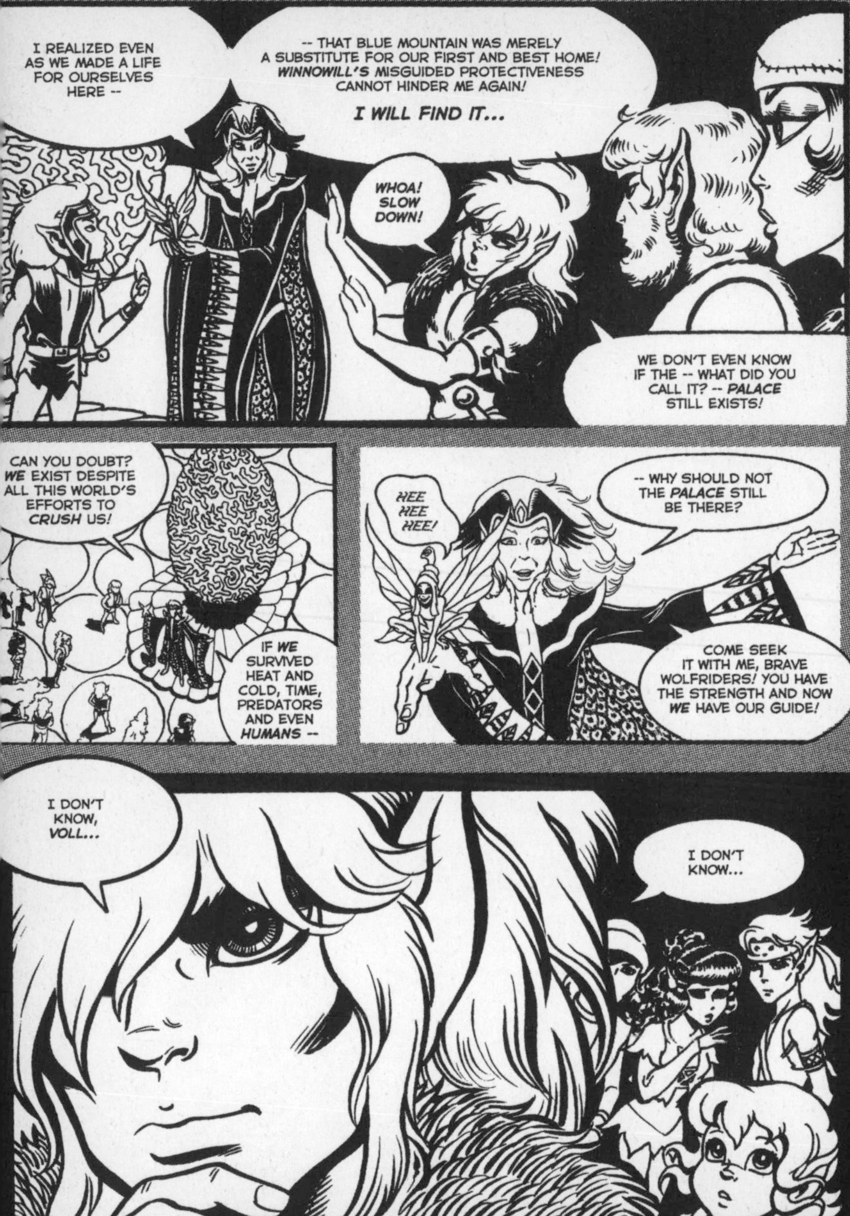
I REALIZED EVEN AS WE MADE A LIFE FOR OURSELVES HERE --
-- THAT BLUE MOUNTAIN WAS MERELY A SUBSTITUTE FOR OUR FIRST AND BEST HOME! WINNOWILL'S MISGUIDED PROTECTIVENESS CANNOT HINDER ME AGAIN!
I WILL FIND IT...
WHOA! SLOW DOWN!
WE DON'T EVEN KNOW IF THE -- WHAT DID YOU CALL IT? -- PALACE STILL EXISTS!
CAN YOU DOUBT? WE EXIST DESPITE ALL THIS WORLD'S EFFORTS TO CRUSH US!
IF WE SURVIVED HEAT AND COLD, TIME, PREDATORS AND EVEN HUMANS --
HEE HEE HEE!
-- WHY SHOULD NOT THE PALACE STILL BE THERE?
COME SEEK IT WITH ME, BRAVE WOLFRIDERS! YOU HAVE THE STRENGTH AND NOW WE HAVE OUR GUIDE!
I DON'T KNOW, VOLL...
I DON'T KNOW...

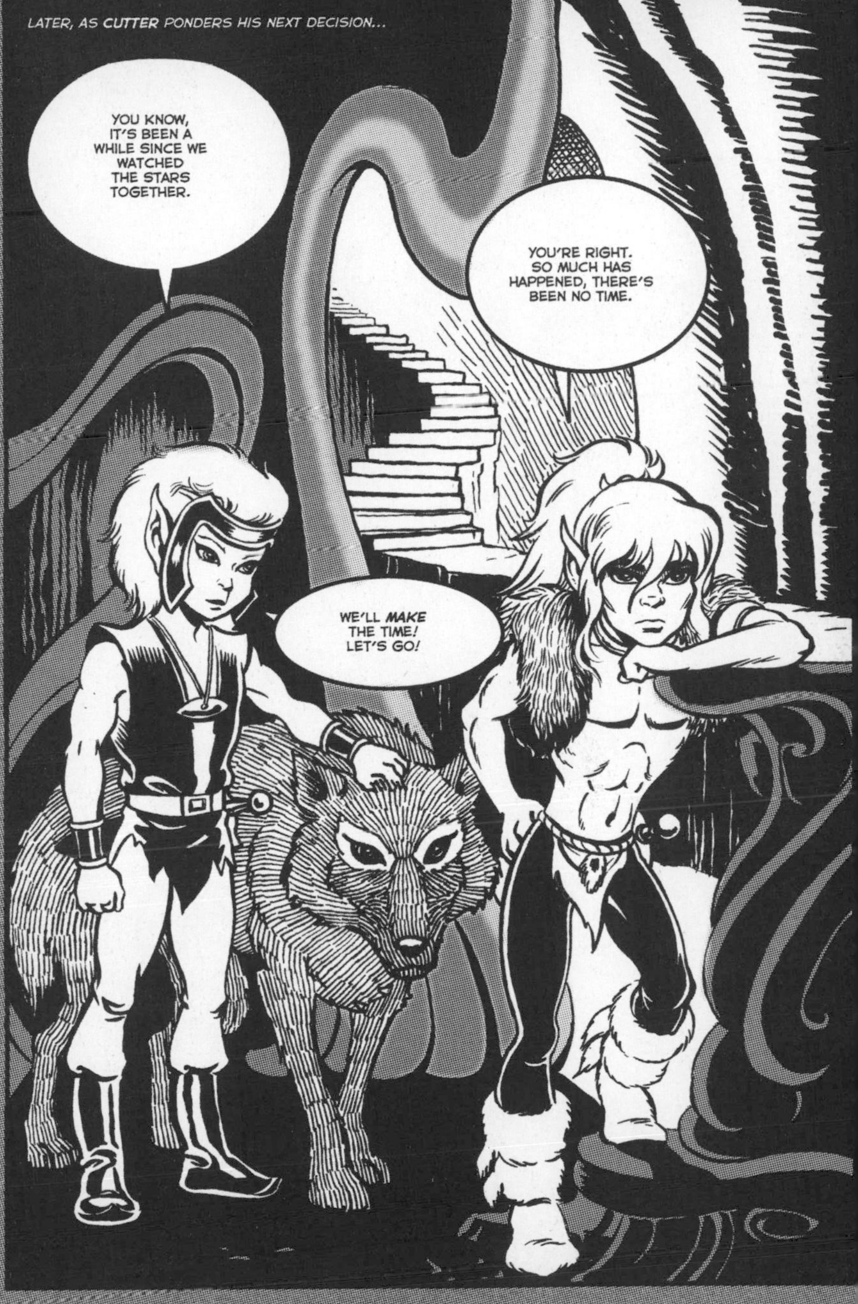
LATER, AS CUTTER PONDERS HIS NEXT DECISION...
YOU KNOW, IT'S BEEN A WHILE SINCE WE WATCHED THE STARS TOGETHER.
YOU'RE RIGHT. SO MUCH HAS HAPPENED, THERE'S BEEN NO TIME.
WE'LL *MAKE* THE TIME! LET'S GO!

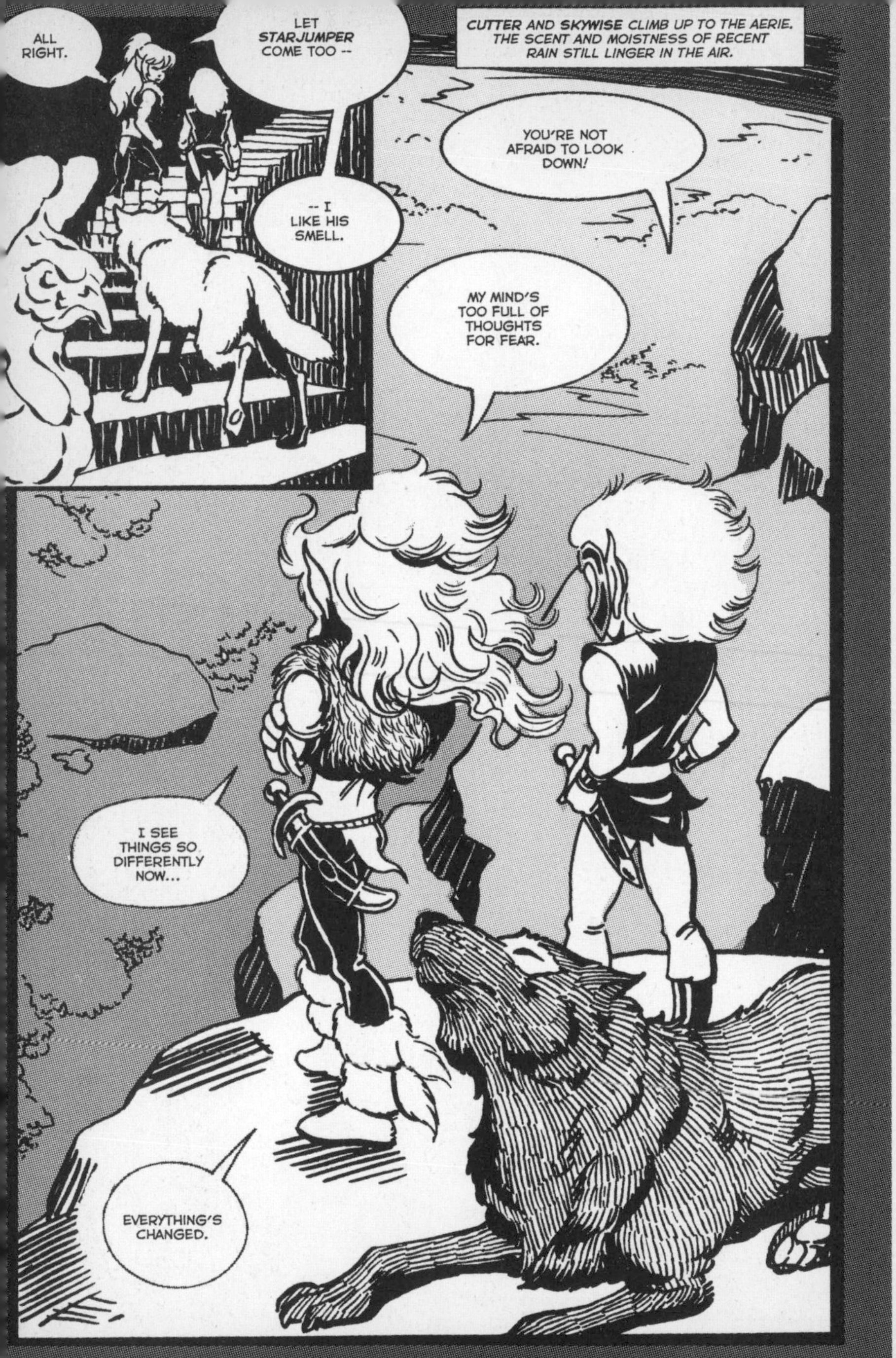

ALL RIGHT.
LET STARJUMPER COME TOO --
-- I LIKE HIS SMELL.
CUTTER AND SKYWISE CLIMB UP TO THE AERIE. THE SCENT AND MOISTNESS OF RECENT RAIN STILL LINGER IN THE AIR.
YOU'RE NOT AFRAID TO LOOK DOWN!
MY MIND'S TOO FULL OF THOUGHTS FOR FEAR.
I SEE THINGS SO DIFFERENTLY NOW...
EVERYTHING'S CHANGED.

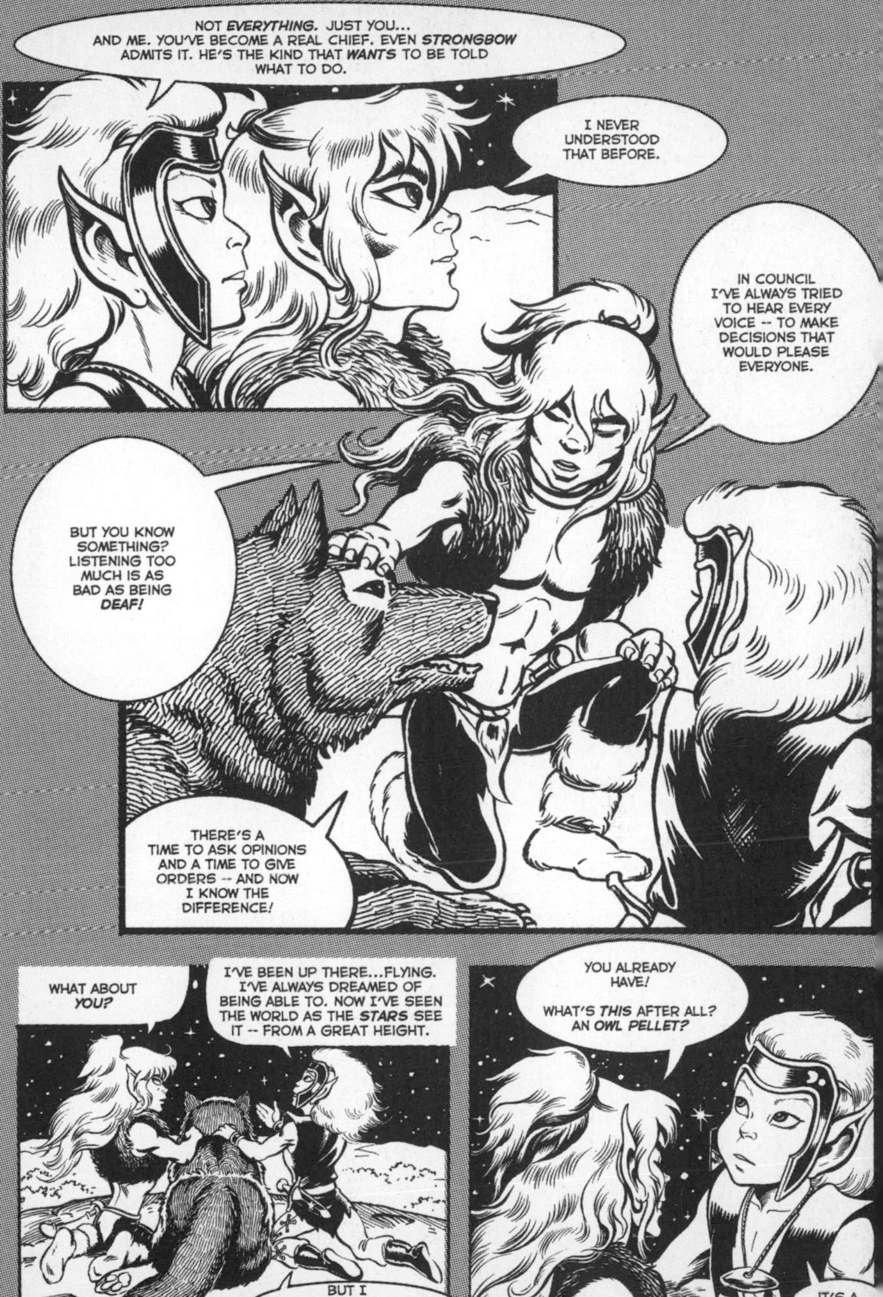
NOT EVERYTHING. JUST YOU... AND ME. YOU'VE BECOME A REAL CHIEF. EVEN STRONGBOW ADMITS IT. HE'S THE KIND THAT WANTS TO BE TOLD WHAT TO DO.
I NEVER UNDERSTOOD THAT BEFORE.
IN COUNCIL I'VE ALWAYS TRIED TO HEAR EVERY VOICE -- TO MAKE DECISIONS THAT WOULD PLEASE EVERYONE.
BUT YOU KNOW SOMETHING? LISTENING TOO MUCH IS AS BAD AS BEING DEAF!
THERE'S A TIME TO ASK OPINIONS AND A TIME TO GIVE ORDERS -- AND NOW I KNOW THE DIFFERENCE!
WHAT ABOUT YOU?
I'VE BEEN UP THERE...FLYING. I'VE ALWAYS DREAMED OF BEING ABLE TO. NOW I'VE SEEN THE WORLD AS THE STARS SEE IT -- FROM A GREAT HEIGHT.
BUT I STILL COULDN'T TOUCH THE STARS.
YOU ALREADY HAVE!
WHAT'S THIS AFTER ALL? AN OWL PELLET?
IT'S A KEY --

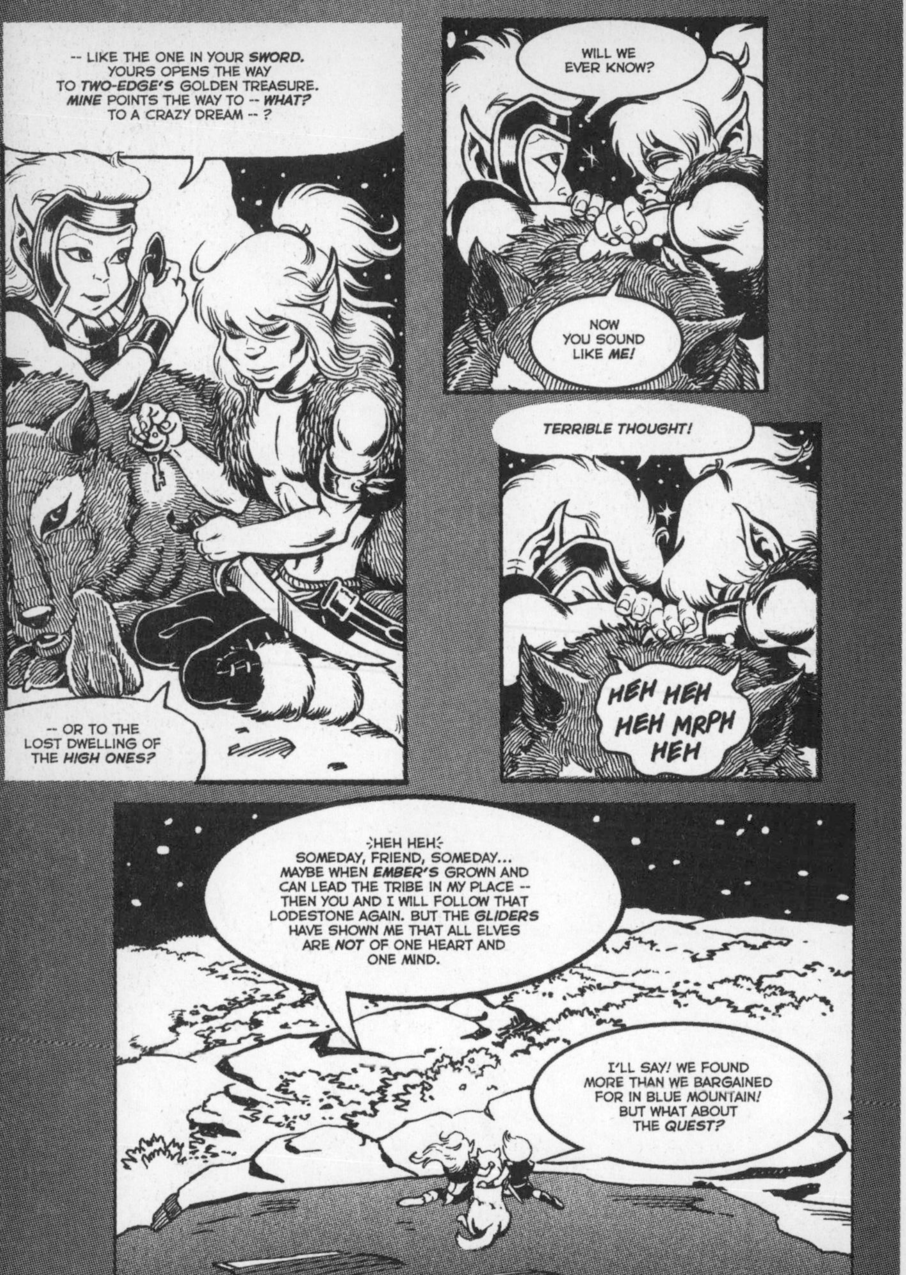
-- LIKE THE ONE IN YOUR SWORD. YOURS OPENS THE WAY TO TWO-EDGE'S GOLDEN TREASURE. MINE POINTS THE WAY TO -- WHAT? TO A CRAZY DREAM -- ?
-- OR TO THE LOST DWELLING OF THE HIGH ONES?
WILL WE EVER KNOW?
NOW YOU SOUND LIKE ME!
TERRIBLE THOUGHT!
HEH HEH HEH MRPH HEH
HEH HEH
SOMEDAY, FRIEND, SOMEDAY... MAYBE WHEN EMBER'S GROWN AND CAN LEAD THE TRIBE IN MY PLACE -- THEN YOU AND I WILL FOLLOW THAT LODESTONE AGAIN. BUT THE GLIDERS HAVE SHOWN ME THAT ALL ELVES ARE NOT OF ONE HEART AND ONE MIND.
I'LL SAY! WE FOUND MORE THAN WE BARGAINED FOR IN BLUE MOUNTAIN! BUT WHAT ABOUT THE QUEST?

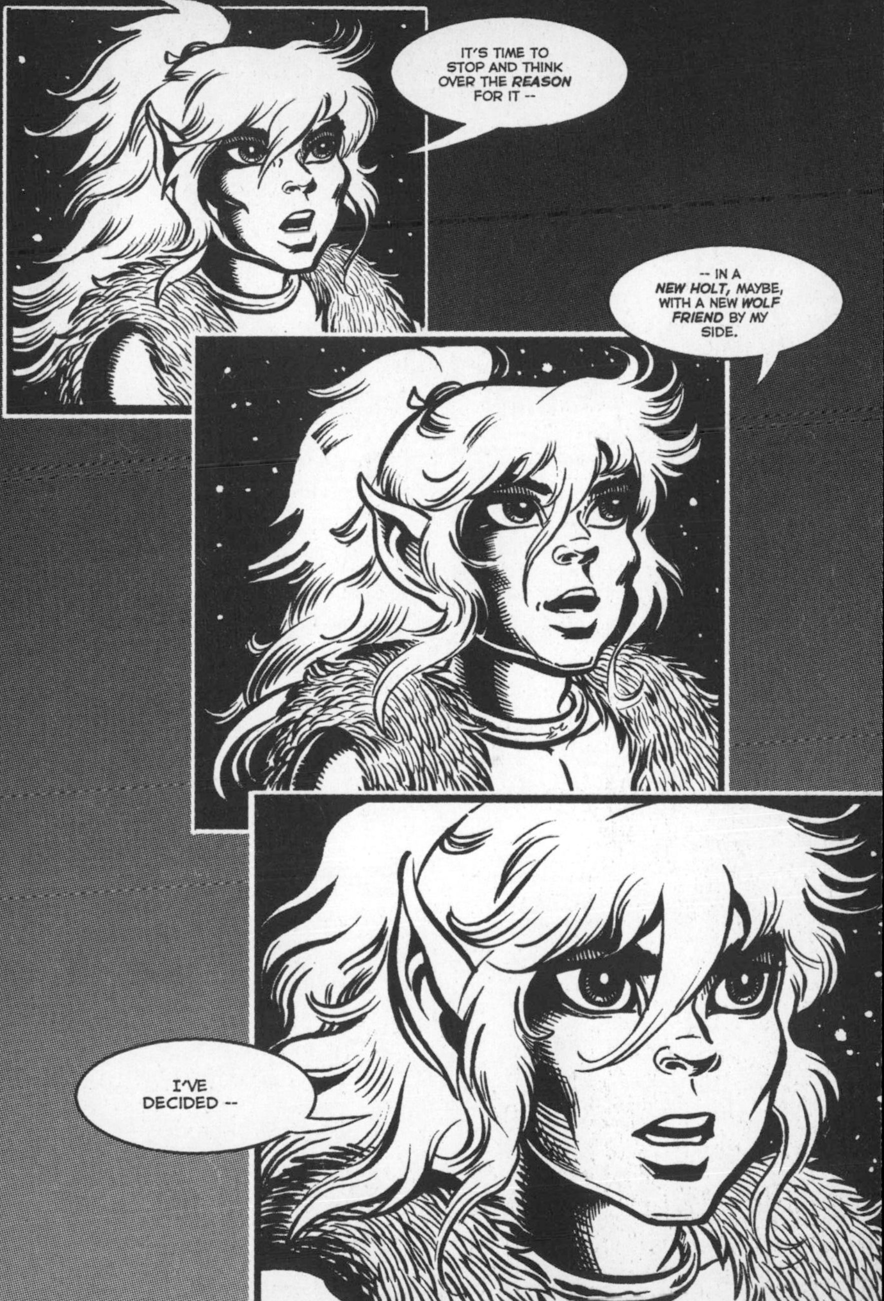
IT'S TIME TO STOP AND THINK OVER THE REASON FOR IT --
-- IN A NEW HOLT, MAYBE, WITH A NEW WOLF FRIEND BY MY SIDE.
I'VE DECIDED --

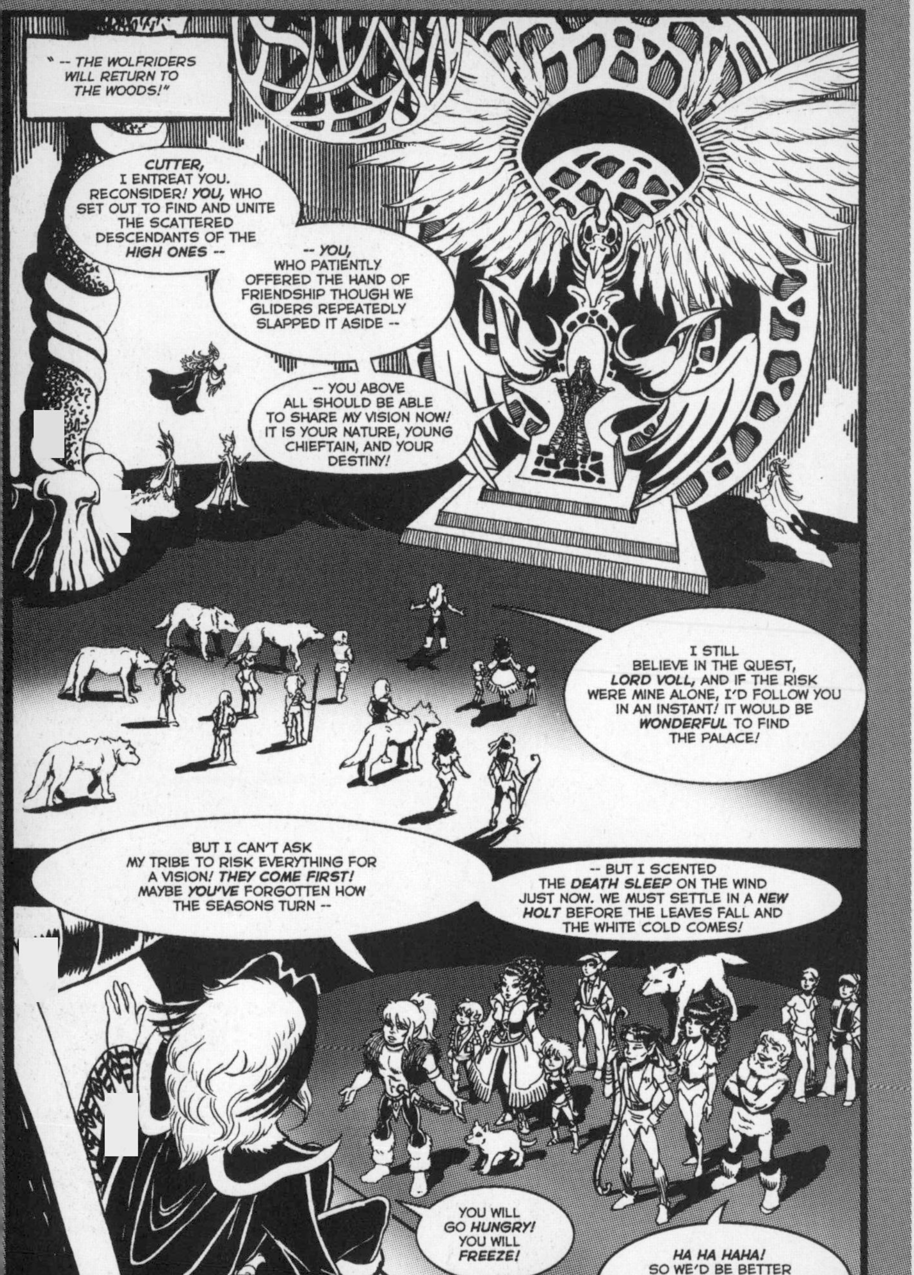
" -- THE WOLFRIDERS WILL RETURN TO THE WOODS!"
CUTTER, I ENTREAT YOU. RECONSIDER! YOU, WHO SET OUT TO FIND AND UNITE THE SCATTERED DESCENDANTS OF THE HIGH ONES --
-- YOU, WHO PATIENTLY OFFERED THE HAND OF FRIENDSHIP THOUGH WE GLIDERS REPEATEDLY SLAPPED IT ASIDE --
-- YOU ABOVE ALL SHOULD BE ABLE TO SHARE MY VISION NOW! IT IS YOUR NATURE, YOUNG CHIEFTAIN, AND YOUR DESTINY!
I STILL BELIEVE IN THE QUEST, LORD VOLL, AND IF THE RISK WERE MINE ALONE, I'D FOLLOW YOU IN AN INSTANT! IT WOULD BE WONDERFUL TO FIND THE PALACE!
BUT I CAN'T ASK MY TRIBE TO RISK EVERYTHING FOR A VISION! THEY COME FIRST! MAYBE YOU'VE FORGOTTEN HOW THE SEASONS TURN --
-- BUT I SCENTED THE DEATH SLEEP ON THE WIND JUST NOW. WE MUST SETTLE IN A NEW HOLT BEFORE THE LEAVES FALL AND THE WHITE COLD COMES!
YOU WILL GO HUNGRY! YOU WILL FREEZE!
HA HA HAHA! SO WE'D BE BETTER OFF CHASING AFTER THE HIGH ONES' MOUNTAIN THING WITH YOU?!

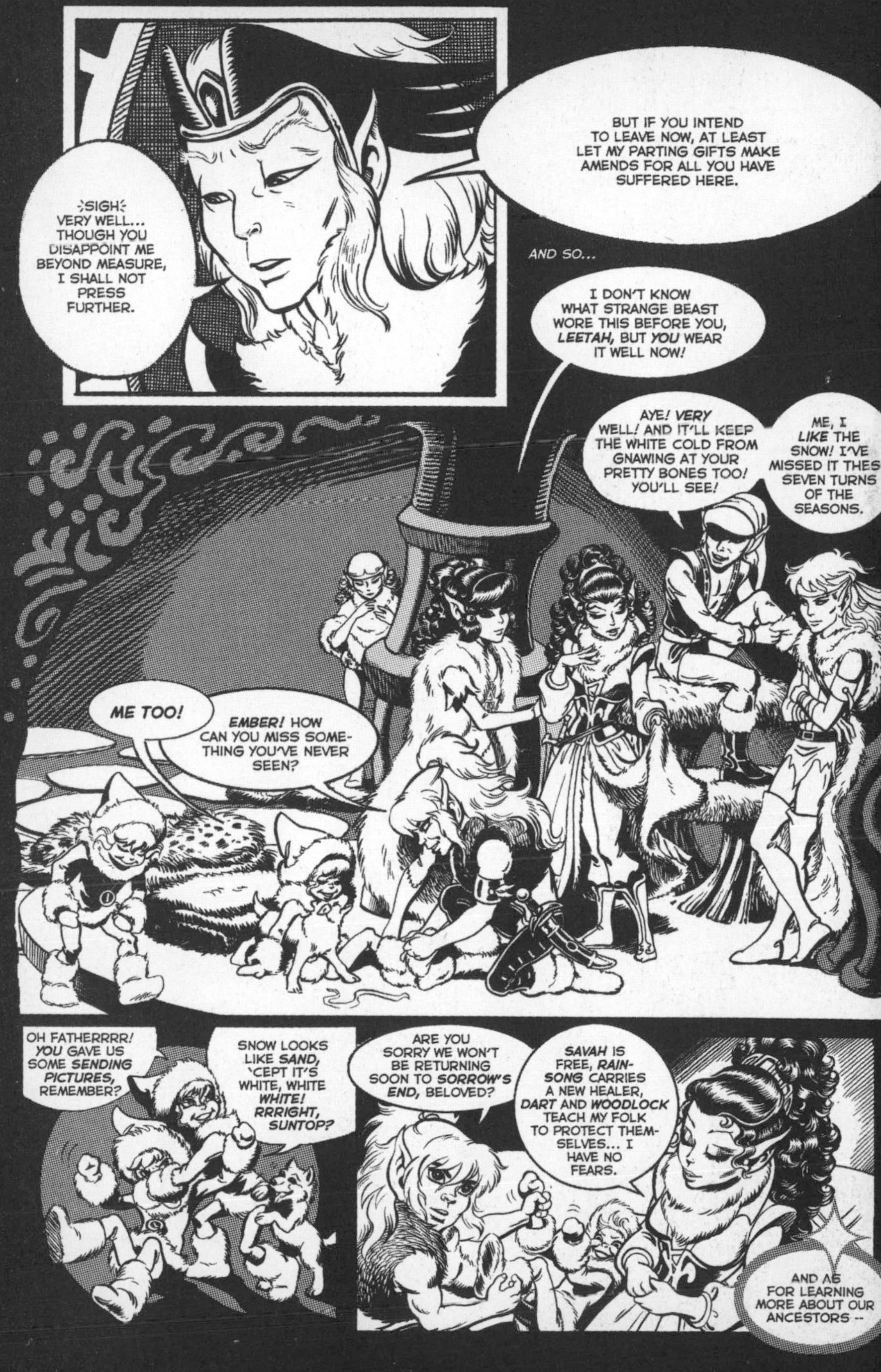

BUT IF YOU INTEND TO LEAVE NOW, AT LEAST LET MY PARTING GIFTS MAKE AMENDS FOR ALL YOU HAVE SUFFERED HERE.
:SIGH: VERY WELL... THOUGH YOU DISAPPOINT ME BEYOND MEASURE, I SHALL NOT PRESS FURTHER.
AND SO...
I DON'T KNOW WHAT STRANGE BEAST WORE THIS BEFORE YOU, LEETAH, BUT YOU WEAR IT WELL NOW!
AYE! VERY WELL! AND IT'LL KEEP THE WHITE COLD FROM GNAWING AT YOUR PRETTY BONES TOO! YOU'LL SEE!
ME, I LIKE THE SNOW! I'VE MISSED IT THES SEVEN TURNS OF THE SEASONS.
ME TOO!
EMBER! HOW CAN YOU MISS SOMETHING YOU'VE NEVER SEEN?
OH FATHERRRR! YOU GAVE US SOME SENDING PICTURES, REMEMBER?
SNOW LOOKS LIKE SAND, 'CEPT IT'S WHITE, WHITE WHITE! RRRIGHT, SUNTOP?
ARE YOU SORRY WE WON'T BE RETURNING SOON TO SORROW'S END, BELOVED?
SAVAH IS FREE, RAINSONG CARRIES A NEW HEALER, DART AND WOODLOCK TEACH MY FOLK TO PROTECT THEMSELVES... I HAVE NO FEARS.
AND AS FOR LEARNING MORE ABOUT OUR ANCESTORS --

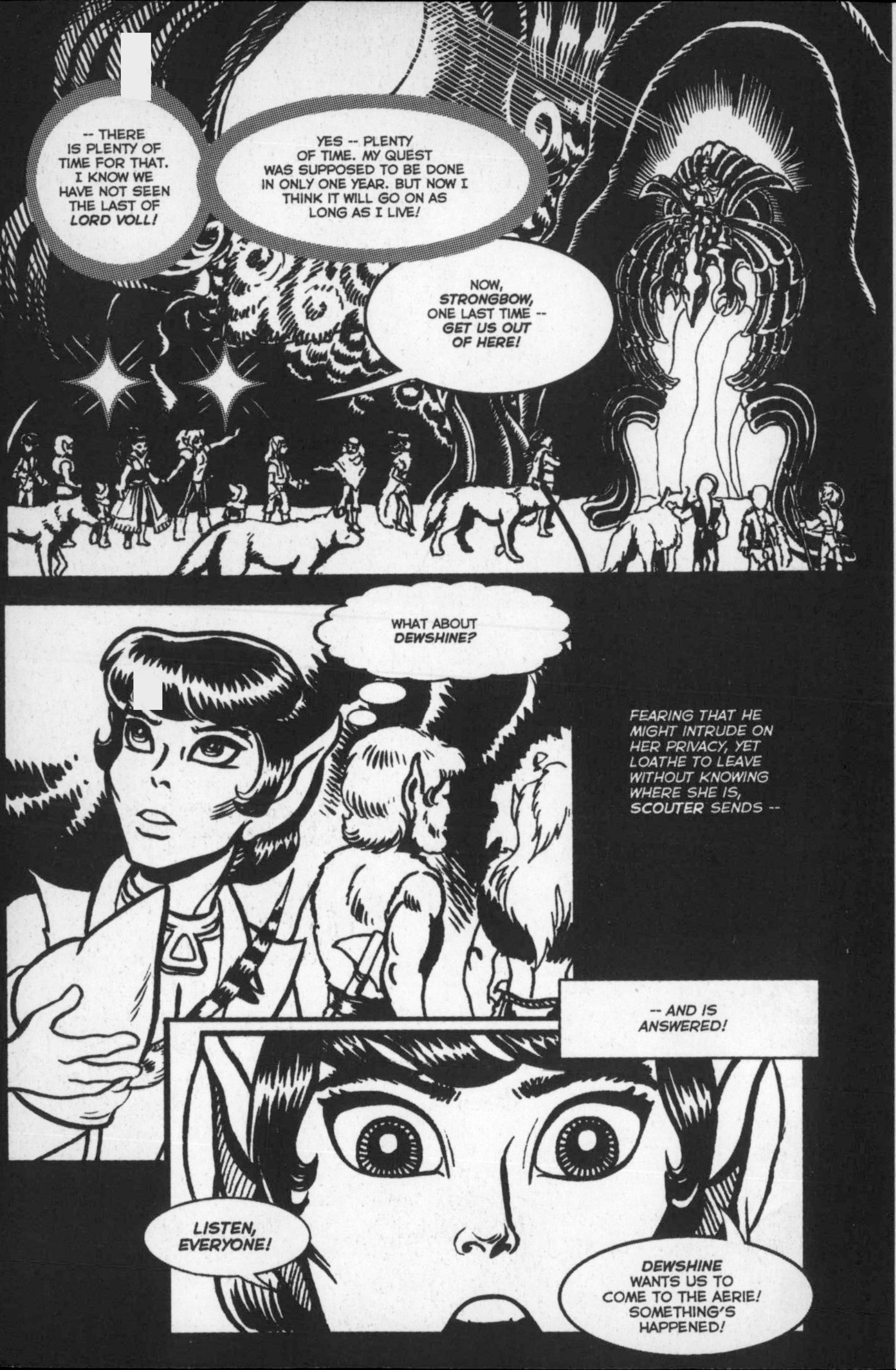

-- THERE IS PLENTY OF TIME FOR THAT. I KNOW WE HAVE NOT SEEN THE LAST OF *LORD VOLL!*
YES -- PLENTY OF TIME. MY QUEST WAS SUPPOSED TO BE DONE IN ONLY ONE YEAR. BUT NOW I THINK IT WILL GO ON AS LONG AS I LIVE!
NOW, *STRONGBOW,* ONE LAST TIME -- *GET US OUT OF HERE!*
WHAT ABOUT *DEWSHINE?*
FEARING THAT HE MIGHT INTRUDE ON HER PRIVACY, YET LOATHE TO LEAVE WITHOUT KNOWING WHERE SHE IS, SCOUTER SENDS --
-- AND IS ANSWERED!
LISTEN, EVERYONE!
DEWSHINE WANTS US TO COME TO THE AERIE! SOMETHING'S HAPPENED!

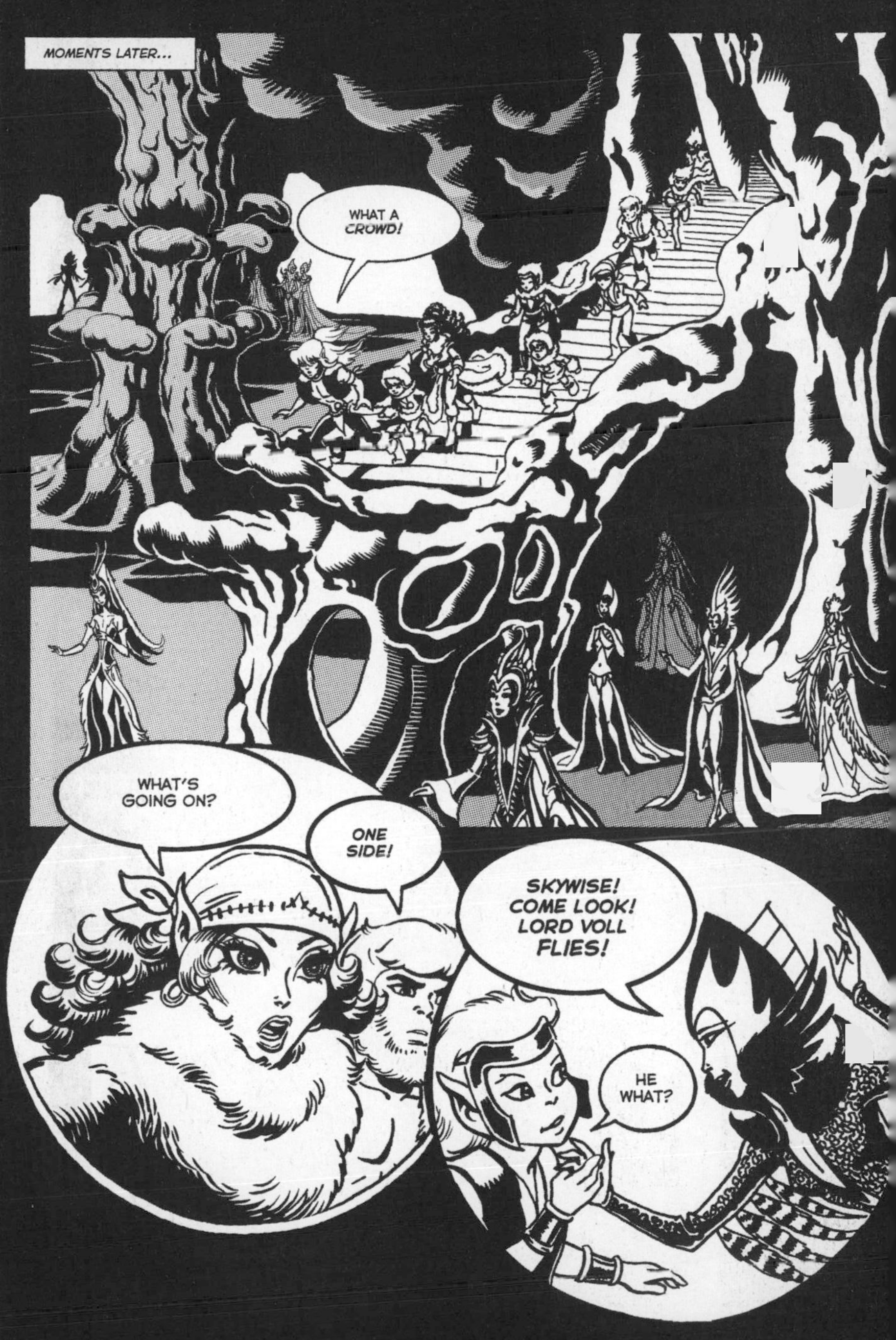

MOMENTS LATER...
WHAT A CROWD!
WHAT'S GOING ON?
ONE SIDE!
SKYWISE! COME LOOK! LORD VOLL FLIES!
HE WHAT?

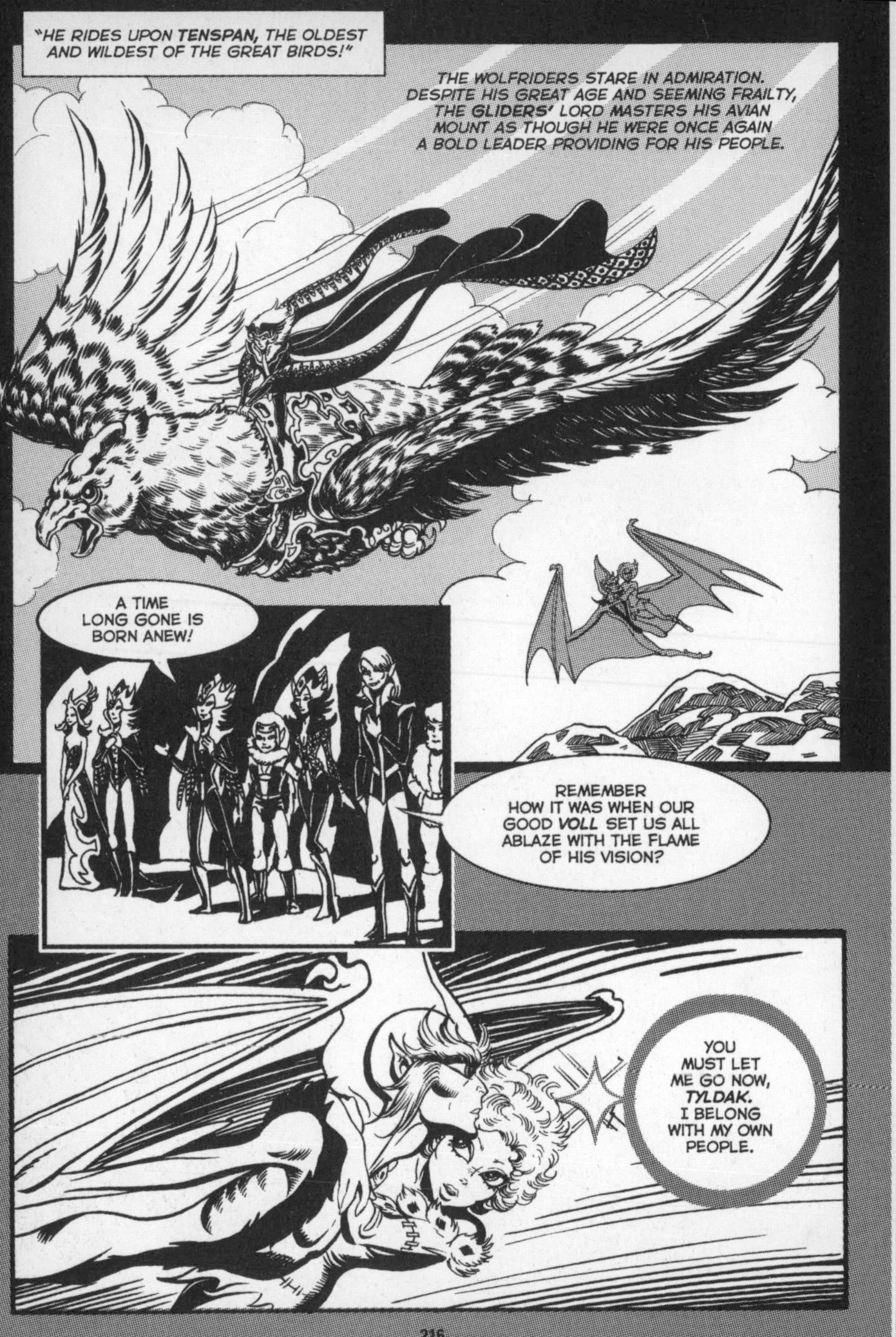
"HE RIDES UPON TENSPAN, THE OLDEST AND WILDEST OF THE GREAT BIRDS!"
THE WOLFRIDERS STARE IN ADMIRATION. DESPITE HIS GREAT AGE AND SEEMING FRAILTY, THE GLIDERS' LORD MASTERS HIS AVIAN MOUNT AS THOUGH HE WERE ONCE AGAIN A BOLD LEADER PROVIDING FOR HIS PEOPLE.
A TIME LONG GONE IS BORN ANEW!
REMEMBER HOW IT WAS WHEN OUR GOOD VOLL SET US ALL ABLAZE WITH THE FLAME OF HIS VISION?
YOU MUST LET ME GO NOW, TYLDAK. I BELONG WITH MY OWN PEOPLE.

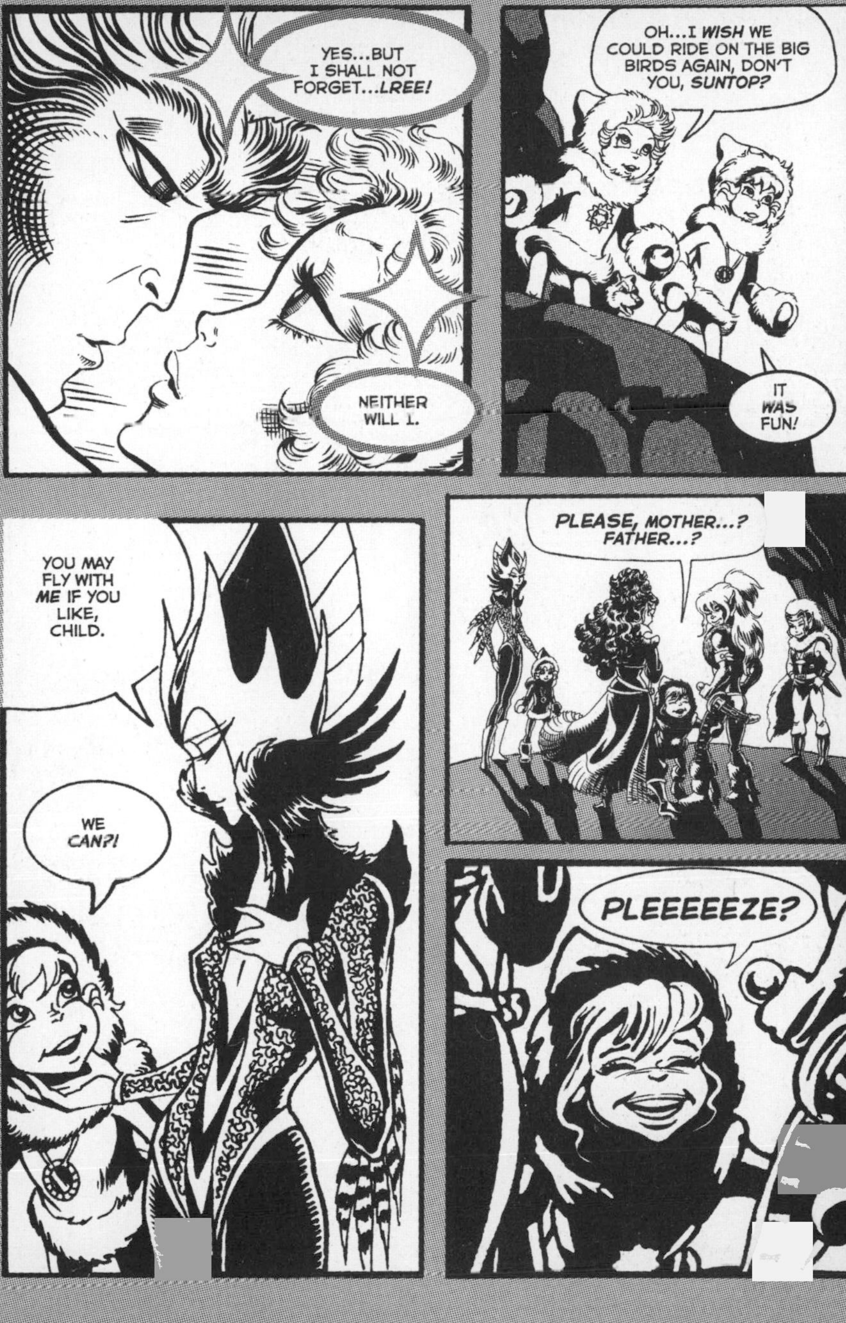
YES...BUT I SHALL NOT FORGET...LREE!
NEITHER WILL I.
OH...I WISH WE COULD RIDE ON THE BIG BIRDS AGAIN, DON'T YOU, SUNTOP?
IT WAS FUN!
YOU MAY FLY WITH ME IF YOU LIKE, CHILD.
WE CAN?!
PLEASE, MOTHER...? FATHER...?
PLEEEEEEZE?

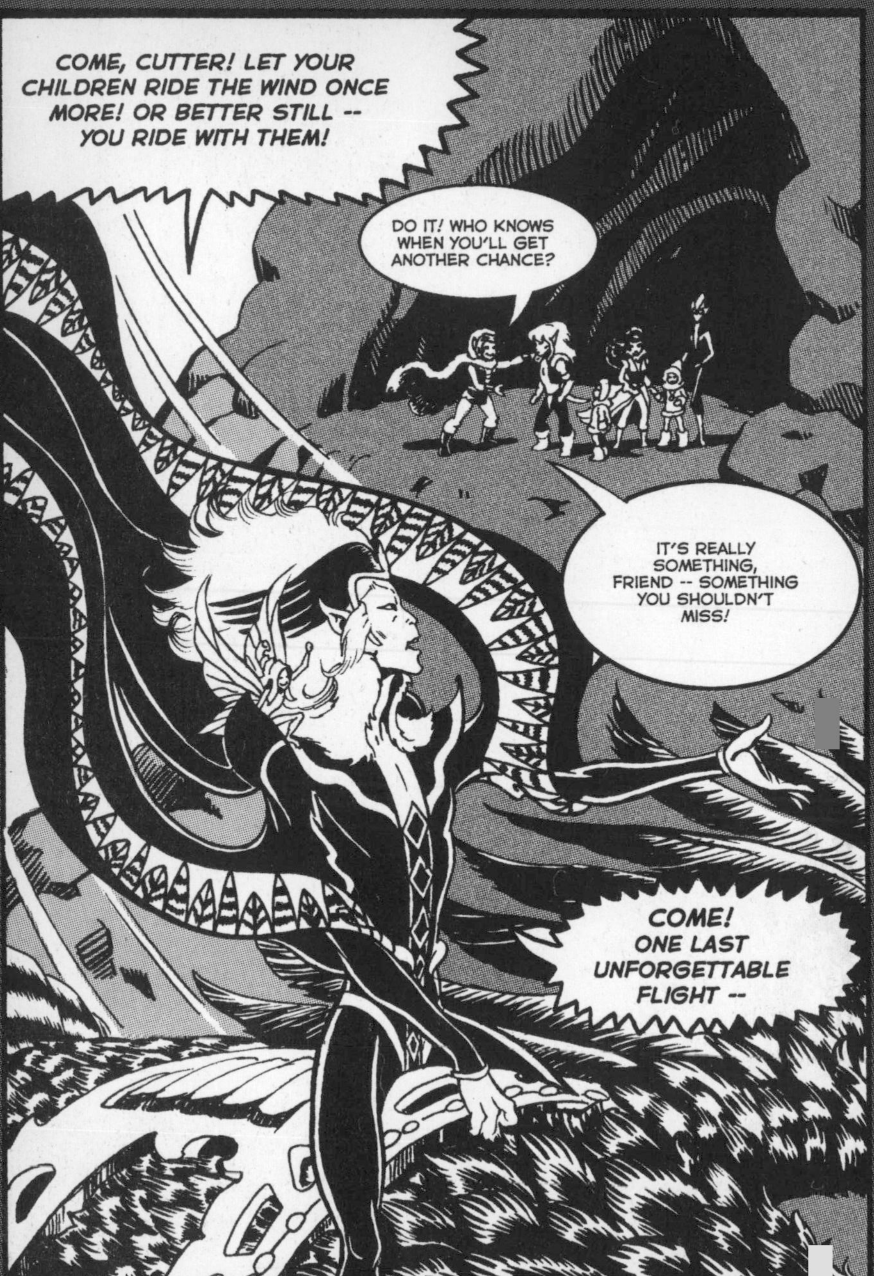
COME, CUTTER! LET YOUR CHILDREN RIDE THE WIND ONCE MORE! OR BETTER STILL -- YOU RIDE WITH THEM!
DO IT! WHO KNOWS WHEN YOU'LL GET ANOTHER CHANCE?
IT'S REALLY SOMETHING, FRIEND -- SOMETHING YOU SHOULDN'T MISS!
COME! ONE LAST UNFORGETTABLE FLIGHT --

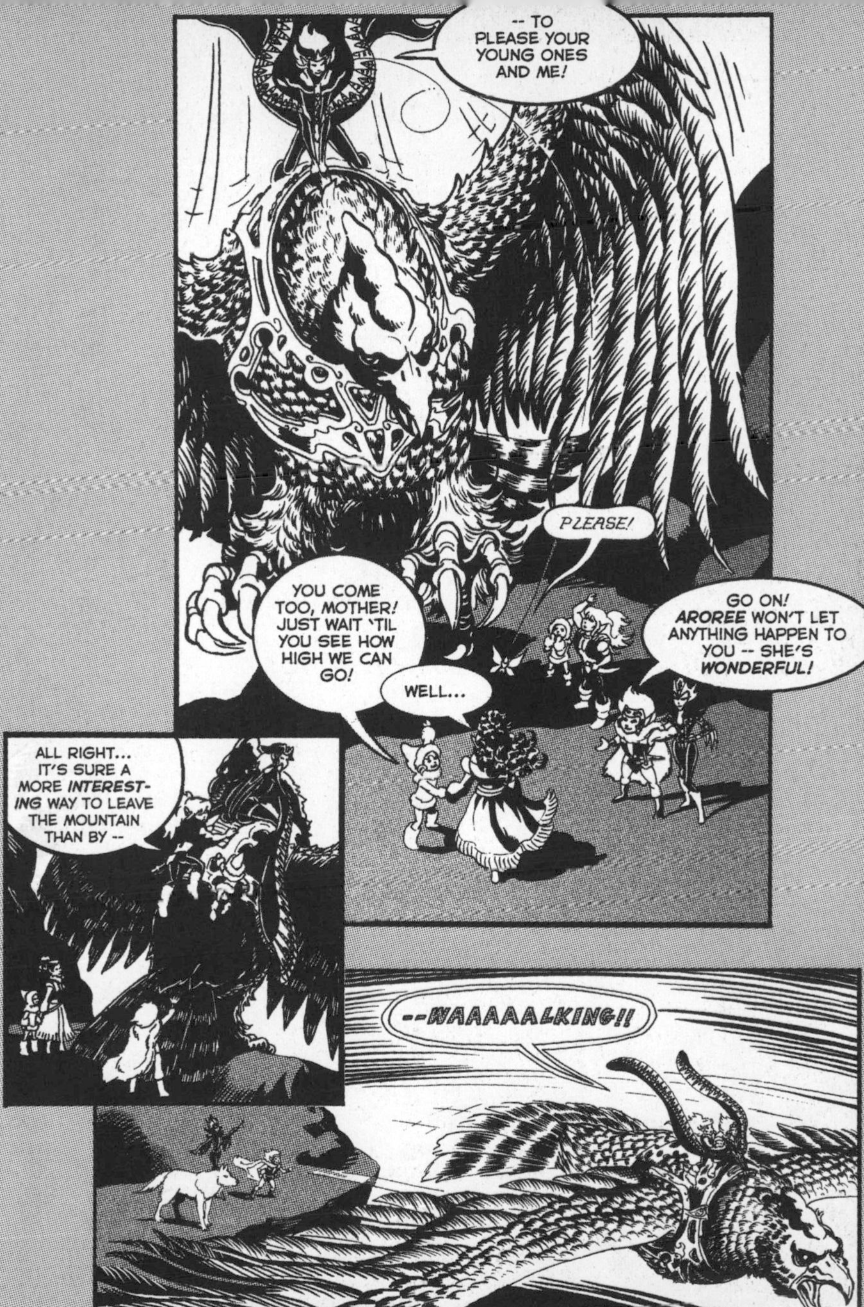
-- TO PLEASE YOUR YOUNG ONES AND ME!
PLEASE!
YOU COME TOO, MOTHER! JUST WAIT 'TIL YOU SEE HOW HIGH WE CAN GO!
GO ON! AROREE WON'T LET ANYTHING HAPPEN TO YOU -- SHE'S WONDERFUL!
WELL...
ALL RIGHT... IT'S SURE A MORE INTERESTING WAY TO LEAVE THE MOUNTAIN THAN BY --
--WAAAAALKING!!

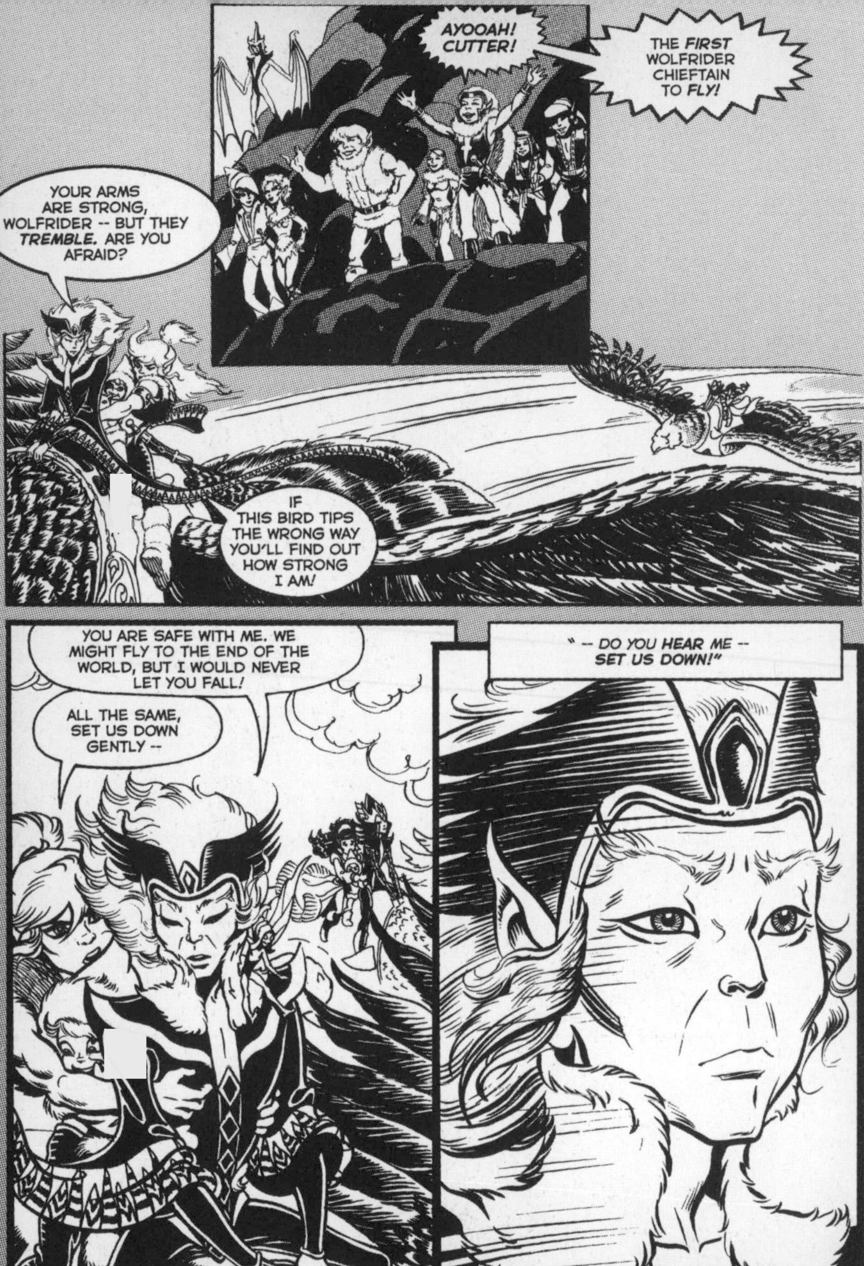
AYOOAH! CUTTER!
THE FIRST WOLFRIDER CHIEFTAIN TO FLY!
YOUR ARMS ARE STRONG, WOLFRIDER -- BUT THEY TREMBLE. ARE YOU AFRAID?
IF THIS BIRD TIPS THE WRONG WAY YOU'LL FIND OUT HOW STRONG I AM!
YOU ARE SAFE WITH ME. WE MIGHT FLY TO THE END OF THE WORLD, BUT I WOULD NEVER LET YOU FALL!
ALL THE SAME, SET US DOWN GENTLY --
" -- DO YOU HEAR ME -- SET US DOWN!"

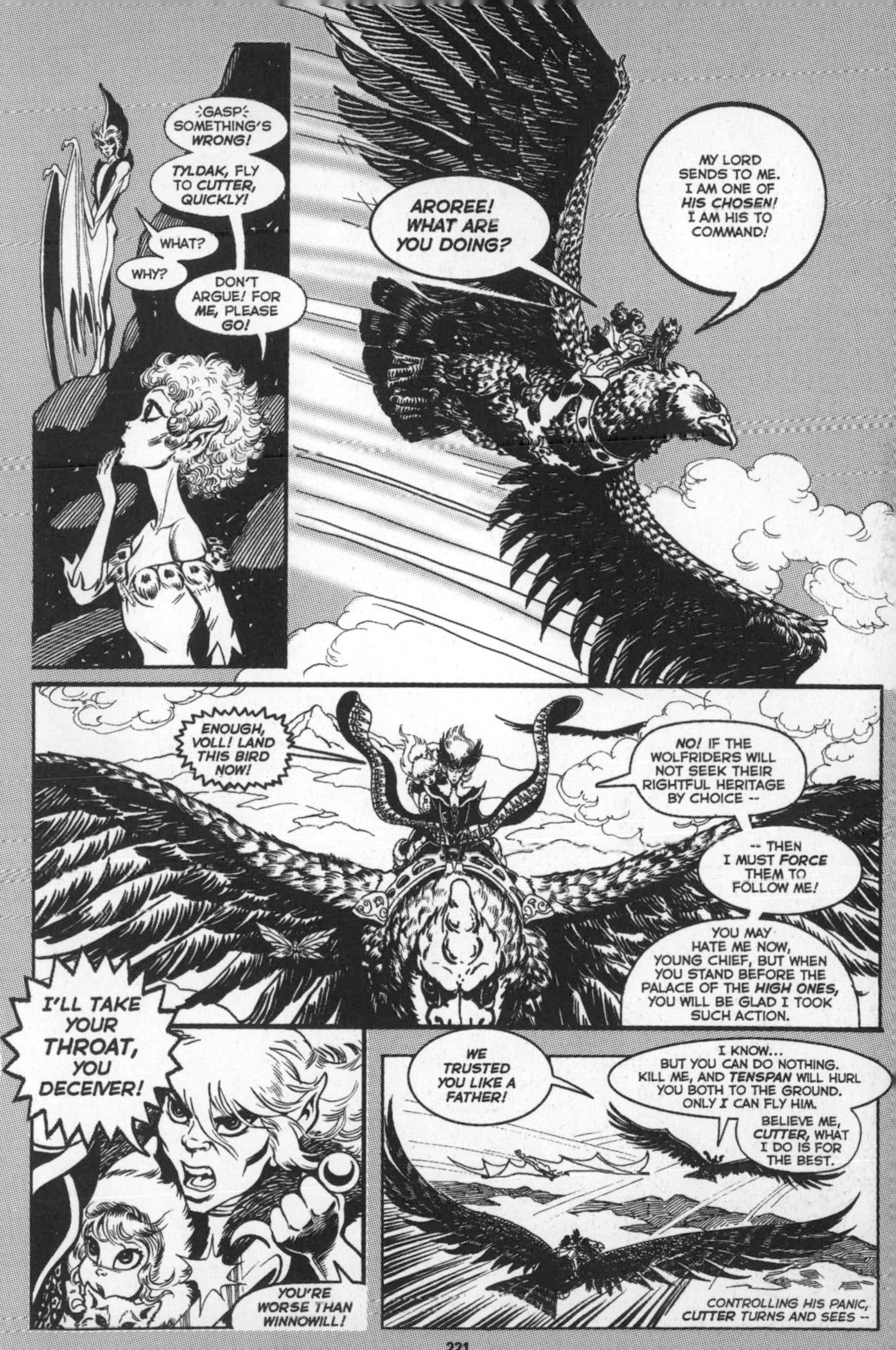

-GASP- SOMETHING'S WRONG!
TYLDAK, FLY TO CUTTER, QUICKLY!
WHAT?
WHY?
DON'T ARGUE! FOR ME, PLEASE GO!
AROREE! WHAT ARE YOU DOING?
MY LORD SENDS TO ME. I AM ONE OF HIS CHOSEN! I AM HIS TO COMMAND!
ENOUGH, VOLL! LAND THIS BIRD NOW!
NO! IF THE WOLFRIDERS WILL NOT SEEK THEIR RIGHTFUL HERITAGE BY CHOICE --
-- THEN I MUST FORCE THEM TO FOLLOW ME!
YOU MAY HATE ME NOW, YOUNG CHIEF, BUT WHEN YOU STAND BEFORE THE PALACE OF THE HIGH ONES, YOU WILL BE GLAD I TOOK SUCH ACTION.
I'LL TAKE YOUR THROAT, YOU DECEIVER!
YOU'RE WORSE THAN WINNOWILL!
WE TRUSTED YOU LIKE A FATHER!
I KNOW... BUT YOU CAN DO NOTHING. KILL ME, AND TENSPAN WILL HURL YOU BOTH TO THE GROUND. ONLY I CAN FLY HIM.
BELIEVE ME, CUTTER, WHAT I DO IS FOR THE BEST.
CONTROLLING HIS PANIC, CUTTER TURNS AND SEES --

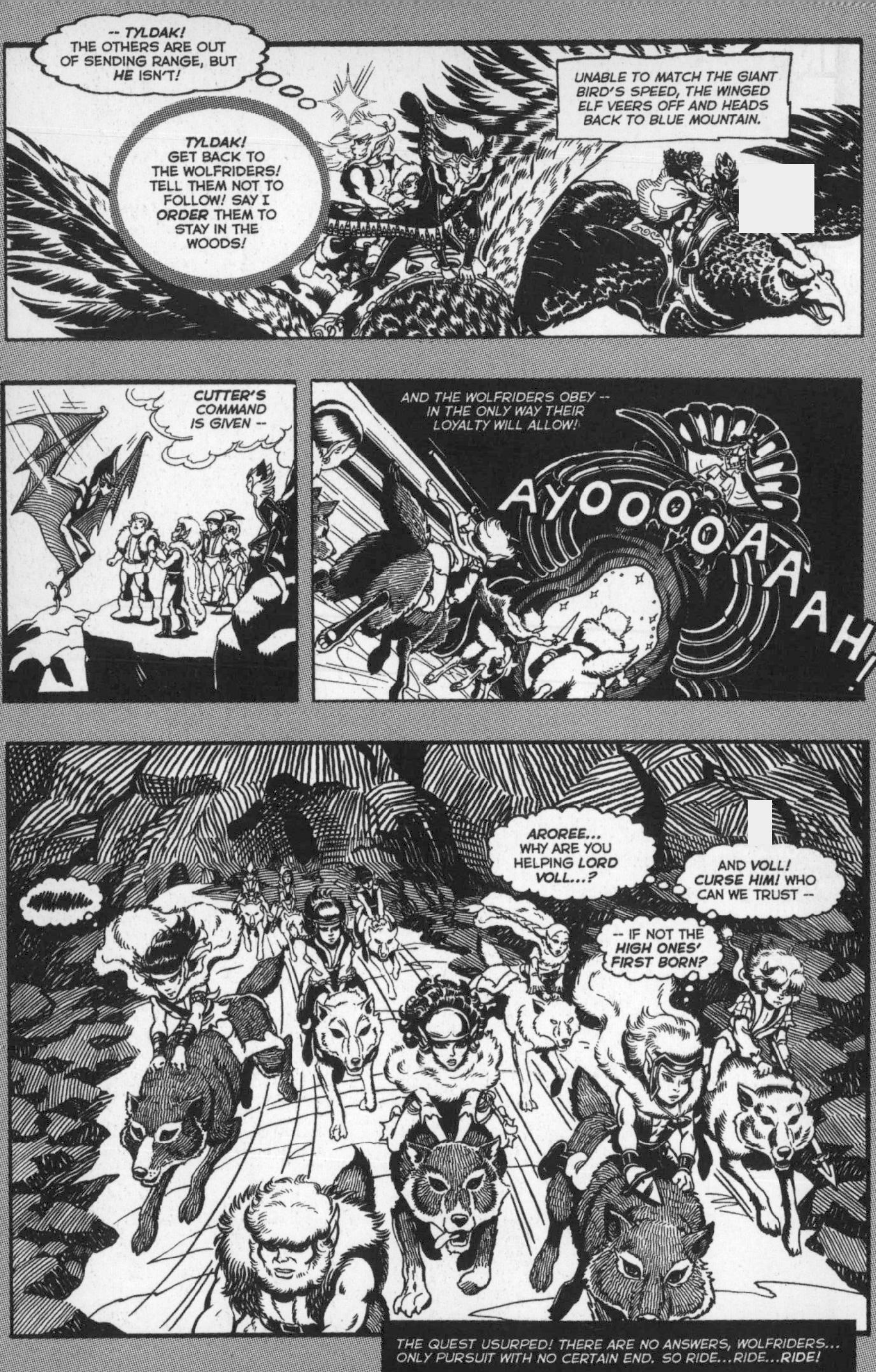
-- TYLDAK! THE OTHERS ARE OUT OF SENDING RANGE, BUT HE ISN'T!
TYLDAK! GET BACK TO THE WOLFRIDERS! TELL THEM NOT TO FOLLOW! SAY I ORDER THEM TO STAY IN THE WOODS!
UNABLE TO MATCH THE GIANT BIRD'S SPEED, THE WINGED ELF VEERS OFF AND HEADS BACK TO BLUE MOUNTAIN.
CUTTER'S COMMAND IS GIVEN --
AND THE WOLFRIDERS OBEY -- IN THE ONLY WAY THEIR LOYALTY WILL ALLOW!
AYOOOOAAAAH!
AROREE... WHY ARE YOU HELPING LORD VOLL...?
AND VOLL! CURSE HIM! WHO CAN WE TRUST --
-- IF NOT THE HIGH ONES' FIRST BORN?
THE QUEST USURPED! THERE ARE NO ANSWERS, WOLFRIDERS... ONLY PURSUIT WITH NO CERTAIN END. SO RIDE...RIDE...RIDE!

IN THE
NEXT VOLUME

The Wolfriders are reunited after their harrowing trial within Blue Mountain. Onward they quest, certain that they will find not only other elfin wanderers, but also the true safe-home of all elves – the legendary Palace of the High Ones. But the Wolfriders and their newfound allies the Go-Backs are driven into a brutal conflict against murderous mountain trolls who guard the palace with a vengeance!

Look for this latest addition in DC Comics' new library of ElfQuest stories in

OCTOBER
2004